THAT TIME I GOT REINCARNATED AS A
SLIME

17

Author: FUSE
Artist: TAIKI KAWAKAMI
Character design: MITZ VAH

D1638910

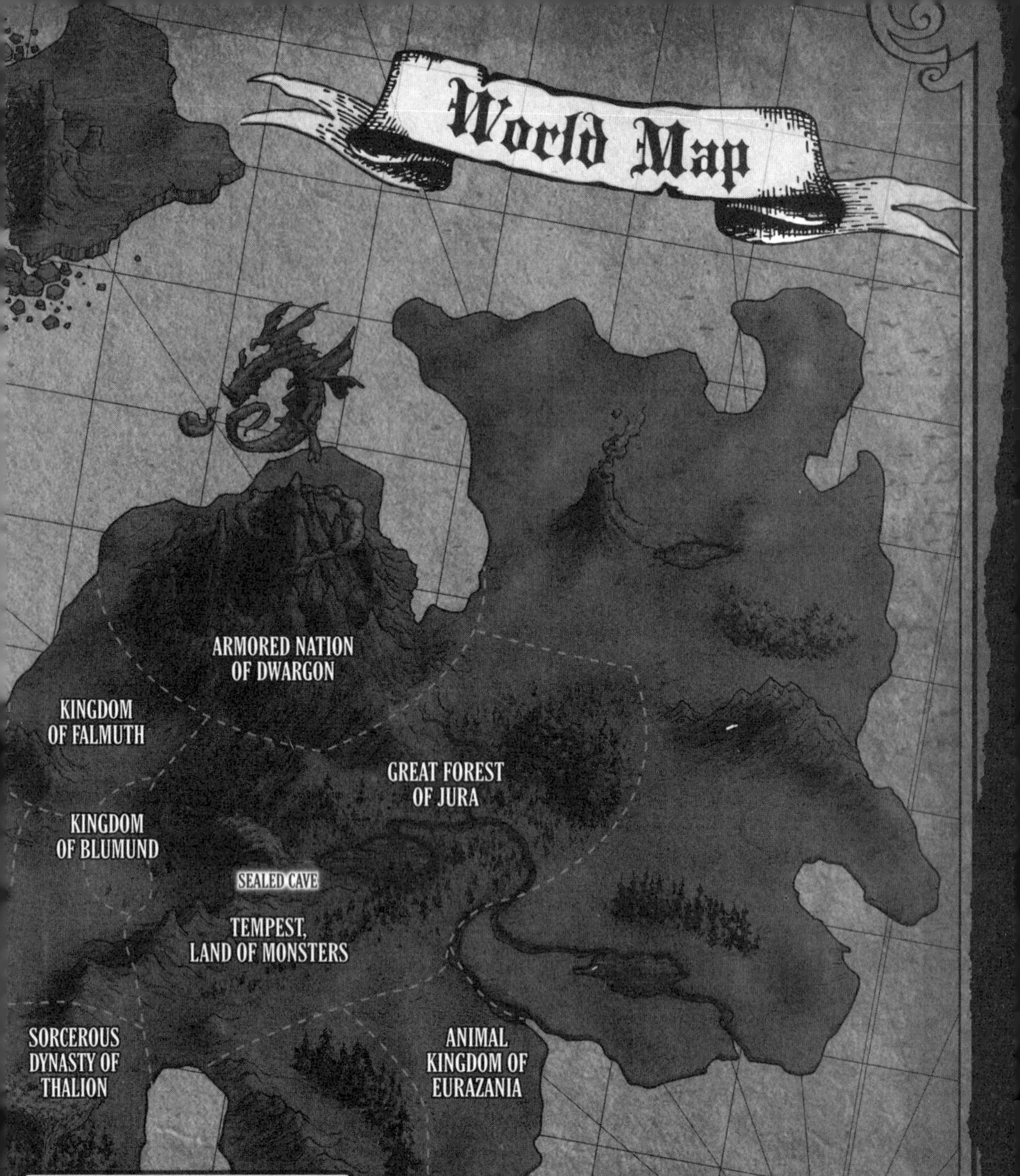
World Map
ARMORED NATION OF DWARGON
KINGDOM OF FALMUTH
GREAT FOREST OF JURA
KINGDOM OF BLUMUND
SEALED CAVE
TEMPEST, LAND OF MONSTERS
SORCEROUS DYNASTY OF THALION
ANIMAL KINGDOM OF EURAZANIA

PLOT SUMMARY

When Rimuru became a Demon Lord, Great Sage evolved into the Ultimate Skill "Raphael," Lord of Wisdom. Raphael then finished decoding Unlimited Imprisonment, freeing Veldora at last. Rimuru was delighted to see his old friend again, but the situation threatening Tempest allowed no time for catching up. The other Demon Lords' attention has fallen onto Rimuru, and they convene their council, called "Walpurgis", at the urging of Demon Lord Clayman—the secret mastermind who has finally made clear his intention to purge Rimuru once and for all. ▼

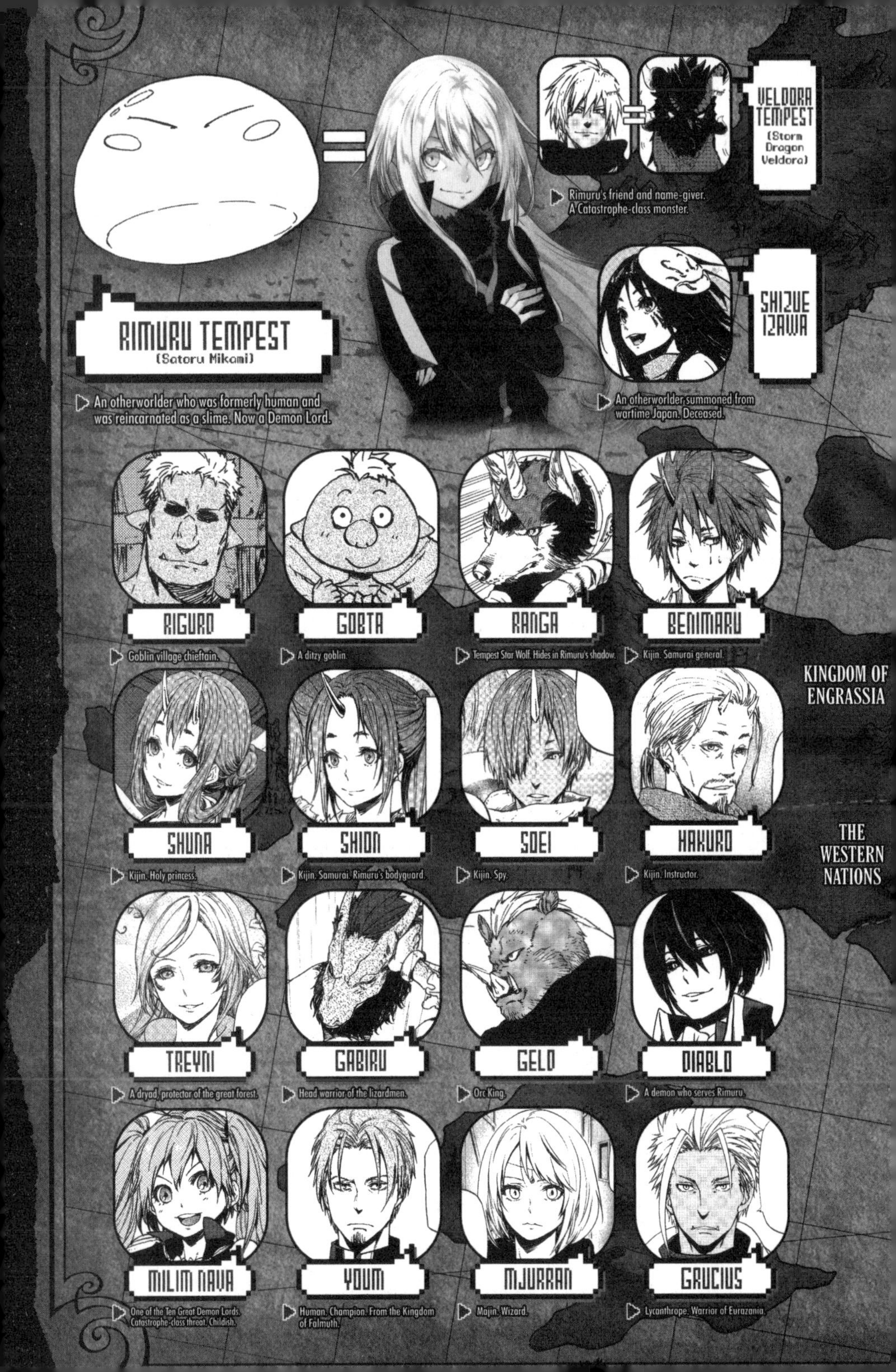
RIMURU TEMPEST
(Satoru Mikami)
An otherworlder who was formerly human and was reincarnated as a slime. Now a Demon Lord.
VELDORA TEMPEST
(Storm Dragon Veldora)
Rimuru's friend and name-giver. A Catastrophe-class monster.
SHIZUE IZAWA
An otherworlder summoned from wartime Japan. Deceased.
RIGURD
Goblin village chieftain.
GOBTA
A ditzy goblin.
RANGA
Tempest Star Wolf. Hides in Rimuru's shadow.
BENIMARU
Kijin. Samurai general.
KINGDOM OF ENGRASSIA
SHUNA
Kijin. Holy princess.
SHION
Kijin. Samurai. Rimuru's bodyguard.
SOEI
Kijin. Spy.
HAKURO
Kijin. Instructor.
THE WESTERN NATIONS
TREYNI
A dryad, protector of the great forest.
GABIRU
Head warrior of the lizardmen.
GELD
Orc King.
DIABLO
A demon who serves Rimuru.
MILIM NAVA
One of the Ten Great Demon Lords. Catastrophe-class threat. Childish.
YOUM
Human. Champion. From the Kingdom of Falmuth.
MJURRAN
Majin. Wizard.
GRUCIUS
Lycanthrope. Warrior of Eurazania.

CONTENTS

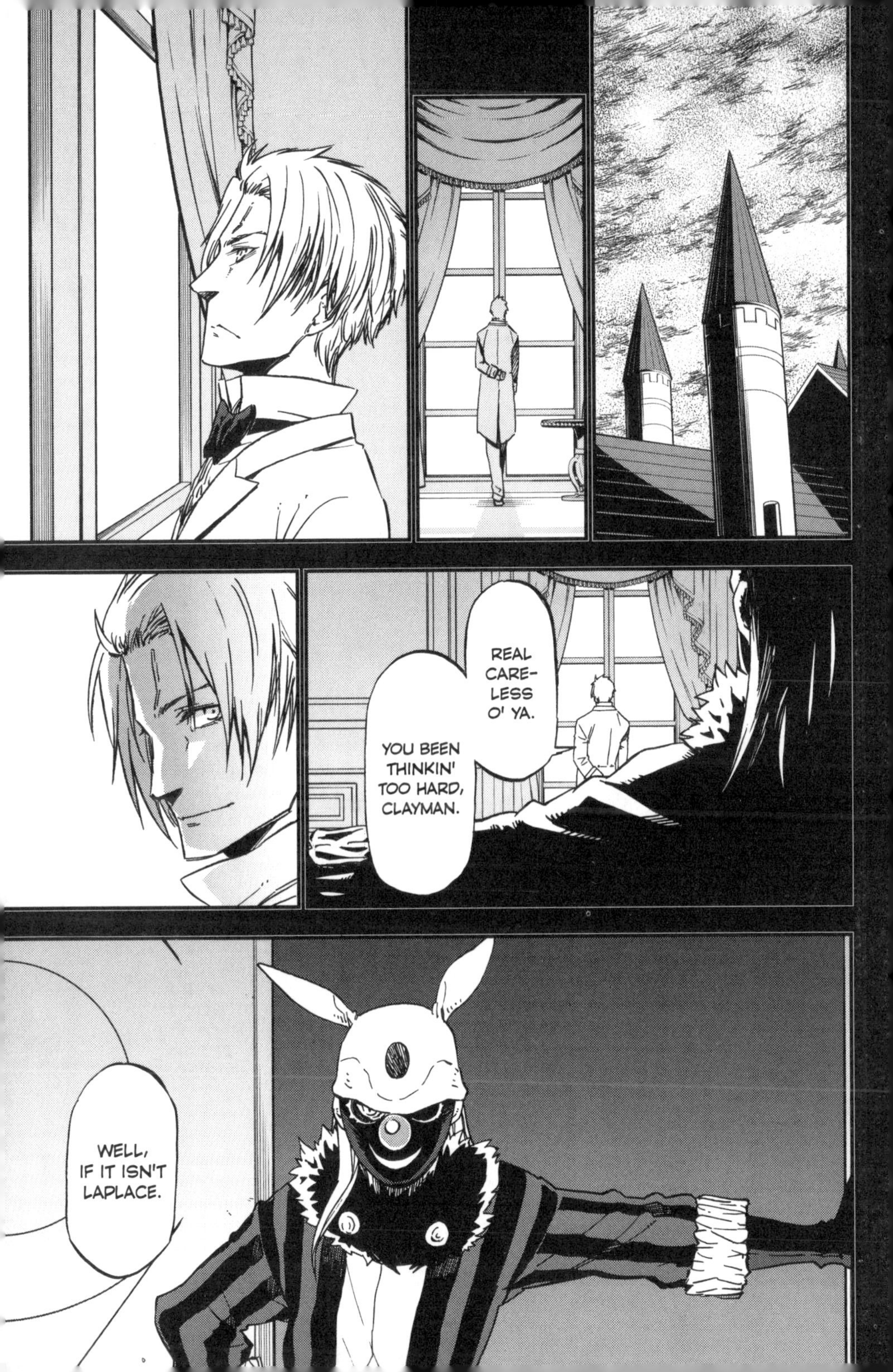
REAL CARE-LESS O' YA.
YOU BEEN THINKIN' TOO HARD, CLAYMAN.
WELL, IF IT ISN'T LAPLACE.

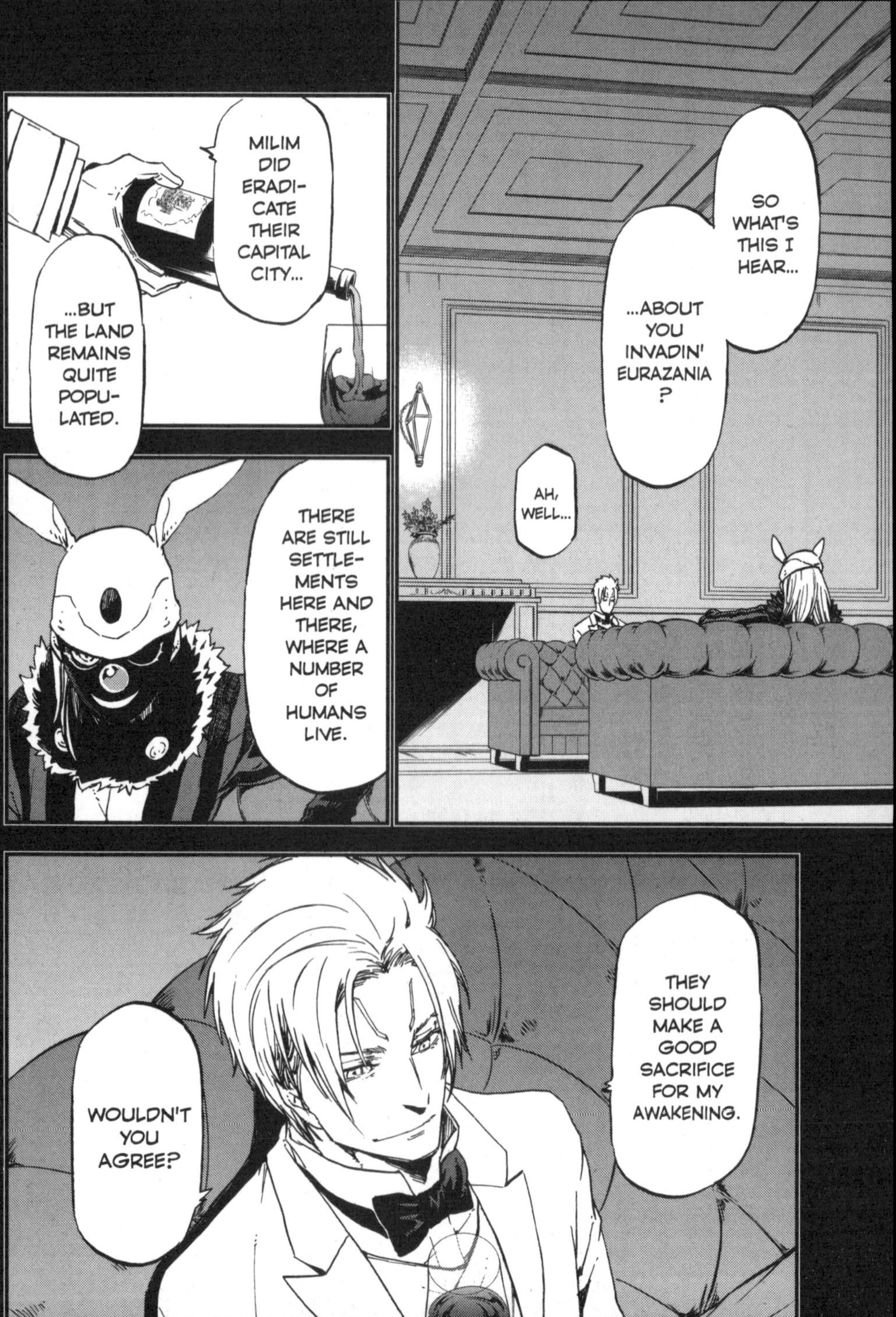
SO WHAT'S THIS I HEAR...
...ABOUT YOU INVADIN' EURAZANIA?
AH, WELL...
MILIM DID ERADICATE THEIR CAPITAL CITY...
...BUT THE LAND REMAINS QUITE POPULATED.
THERE ARE STILL SETTLEMENTS HERE AND THERE, WHERE A NUMBER OF HUMANS LIVE.
THEY SHOULD MAKE A GOOD SACRIFICE FOR MY AWAKENING.
WOULDN'T YOU AGREE?

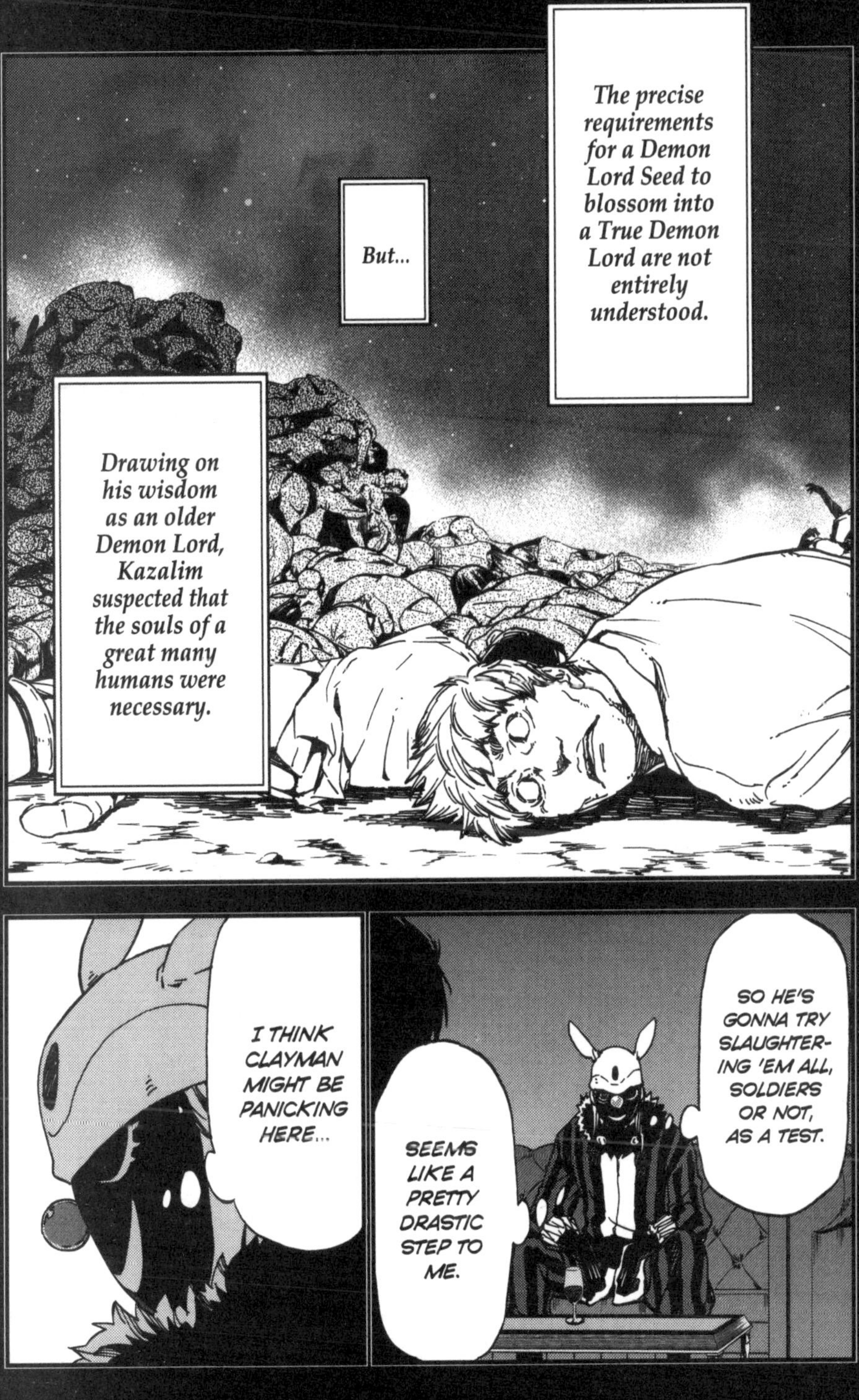
The precise requirements for a Demon Lord Seed to blossom into a True Demon Lord are not entirely understood.
But...
Drawing on his wisdom as an older Demon Lord, Kazalim suspected that the souls of a great many humans were necessary.
SO HE'S GONNA TRY SLAUGHTER-ING 'EM ALL, SOLDIERS OR NOT, AS A TEST.
SEEMS LIKE A PRETTY DRASTIC STEP TO ME.
I THINK CLAYMAN MIGHT BE PANICKING HERE...

SAY...

YOU DON'T HAFTA DO THIS *RIGHT* BEFORE SUCH A CRUCIAL JUNCTURE, DO YA?

YOU'VE GOT THE WALPURGIS COMING UP IN JUST A WEEK, RIGHT?

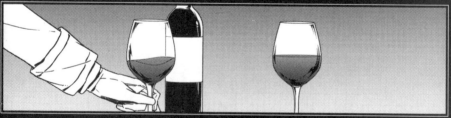

AND THERE'S THAT NON-INTERFERENCE TREATY BETWEEN DEMON LORDS.

IF YA BREAK THAT TREATY BY INVADING EURAZANIA FURTHER, THE OTHER LORDS'LL HAVE THEIR SAY, WON'T THEY?

TRUE, BUT THAT WILL NOT BE A PROBLEM.

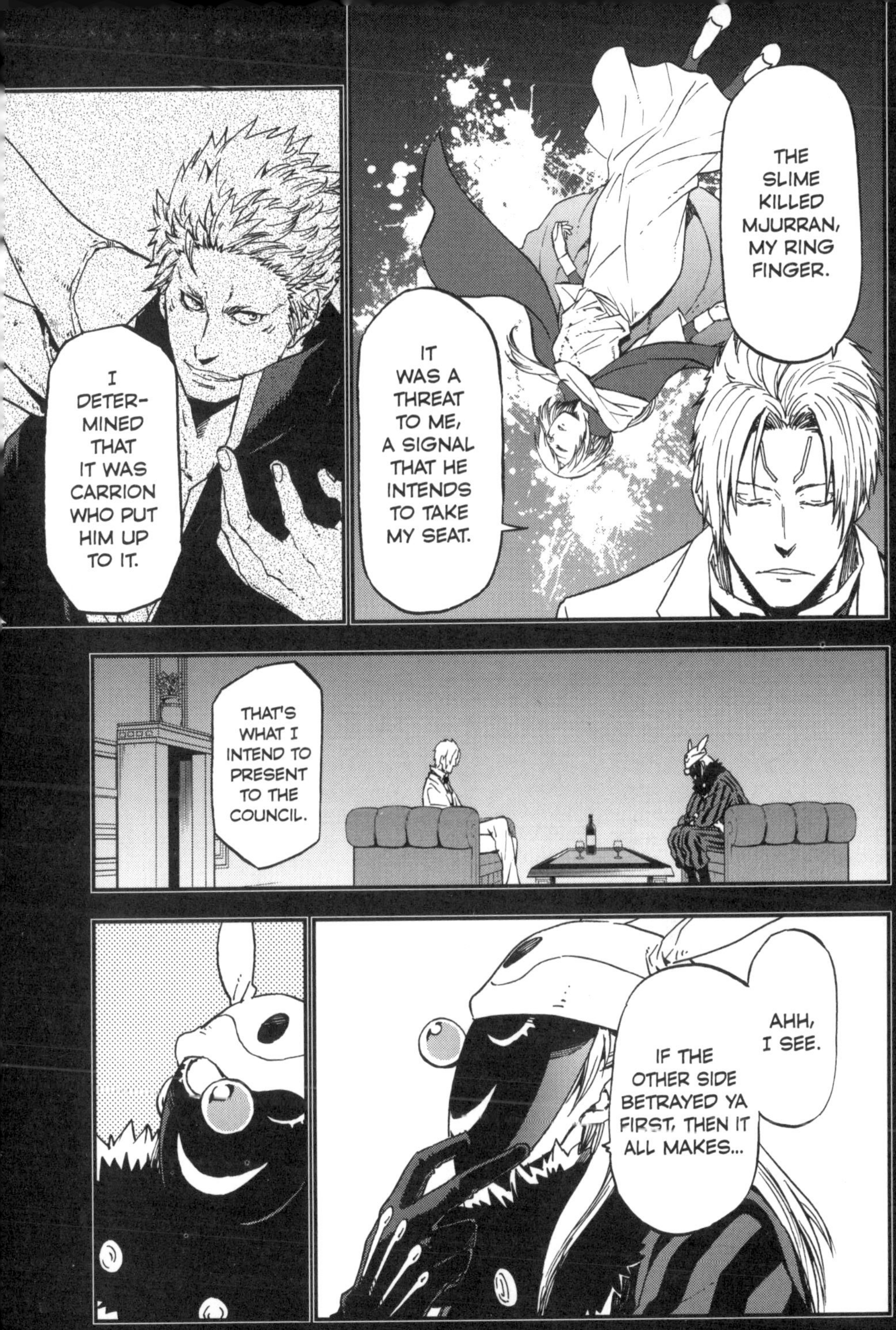
THE SLIME KILLED MJURRAN, MY RING FINGER.
IT WAS A THREAT TO ME, A SIGNAL THAT HE INTENDS TO TAKE MY SEAT.
I DETER-MINED THAT IT WAS CARRION WHO PUT HIM UP TO IT.
THAT'S WHAT I INTEND TO PRESENT TO THE COUNCIL.
AHH, I SEE.
IF THE OTHER SIDE BETRAYED YA FIRST, THEN IT ALL MAKES...

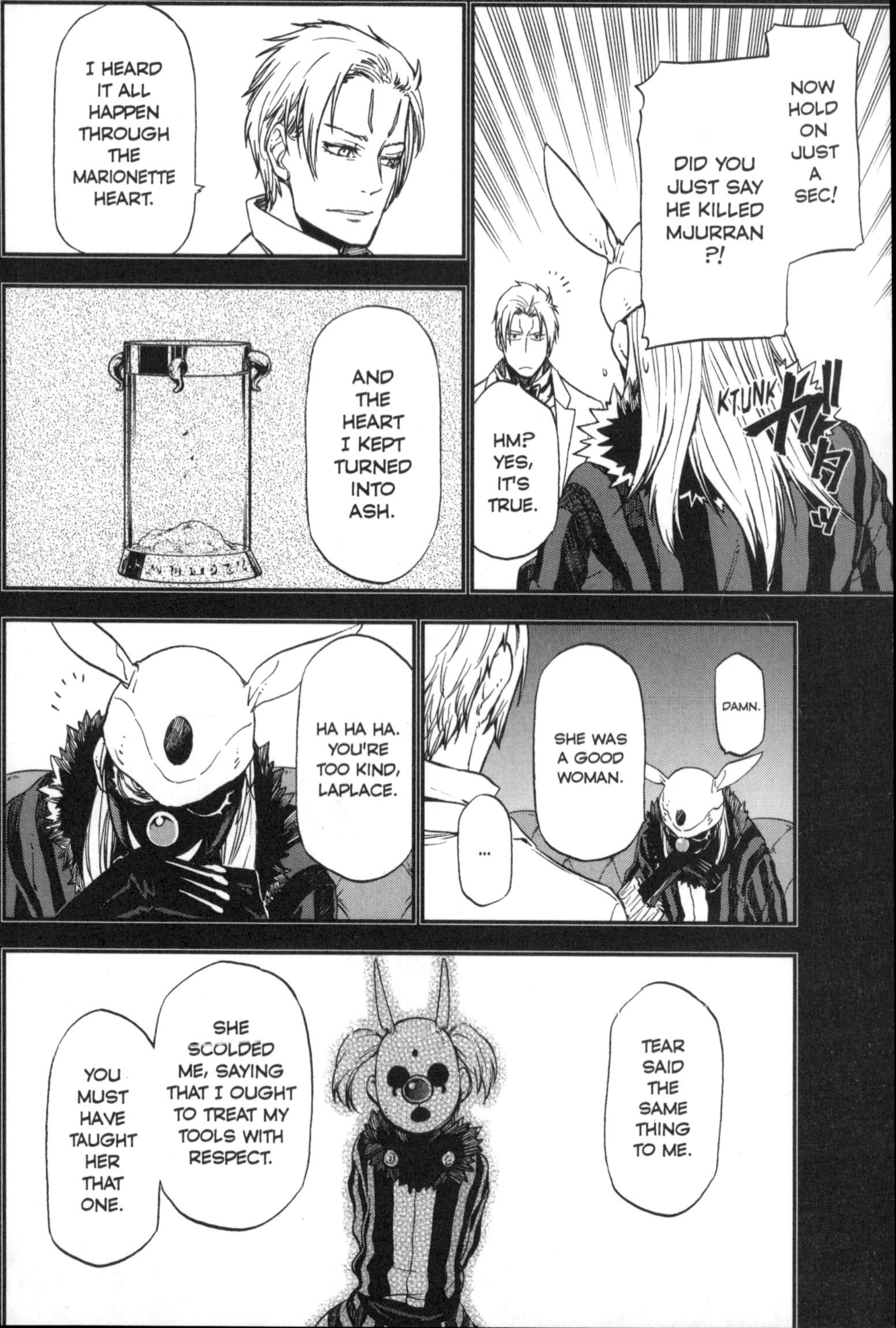
NOW HOLD ON JUST A SEC!
DID YOU JUST SAY HE KILLED MJURRAN?!
KTUNK
HM? YES, IT'S TRUE.
I HEARD IT ALL HAPPEN THROUGH THE MARIONETTE HEART.
AND THE HEART I KEPT TURNED INTO ASH.
DAMN.
SHE WAS A GOOD WOMAN.
...
HA HA HA. YOU'RE TOO KIND, LAPLACE.
TEAR SAID THE SAME THING TO ME.
SHE SCOLDED ME, SAYING THAT I OUGHT TO TREAT MY TOOLS WITH RESPECT.
YOU MUST HAVE TAUGHT HER THAT ONE.

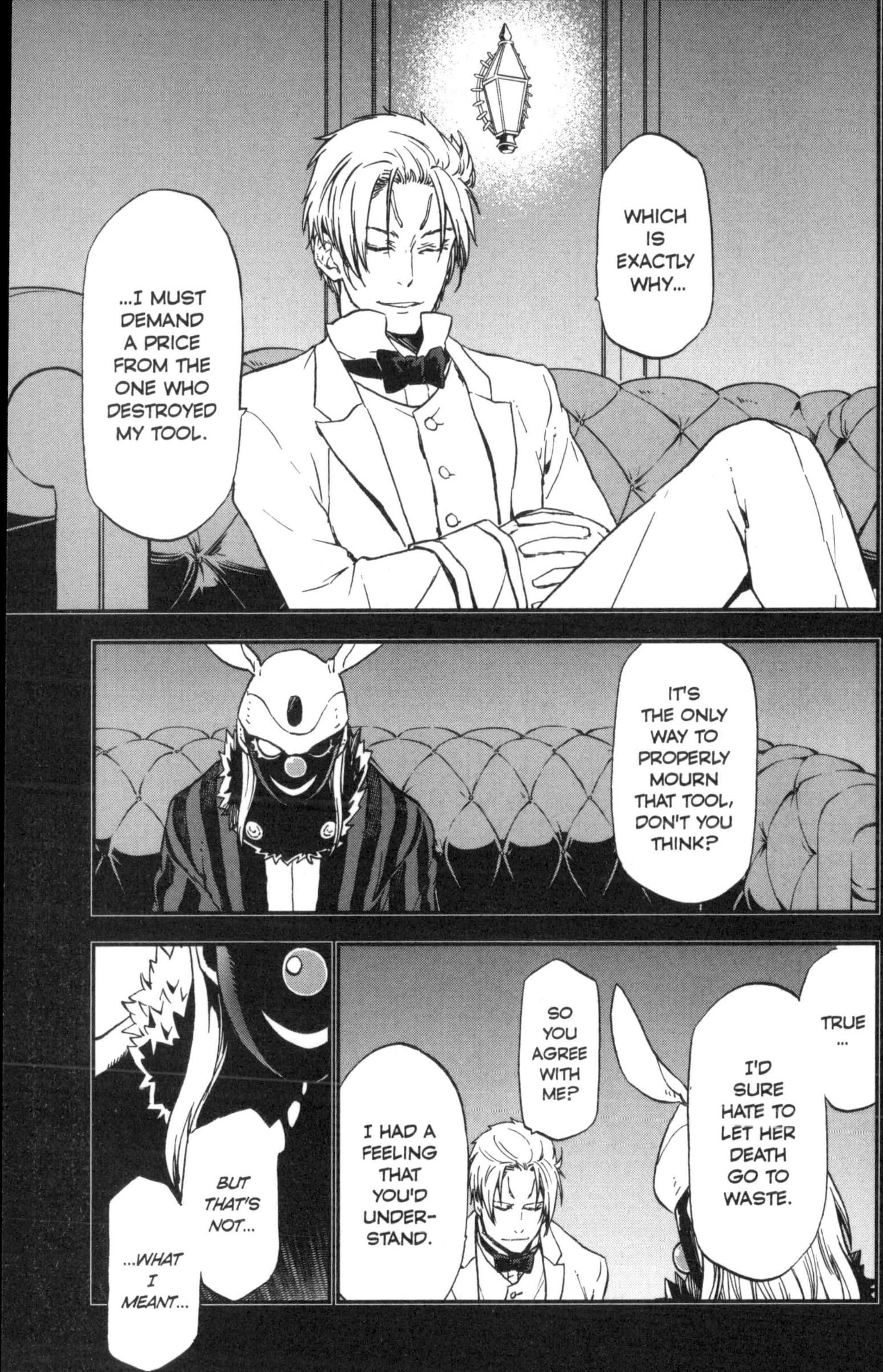
WHICH IS EXACTLY WHY...
...I MUST DEMAND A PRICE FROM THE ONE WHO DESTROYED MY TOOL.
IT'S THE ONLY WAY TO PROPERLY MOURN THAT TOOL, DON'T YOU THINK?
TRUE...
I'D SURE HATE TO LET HER DEATH GO TO WASTE.
SO YOU AGREE WITH ME?
I HAD A FEELING THAT YOU'D UNDER-STAND.
BUT THAT'S NOT...
...WHAT I MEANT...

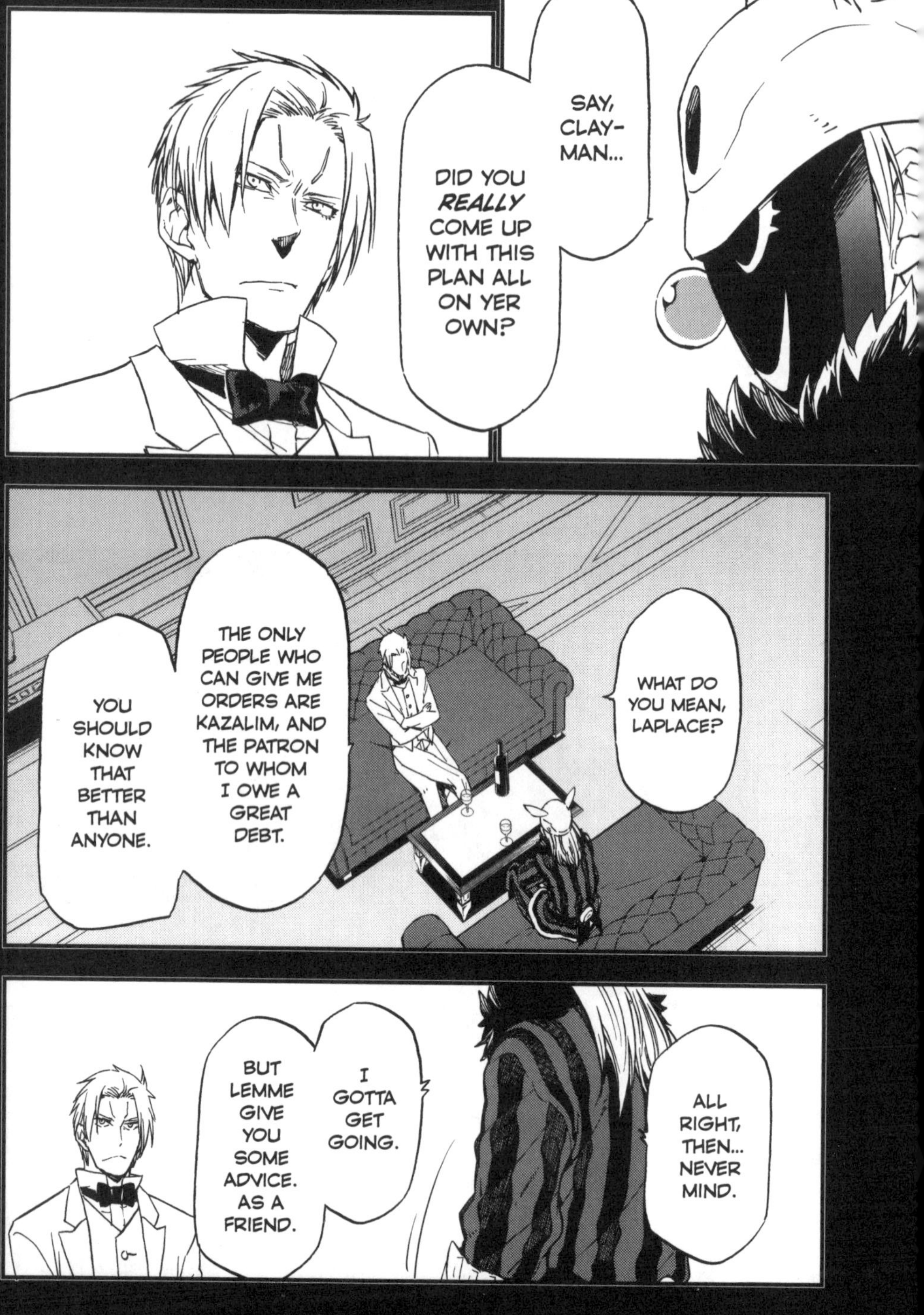
SAY, CLAY-MAN...
DID YOU *REALLY* COME UP WITH THIS PLAN ALL ON YER OWN?
WHAT DO YOU MEAN, LAPLACE?
THE ONLY PEOPLE WHO CAN GIVE ME ORDERS ARE KAZALIM, AND THE PATRON TO WHOM I OWE A GREAT DEBT.
YOU SHOULD KNOW THAT BETTER THAN ANYONE.
ALL RIGHT, THEN... NEVER MIND.
I GOTTA GET GOING.
BUT LEMME GIVE YOU SOME ADVICE. AS A FRIEND.

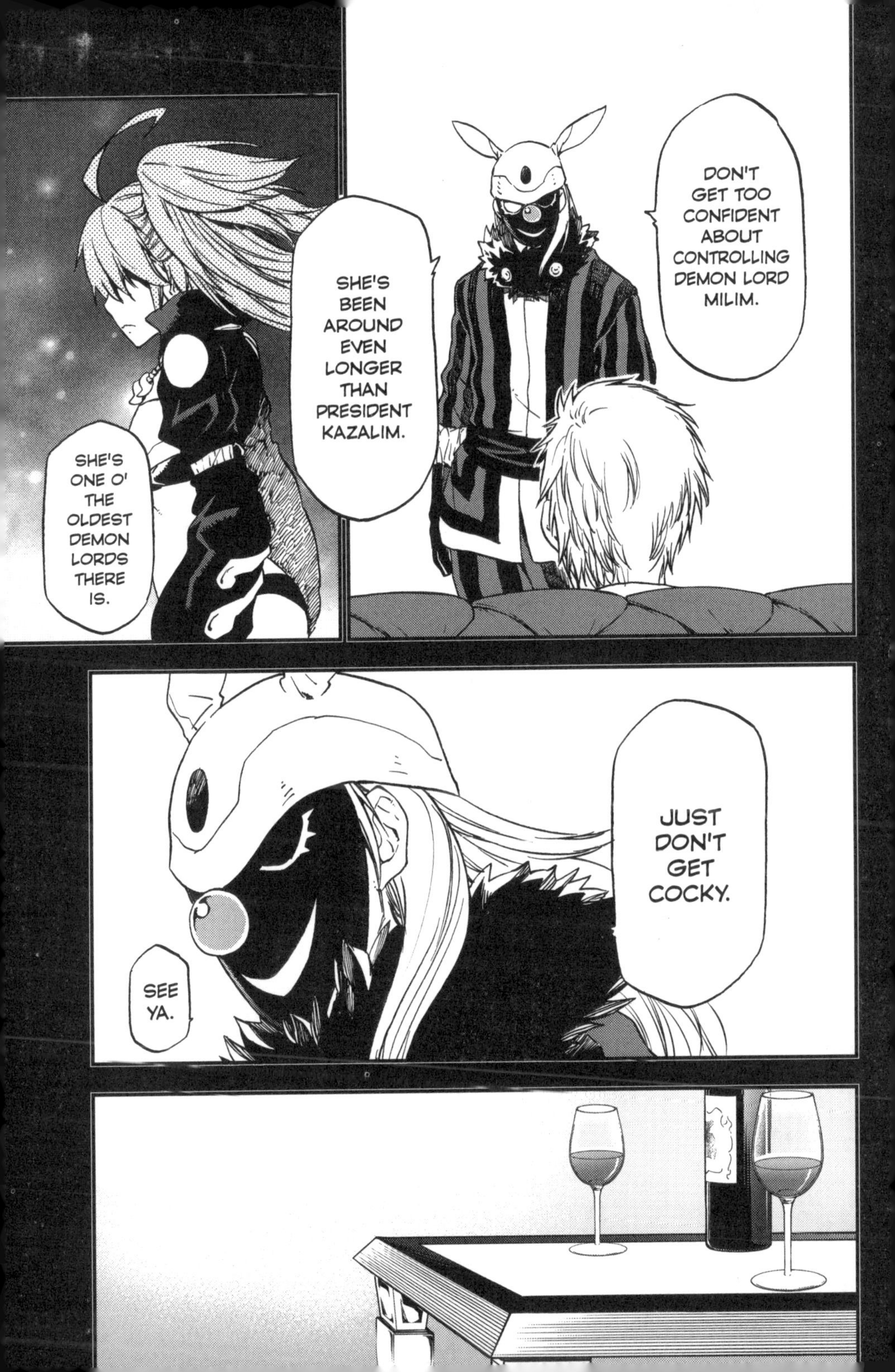
DON'T GET TOO CONFIDENT ABOUT CONTROLLING DEMON LORD MILIM.
SHE'S BEEN AROUND EVEN LONGER THAN PRESIDENT KAZALIM.
SHE'S ONE O' THE OLDEST DEMON LORDS THERE IS.
JUST DON'T GET COCKY.
SEE YA.

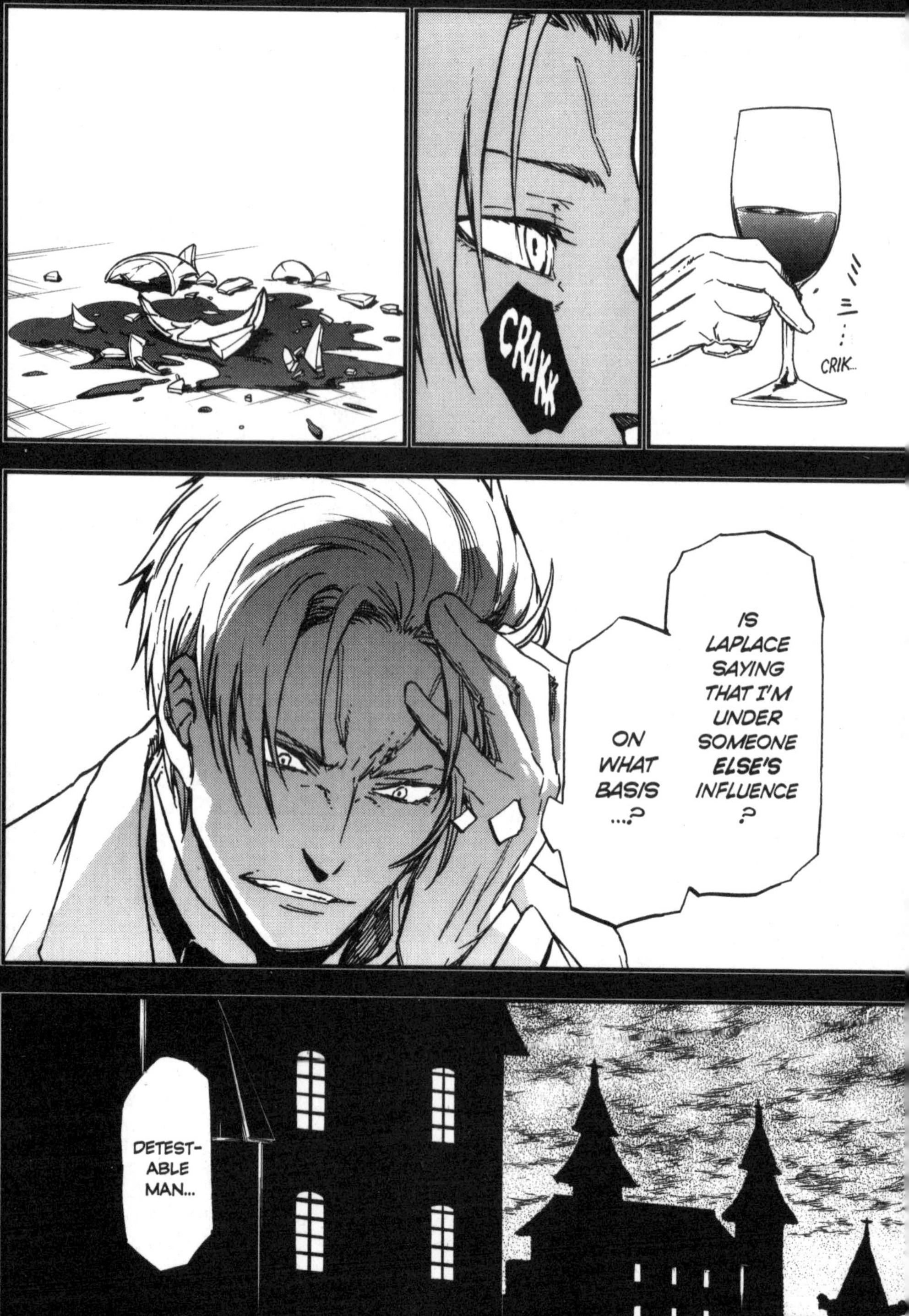
CRIK...
CRAKK
IS LAPLACE SAYING THAT I'M UNDER SOMEONE ELSE'S INFLUENCE?
ON WHAT BASIS...?
DETEST-ABLE MAN...

CHAPTER 75 Monster-and-Man Summit II

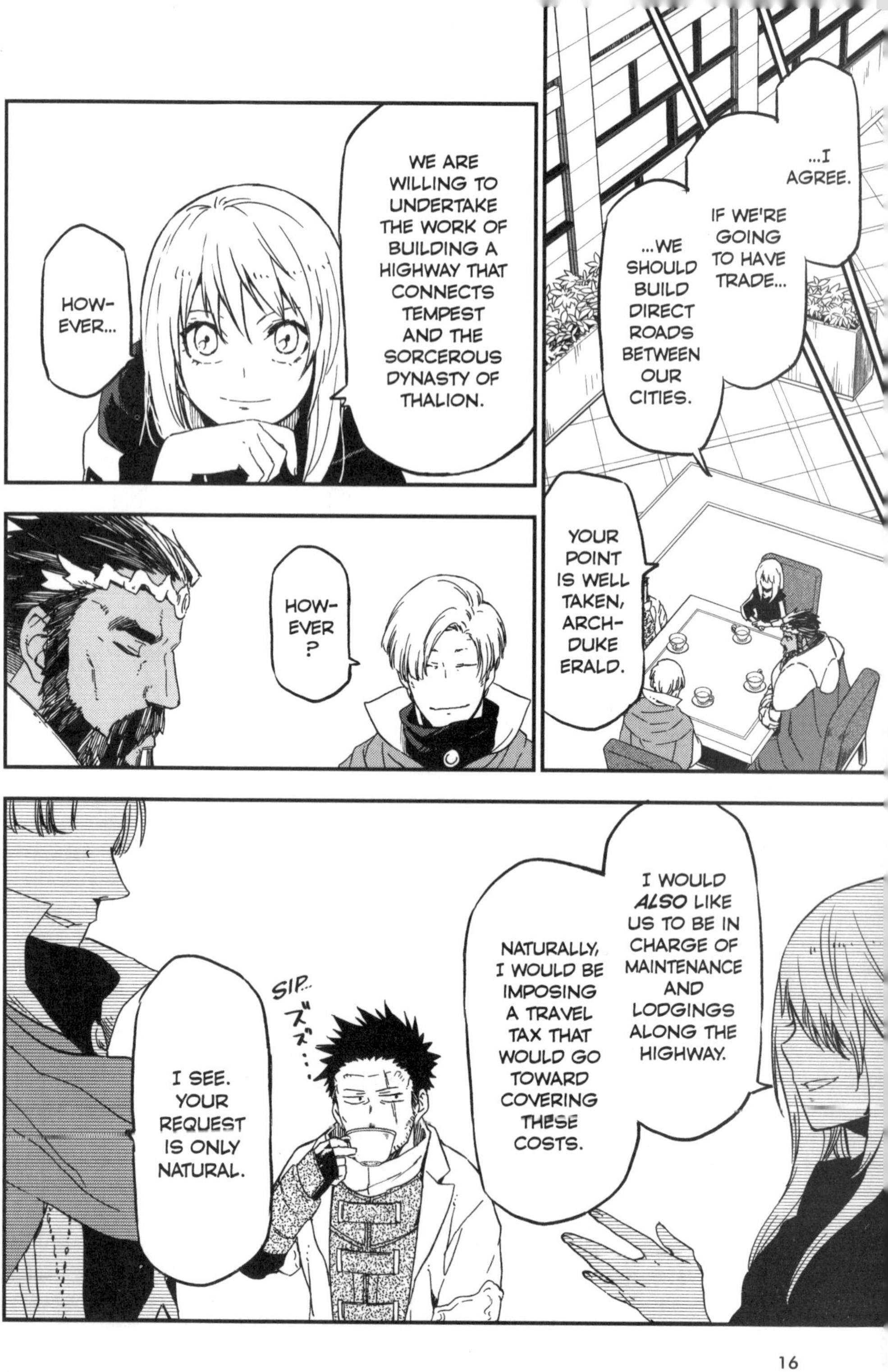
...I AGREE.
IF WE'RE GOING TO HAVE TRADE...
...WE SHOULD BUILD DIRECT ROADS BETWEEN OUR CITIES.
YOUR POINT IS WELL TAKEN, ARCHDUKE ERALD.
WE ARE WILLING TO UNDERTAKE THE WORK OF BUILDING A HIGHWAY THAT CONNECTS TEMPEST AND THE SORCEROUS DYNASTY OF THALION.
HOWEVER...
HOWEVER?
I WOULD *ALSO* LIKE US TO BE IN CHARGE OF MAINTENANCE AND LODGINGS ALONG THE HIGHWAY.
NATURALLY, I WOULD BE IMPOSING A TRAVEL TAX THAT WOULD GO TOWARD COVERING THESE COSTS.
SIP...
ズズ…
I SEE. YOUR REQUEST IS ONLY NATURAL.

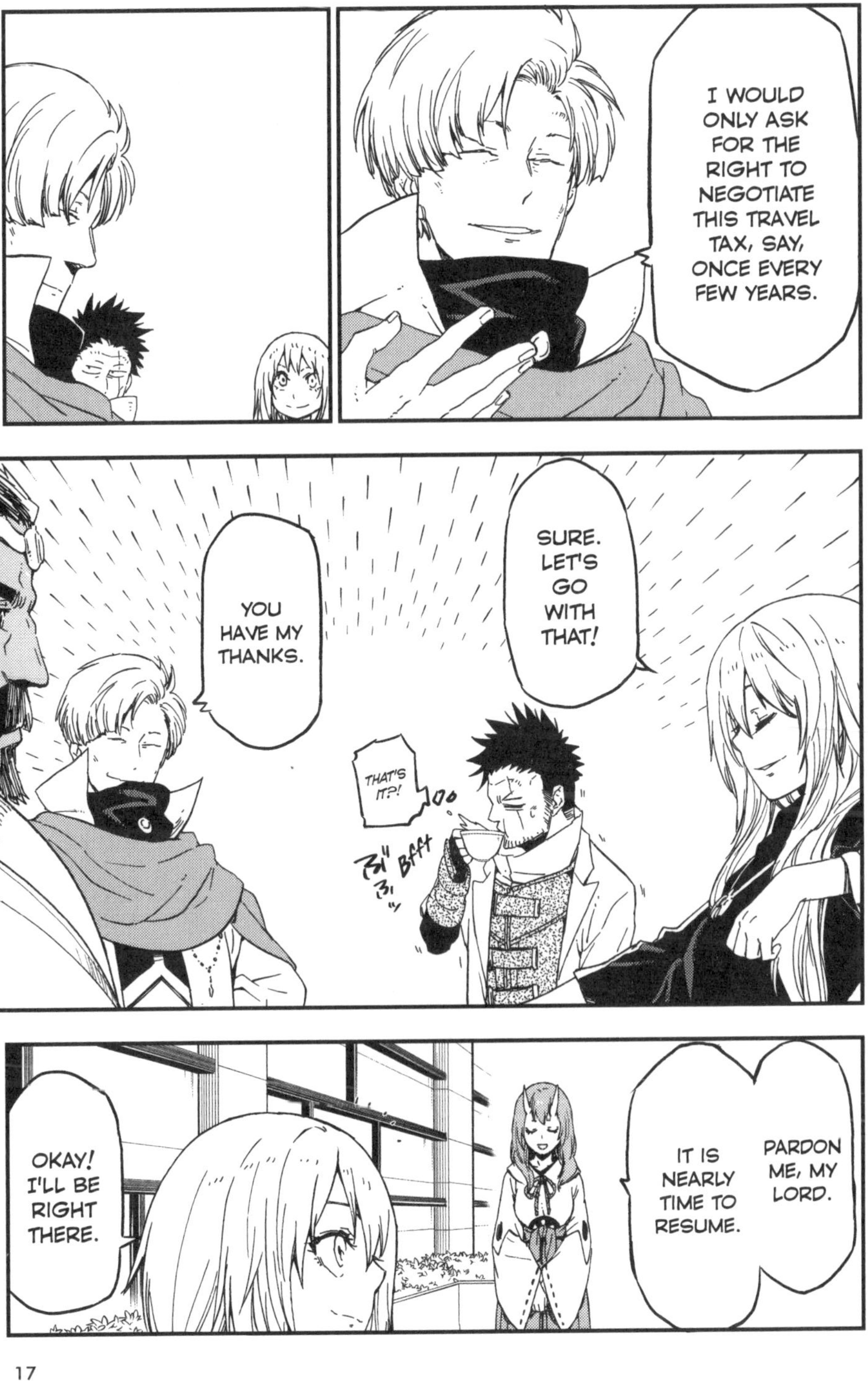
I WOULD ONLY ASK FOR THE RIGHT TO NEGOTIATE THIS TRAVEL TAX, SAY, ONCE EVERY FEW YEARS.
SURE. LET'S GO WITH THAT!
YOU HAVE MY THANKS.
THAT'S IT?!
Bfft
PARDON ME, MY LORD.
IT IS NEARLY TIME TO RESUME.
OKAY! I'LL BE RIGHT THERE.

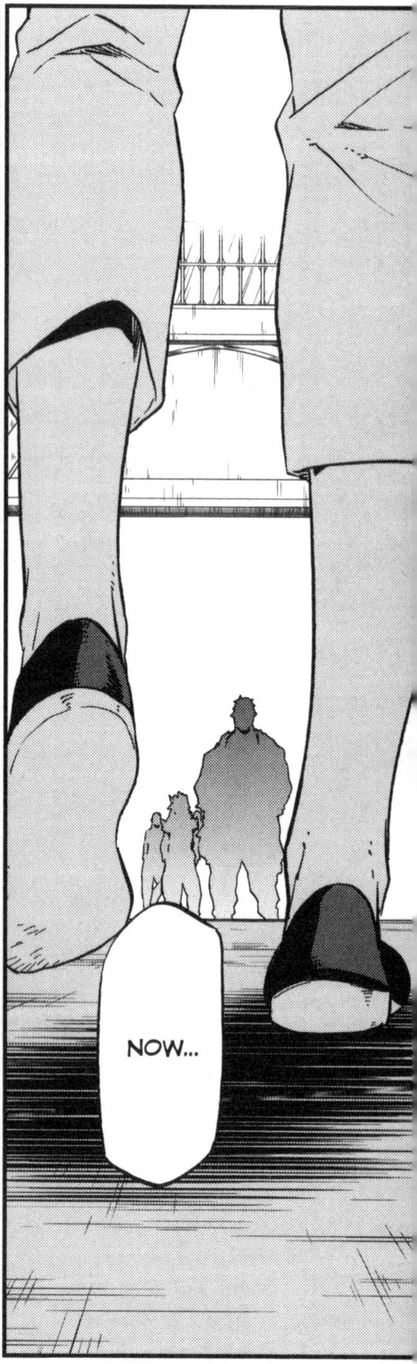
NOW...

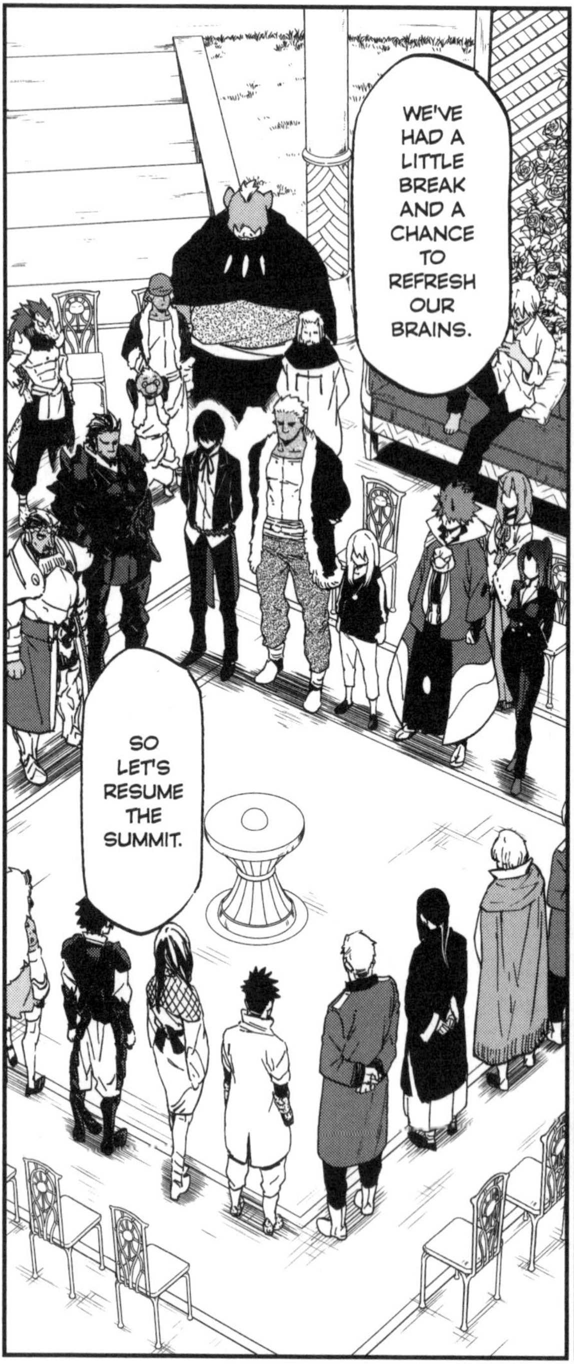
WE'VE HAD A LITTLE BREAK AND A CHANCE TO REFRESH OUR BRAINS.
SO LET'S RESUME THE SUMMIT.

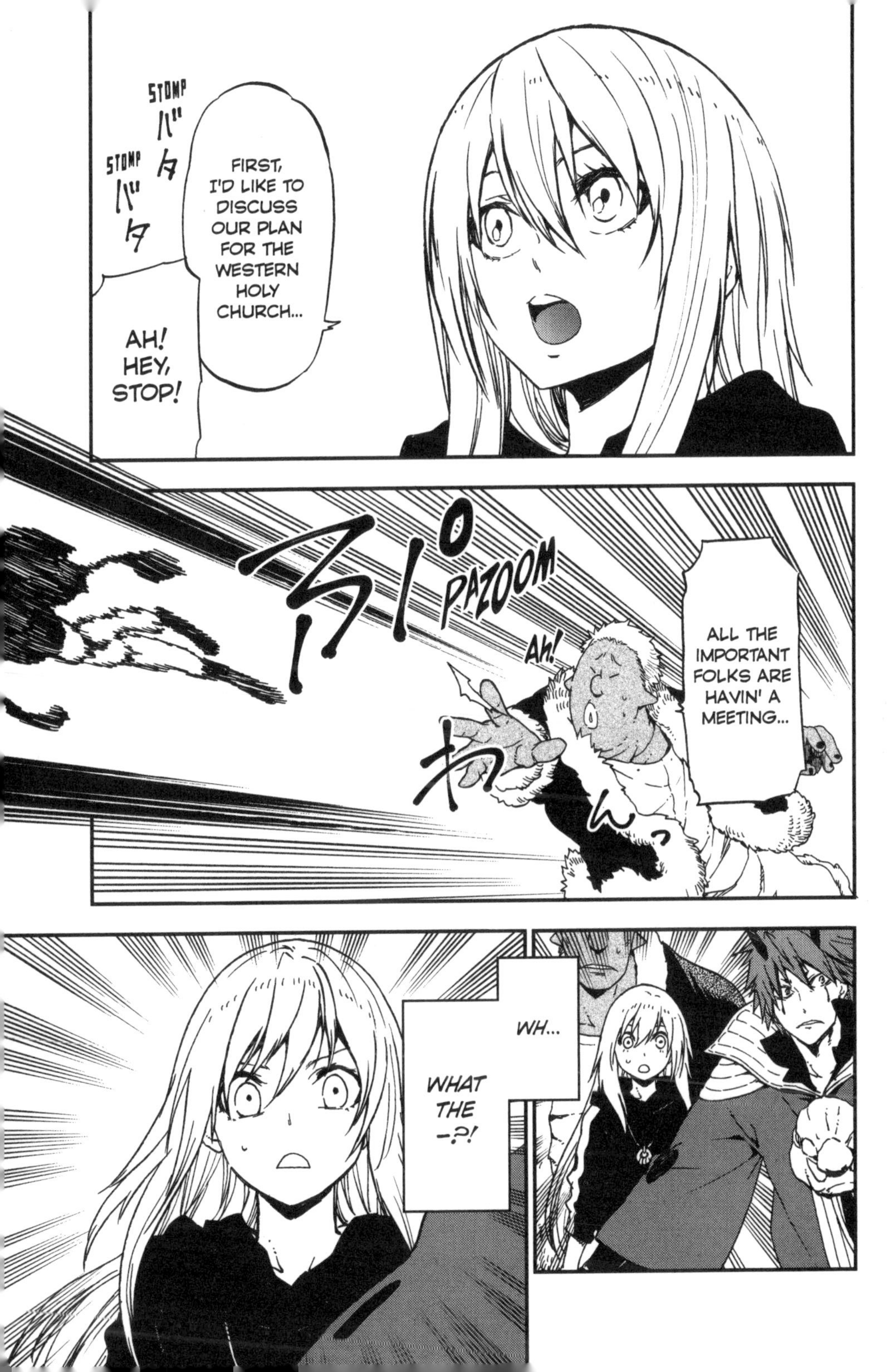
FIRST, I'D LIKE TO DISCUSS OUR PLAN FOR THE WESTERN HOLY CHURCH...
STOMP
STOMP
AH! HEY, STOP!
ALL THE IMPORTANT FOLKS ARE HAVIN' A MEETING...
Ah!
PAZOOM
WH...
WHAT THE —?!

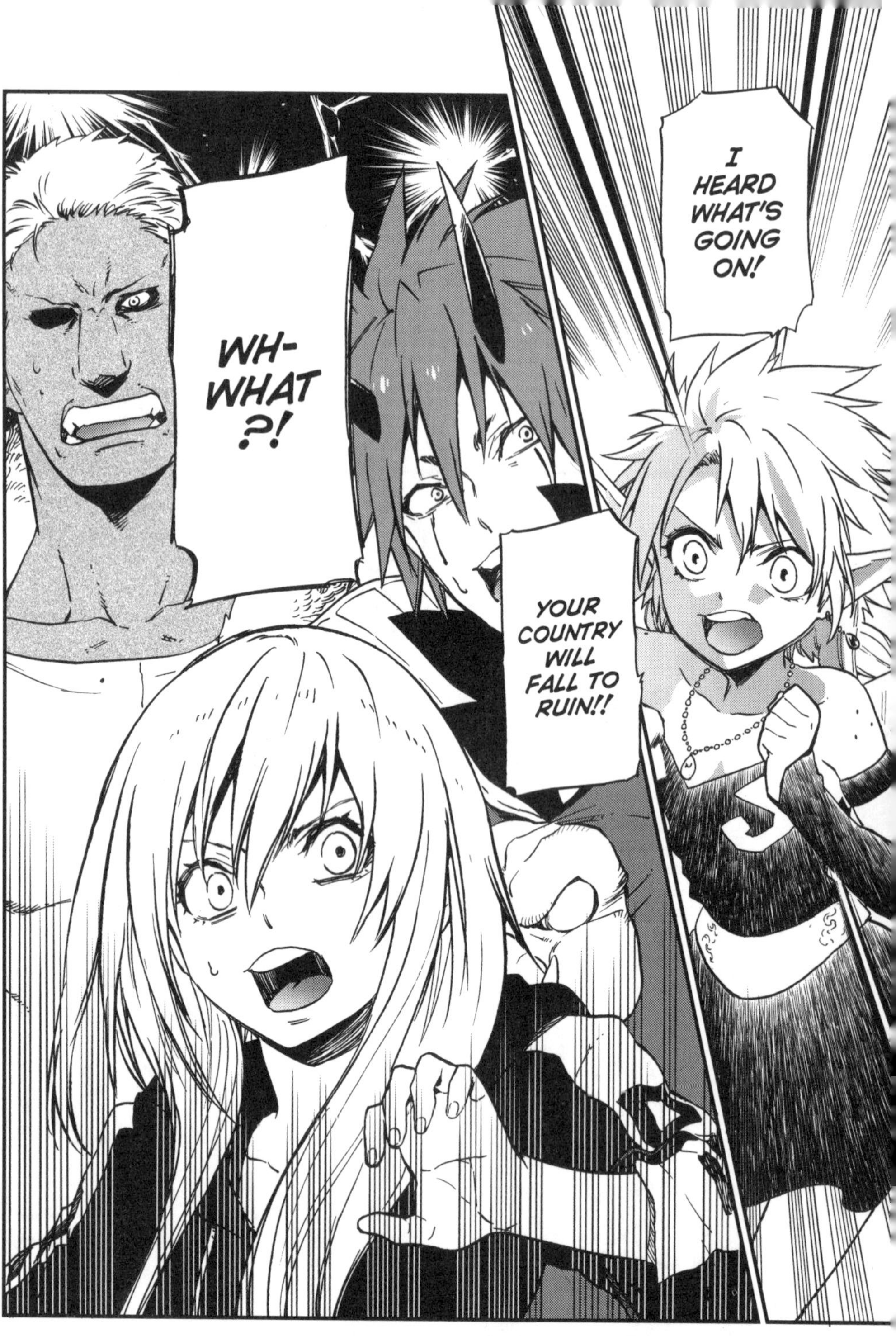
I HEARD WHAT'S GOING ON!
YOUR COUNTRY WILL FALL TO RUIN!!
WH- WHAT ?!

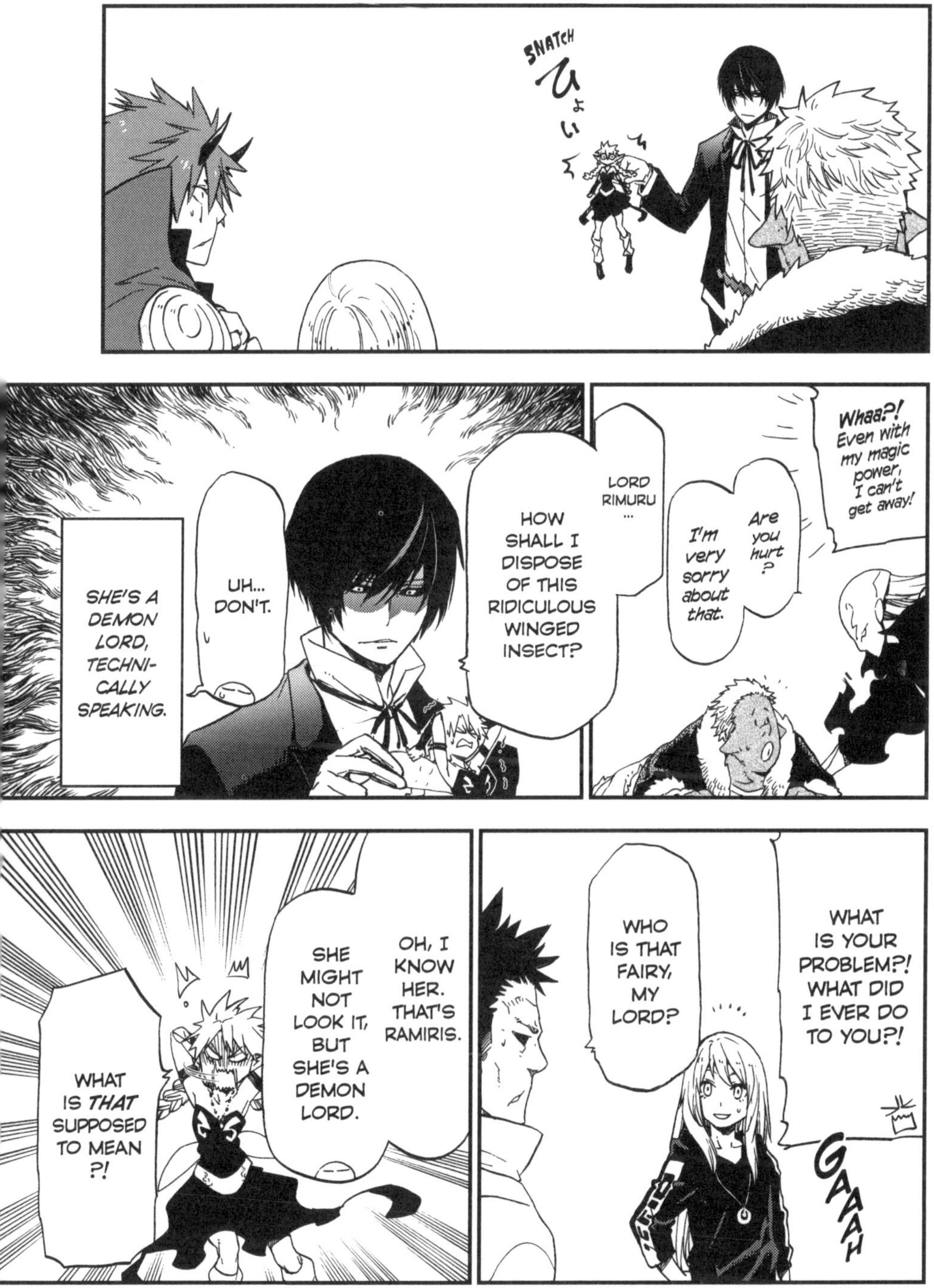

SNATCH
ひょい
Whaa?! Even with my magic power, I can't get away!
Are you hurt?
I'm very sorry about that.
LORD RIMURU...
HOW SHALL I DISPOSE OF THIS RIDICULOUS WINGED INSECT?
UH... DON'T.
SHE'S A DEMON LORD, TECHNICALLY SPEAKING.
WHAT IS YOUR PROBLEM?! WHAT DID I EVER DO TO YOU?!
GAAAH
WHO IS THAT FAIRY, MY LORD?
OH, I KNOW HER. THAT'S RAMIRIS.
SHE MIGHT NOT LOOK IT, BUT SHE'S A DEMON LORD.
WHAT IS *THAT* SUPPOSED TO MEAN?!

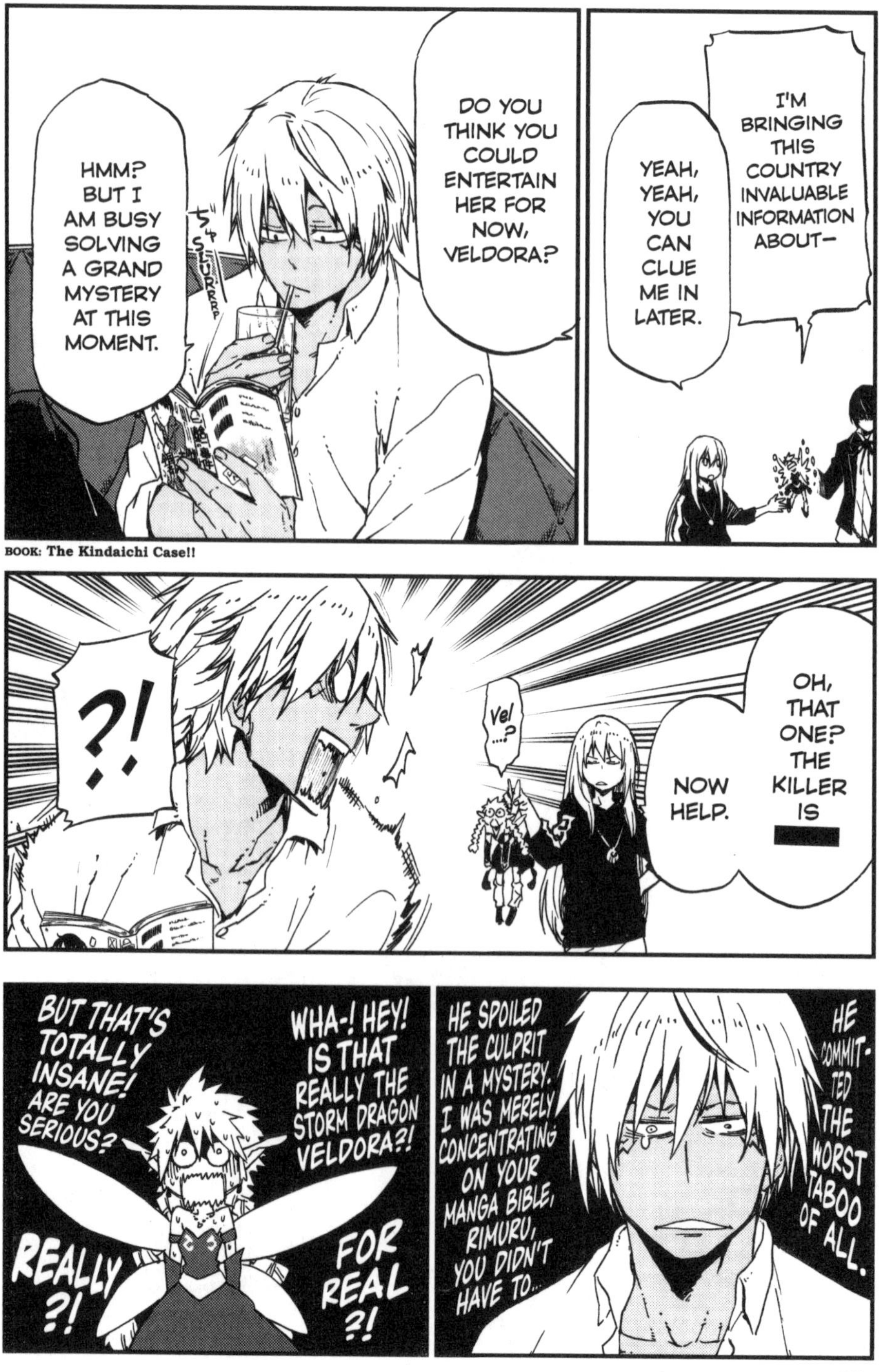

I'M BRINGING THIS COUNTRY INVALUABLE INFORMATION ABOUT–
YEAH, YEAH, YOU CAN CLUE ME IN LATER.
DO YOU THINK YOU COULD ENTERTAIN HER FOR NOW, VELDORA?
SLURRRP
HMM? BUT I AM BUSY SOLVING A GRAND MYSTERY AT THIS MOMENT.
OH, THAT ONE? THE KILLER IS [redacted]
NOW HELP.
Vel ...?
?!
HE COMMITTED THE WORST TABOO OF ALL.
HE SPOILED THE CULPRIT IN A MYSTERY. I WAS MERELY CONCENTRATING ON YOUR MANGA BIBLE, RIMURU, YOU DIDN'T HAVE TO...
WHA-! HEY! IS THAT REALLY THE STORM DRAGON VELDORA?!
FOR REAL?!
BUT THAT'S TOTALLY INSANE! ARE YOU SERIOUS?
REALLY?!

BOOK: The Kindaichi Case!!

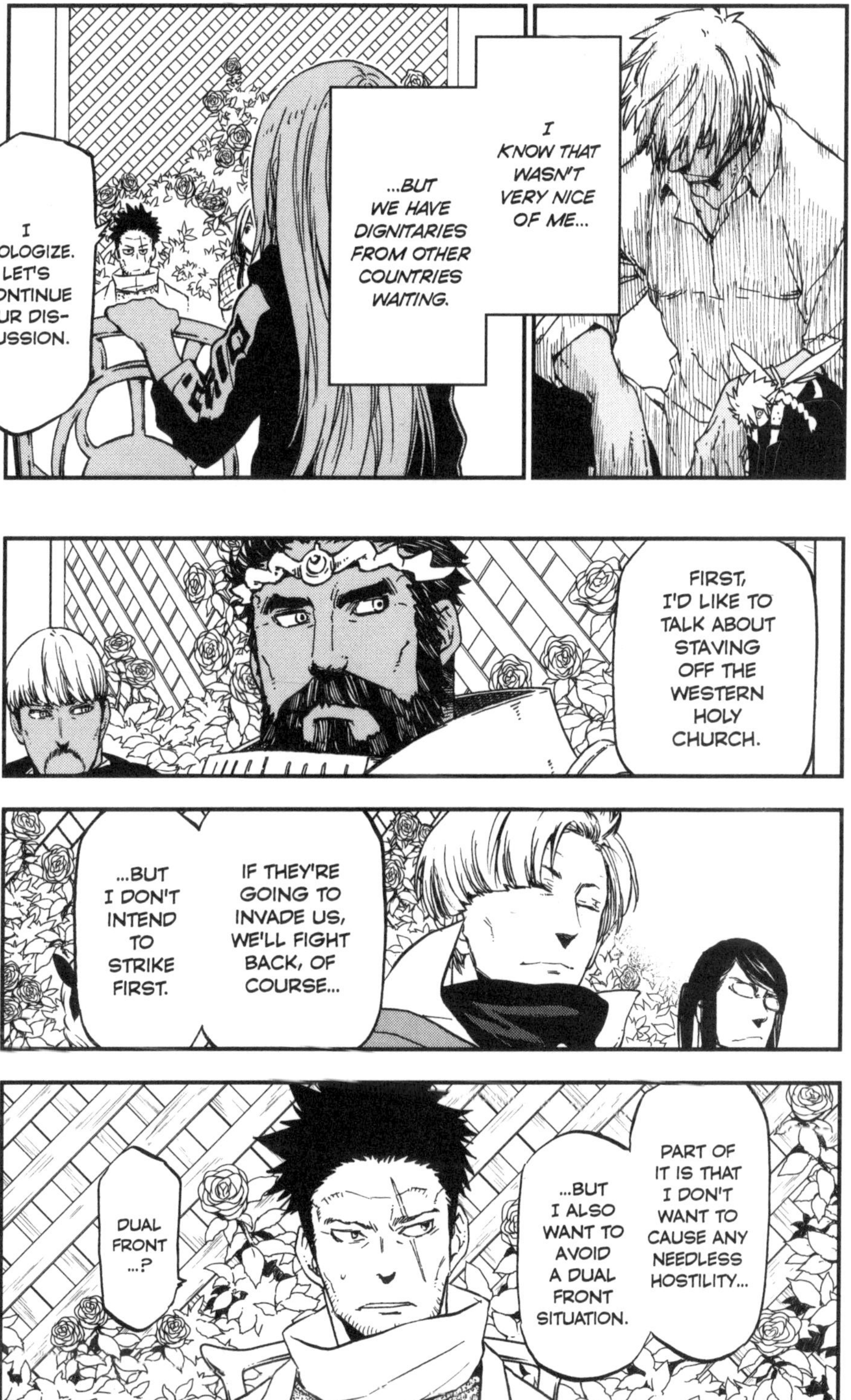
I KNOW THAT WASN'T VERY NICE OF ME...
...BUT WE HAVE DIGNITARIES FROM OTHER COUNTRIES WAITING.
I APOLOGIZE. LET'S CONTINUE OUR DISCUSSION.
FIRST, I'D LIKE TO TALK ABOUT STAVING OFF THE WESTERN HOLY CHURCH.
IF THEY'RE GOING TO INVADE US, WE'LL FIGHT BACK, OF COURSE...
...BUT I DON'T INTEND TO STRIKE FIRST.
PART OF IT IS THAT I DON'T WANT TO CAUSE ANY NEEDLESS HOSTILITY...
...BUT I ALSO WANT TO AVOID A DUAL FRONT SITUATION.
DUAL FRONT ...?

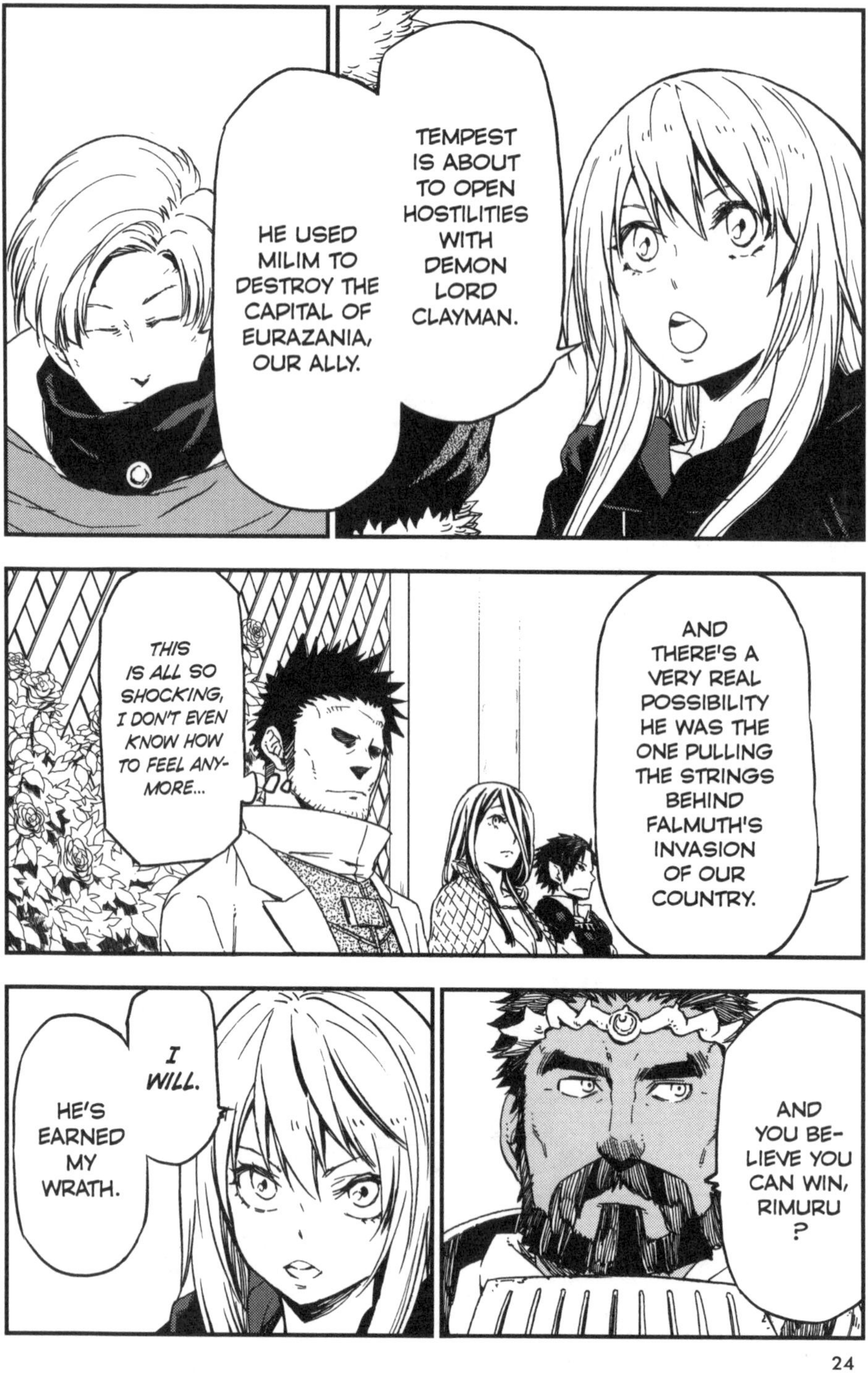
TEMPEST IS ABOUT TO OPEN HOSTILITIES WITH DEMON LORD CLAYMAN.
HE USED MILIM TO DESTROY THE CAPITAL OF EURAZANIA, OUR ALLY.
AND THERE'S A VERY REAL POSSIBILITY HE WAS THE ONE PULLING THE STRINGS BEHIND FALMUTH'S INVASION OF OUR COUNTRY.
THIS IS ALL SO SHOCKING, I DON'T EVEN KNOW HOW TO FEEL ANY-MORE...
AND YOU BE-LIEVE YOU CAN WIN, RIMURU?
I WILL.
HE'S EARNED MY WRATH.

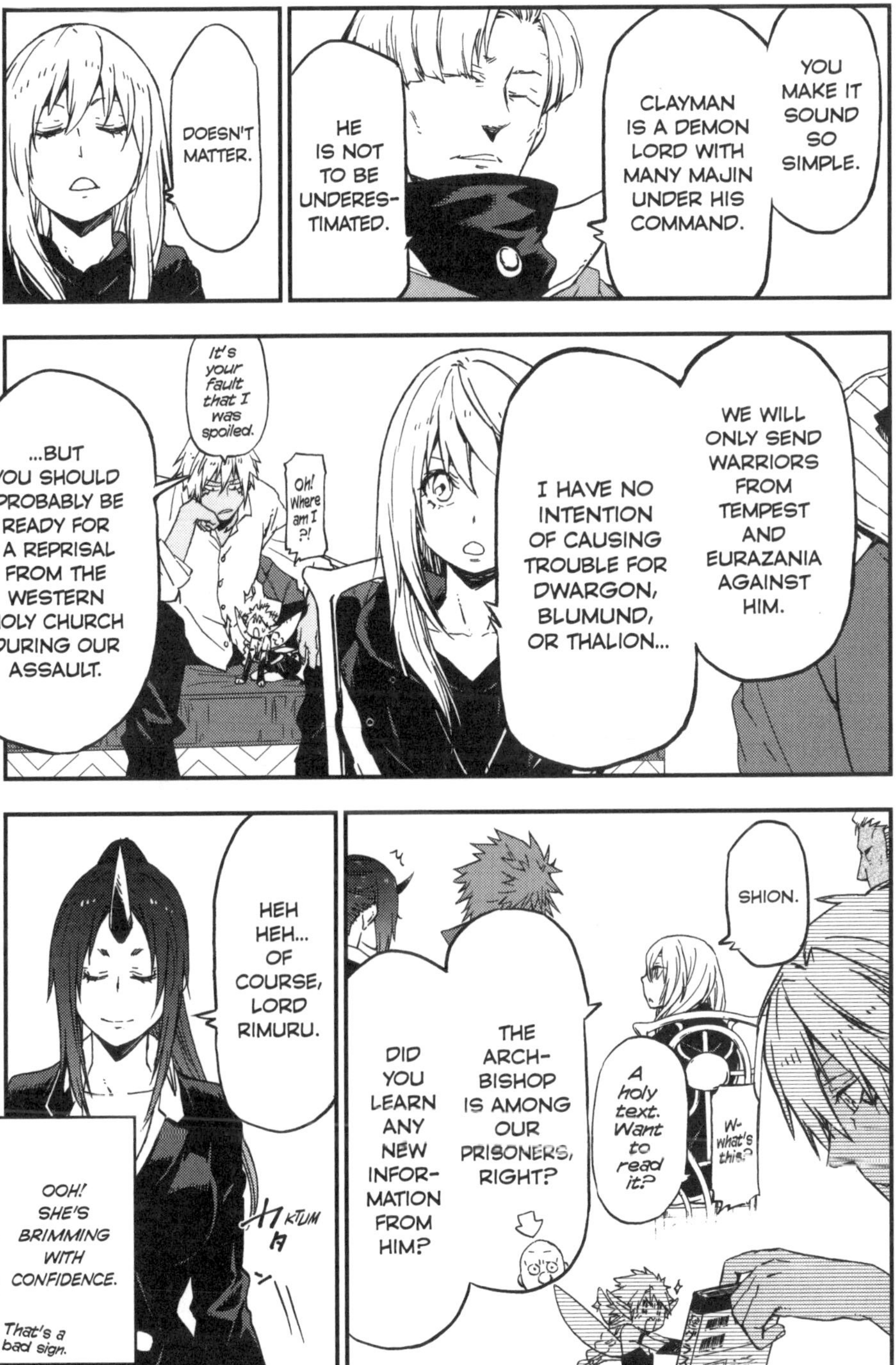
YOU MAKE IT SOUND SO SIMPLE.
CLAYMAN IS A DEMON LORD WITH MANY MAJIN UNDER HIS COMMAND.
HE IS NOT TO BE UNDERES-TIMATED.
DOESN'T MATTER.
WE WILL ONLY SEND WARRIORS FROM TEMPEST AND EURAZANIA AGAINST HIM.
I HAVE NO INTENTION OF CAUSING TROUBLE FOR DWARGON, BLUMUND, OR THALION...
It's your fault that I was spoiled.
Oh! Where am I ?!
...BUT YOU SHOULD PROBABLY BE READY FOR A REPRISAL FROM THE WESTERN HOLY CHURCH DURING OUR ASSAULT.
SHION.
THE ARCH-BISHOP IS AMONG OUR PRISONERS, RIGHT?
DID YOU LEARN ANY NEW INFOR-MATION FROM HIM?
A holy text. Want to read it?
W-what's this?
HEH HEH... OF COURSE, LORD RIMURU.
KTUM
OOH! SHE'S BRIMMING WITH CONFIDENCE.
That's a bad sign.

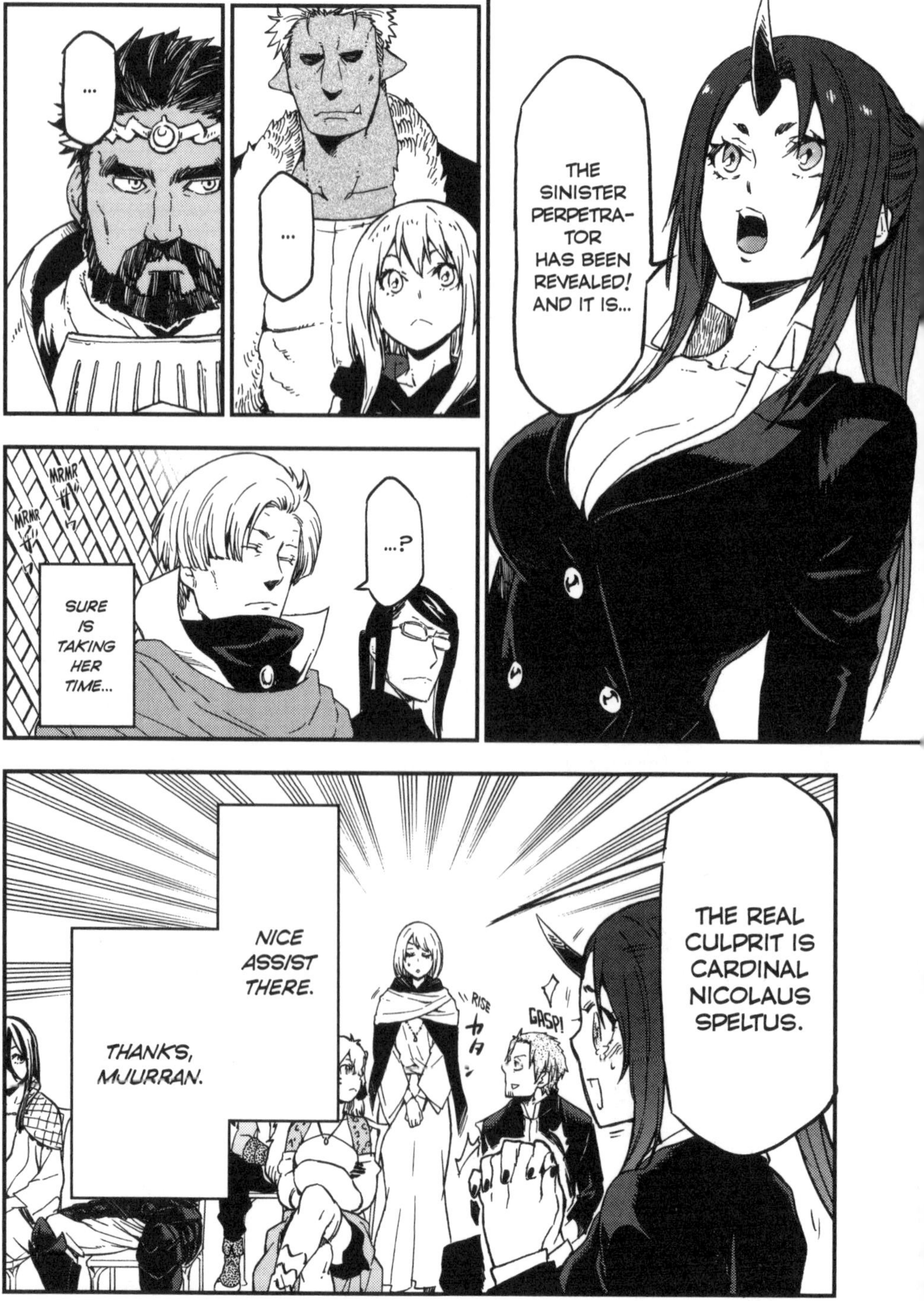
THE SINISTER PERPETRATOR HAS BEEN REVEALED! AND IT IS...
...
...
...?
MRMR
MRMR
SURE IS TAKING HER TIME...
THE REAL CULPRIT IS CARDINAL NICOLAUS SPELTUS.
GASP!
RISE
NICE ASSIST THERE.
THANKS, MJURRAN.

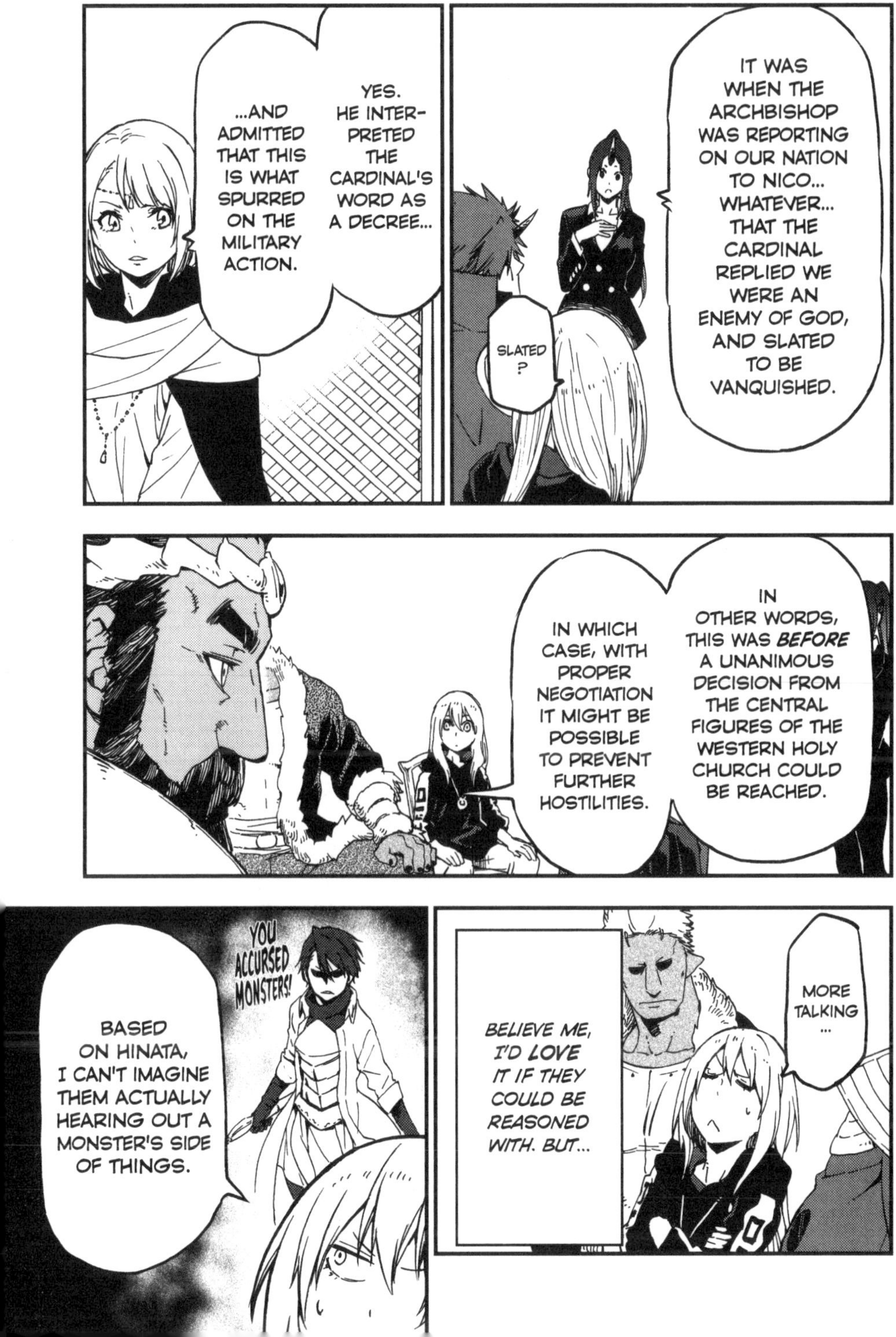
IT WAS WHEN THE ARCHBISHOP WAS REPORTING ON OUR NATION TO NICO... WHATEVER... THAT THE CARDINAL REPLIED WE WERE AN ENEMY OF GOD, AND SLATED TO BE VANQUISHED.
SLATED?
YES. HE INTER-PRETED THE CARDINAL'S WORD AS A DECREE...
...AND ADMITTED THAT THIS IS WHAT SPURRED ON THE MILITARY ACTION.
IN OTHER WORDS, THIS WAS *BEFORE* A UNANIMOUS DECISION FROM THE CENTRAL FIGURES OF THE WESTERN HOLY CHURCH COULD BE REACHED.
IN WHICH CASE, WITH PROPER NEGOTIATION IT MIGHT BE POSSIBLE TO PREVENT FURTHER HOSTILITIES.
MORE TALKING...
BELIEVE ME, I'D ***LOVE*** *IT IF THEY COULD BE REASONED WITH. BUT...*
YOU ACCURSED MONSTERS!
BASED ON HINATA, I CAN'T IMAGINE THEM ACTUALLY HEARING OUT A MONSTER'S SIDE OF THINGS.

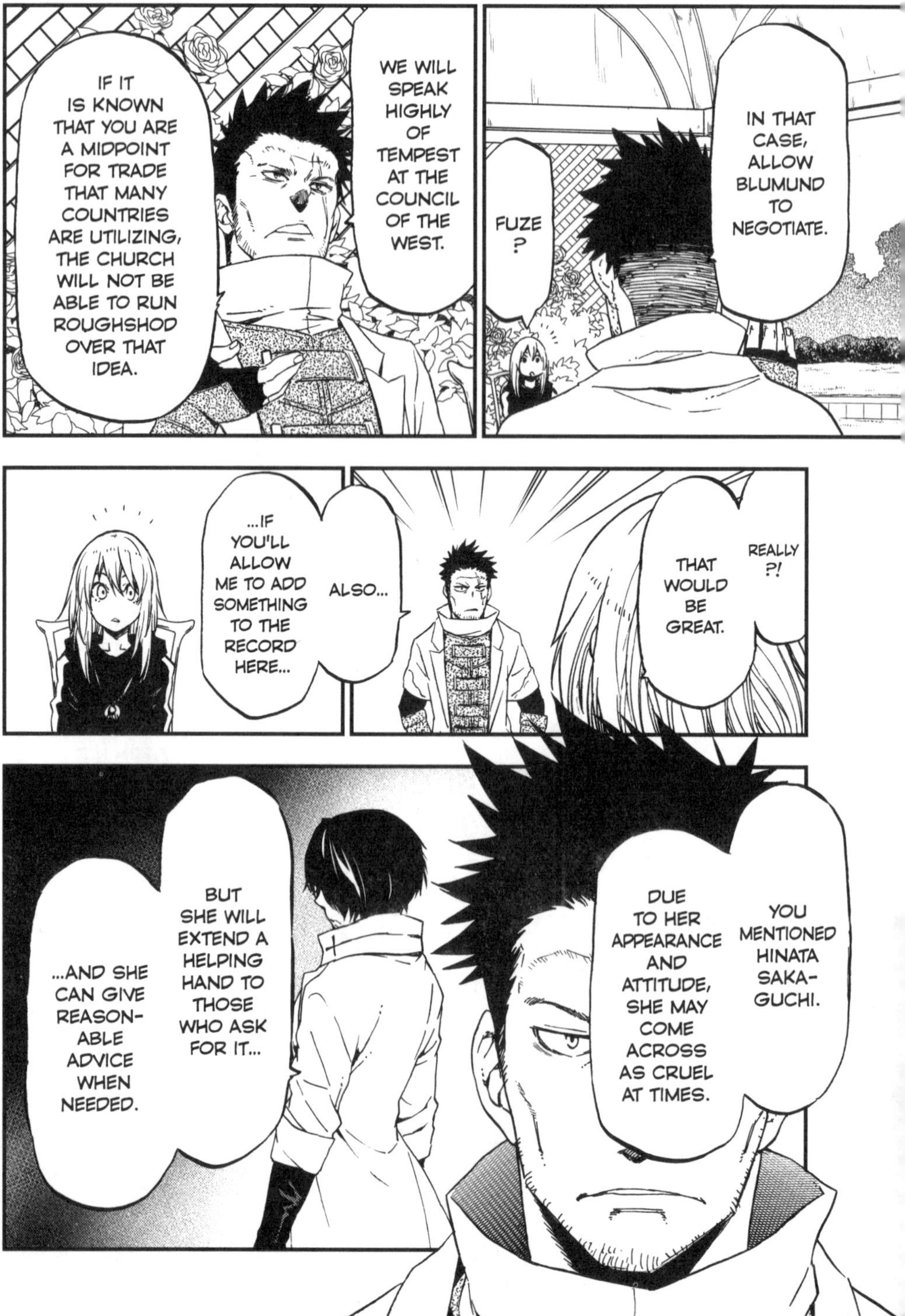
IN THAT CASE, ALLOW BLUMUND TO NEGOTIATE.
FUZE?
WE WILL SPEAK HIGHLY OF TEMPEST AT THE COUNCIL OF THE WEST.
IF IT IS KNOWN THAT YOU ARE A MIDPOINT FOR TRADE THAT MANY COUNTRIES ARE UTILIZING, THE CHURCH WILL NOT BE ABLE TO RUN ROUGHSHOD OVER THAT IDEA.
REALLY?!
THAT WOULD BE GREAT.
ALSO...
...IF YOU'LL ALLOW ME TO ADD SOMETHING TO THE RECORD HERE...
YOU MENTIONED HINATA SAKA-GUCHI.
DUE TO HER APPEARANCE AND ATTITUDE, SHE MAY COME ACROSS AS CRUEL AT TIMES.
BUT SHE WILL EXTEND A HELPING HAND TO THOSE WHO ASK FOR IT...
...AND SHE CAN GIVE REASON-ABLE ADVICE WHEN NEEDED.

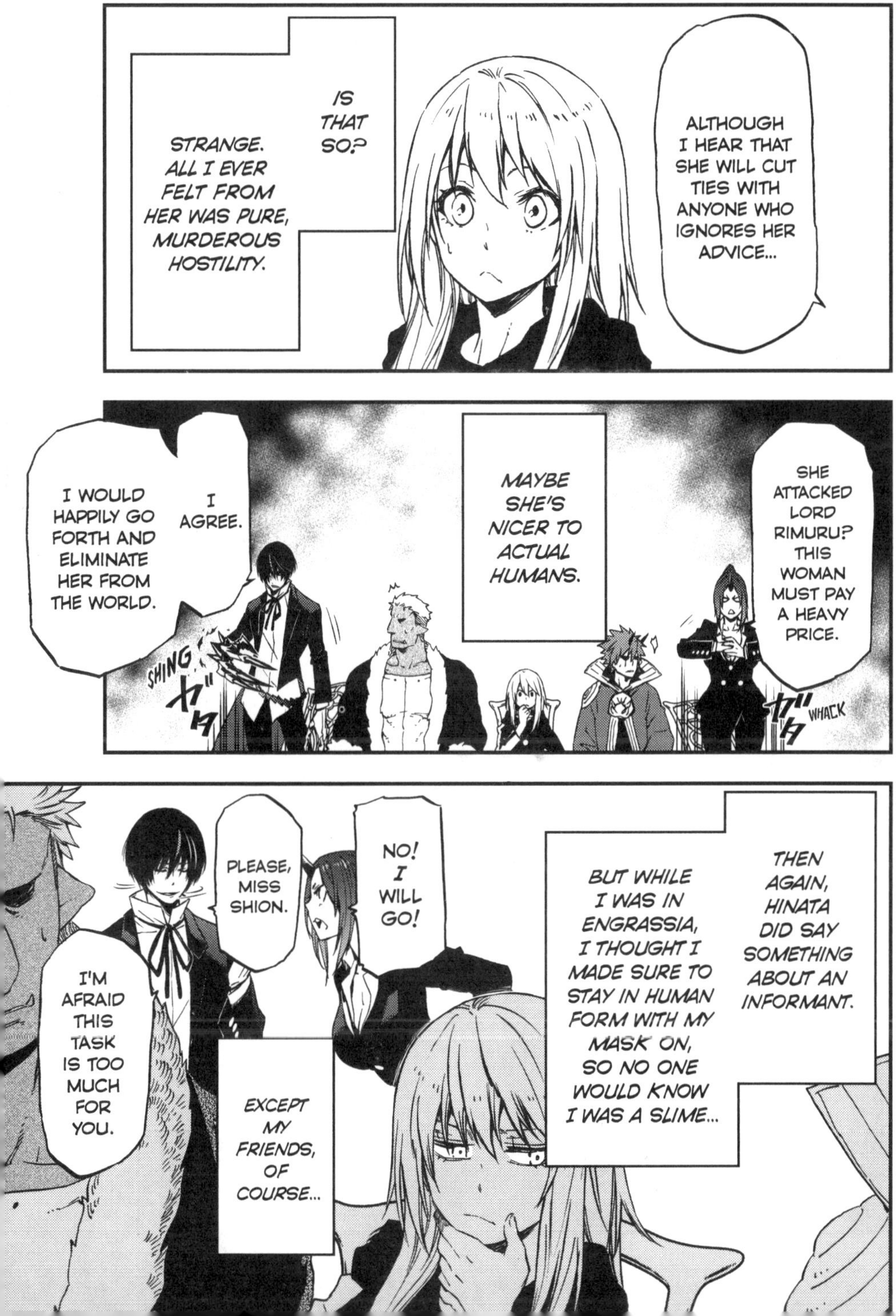
ALTHOUGH I HEAR THAT SHE WILL CUT TIES WITH ANYONE WHO IGNORES HER ADVICE...
IS THAT SO?
STRANGE. ALL I EVER FELT FROM HER WAS PURE, MURDEROUS HOSTILITY.
SHE ATTACKED LORD RIMURU? THIS WOMAN MUST PAY A HEAVY PRICE.
WHACK
MAYBE SHE'S NICER TO ACTUAL HUMANS.
I AGREE.
I WOULD HAPPILY GO FORTH AND ELIMINATE HER FROM THE WORLD.
SHING
THEN AGAIN, HINATA DID SAY SOMETHING ABOUT AN INFORMANT.
BUT WHILE I WAS IN ENGRASSIA, I THOUGHT I MADE SURE TO STAY IN HUMAN FORM WITH MY MASK ON, SO NO ONE WOULD KNOW I WAS A SLIME...
NO! I WILL GO!
PLEASE, MISS SHION.
I'M AFRAID THIS TASK IS TOO MUCH FOR YOU.
EXCEPT MY FRIENDS, OF COURSE...

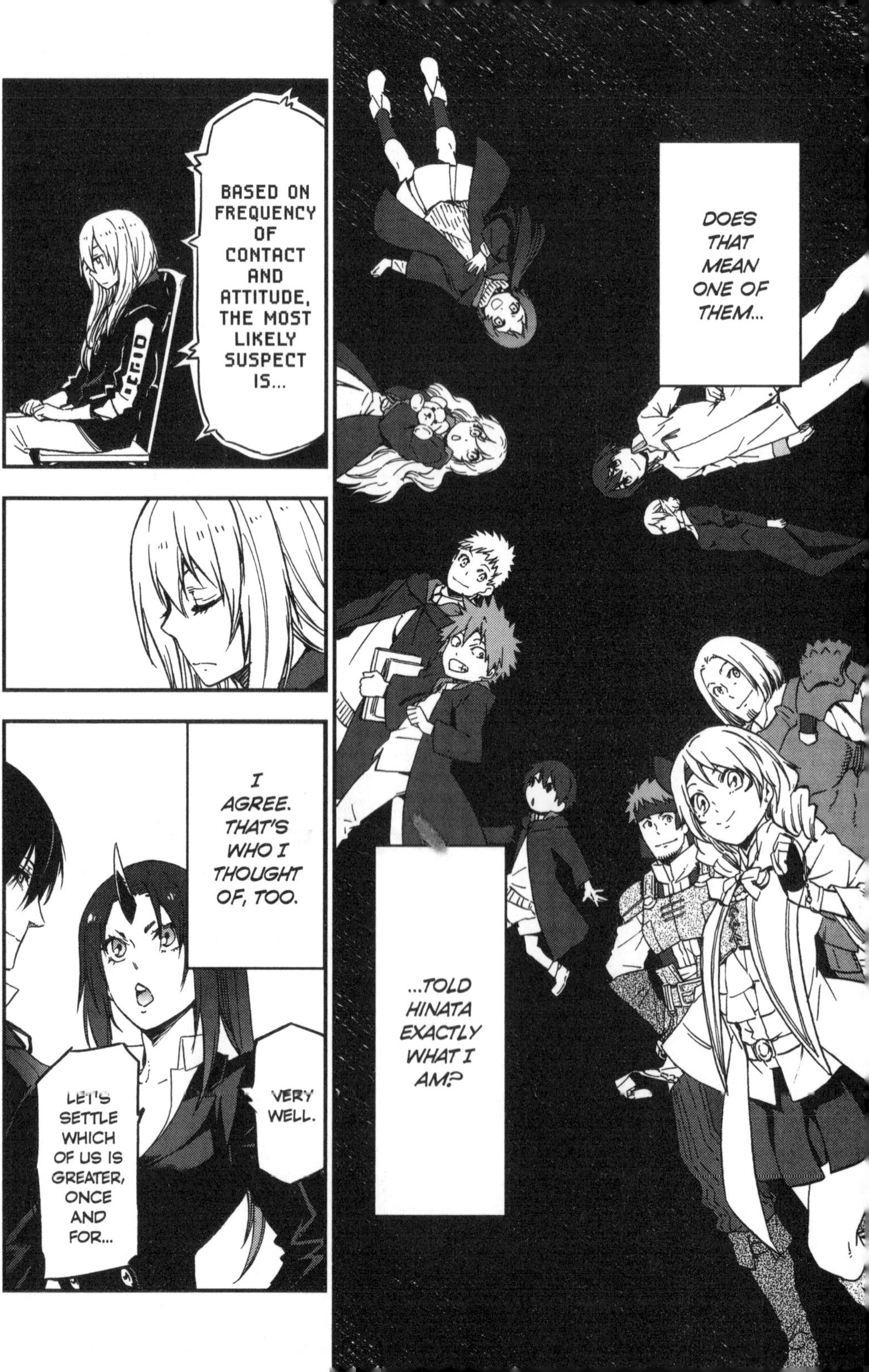
DOES THAT MEAN ONE OF THEM...
...TOLD HINATA EXACTLY WHAT I AM?
BASED ON FREQUENCY OF CONTACT AND ATTITUDE, THE MOST LIKELY SUSPECT IS...
I AGREE. THAT'S WHO I THOUGHT OF, TOO.
VERY WELL.
LET'S SETTLE WHICH OF US IS GREATER, ONCE AND FOR...

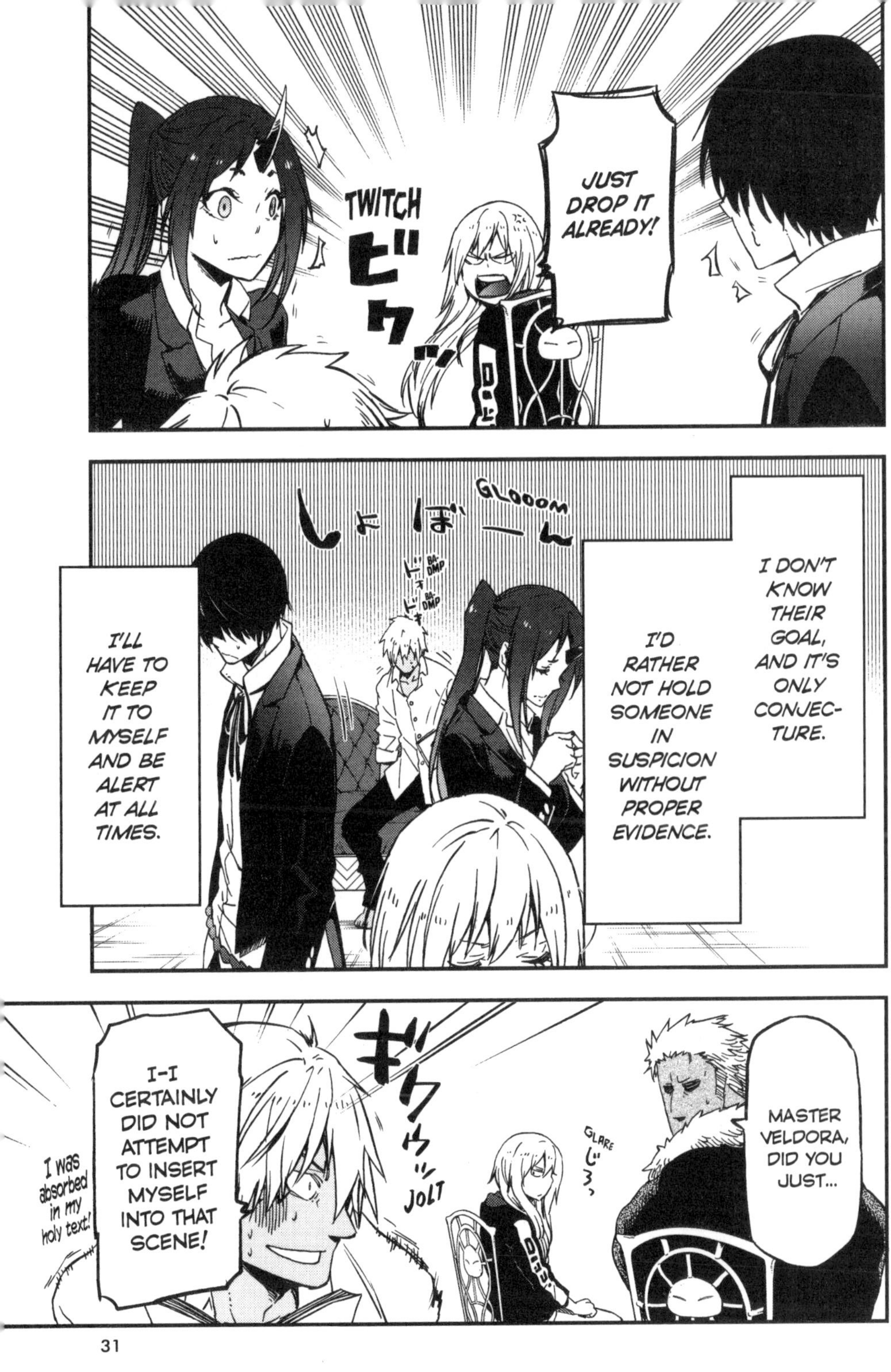
JUST DROP IT ALREADY!
TWITCH
GLOOOM
I DON'T KNOW THEIR GOAL, AND IT'S ONLY CONJECTURE.
I'D RATHER NOT HOLD SOMEONE IN SUSPICION WITHOUT PROPER EVIDENCE.
BA-DMP BA-DMP
I'LL HAVE TO KEEP IT TO MYSELF AND BE ALERT AT ALL TIMES.
MASTER VELDORA, DID YOU JUST...
GLARE
JOLT
I-I CERTAINLY DID NOT ATTEMPT TO INSERT MYSELF INTO THAT SCENE!
I was absorbed in my holy text!

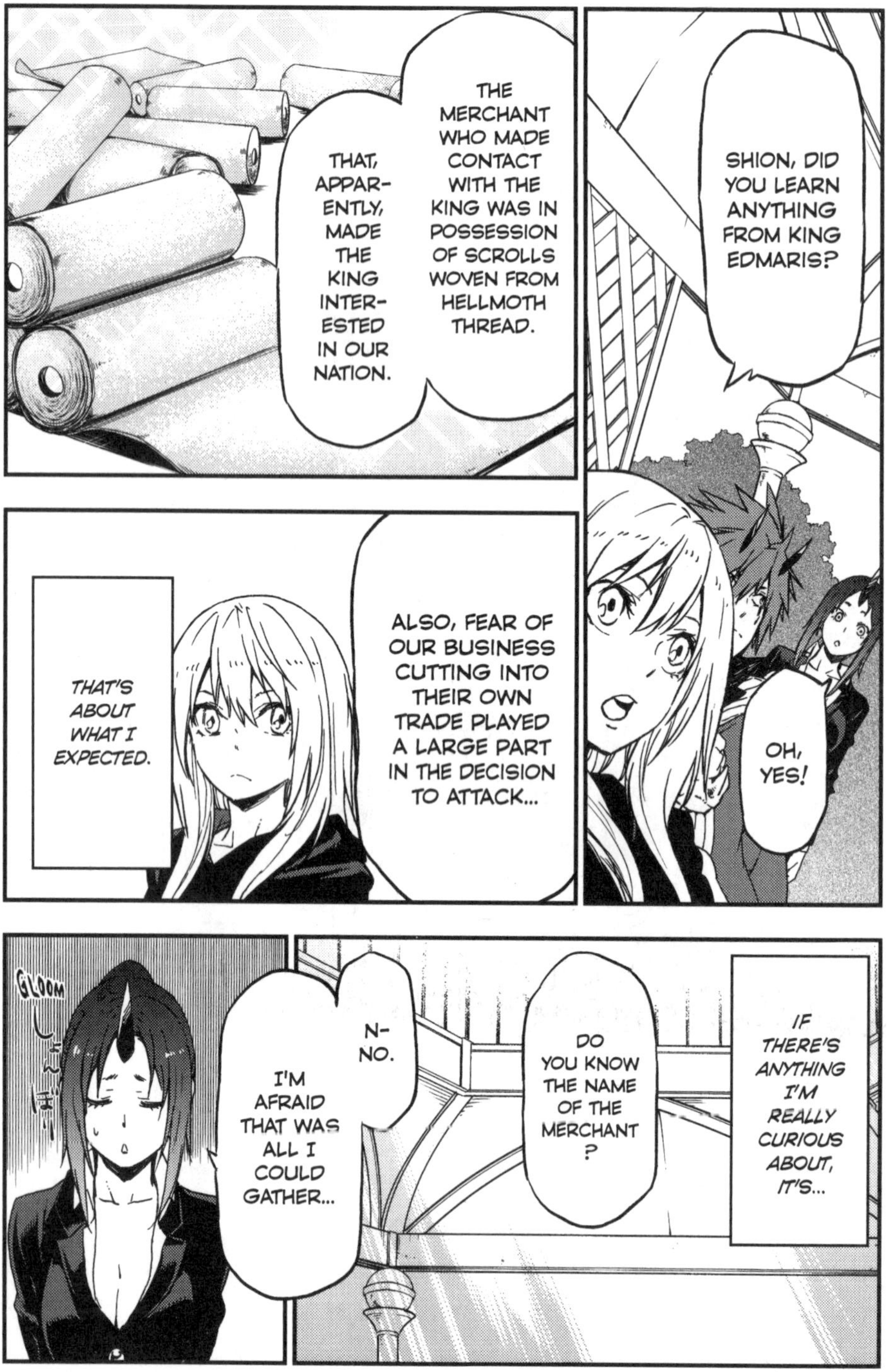

SHION, DID YOU LEARN ANYTHING FROM KING EDMARIS?
OH, YES!
THE MERCHANT WHO MADE CONTACT WITH THE KING WAS IN POSSESSION OF SCROLLS WOVEN FROM HELLMOTH THREAD.
THAT, APPARENTLY, MADE THE KING INTERESTED IN OUR NATION.
ALSO, FEAR OF OUR BUSINESS CUTTING INTO THEIR OWN TRADE PLAYED A LARGE PART IN THE DECISION TO ATTACK...
THAT'S ABOUT WHAT I EXPECTED.
IF THERE'S ANYTHING I'M REALLY CURIOUS ABOUT, IT'S...
DO YOU KNOW THE NAME OF THE MERCHANT?
N-NO.
I'M AFRAID THAT WAS ALL I COULD GATHER...
GLOOM

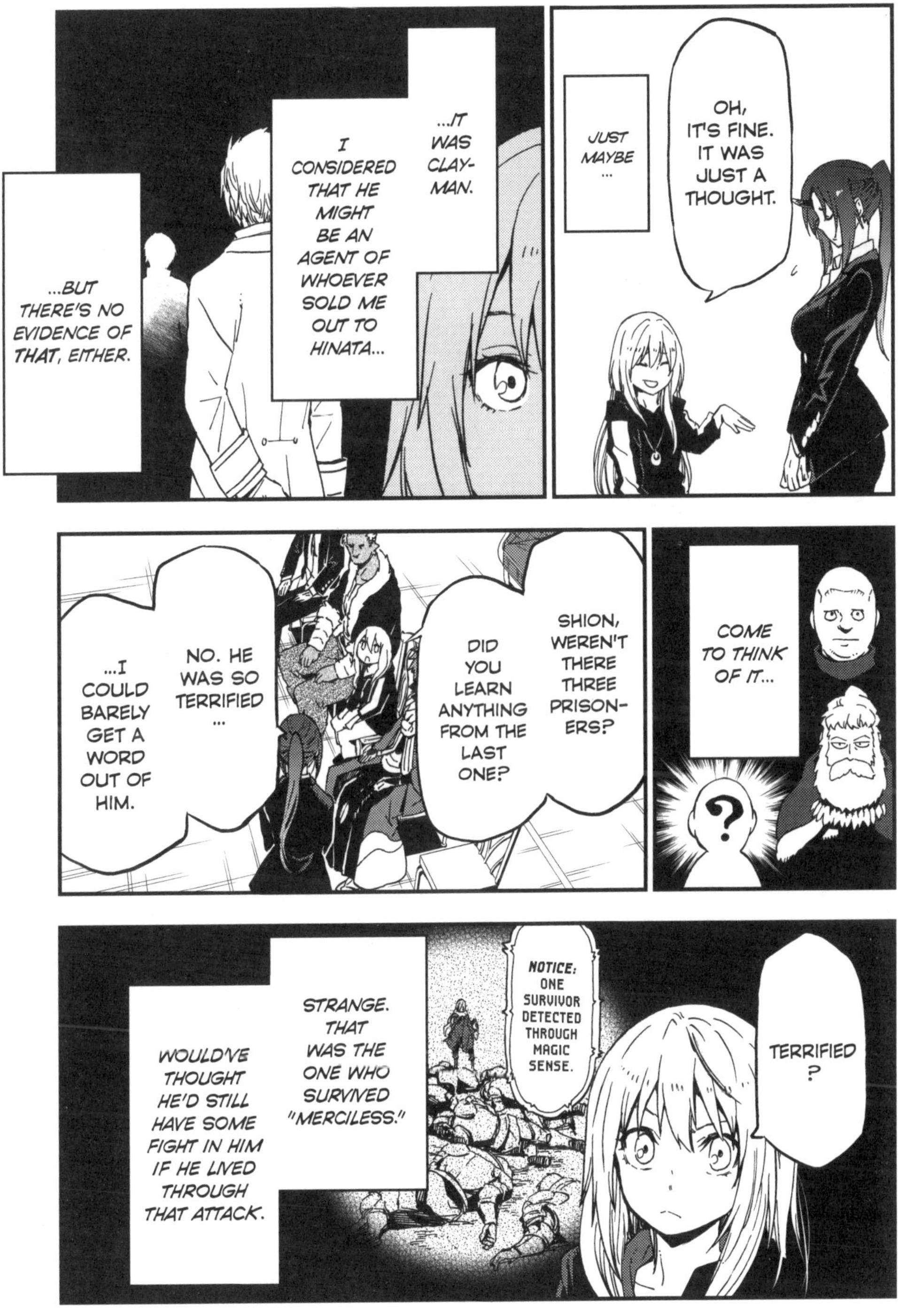
OH, IT'S FINE. IT WAS JUST A THOUGHT.
JUST MAYBE ...
...IT WAS CLAY-MAN.
I CONSIDERED THAT HE MIGHT BE AN AGENT OF WHOEVER SOLD ME OUT TO HINATA...
...BUT THERE'S NO EVIDENCE OF THAT, EITHER.
COME TO THINK OF IT...
?
SHION, WEREN'T THERE THREE PRISON-ERS?
DID YOU LEARN ANYTHING FROM THE LAST ONE?
NO. HE WAS SO TERRIFIED ...
...I COULD BARELY GET A WORD OUT OF HIM.
TERRIFIED ?
NOTICE: ONE SURVIVOR DETECTED THROUGH MAGIC SENSE.
STRANGE. THAT WAS THE ONE WHO SURVIVED "MERCILESS."
WOULD'VE THOUGHT HE'D STILL HAVE SOME FIGHT IN HIM IF HE LIVED THROUGH THAT ATTACK.

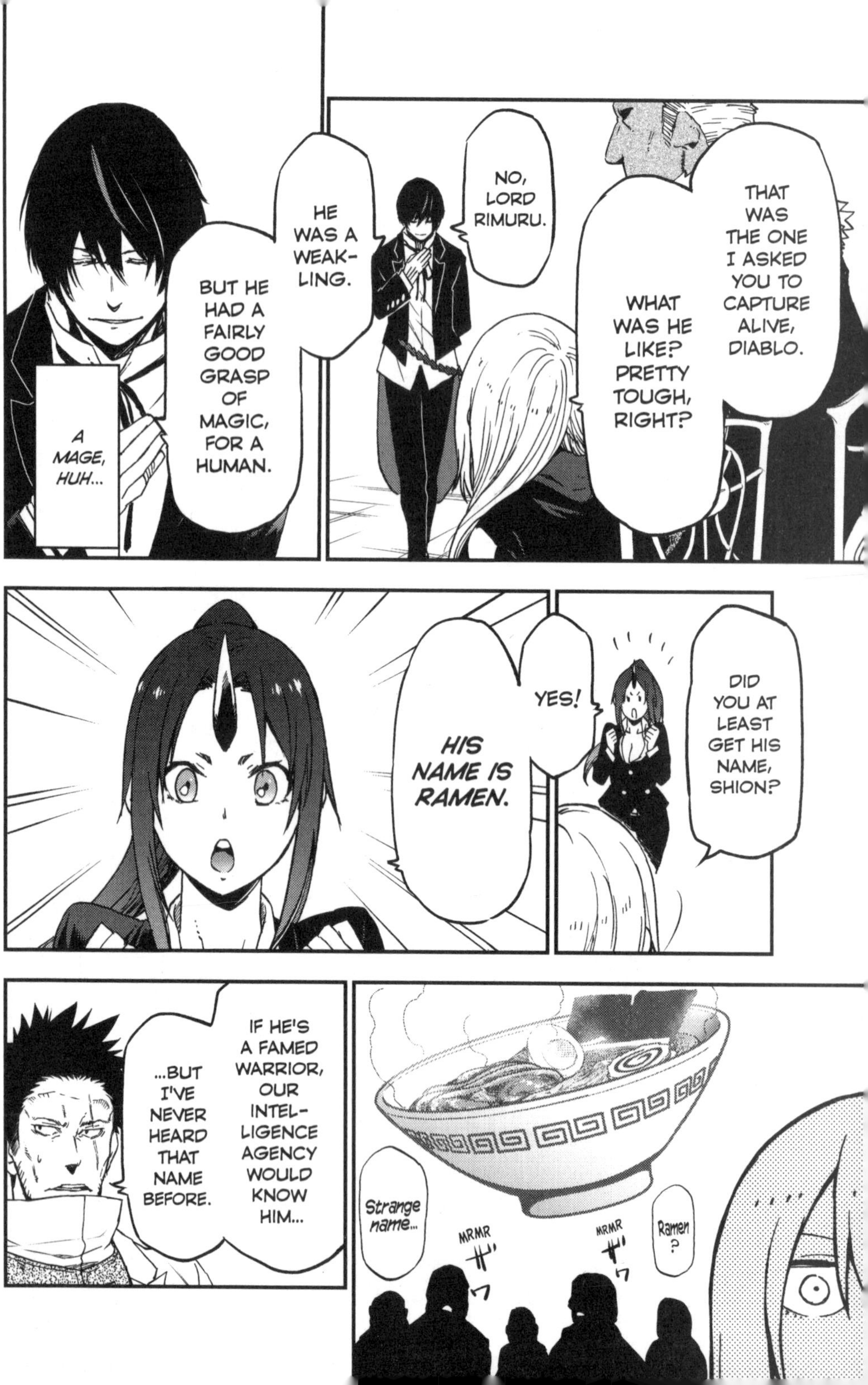
THAT WAS THE ONE I ASKED YOU TO CAPTURE ALIVE, DIABLO.
WHAT WAS HE LIKE? PRETTY TOUGH, RIGHT?
NO, LORD RIMURU.
HE WAS A WEAKLING.
BUT HE HAD A FAIRLY GOOD GRASP OF MAGIC, FOR A HUMAN.
A MAGE, HUH...
DID YOU AT LEAST GET HIS NAME, SHION?
YES!
HIS NAME IS RAMEN.
Ramen?
MRMR
MRMR
Strange name...
IF HE'S A FAMED WARRIOR, OUR INTEL-LIGENCE AGENCY WOULD KNOW HIM...
...BUT I'VE NEVER HEARD THAT NAME BEFORE.

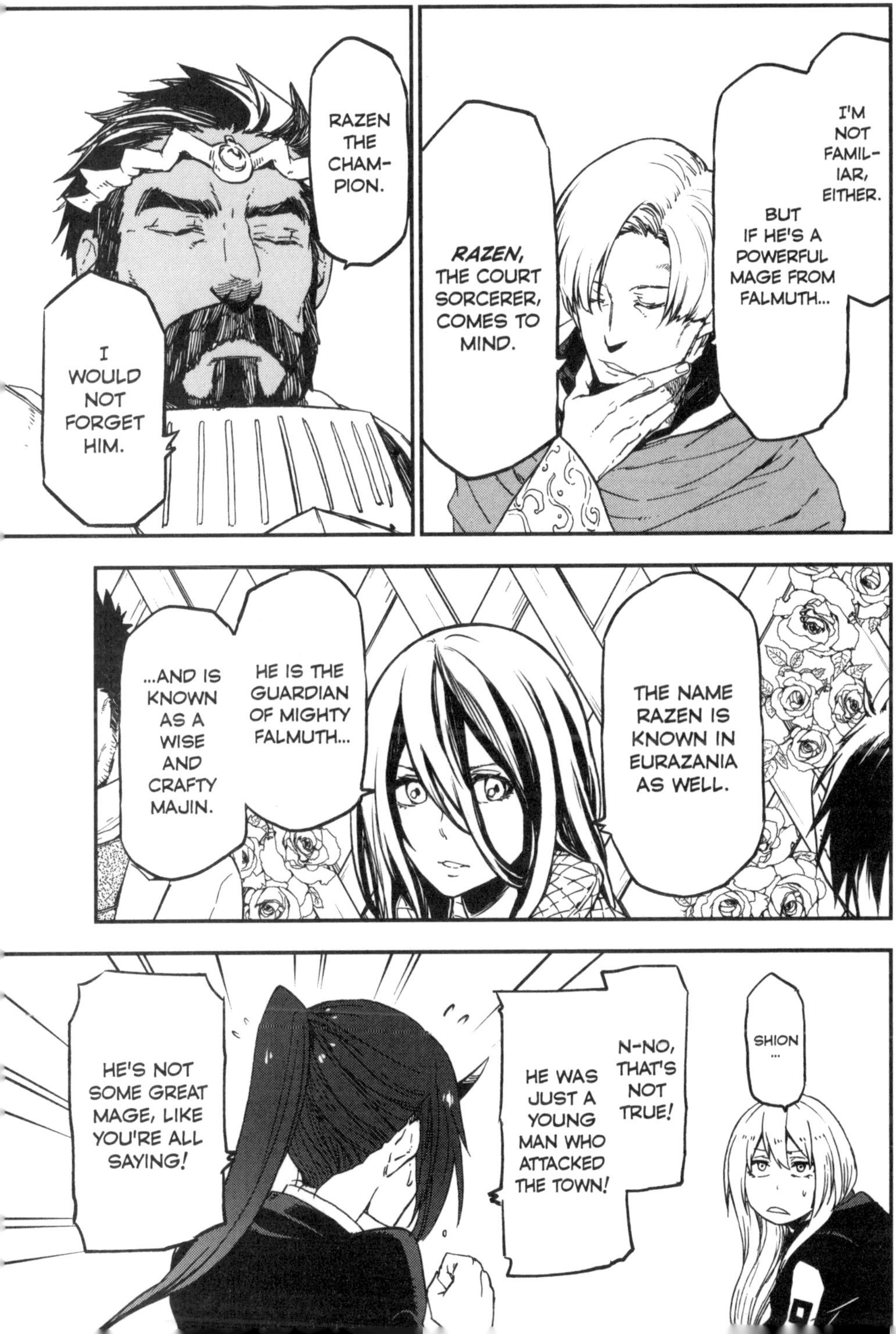
I'M NOT FAMILIAR, EITHER.
BUT IF HE'S A POWERFUL MAGE FROM FALMUTH...
RAZEN, THE COURT SORCERER, COMES TO MIND.
RAZEN THE CHAMPION.
I WOULD NOT FORGET HIM.
THE NAME RAZEN IS KNOWN IN EURAZANIA AS WELL.
HE IS THE GUARDIAN OF MIGHTY FALMUTH...
...AND IS KNOWN AS A WISE AND CRAFTY MAJIN.
SHION...
N-NO, THAT'S NOT TRUE!
HE WAS JUST A YOUNG MAN WHO ATTACKED THE TOWN!
HE'S NOT SOME GREAT MAGE, LIKE YOU'RE ALL SAYING!

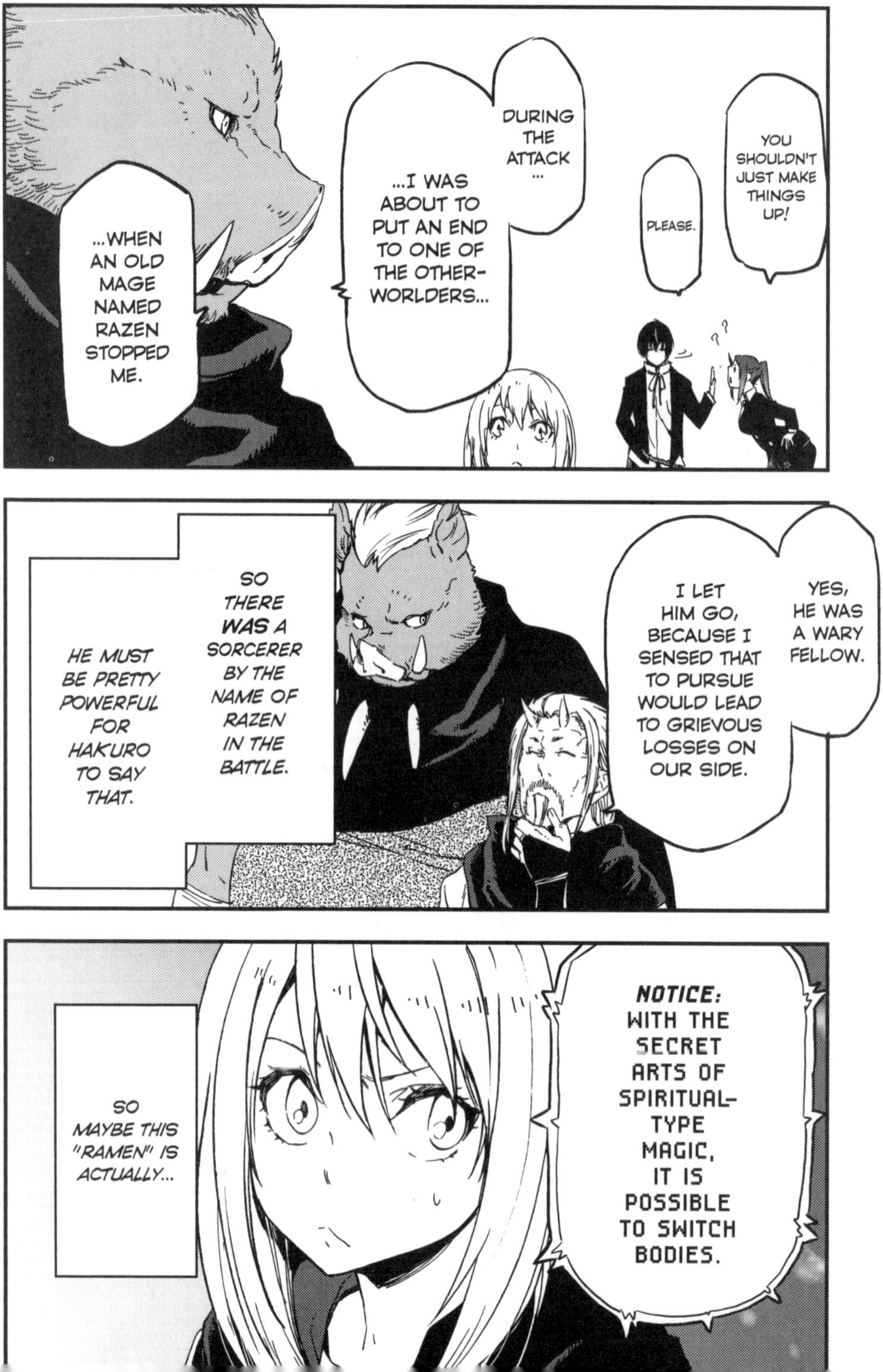
YOU SHOULDN'T JUST MAKE THINGS UP!
PLEASE.
DURING THE ATTACK...
...I WAS ABOUT TO PUT AN END TO ONE OF THE OTHER-WORLDERS...
...WHEN AN OLD MAGE NAMED RAZEN STOPPED ME.
YES, HE WAS A WARY FELLOW.
I LET HIM GO, BECAUSE I SENSED THAT TO PURSUE WOULD LEAD TO GRIEVOUS LOSSES ON OUR SIDE.
SO THERE WAS A SORCERER BY THE NAME OF RAZEN IN THE BATTLE.
HE MUST BE PRETTY POWERFUL FOR HAKURO TO SAY THAT.
NOTICE: WITH THE SECRET ARTS OF SPIRITUAL-TYPE MAGIC, IT IS POSSIBLE TO SWITCH BODIES.
SO MAYBE THIS "RAMEN" IS ACTUALLY...

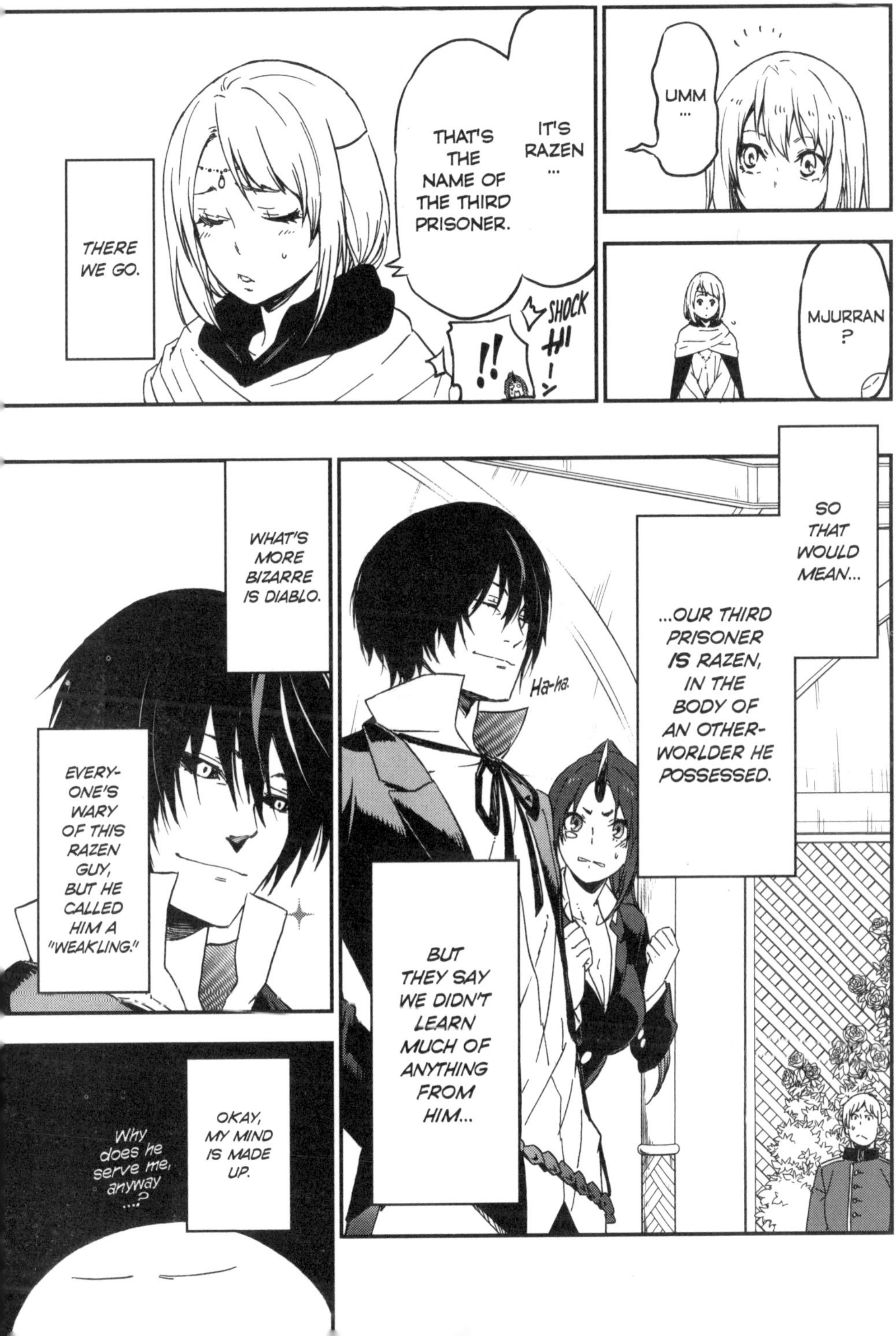
UMM ...
MJURRAN ?
IT'S RAZEN ...
THAT'S THE NAME OF THE THIRD PRISONER.
SHOCK
!!
THERE WE GO.
SO THAT WOULD MEAN...
...OUR THIRD PRISONER IS RAZEN, IN THE BODY OF AN OTHER-WORLDER HE POSSESSED.
Ha-ha.
BUT THEY SAY WE DIDN'T LEARN MUCH OF ANYTHING FROM HIM...
WHAT'S MORE BIZARRE IS DIABLO.
EVERYONE'S WARY OF THIS RAZEN GUY, BUT HE CALLED HIM A "WEAKLING."
OKAY, MY MIND IS MADE UP.
Why does he serve me, anyway ...?

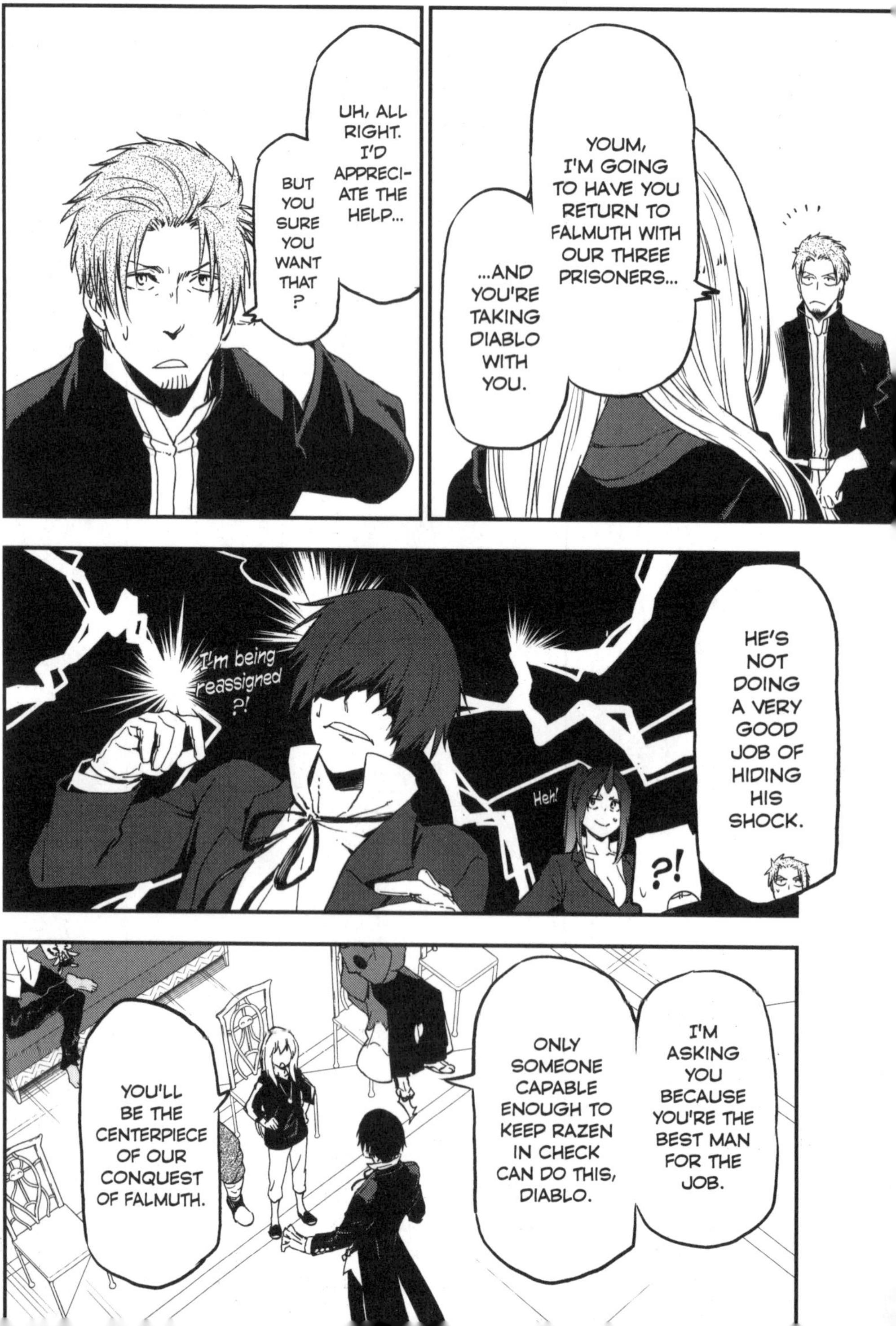
YOUM, I'M GOING TO HAVE YOU RETURN TO FALMUTH WITH OUR THREE PRISONERS...
...AND YOU'RE TAKING DIABLO WITH YOU.
UH, ALL RIGHT. I'D APPRECIATE THE HELP...
BUT YOU SURE YOU WANT THAT?
HE'S NOT DOING A VERY GOOD JOB OF HIDING HIS SHOCK.
?!
Heh!
I'm being reassigned?!
I'M ASKING YOU BECAUSE YOU'RE THE BEST MAN FOR THE JOB.
ONLY SOMEONE CAPABLE ENOUGH TO KEEP RAZEN IN CHECK CAN DO THIS, DIABLO.
YOU'LL BE THE CENTERPIECE OF OUR CONQUEST OF FALMUTH.

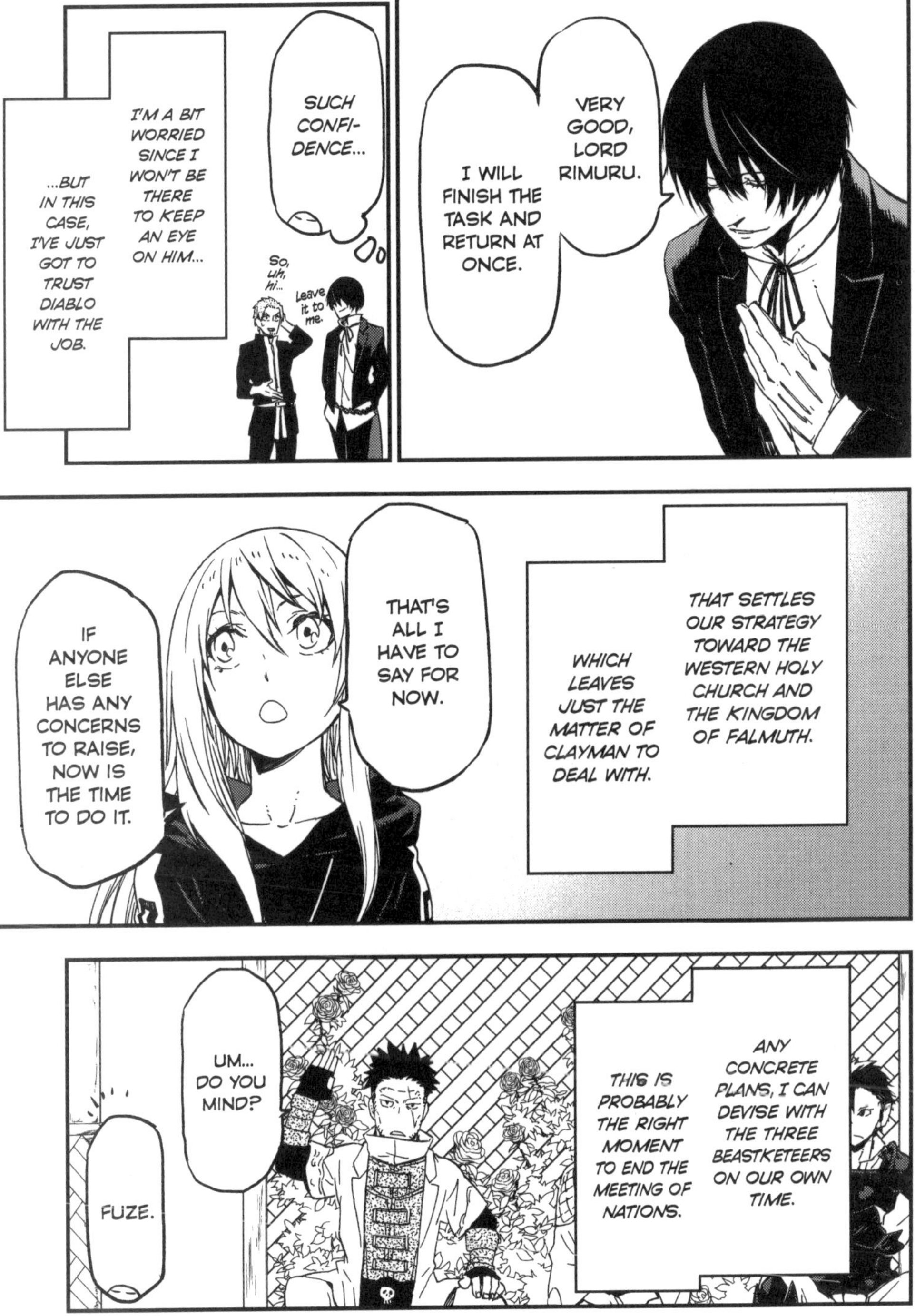
VERY GOOD, LORD RIMURU.
I WILL FINISH THE TASK AND RETURN AT ONCE.
SUCH CONFIDENCE...
I'M A BIT WORRIED SINCE I WON'T BE THERE TO KEEP AN EYE ON HIM...
Leave it to me.
So, uh, hi...
...BUT IN THIS CASE, I'VE JUST GOT TO TRUST DIABLO WITH THE JOB.
THAT SETTLES OUR STRATEGY TOWARD THE WESTERN HOLY CHURCH AND THE KINGDOM OF FALMUTH.
WHICH LEAVES JUST THE MATTER OF CLAYMAN TO DEAL WITH.
THAT'S ALL I HAVE TO SAY FOR NOW.
IF ANYONE ELSE HAS ANY CONCERNS TO RAISE, NOW IS THE TIME TO DO IT.
ANY CONCRETE PLANS, I CAN DEVISE WITH THE THREE BEASTKETEERS ON OUR OWN TIME.
THIS IS PROBABLY THE RIGHT MOMENT TO END THE MEETING OF NATIONS.
UM... DO YOU MIND?
FUZE.

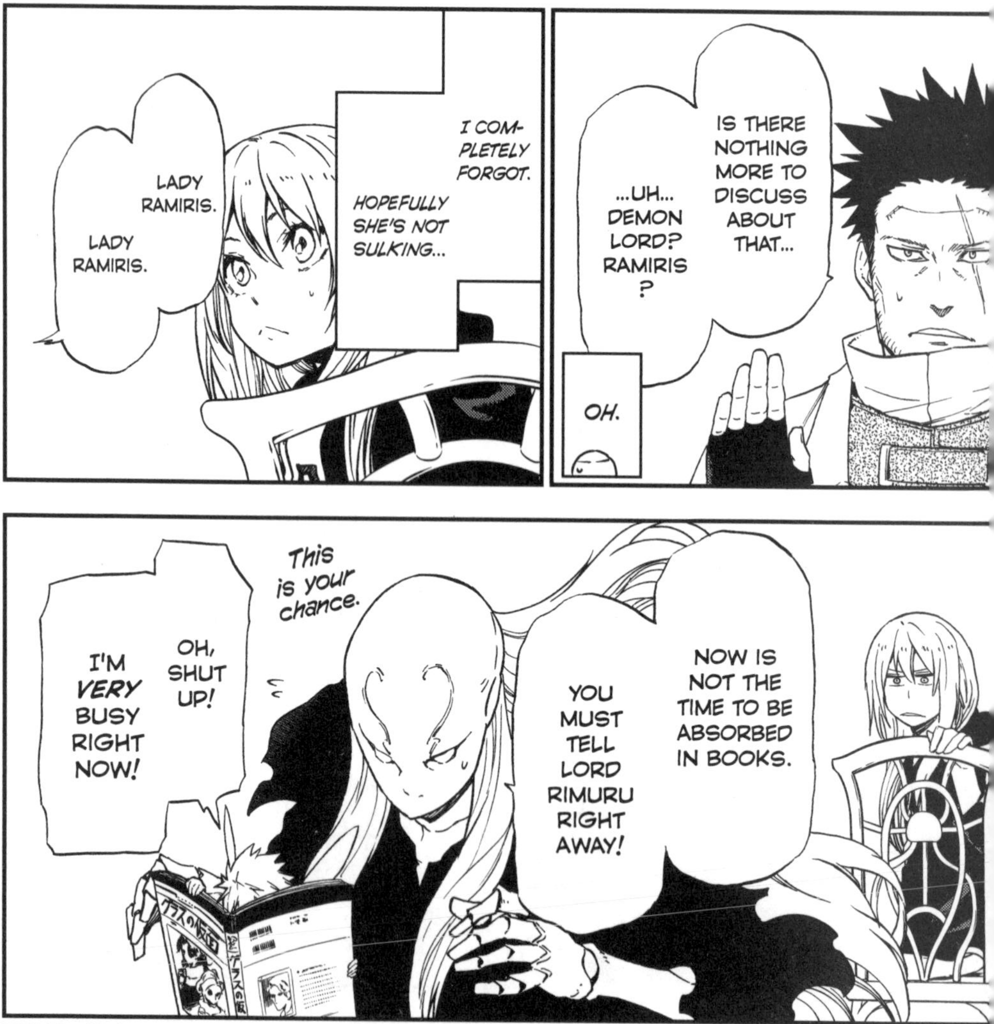
IS THERE NOTHING MORE TO DISCUSS ABOUT THAT...
...UH... DEMON LORD? RAMIRIS?
OH.
I COMPLETELY FORGOT.
HOPEFULLY SHE'S NOT SULKING...
LADY RAMIRIS.
LADY RAMIRIS.
NOW IS NOT THE TIME TO BE ABSORBED IN BOOKS.
YOU MUST TELL LORD RIMURU RIGHT AWAY!
This is your chance.
OH, SHUT UP!
I'M VERY BUSY RIGHT NOW!

BOOK: Glass Mask

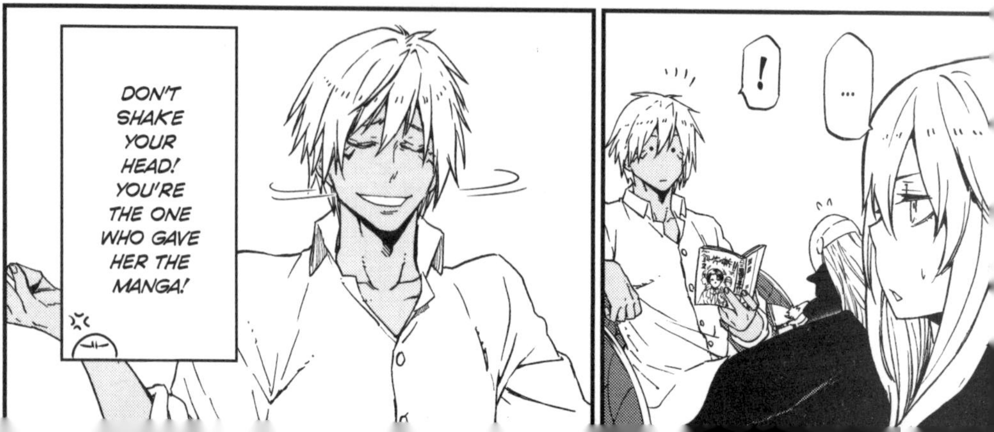
...
!
DON'T SHAKE YOUR HEAD! YOU'RE THE ONE WHO GAVE HER THE MANGA!

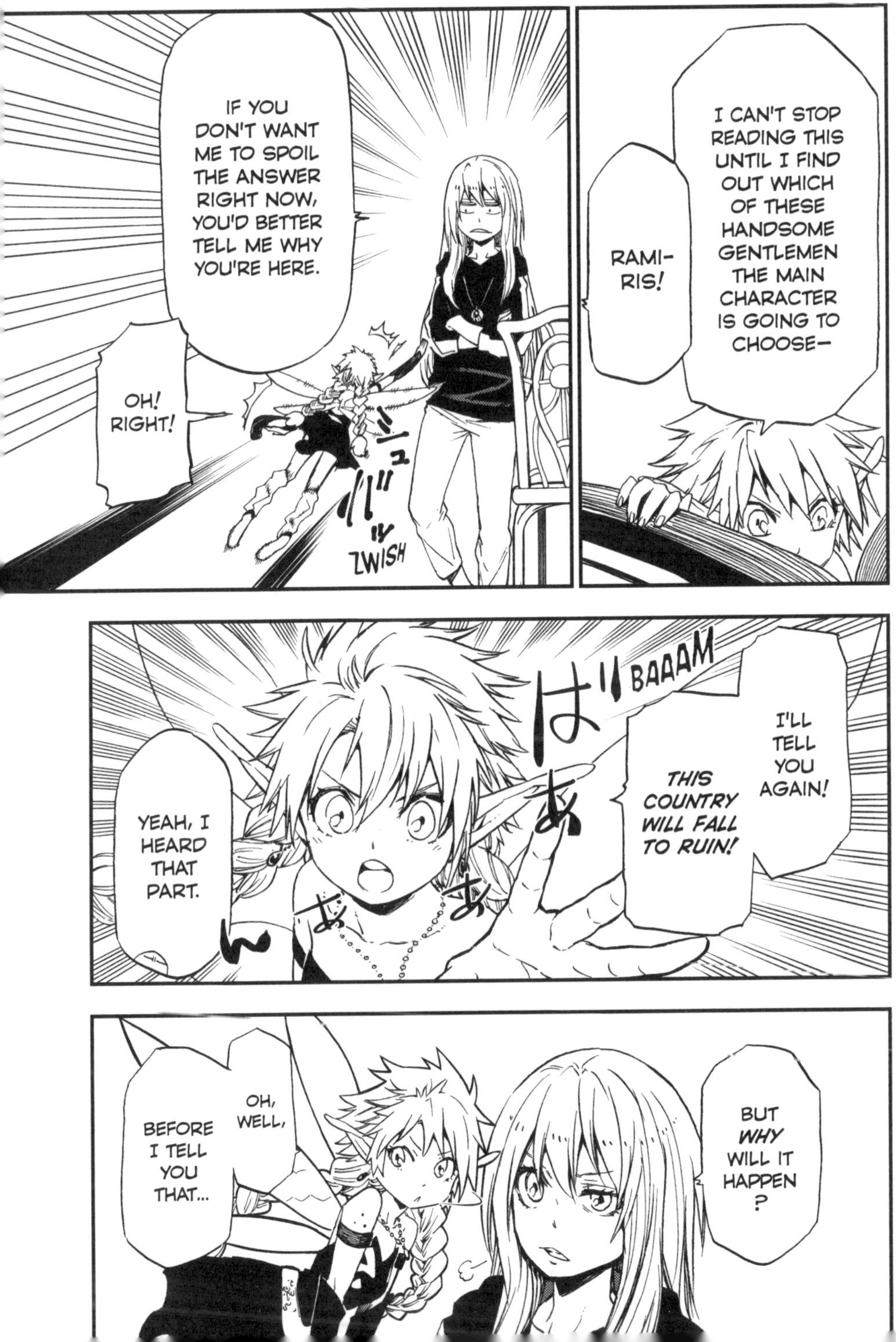
I CAN'T STOP READING THIS UNTIL I FIND OUT WHICH OF THESE HANDSOME GENTLEMEN THE MAIN CHARACTER IS GOING TO CHOOSE—
RAMI-RIS!
IF YOU DON'T WANT ME TO SPOIL THE ANSWER RIGHT NOW, YOU'D BETTER TELL ME WHY YOU'RE HERE.
OH! RIGHT!
ZWISH
BAAAM
I'LL TELL YOU AGAIN!
THIS COUNTRY WILL FALL TO RUIN!
YEAH, I HEARD THAT PART.
BUT *WHY* WILL IT HAPPEN?
OH, WELL,
BEFORE I TELL YOU THAT...

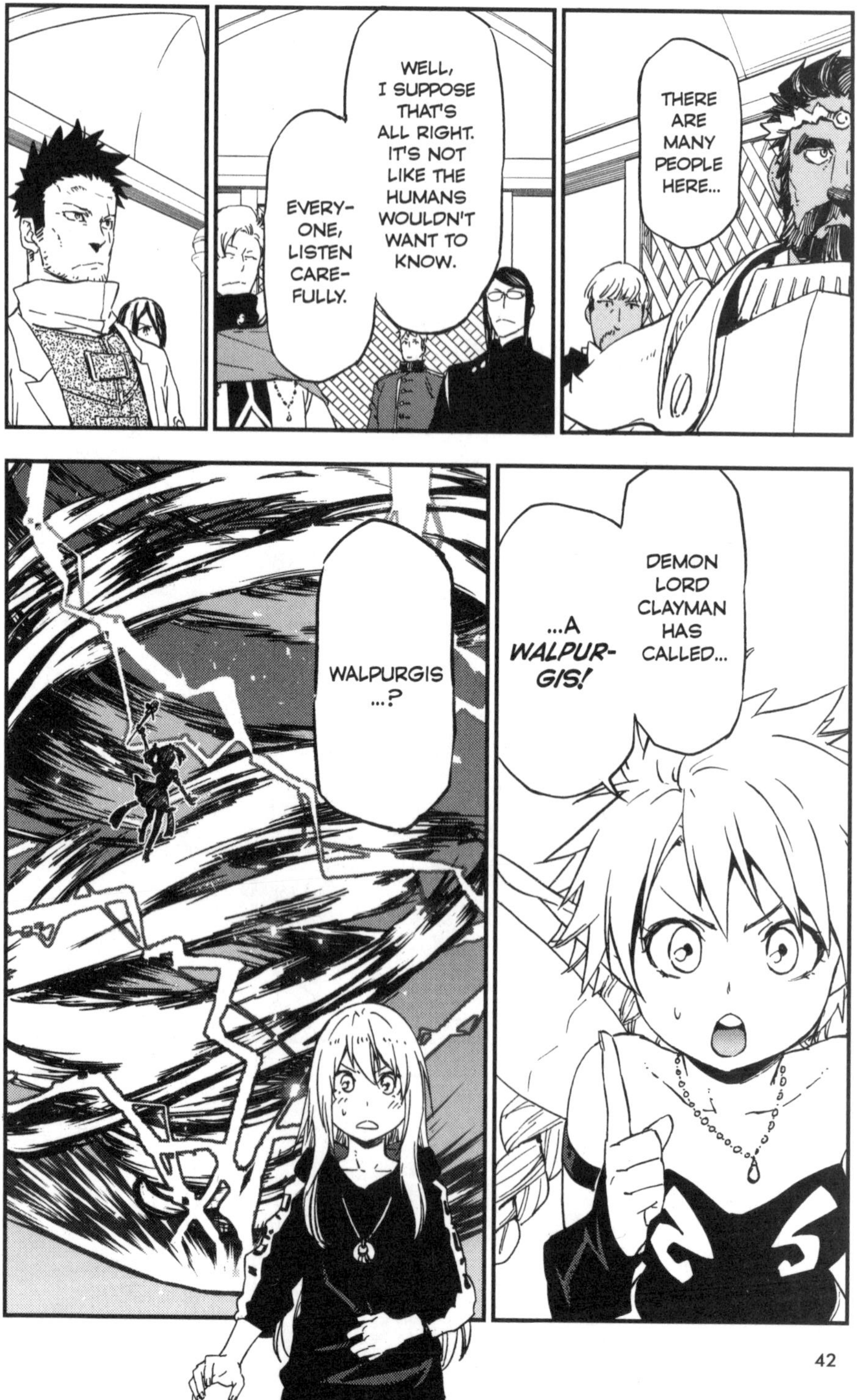
THERE ARE MANY PEOPLE HERE...
WELL, I SUPPOSE THAT'S ALL RIGHT. IT'S NOT LIKE THE HUMANS WOULDN'T WANT TO KNOW.
EVERY-ONE, LISTEN CARE-FULLY.
DEMON LORD CLAYMAN HAS CALLED...
...A *WALPUR-GIS!*
WALPURGIS ...?

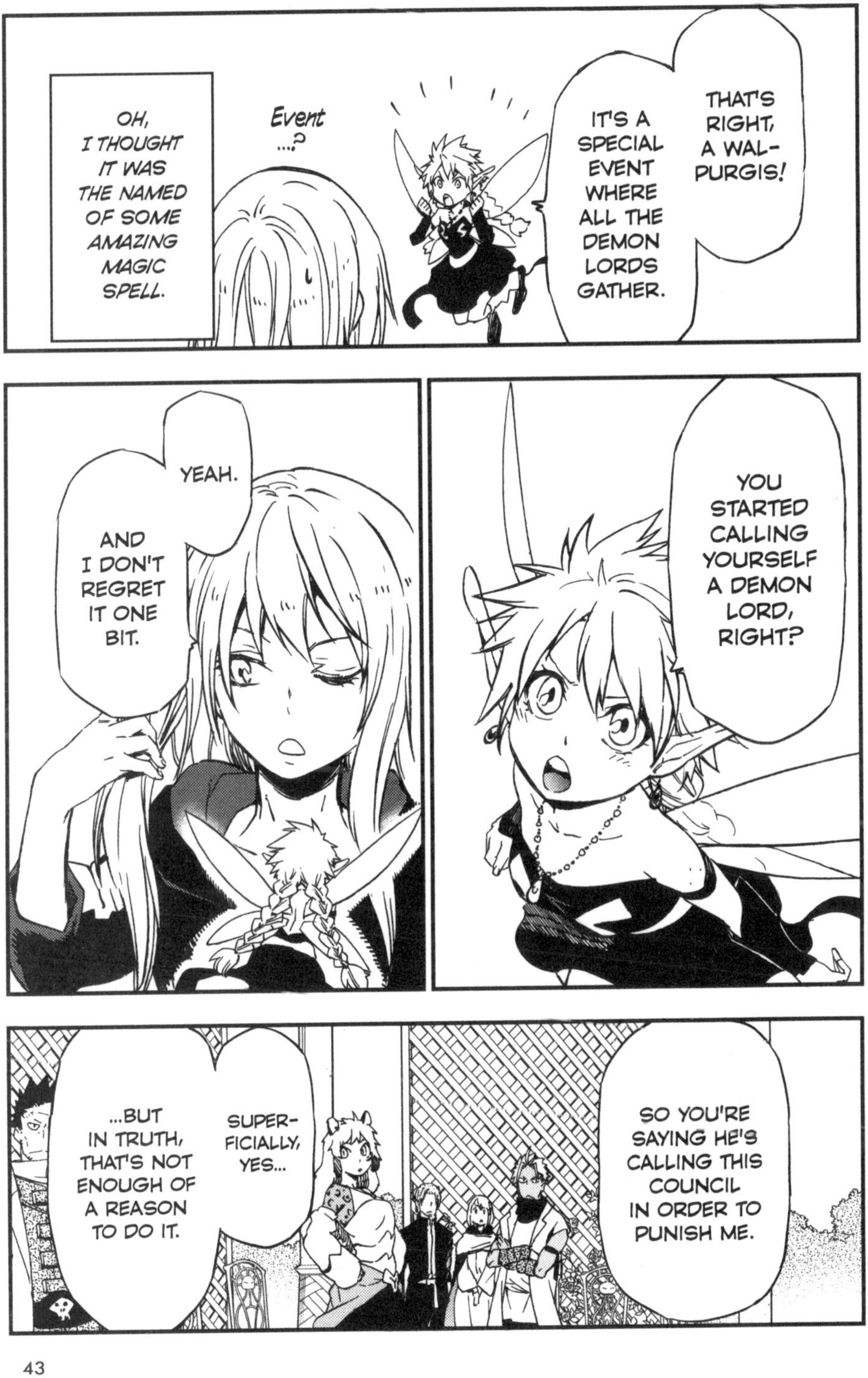
THAT'S RIGHT, A WAL-PURGIS!
IT'S A SPECIAL EVENT WHERE ALL THE DEMON LORDS GATHER.
Event ...?
OH, I THOUGHT IT WAS THE NAMED OF SOME AMAZING MAGIC SPELL.
YOU STARTED CALLING YOURSELF A DEMON LORD, RIGHT?
YEAH.
AND I DON'T REGRET IT ONE BIT.
SO YOU'RE SAYING HE'S CALLING THIS COUNCIL IN ORDER TO PUNISH ME.
SUPER-FICIALLY, YES...
...BUT IN TRUTH, THAT'S NOT ENOUGH OF A REASON TO DO IT.

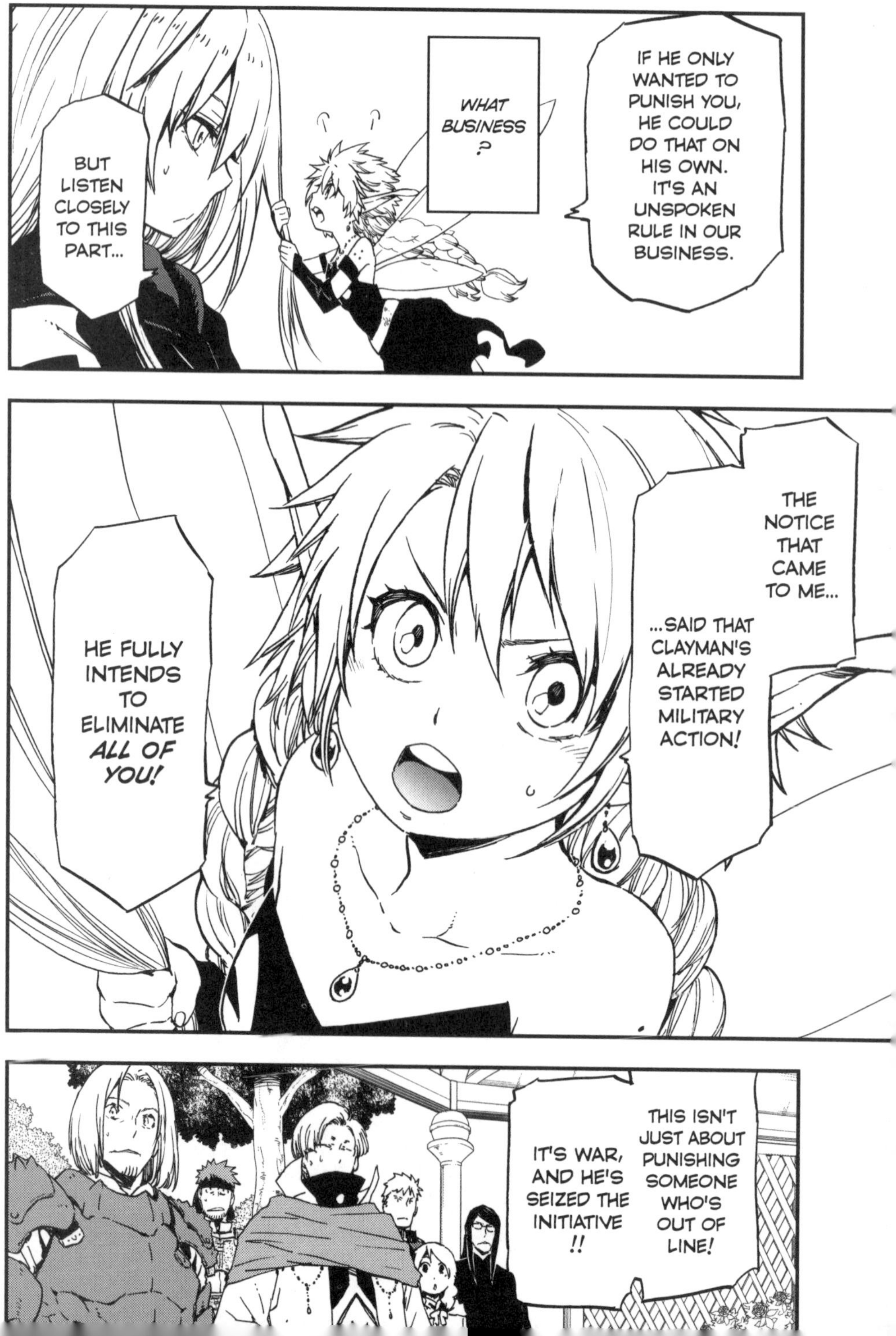
IF HE ONLY WANTED TO PUNISH YOU, HE COULD DO THAT ON HIS OWN. IT'S AN UNSPOKEN RULE IN OUR BUSINESS.
WHAT BUSINESS?
BUT LISTEN CLOSELY TO THIS PART...
THE NOTICE THAT CAME TO ME...
...SAID THAT CLAYMAN'S ALREADY STARTED MILITARY ACTION!
HE FULLY INTENDS TO ELIMINATE ALL OF YOU!
THIS ISN'T JUST ABOUT PUNISHING SOMEONE WHO'S OUT OF LINE!
IT'S WAR, AND HE'S SEIZED THE INITIATIVE!!

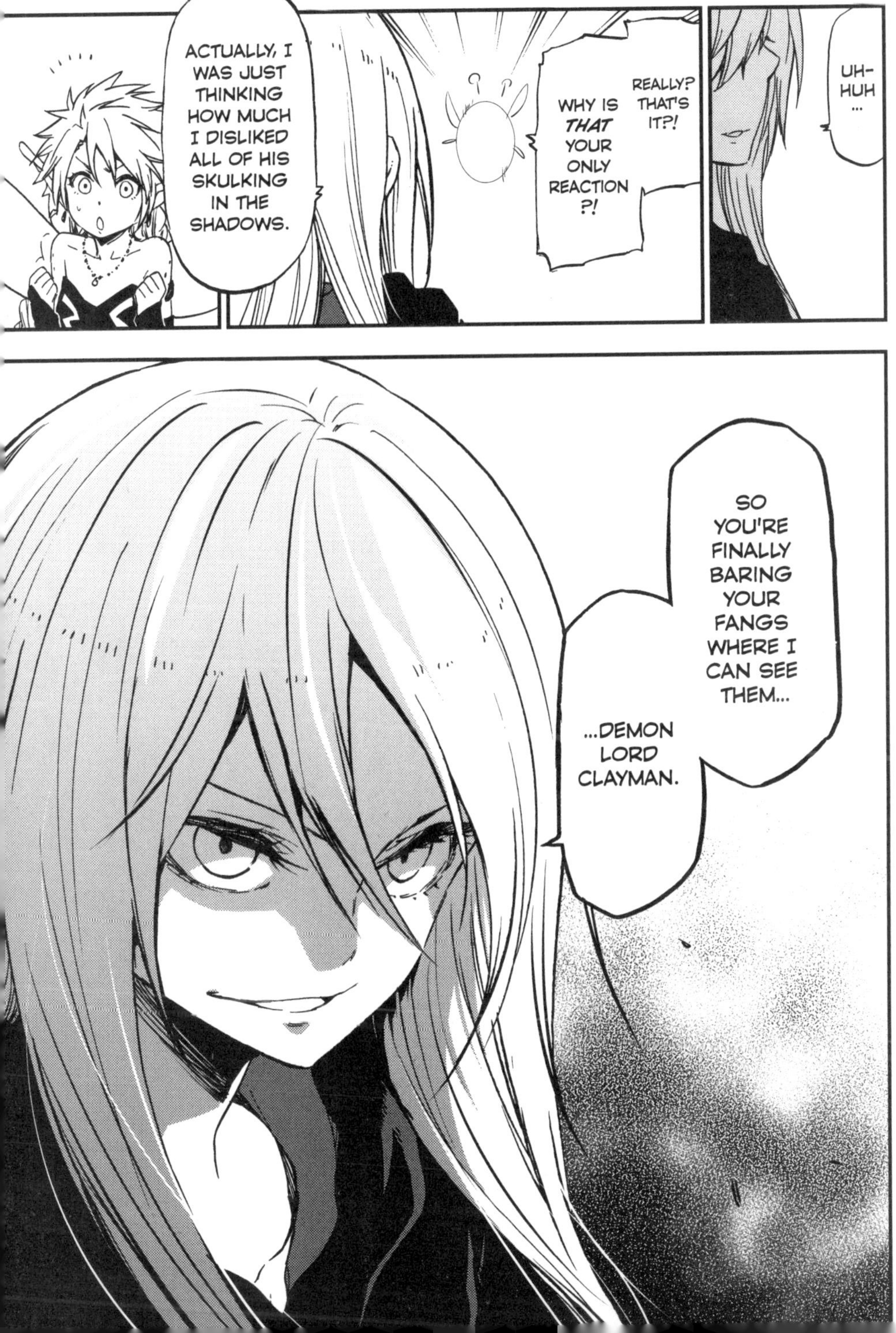
UH-HUH ...
REALLY? THAT'S IT?!
WHY IS *THAT* YOUR ONLY REACTION ?!
ACTUALLY, I WAS JUST THINKING HOW MUCH I DISLIKED ALL OF HIS SKULKING IN THE SHADOWS.
SO YOU'RE FINALLY BARING YOUR FANGS WHERE I CAN SEE THEM...
...DEMON LORD CLAYMAN.

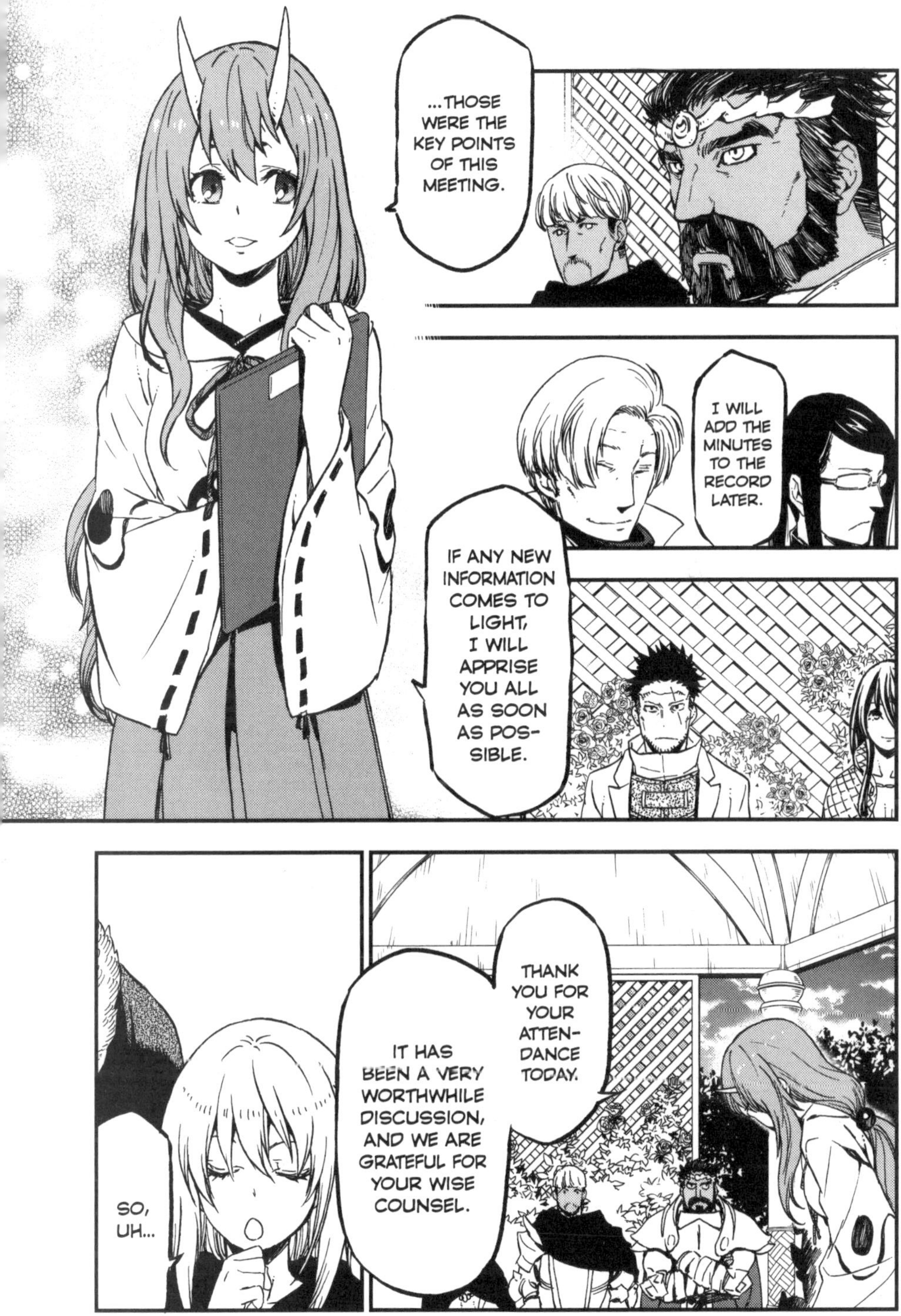

...THOSE WERE THE KEY POINTS OF THIS MEETING.
I WILL ADD THE MINUTES TO THE RECORD LATER.
IF ANY NEW INFORMATION COMES TO LIGHT, I WILL APPRISE YOU ALL AS SOON AS POS-SIBLE.
THANK YOU FOR YOUR ATTEN-DANCE TODAY.
IT HAS BEEN A VERY WORTHWHILE DISCUSSION, AND WE ARE GRATEFUL FOR YOUR WISE COUNSEL.
SO, UH...

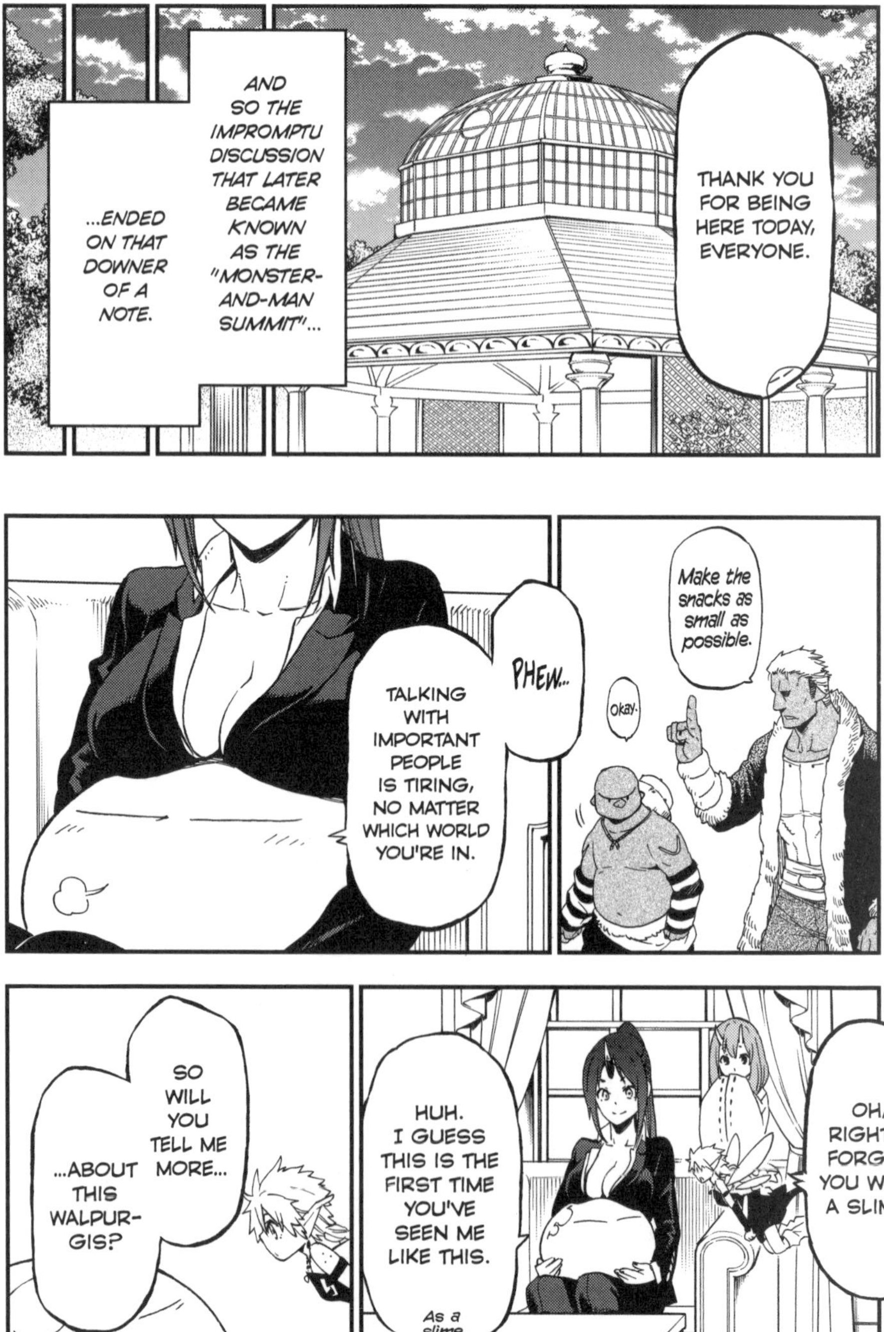
THANK YOU FOR BEING HERE TODAY, EVERYONE.
AND SO THE IMPROMPTU DISCUSSION THAT LATER BECAME KNOWN AS THE "MONSTER-AND-MAN SUMMIT"...
...ENDED ON THAT DOWNER OF A NOTE.
Make the snacks as small as possible.
Okay.
PHEW...
TALKING WITH IMPORTANT PEOPLE IS TIRING, NO MATTER WHICH WORLD YOU'RE IN.
OH, RIGHT, I FORGOT YOU WERE A SLIME.
HUH. I GUESS THIS IS THE FIRST TIME YOU'VE SEEN ME LIKE THIS.
As a slime.
SO WILL YOU TELL ME MORE...
...ABOUT THIS WALPURGIS?

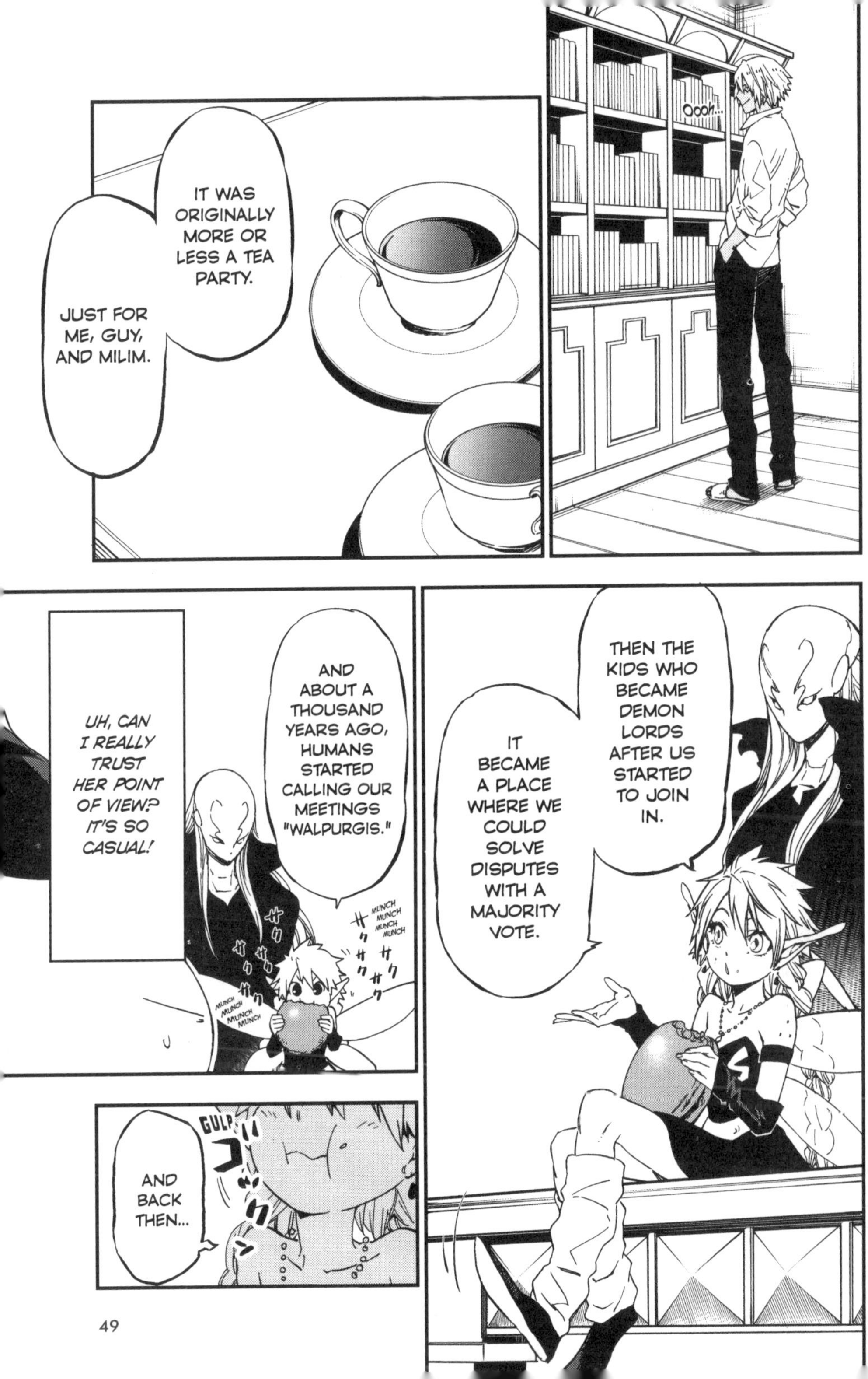
Oooh...
IT WAS ORIGINALLY MORE OR LESS A TEA PARTY.
JUST FOR ME, GUY, AND MILIM.
THEN THE KIDS WHO BECAME DEMON LORDS AFTER US STARTED TO JOIN IN.
IT BECAME A PLACE WHERE WE COULD SOLVE DISPUTES WITH A MAJORITY VOTE.
AND ABOUT A THOUSAND YEARS AGO, HUMANS STARTED CALLING OUR MEETINGS "WALPURGIS."
MUNCH MUNCH MUNCH MUNCH
MUNCH MUNCH MUNCH MUNCH
UH, CAN I REALLY TRUST HER POINT OF VIEW? IT'S SO CASUAL!
GULP
AND BACK THEN...

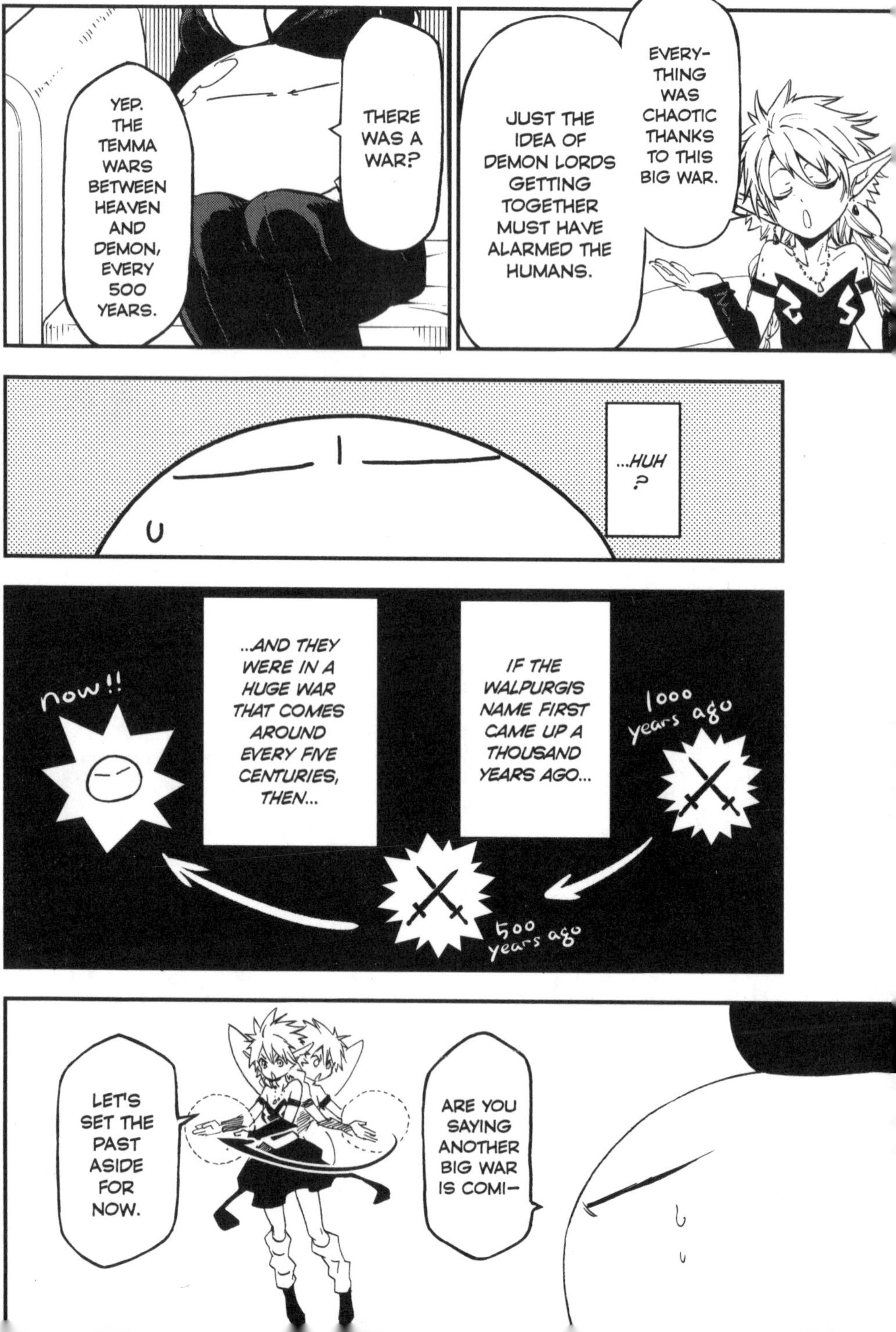
EVERYTHING WAS CHAOTIC THANKS TO THIS BIG WAR.
JUST THE IDEA OF DEMON LORDS GETTING TOGETHER MUST HAVE ALARMED THE HUMANS.
THERE WAS A WAR?
YEP. THE TEMMA WARS BETWEEN HEAVEN AND DEMON, EVERY 500 YEARS.
...HUH?
1000 years ago
IF THE WALPURGIS NAME FIRST CAME UP A THOUSAND YEARS AGO...
500 years ago
...AND THEY WERE IN A HUGE WAR THAT COMES AROUND EVERY FIVE CENTURIES, THEN...
now!!
ARE YOU SAYING ANOTHER BIG WAR IS COMI—
LET'S SET THE PAST ASIDE FOR NOW.

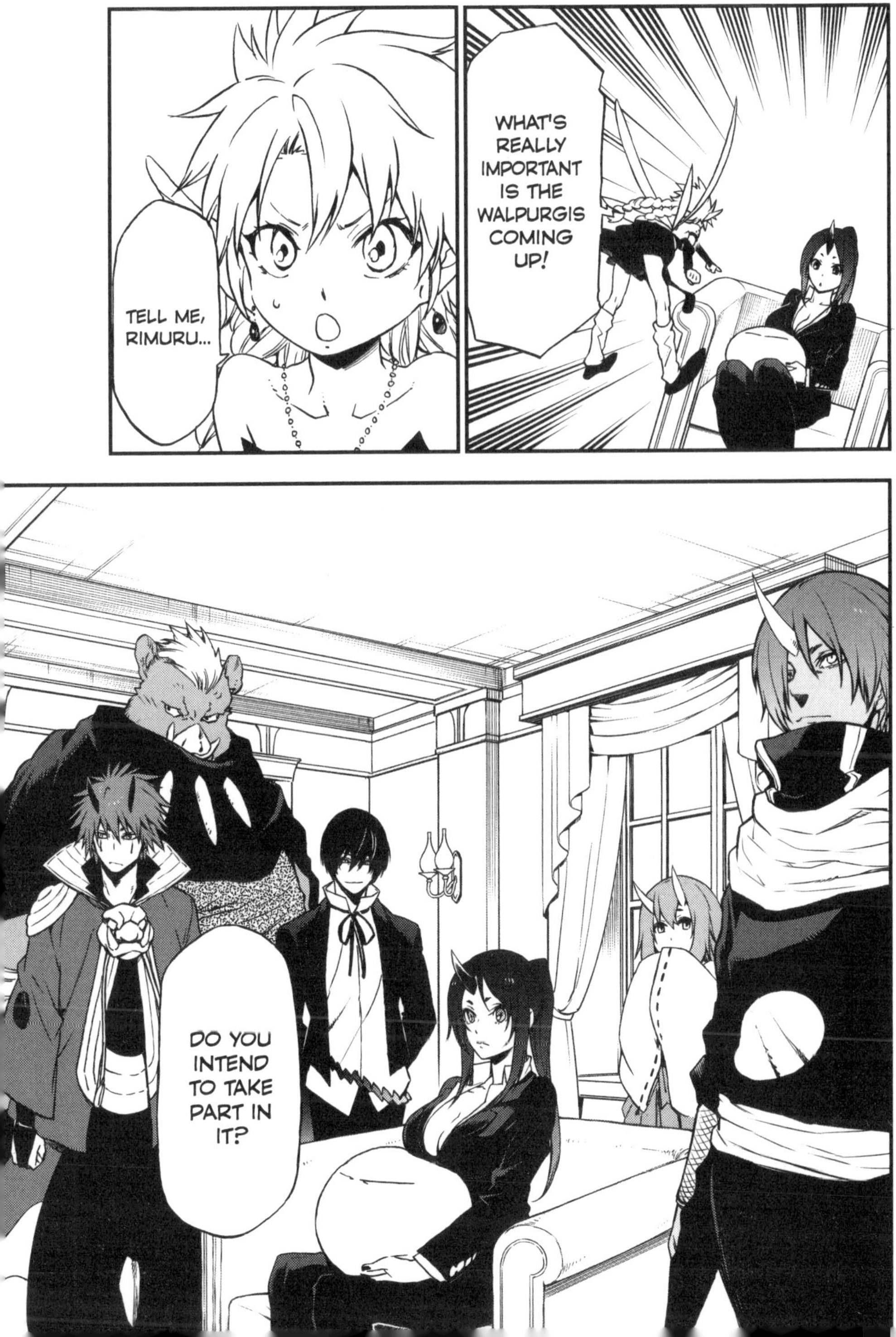
WHAT'S REALLY IMPORTANT IS THE WALPURGIS COMING UP!
TELL ME, RIMURU...
DO YOU INTEND TO TAKE PART IN IT?

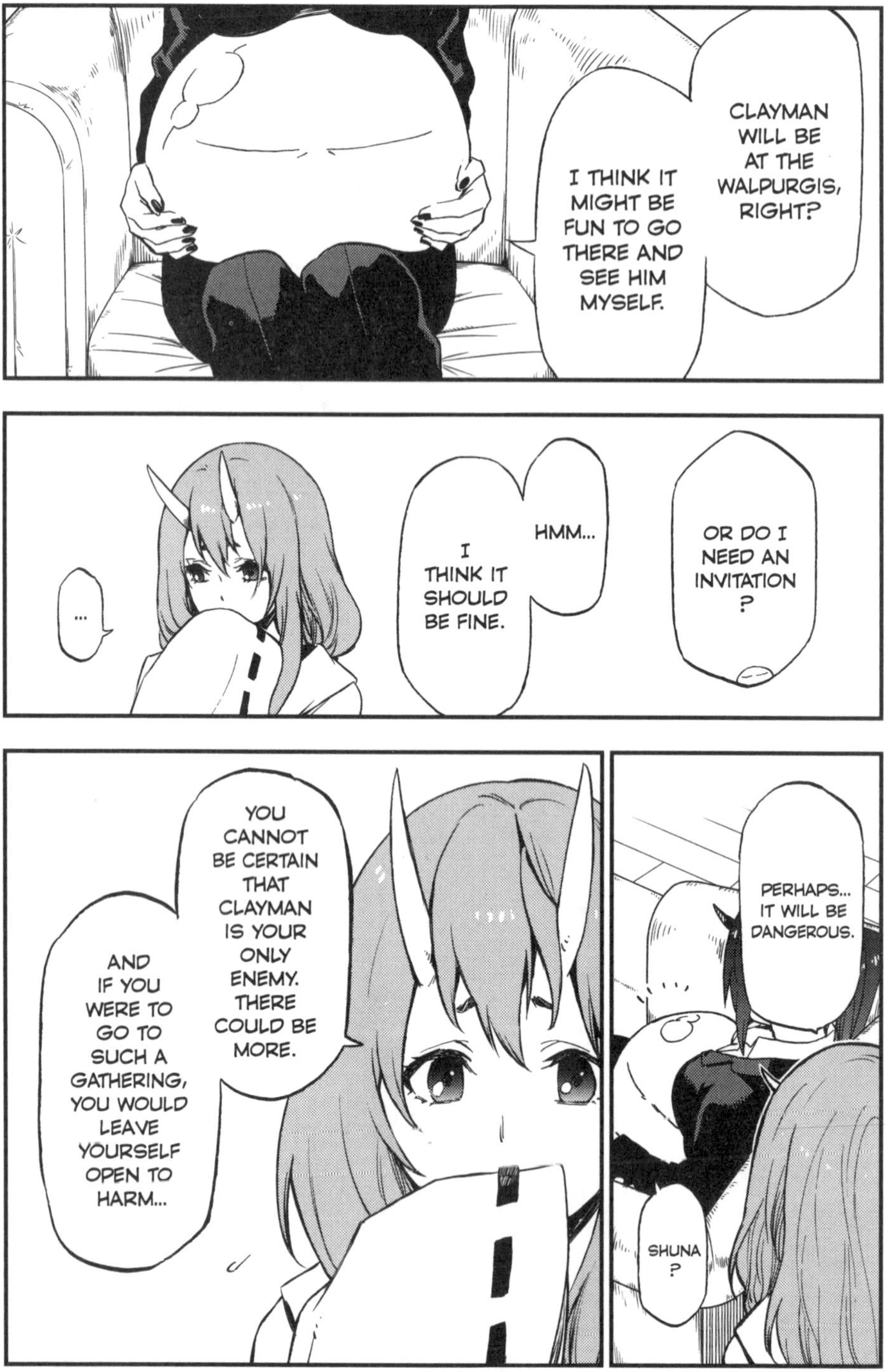
CLAYMAN WILL BE AT THE WALPURGIS, RIGHT?
I THINK IT MIGHT BE FUN TO GO THERE AND SEE HIM MYSELF.
OR DO I NEED AN INVITATION?
HMM... I THINK IT SHOULD BE FINE.
...
PERHAPS... IT WILL BE DANGEROUS.
SHUNA?
YOU CANNOT BE CERTAIN THAT CLAYMAN IS YOUR ONLY ENEMY. THERE COULD BE MORE.
AND IF YOU WERE TO GO TO SUCH A GATHERING, YOU WOULD LEAVE YOURSELF OPEN TO HARM...

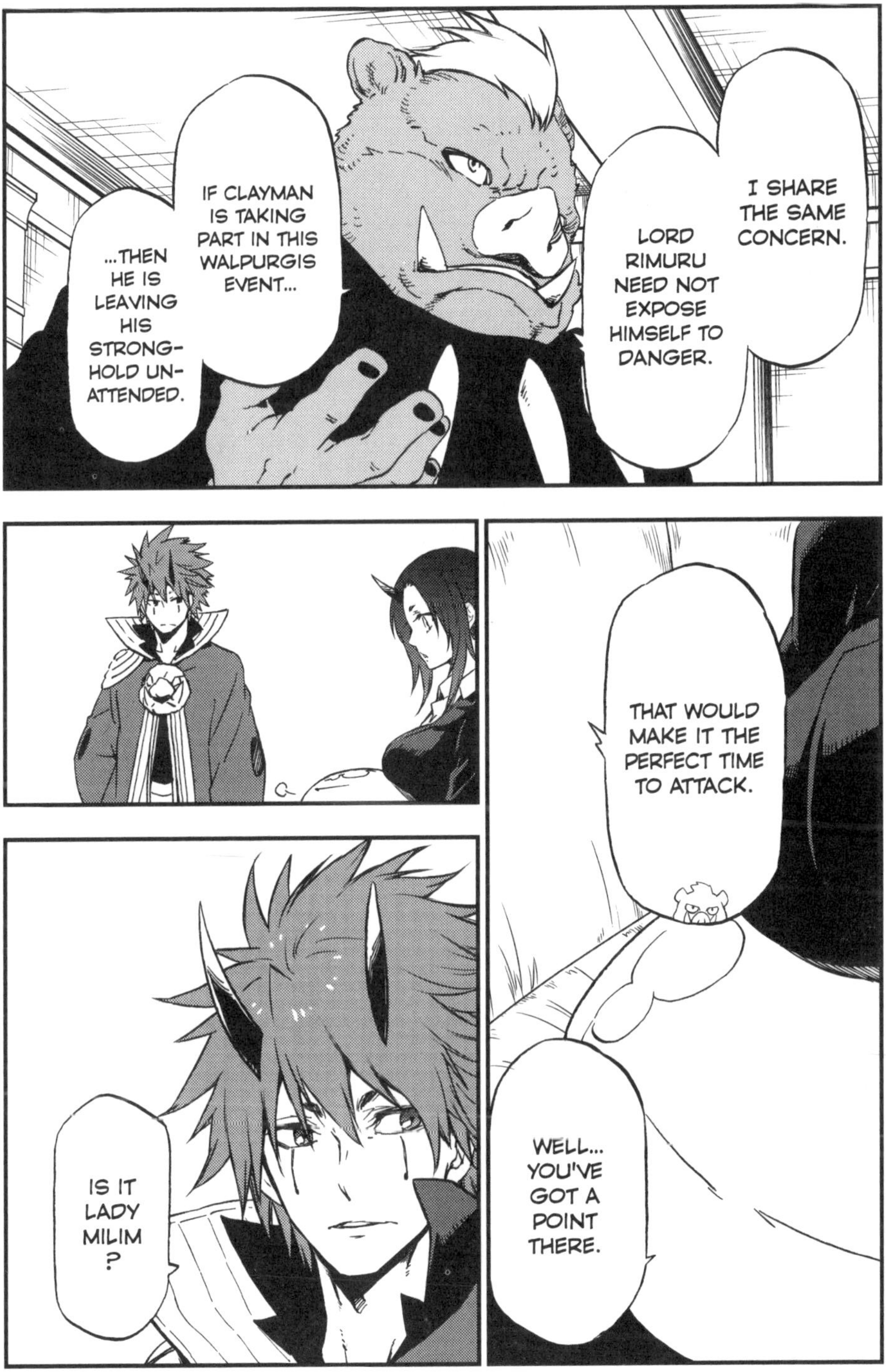
I SHARE THE SAME CONCERN.
LORD RIMURU NEED NOT EXPOSE HIMSELF TO DANGER.
IF CLAYMAN IS TAKING PART IN THIS WALPURGIS EVENT...
...THEN HE IS LEAVING HIS STRONGHOLD UNATTENDED.
THAT WOULD MAKE IT THE PERFECT TIME TO ATTACK.
WELL... YOU'VE GOT A POINT THERE.
IS IT LADY MILIM?

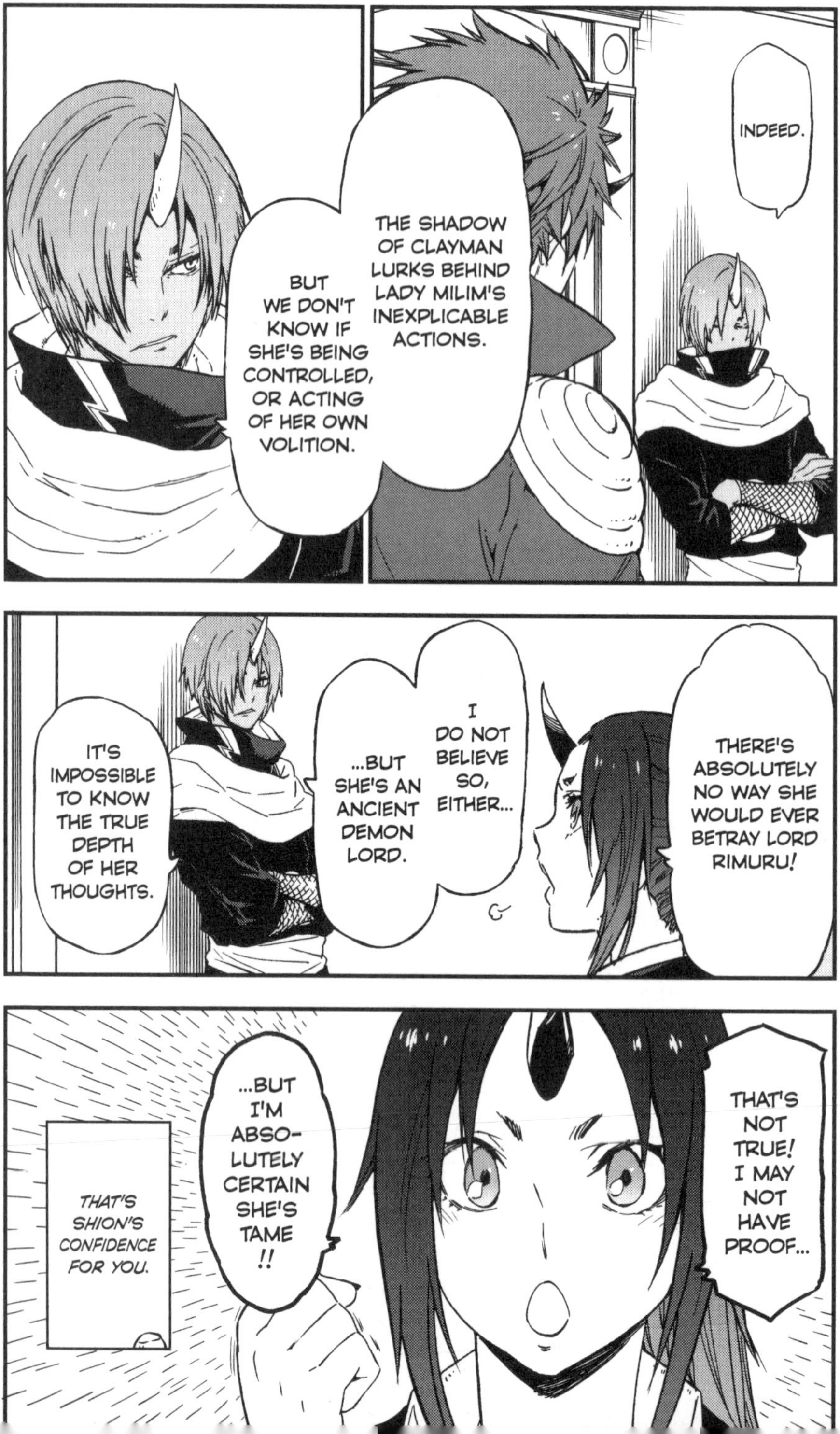
INDEED.
THE SHADOW OF CLAYMAN LURKS BEHIND LADY MILIM'S INEXPLICABLE ACTIONS.
BUT WE DON'T KNOW IF SHE'S BEING CONTROLLED, OR ACTING OF HER OWN VOLITION.
THERE'S ABSOLUTELY NO WAY SHE WOULD EVER BETRAY LORD RIMURU!
I DO NOT BELIEVE SO, EITHER...
...BUT SHE'S AN ANCIENT DEMON LORD.
IT'S IMPOSSIBLE TO KNOW THE TRUE DEPTH OF HER THOUGHTS.
THAT'S NOT TRUE! I MAY NOT HAVE PROOF...
...BUT I'M ABSO-LUTELY CERTAIN SHE'S TAME!!
THAT'S SHION'S CONFIDENCE FOR YOU.

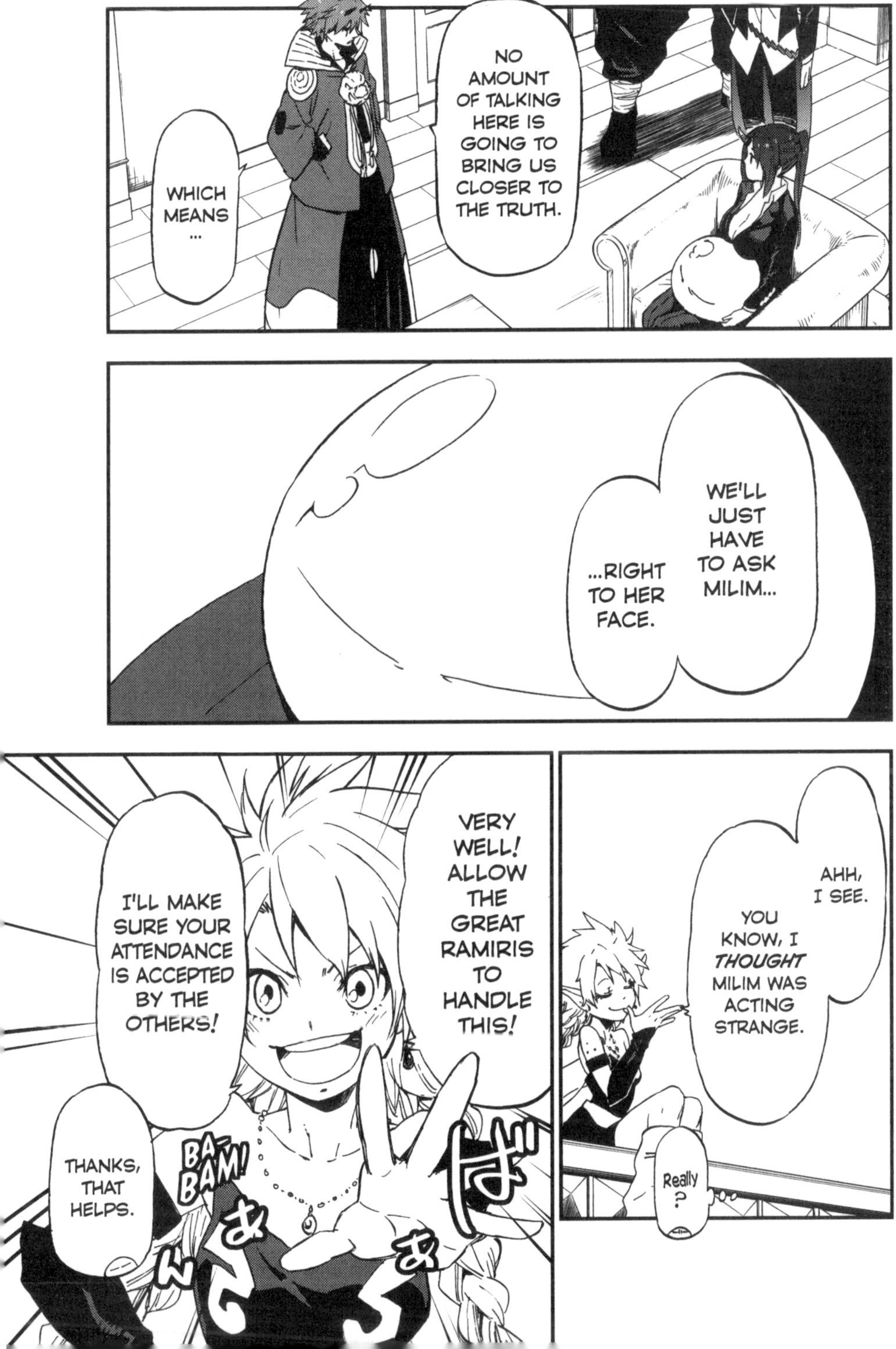
NO AMOUNT OF TALKING HERE IS GOING TO BRING US CLOSER TO THE TRUTH.
WHICH MEANS ...
WE'LL JUST HAVE TO ASK MILIM...
...RIGHT TO HER FACE.
AHH, I SEE.
YOU KNOW, I *THOUGHT* MILIM WAS ACTING STRANGE.
Really?
VERY WELL! ALLOW THE GREAT RAMIRIS TO HANDLE THIS!
I'LL MAKE SURE YOUR ATTENDANCE IS ACCEPTED BY THE OTHERS!
BA-BAM!
THANKS, THAT HELPS.

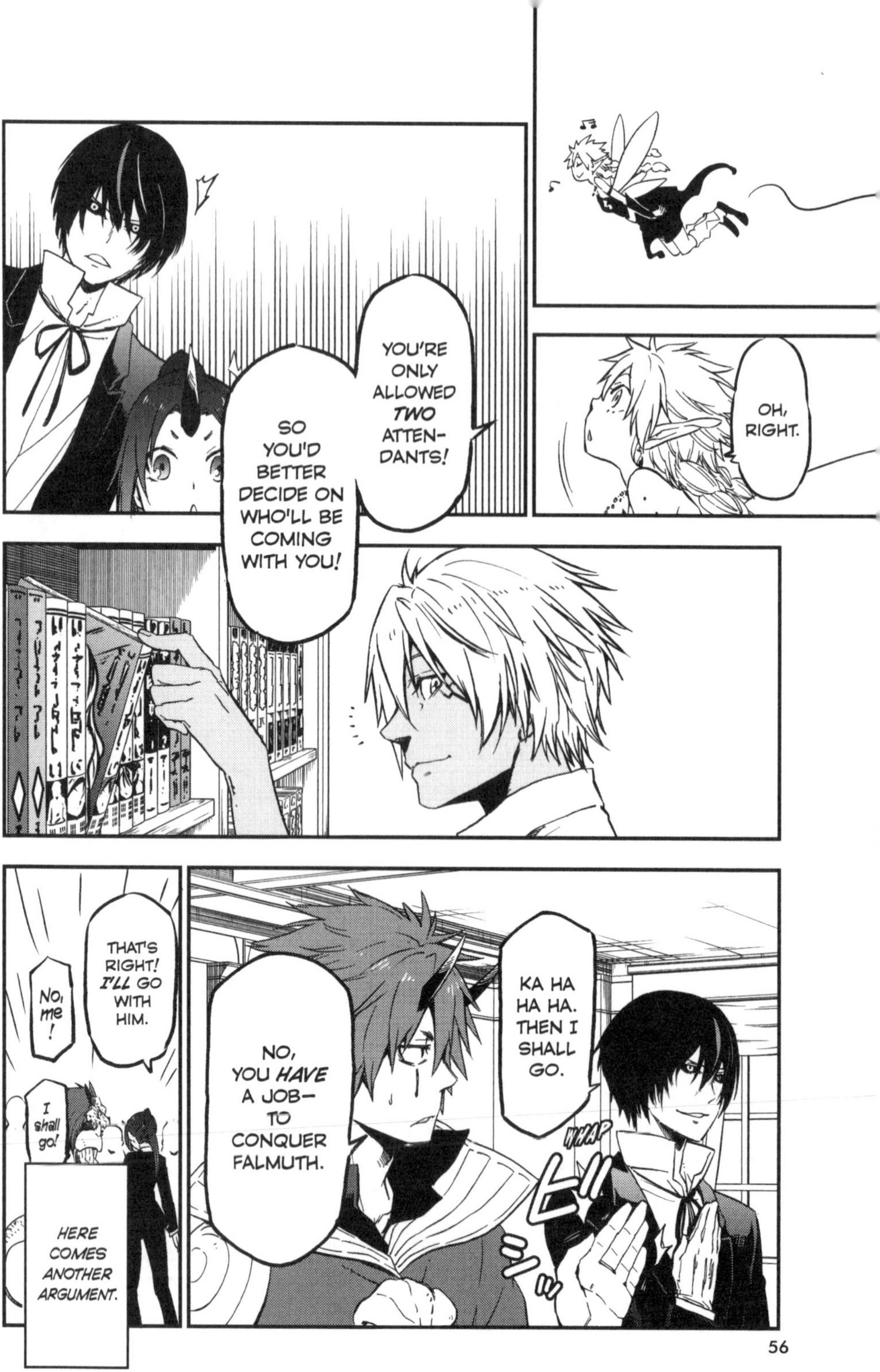
OH, RIGHT.
YOU'RE ONLY ALLOWED *TWO* ATTENDANTS!
SO YOU'D BETTER DECIDE ON WHO'LL BE COMING WITH YOU!
KA HA HA HA. THEN I SHALL GO.
NO, YOU *HAVE* A JOB— TO CONQUER FALMUTH.
WHAP
THAT'S RIGHT! *I'LL* GO WITH HIM.
No, me!
I shall go!
HERE COMES ANOTHER ARGUMENT.

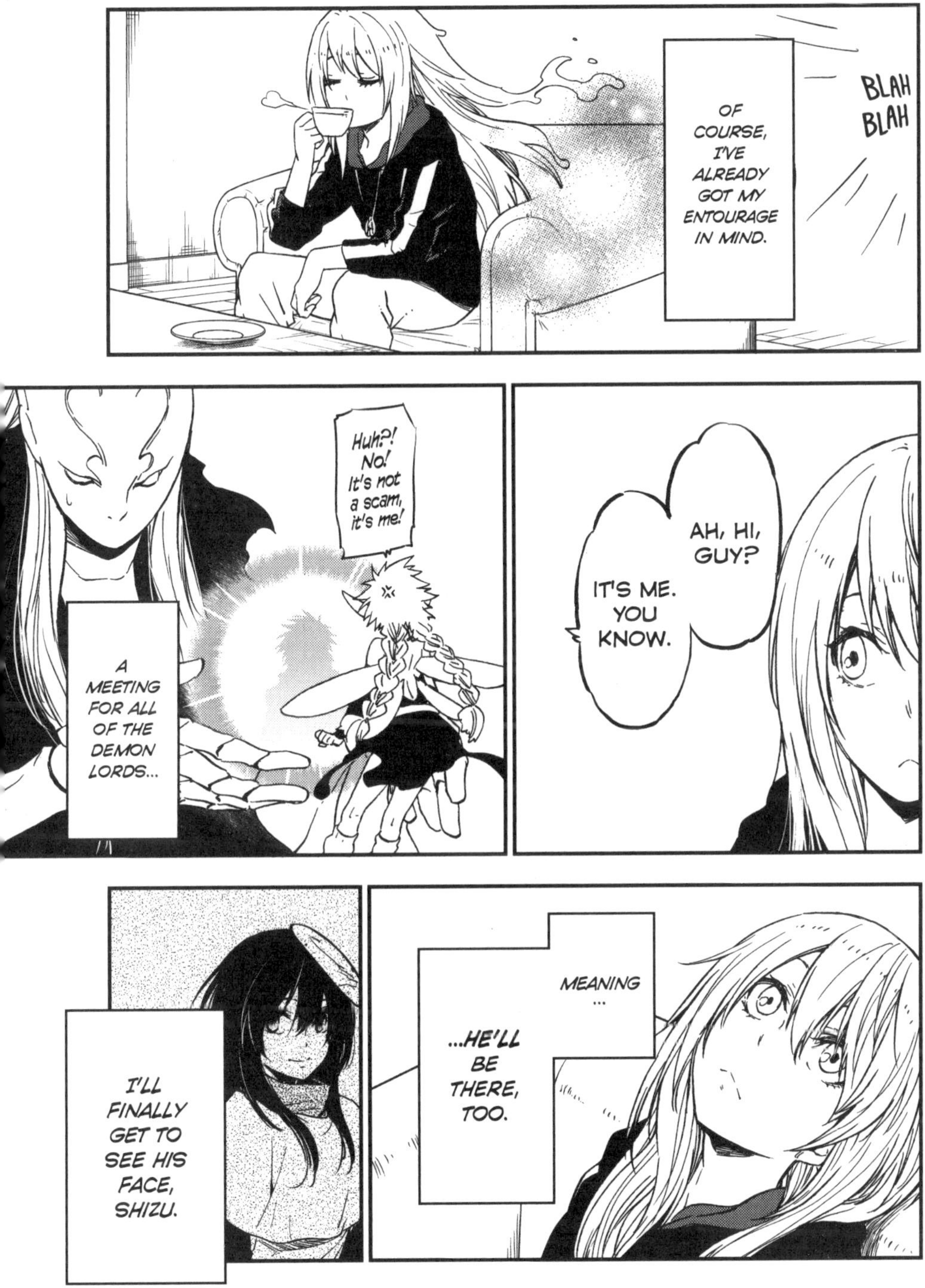
BLAH BLAH
OF COURSE, I'VE ALREADY GOT MY ENTOURAGE IN MIND.
AH, HI, GUY?
IT'S ME. YOU KNOW.
Huh?! No! It's not a scam, it's me!
A MEETING FOR ALL OF THE DEMON LORDS...
MEANING...
...HE'LL BE THERE, TOO.
I'LL FINALLY GET TO SEE HIS FACE, SHIZU.

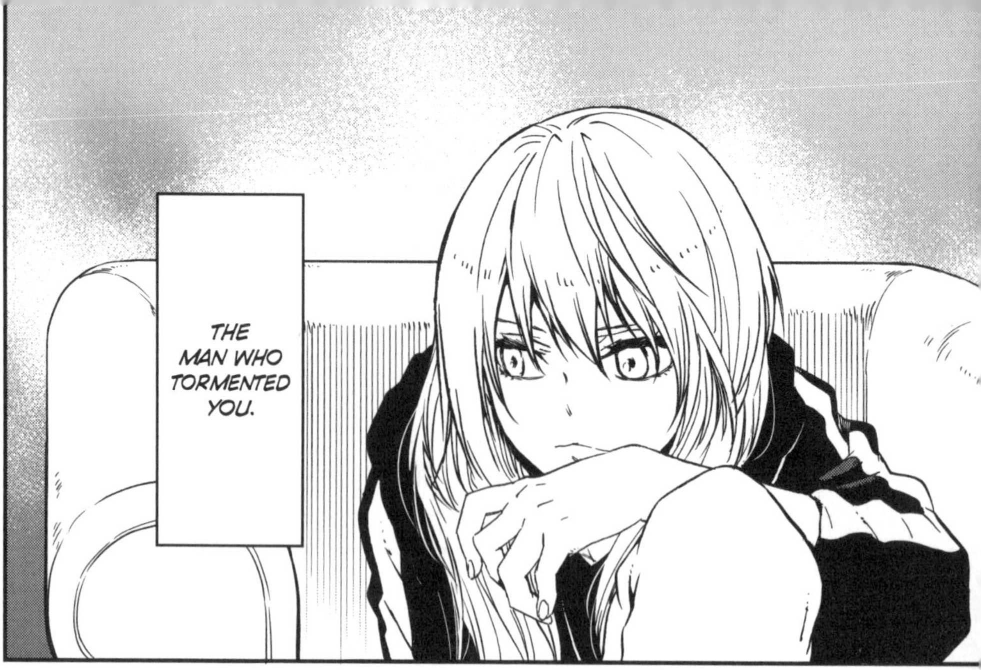
THE MAN WHO TORMENTED YOU.

CHAPTER 76 Demon Lord and True Dragon

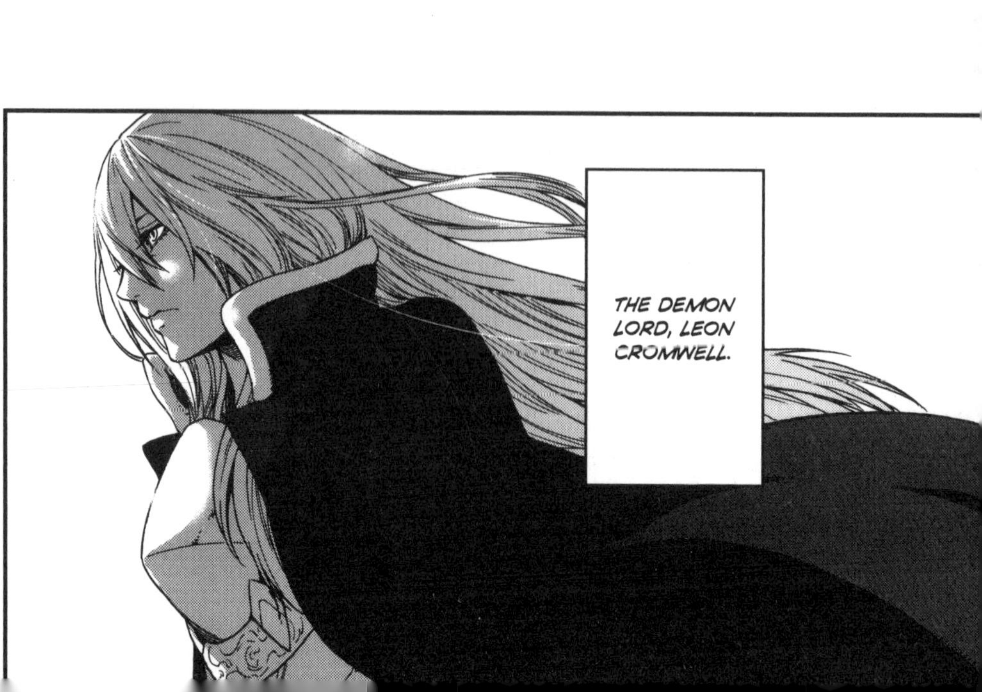
THE DEMON LORD, LEON CROMWELL.

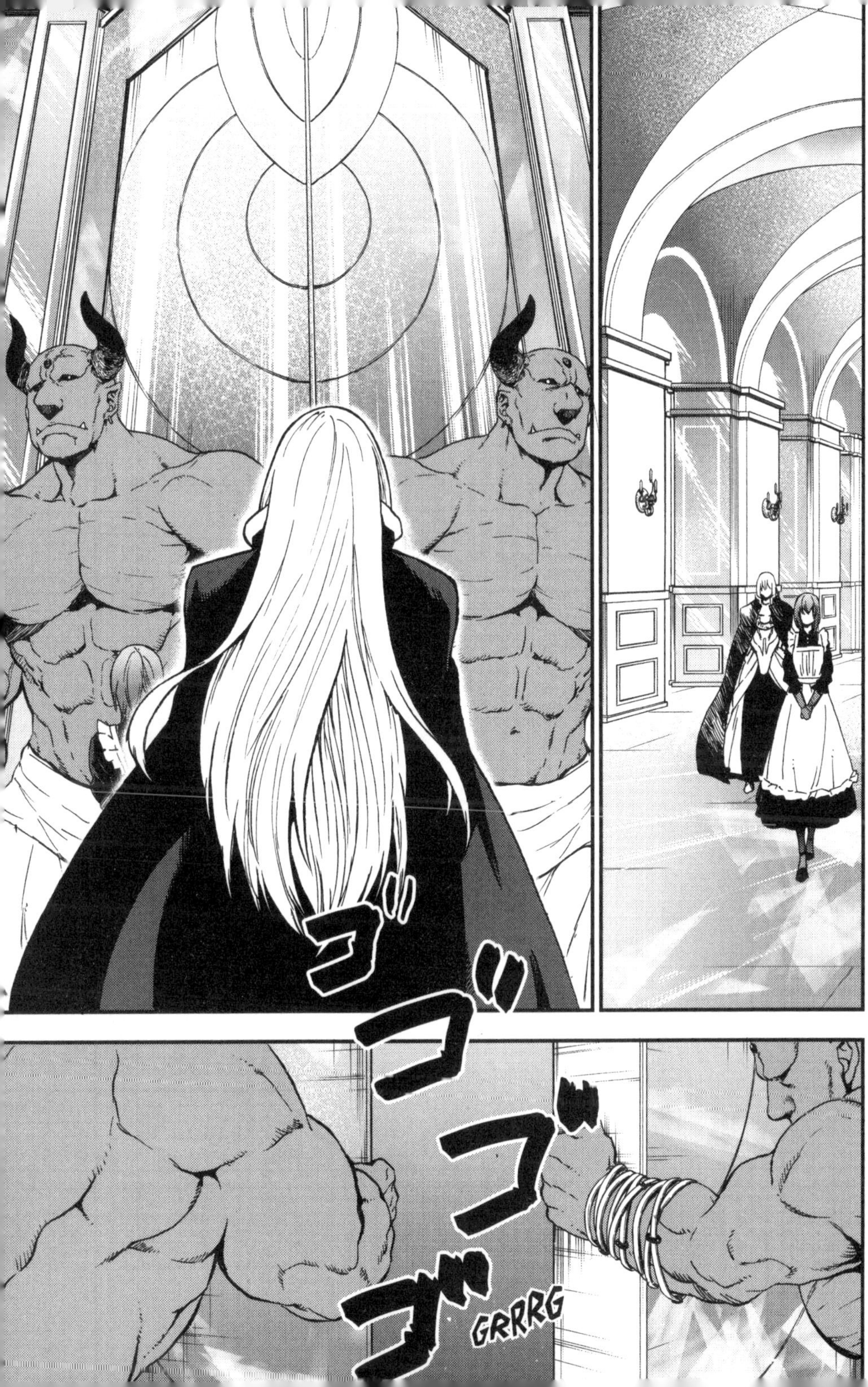
ゴゴゴゴ
GRRRG

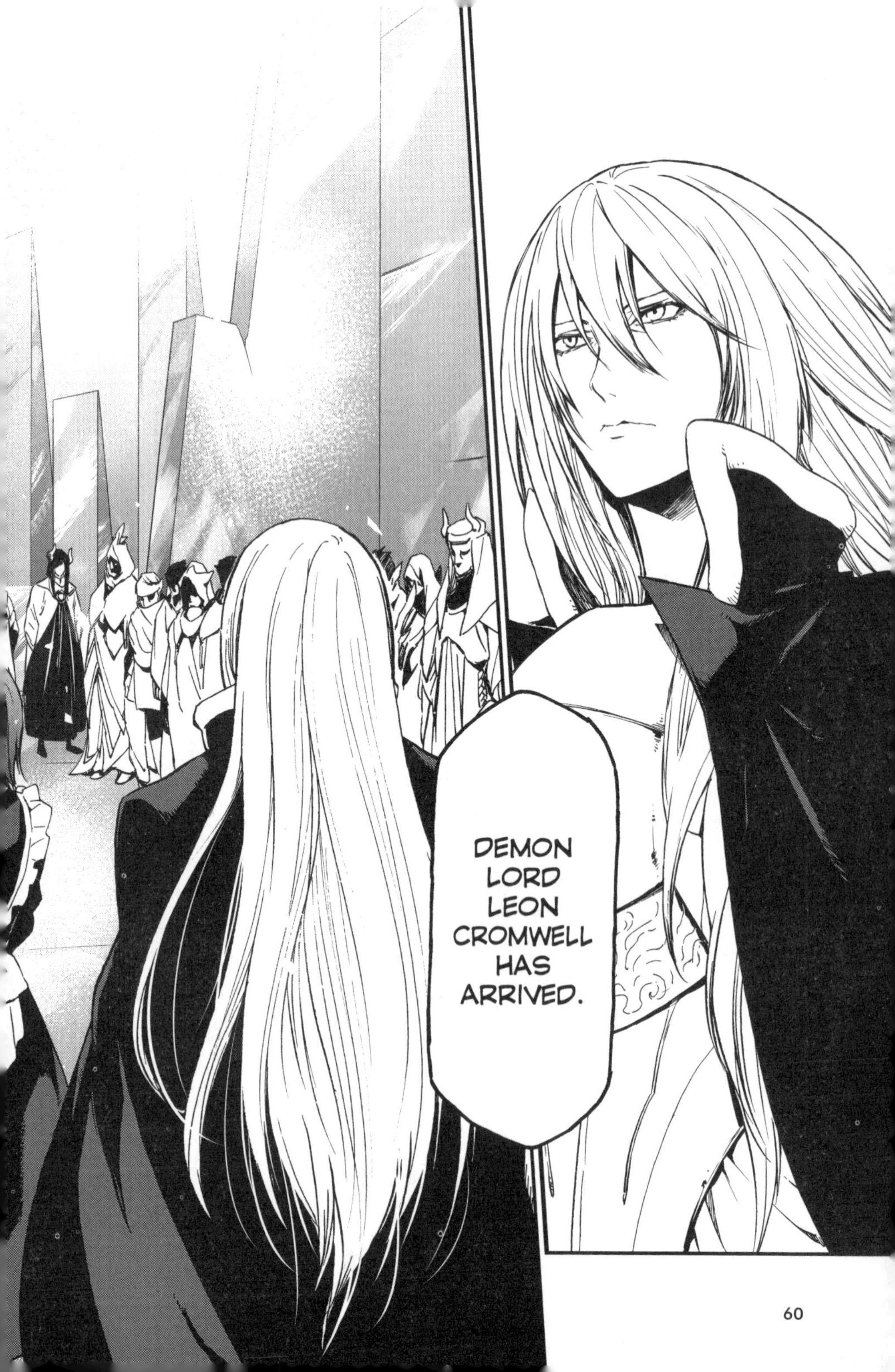
DEMON LORD LEON CROMWELL HAS ARRIVED.

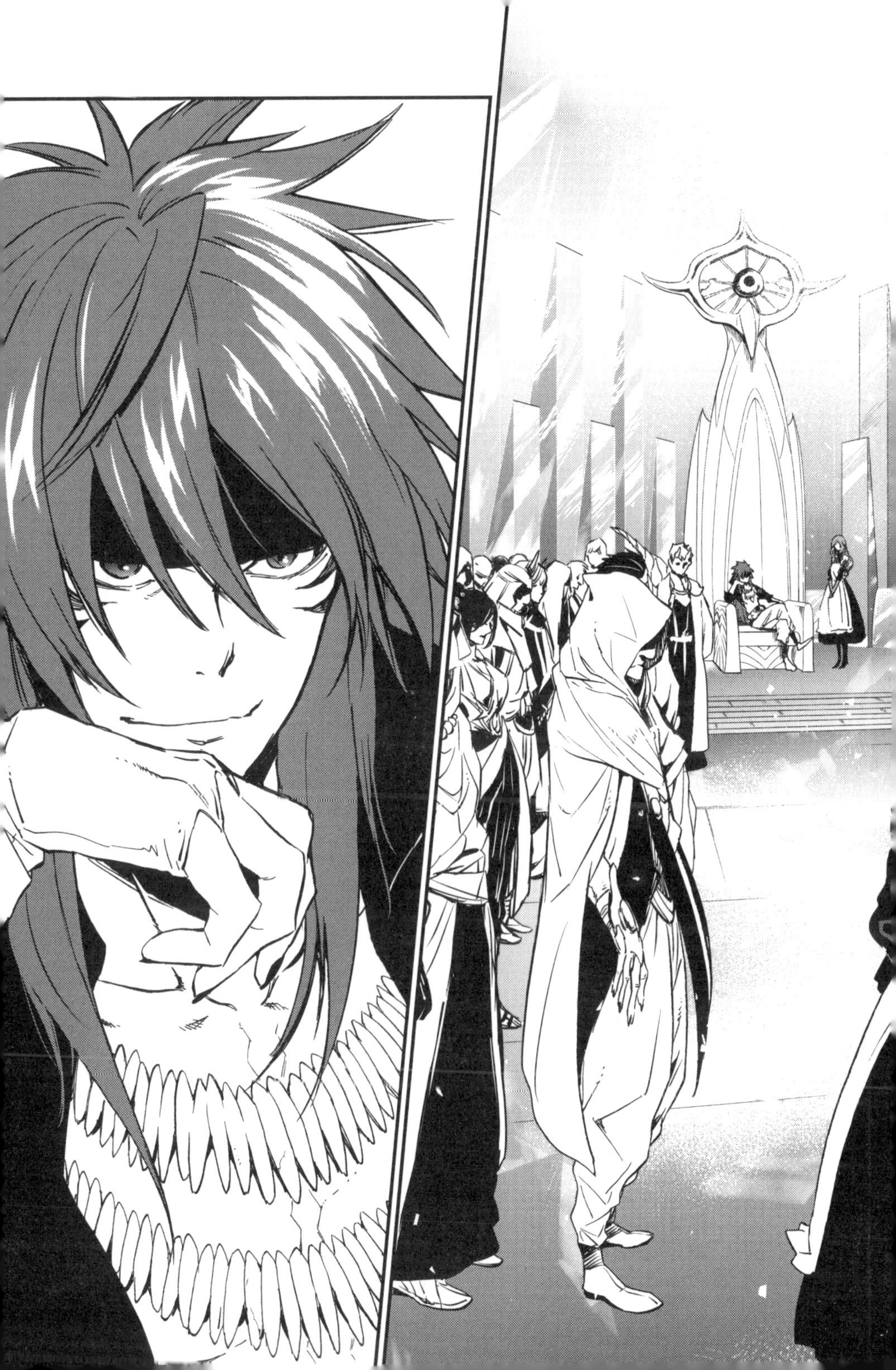

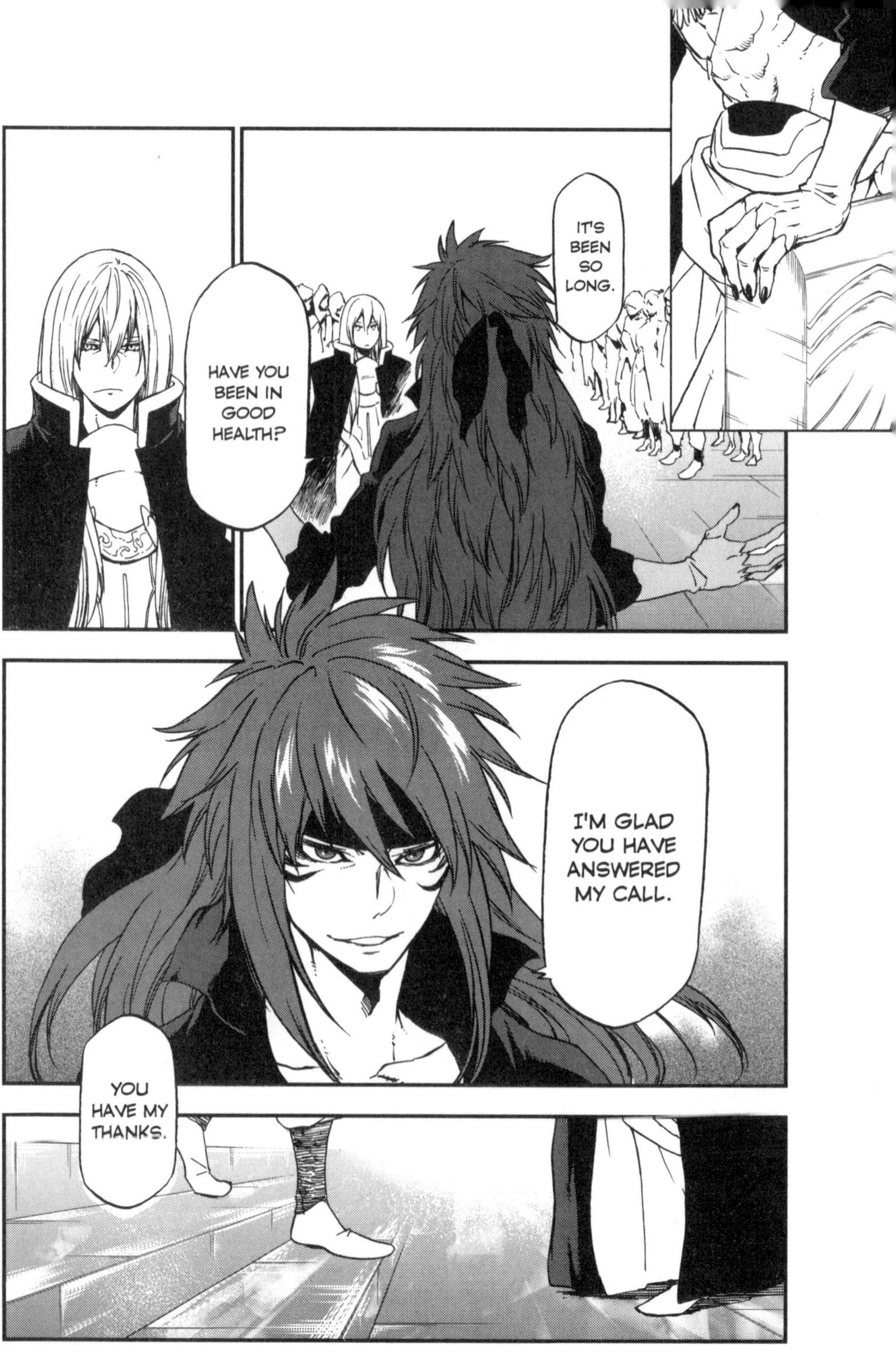
IT'S BEEN SO LONG.
HAVE YOU BEEN IN GOOD HEALTH?
I'M GLAD YOU HAVE ANSWERED MY CALL.
YOU HAVE MY THANKS.

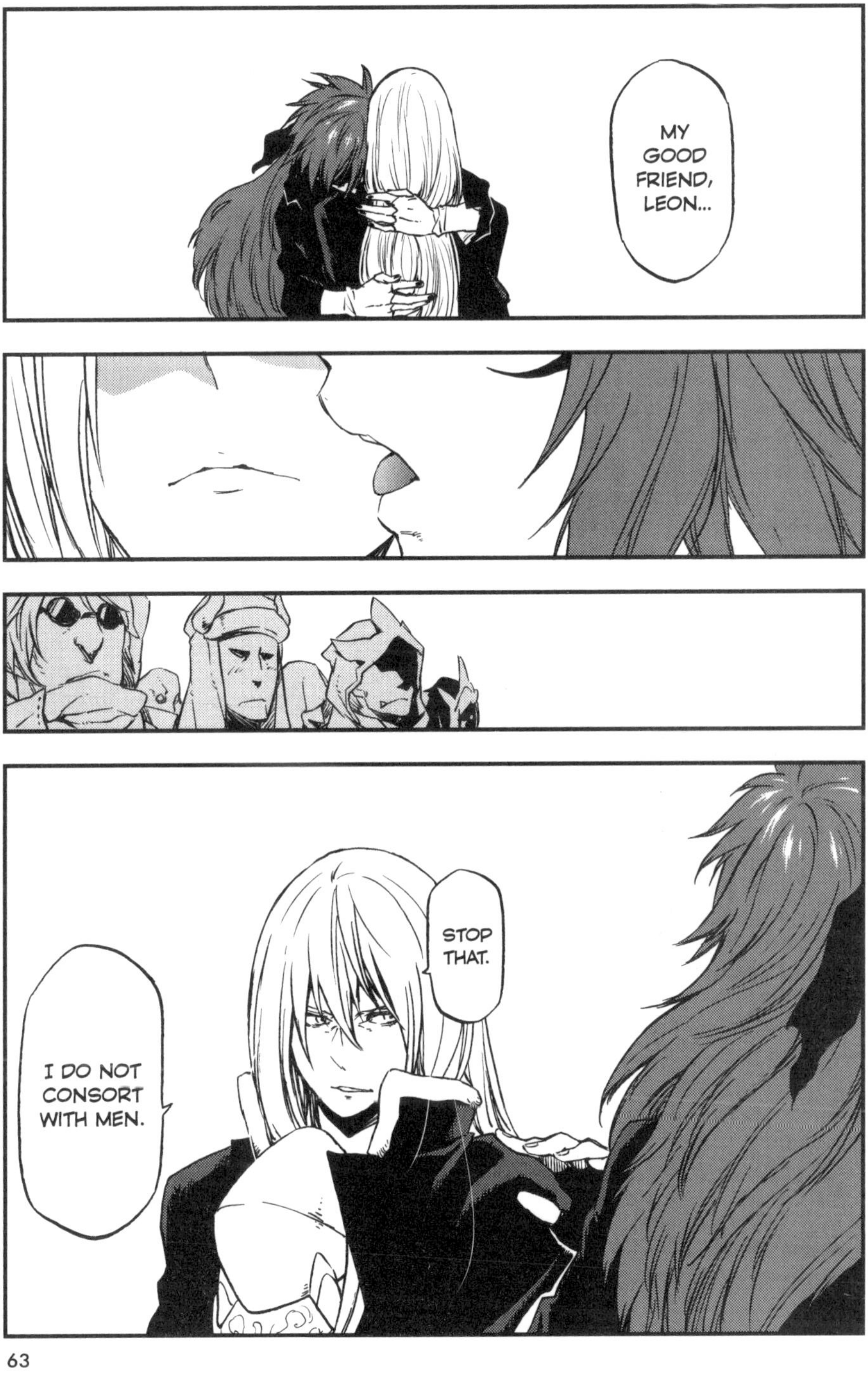
MY GOOD FRIEND, LEON...
STOP THAT.
I DO NOT CONSORT WITH MEN.

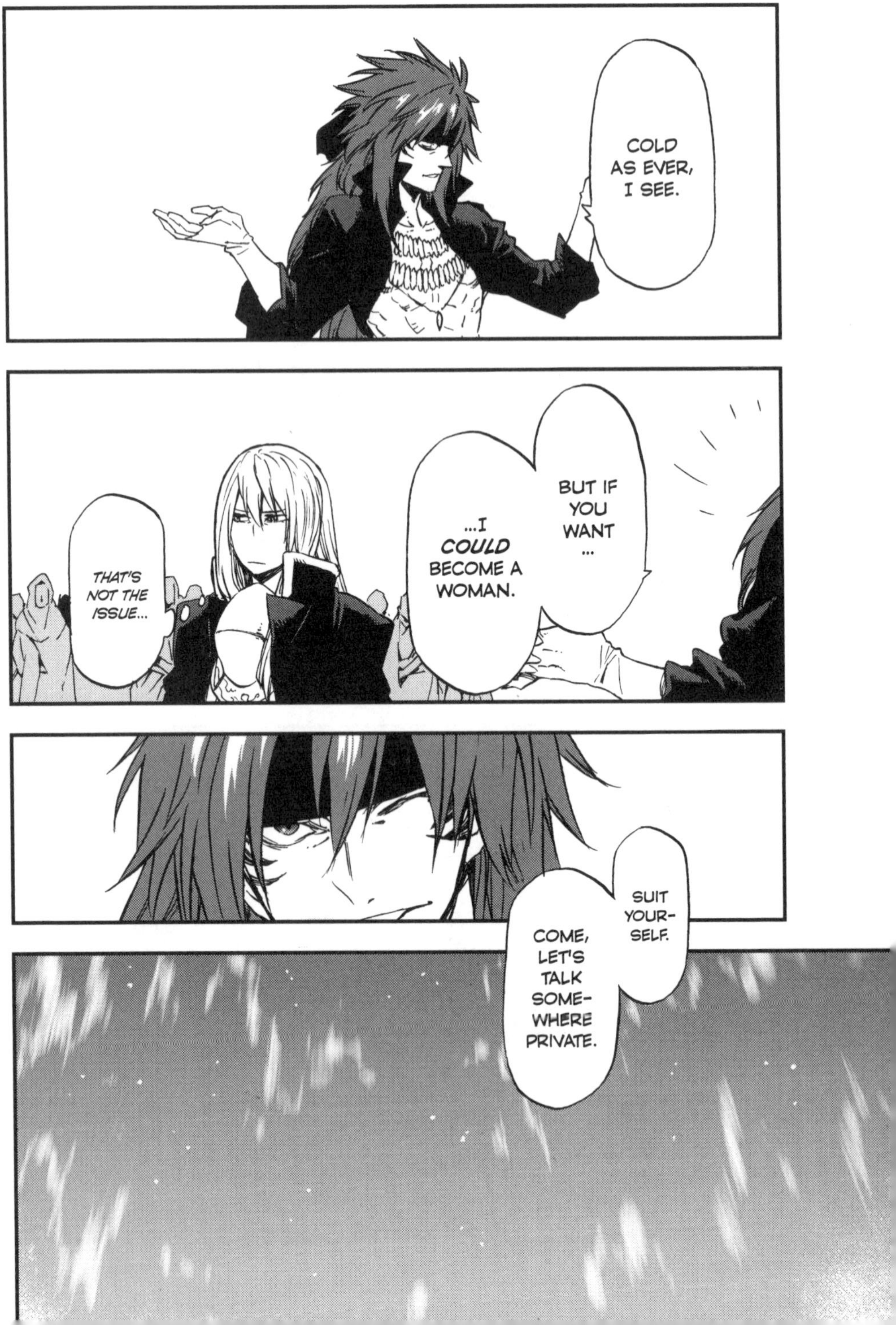
COLD AS EVER, I SEE.
BUT IF YOU WANT ...
...I *COULD* BECOME A WOMAN.
THAT'S NOT THE ISSUE...
SUIT YOURSELF.
COME, LET'S TALK SOMEWHERE PRIVATE.

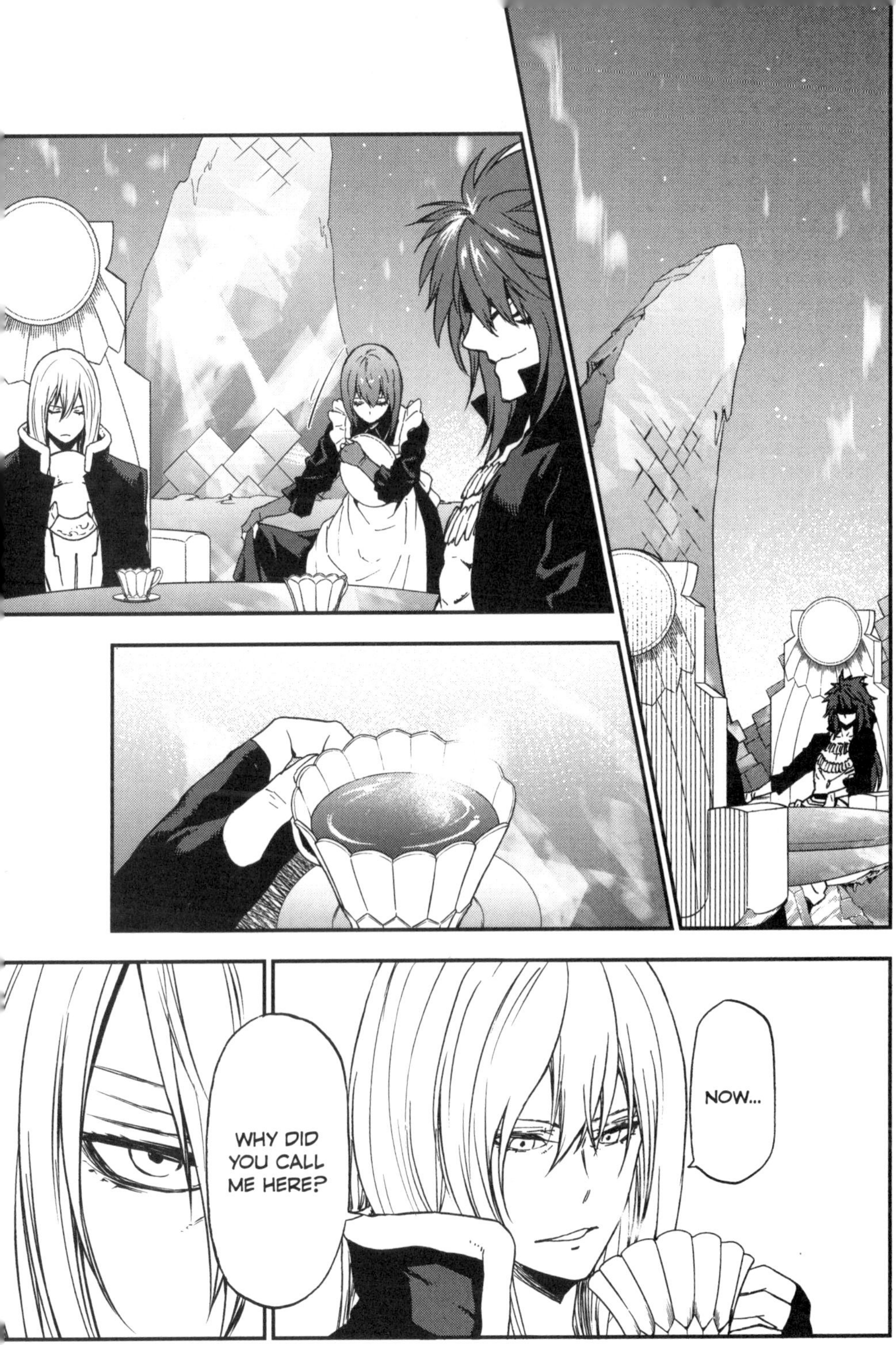
NOW...
WHY DID YOU CALL ME HERE?

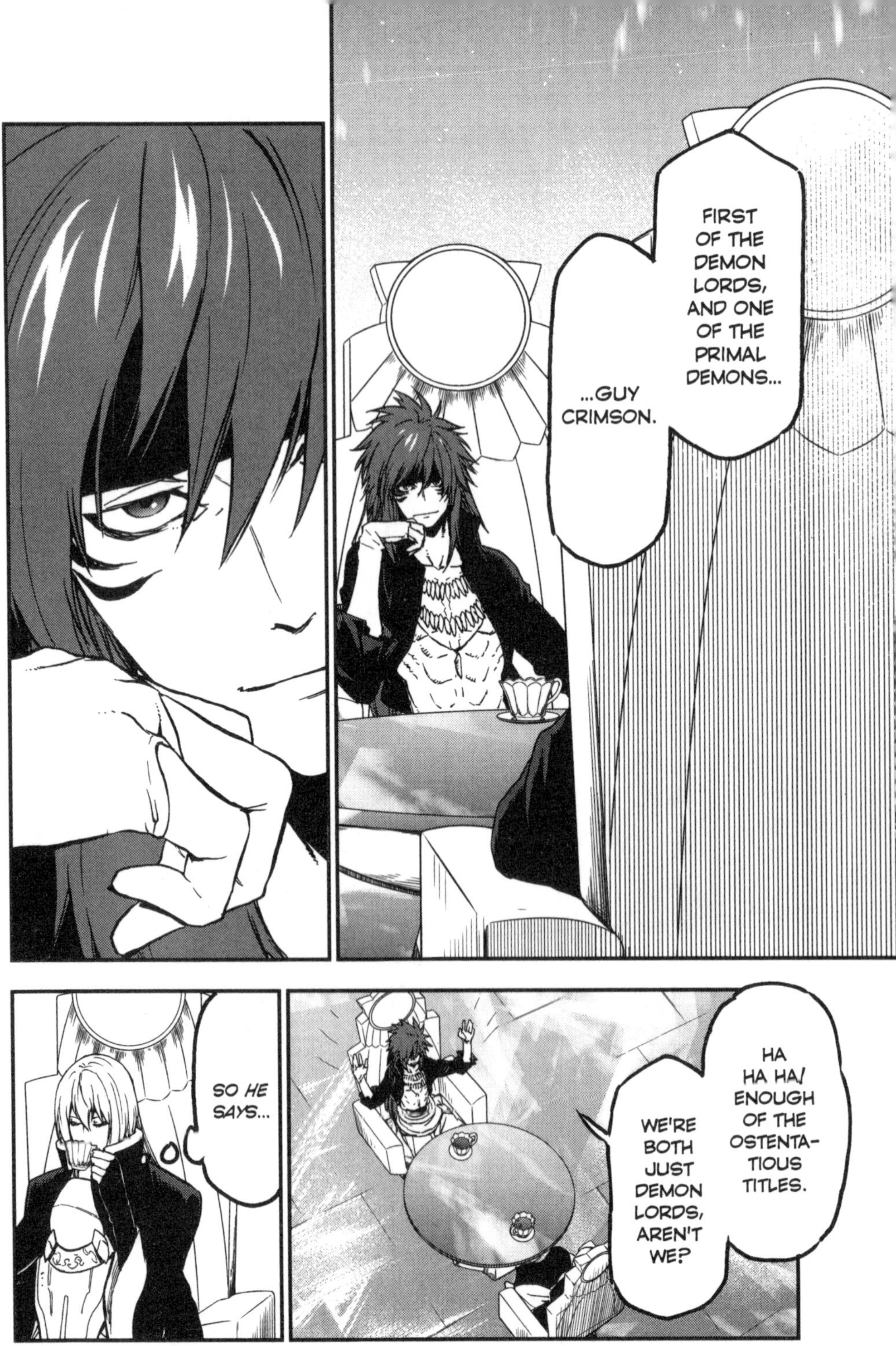
FIRST OF THE DEMON LORDS, AND ONE OF THE PRIMAL DEMONS...
...GUY CRIMSON.
HA HA HA! ENOUGH OF THE OSTENTATIOUS TITLES.
WE'RE BOTH JUST DEMON LORDS, AREN'T WE?
SO HE SAYS...

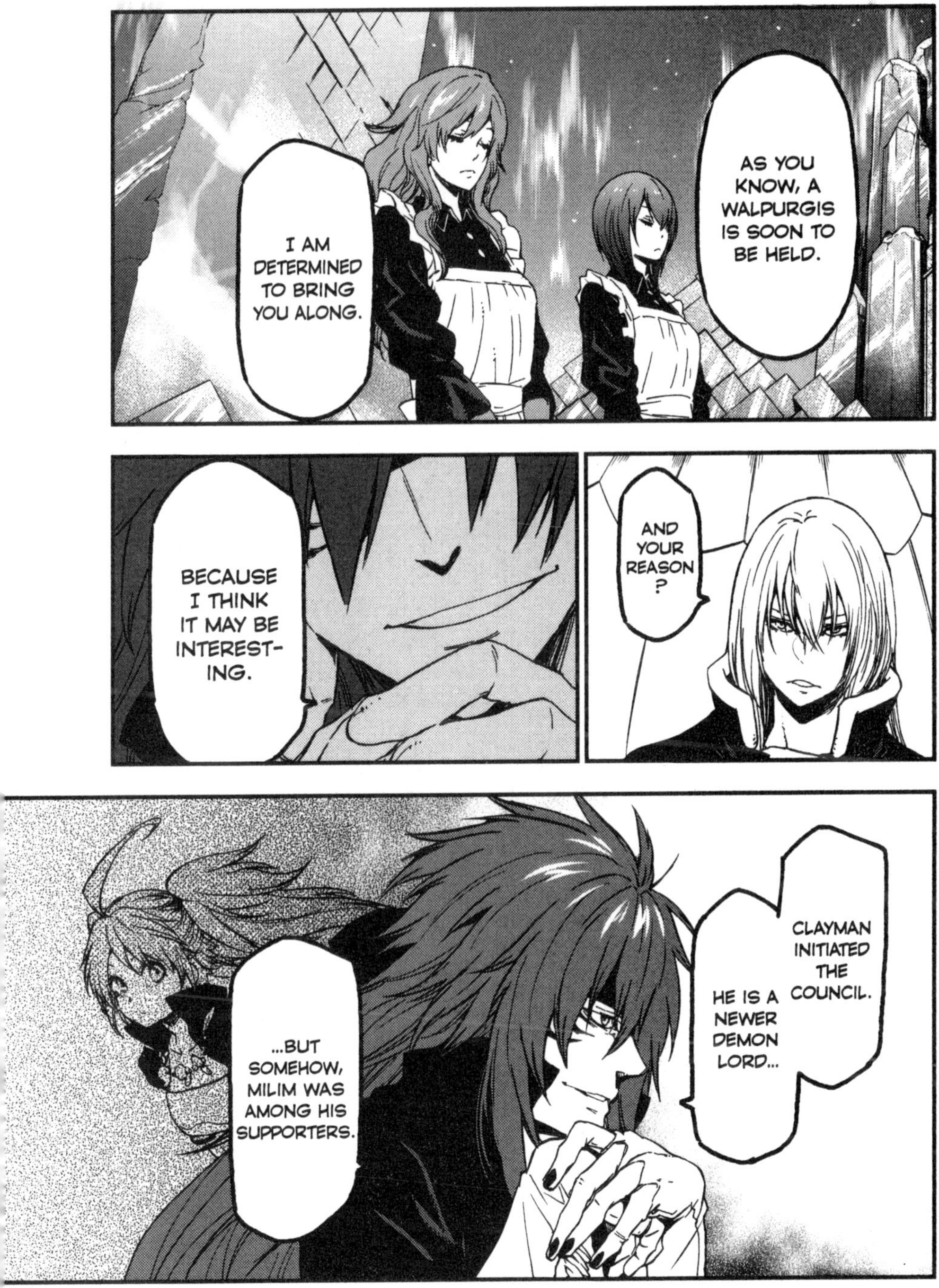
AS YOU KNOW, A WALPURGIS IS SOON TO BE HELD.
I AM DETERMINED TO BRING YOU ALONG.
AND YOUR REASON?
BECAUSE I THINK IT MAY BE INTEREST-ING.
CLAYMAN INITIATED THE COUNCIL.
HE IS A NEWER DEMON LORD...
...BUT SOMEHOW, MILIM WAS AMONG HIS SUPPORTERS.

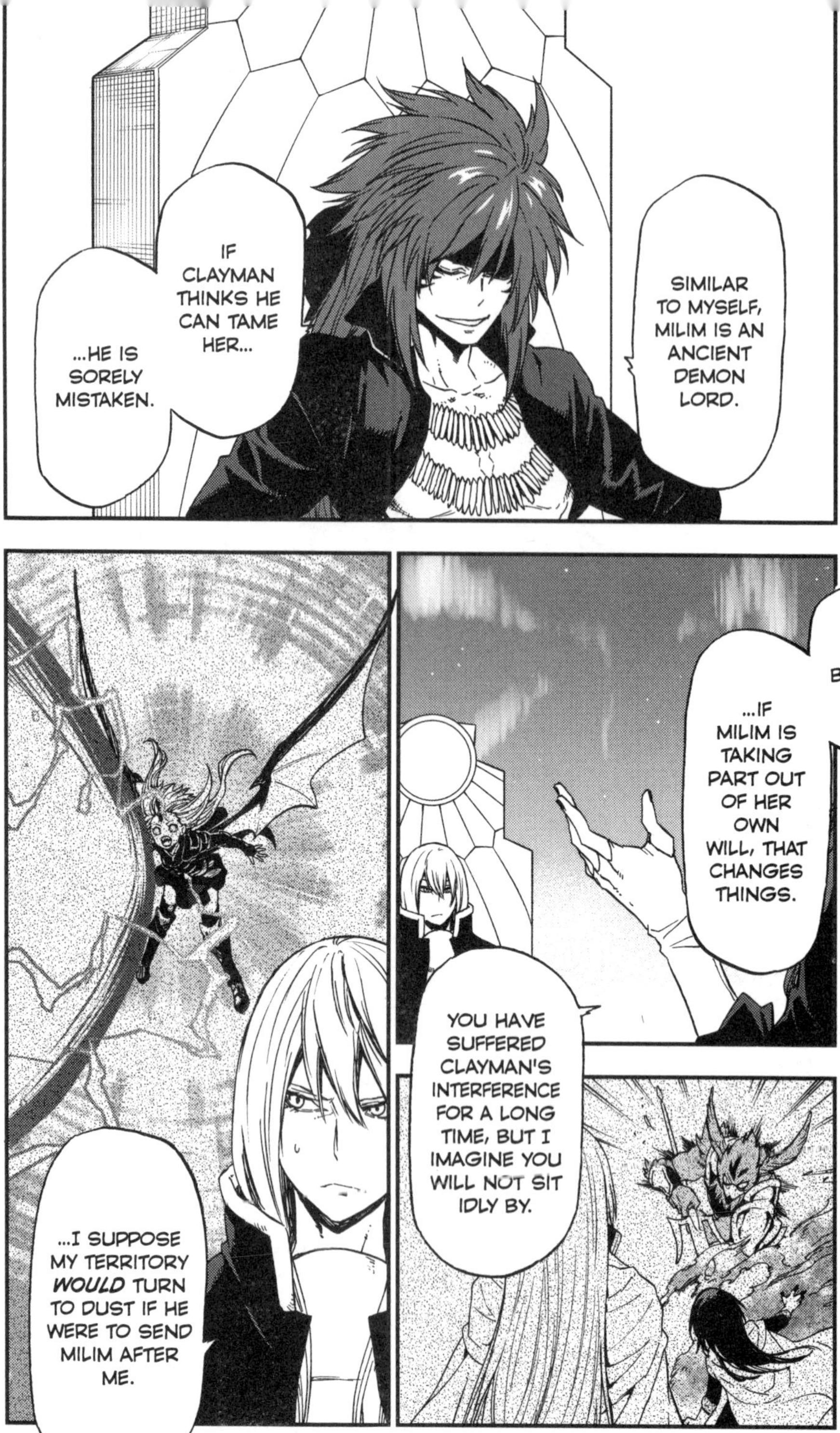
SIMILAR TO MYSELF, MILIM IS AN ANCIENT DEMON LORD.
IF CLAYMAN THINKS HE CAN TAME HER...
...HE IS SORELY MISTAKEN.
BUT...
...IF MILIM IS TAKING PART OUT OF HER OWN WILL, THAT CHANGES THINGS.
YOU HAVE SUFFERED CLAYMAN'S INTERFERENCE FOR A LONG TIME, BUT I IMAGINE YOU WILL NOT SIT IDLY BY.
...I SUPPOSE MY TERRITORY *WOULD* TURN TO DUST IF HE WERE TO SEND MILIM AFTER ME.

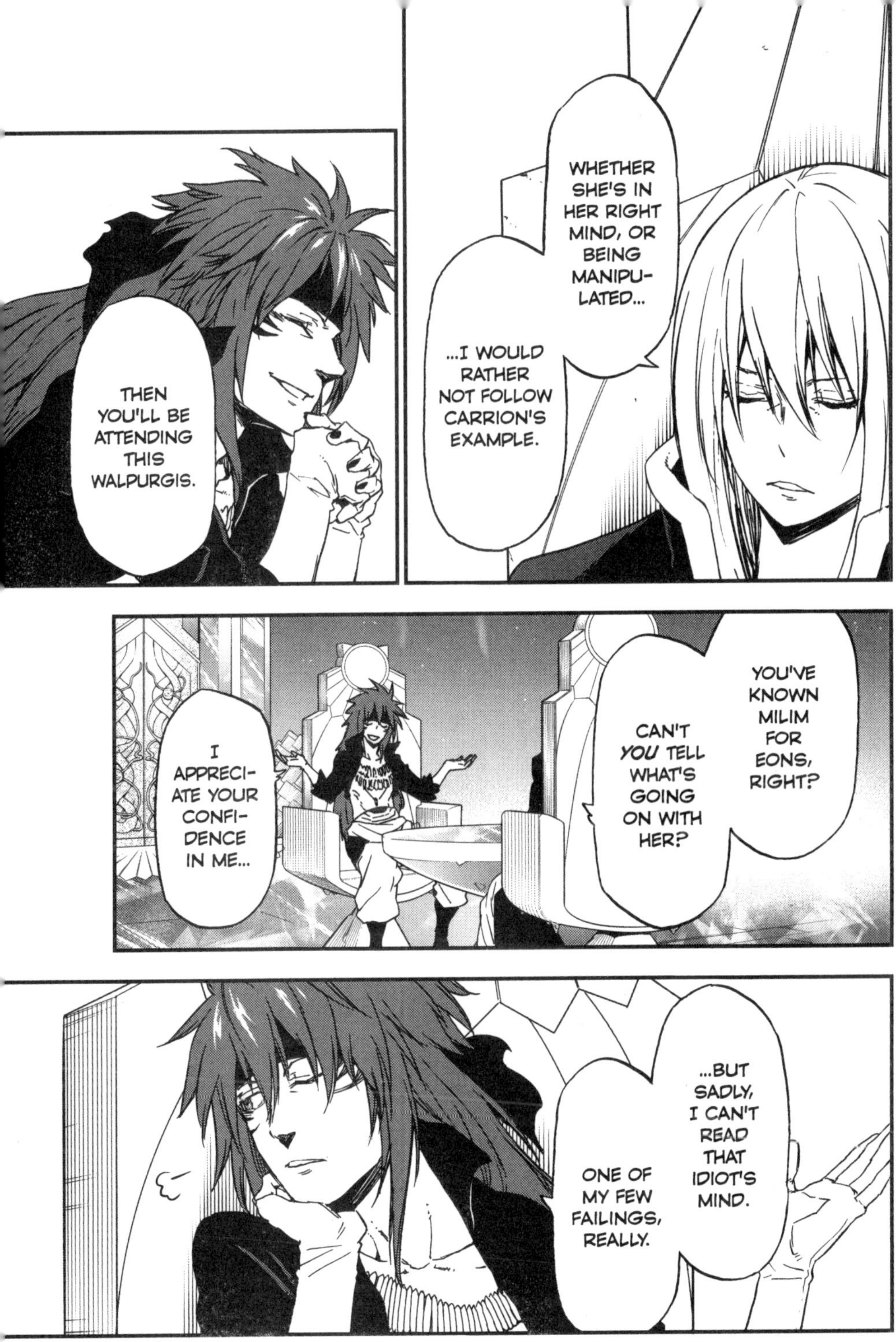
WHETHER SHE'S IN HER RIGHT MIND, OR BEING MANIPULATED...
...I WOULD RATHER NOT FOLLOW CARRION'S EXAMPLE.
THEN YOU'LL BE ATTENDING THIS WALPURGIS.
YOU'VE KNOWN MILIM FOR EONS, RIGHT?
CAN'T *YOU* TELL WHAT'S GOING ON WITH HER?
I APPRECIATE YOUR CONFIDENCE IN ME...
...BUT SADLY, I CAN'T READ THAT IDIOT'S MIND.
ONE OF MY FEW FAILINGS, REALLY.

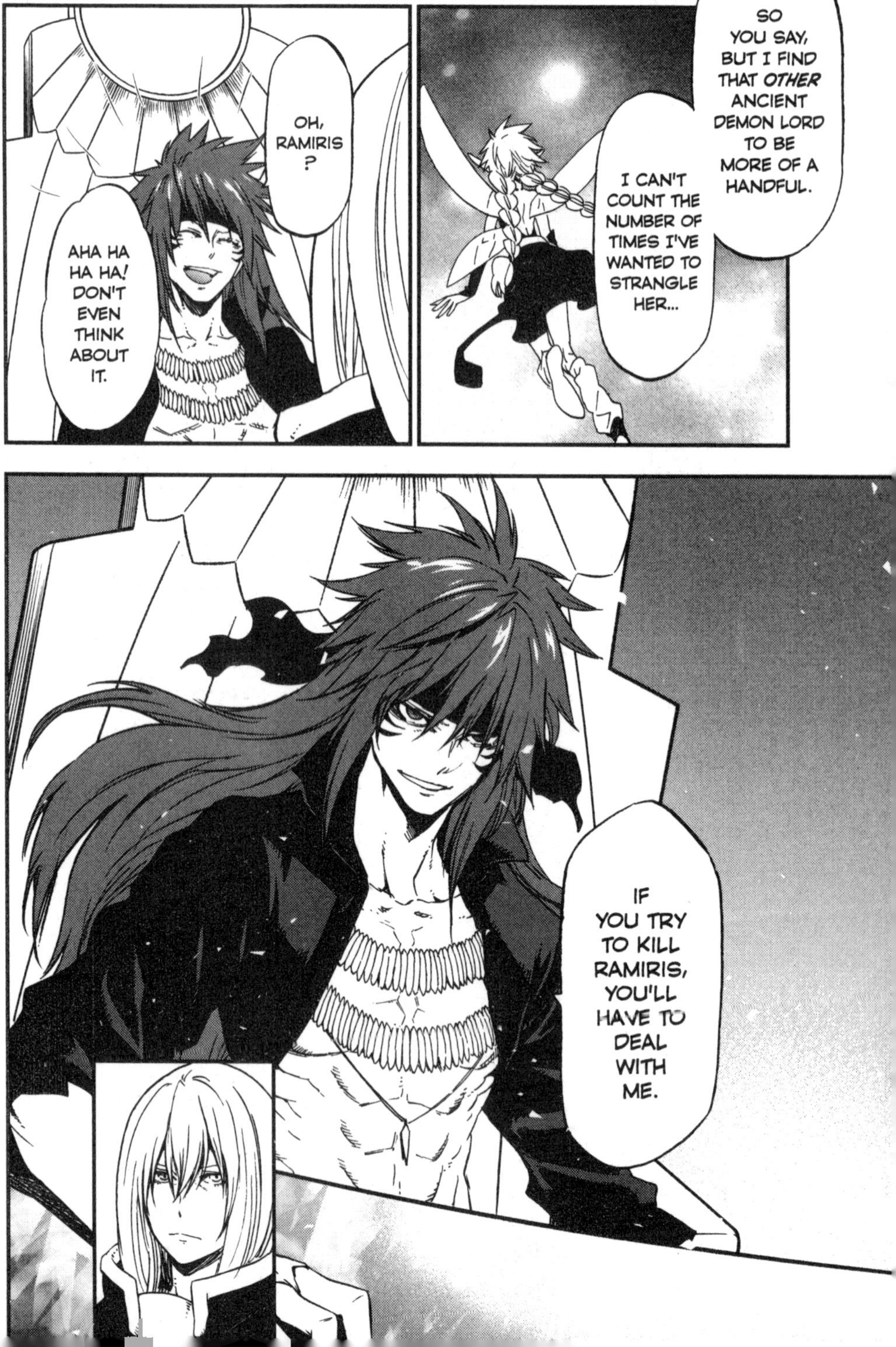
SO YOU SAY, BUT I FIND THAT *OTHER* ANCIENT DEMON LORD TO BE MORE OF A HANDFUL.
I CAN'T COUNT THE NUMBER OF TIMES I'VE WANTED TO STRANGLE HER...
OH, RAMIRIS?
AHA HA HA HA! DON'T EVEN THINK ABOUT IT.
IF YOU TRY TO KILL RAMIRIS, YOU'LL HAVE TO DEAL WITH ME.

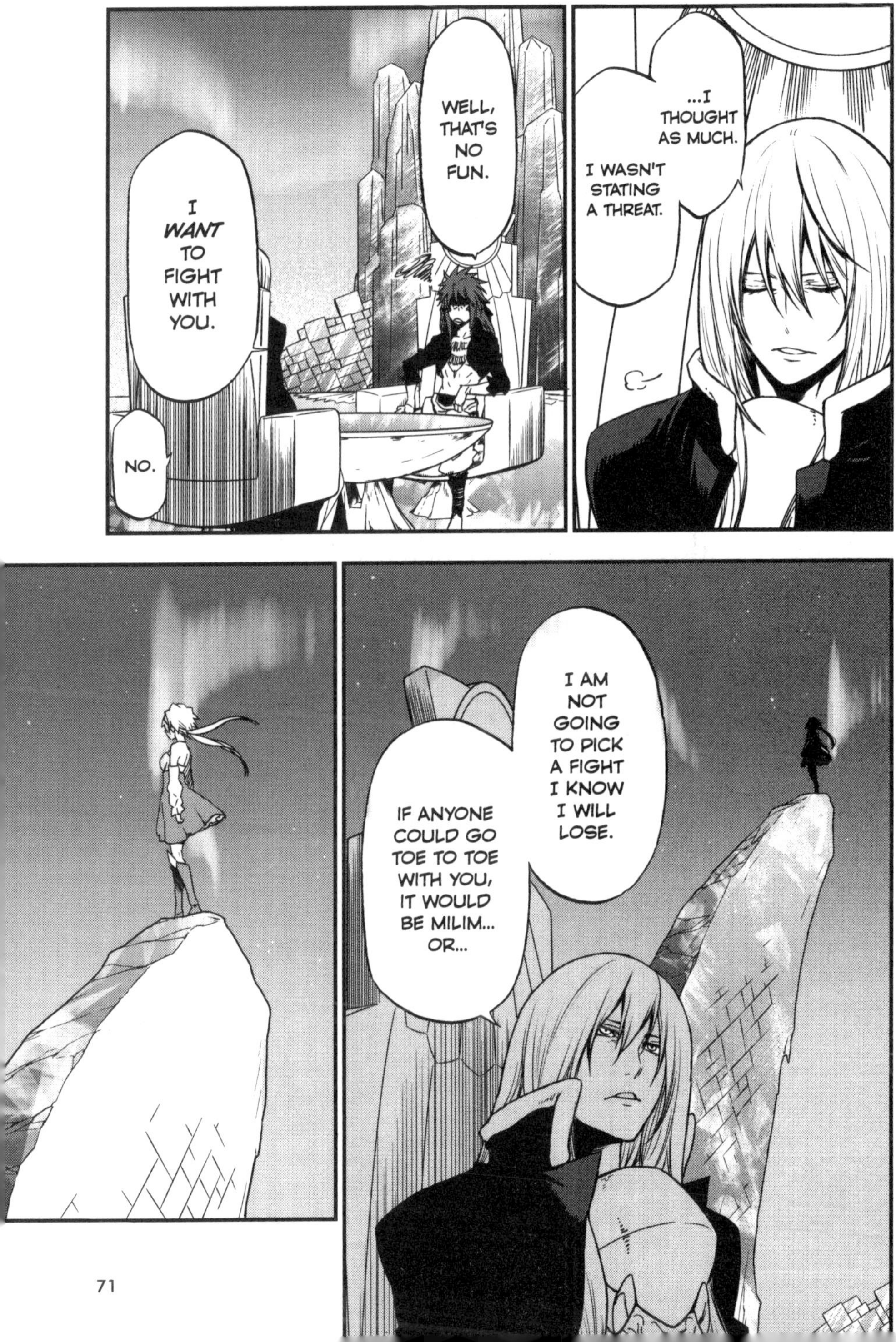
...I THOUGHT AS MUCH.
I WASN'T STATING A THREAT.
WELL, THAT'S NO FUN.
I *WANT* TO FIGHT WITH YOU.
NO.
I AM NOT GOING TO PICK A FIGHT I KNOW I WILL LOSE.
IF ANYONE COULD GO TOE TO TOE WITH YOU, IT WOULD BE MILIM... OR...

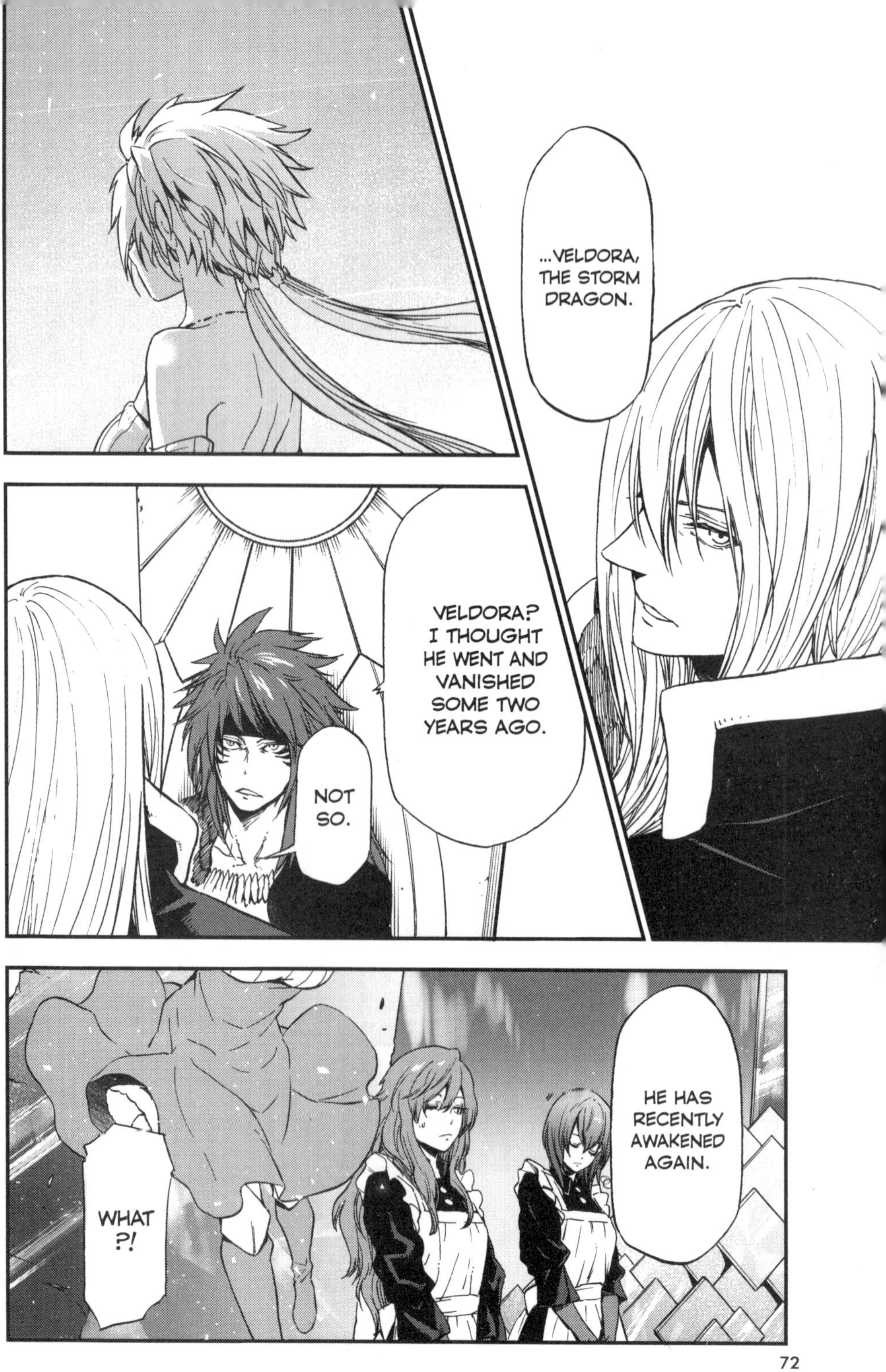

...VELDORA, THE STORM DRAGON.
VELDORA? I THOUGHT HE WENT AND VANISHED SOME TWO YEARS AGO.
NOT SO.
HE HAS RECENTLY AWAKENED AGAIN.
WHAT ?!

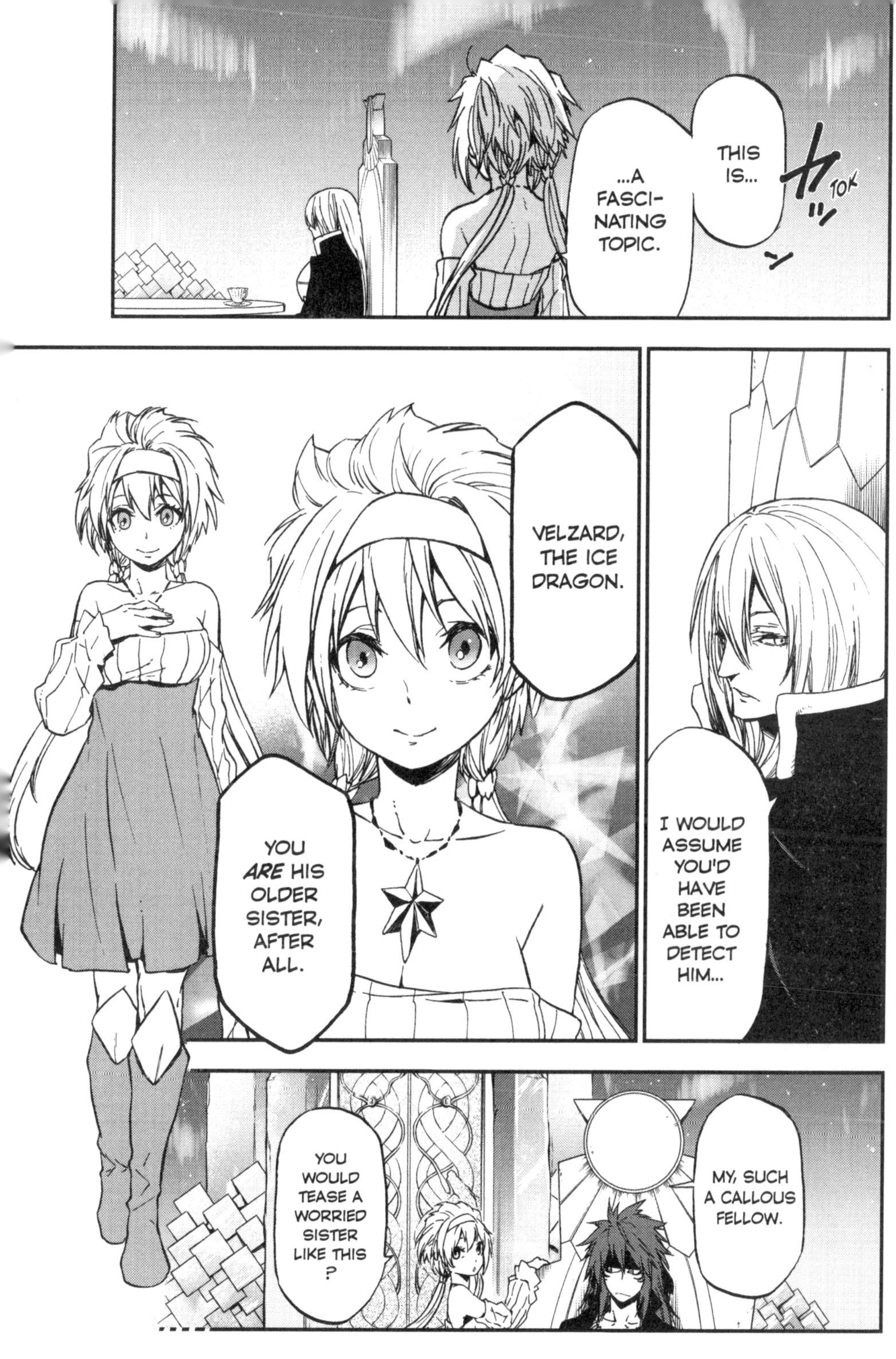
TOK
THIS IS...
...A FASCINATING TOPIC.
I WOULD ASSUME YOU'D HAVE BEEN ABLE TO DETECT HIM...
VELZARD, THE ICE DRAGON.
YOU *ARE* HIS OLDER SISTER, AFTER ALL.
MY, SUCH A CALLOUS FELLOW.
YOU WOULD TEASE A WORRIED SISTER LIKE THIS?

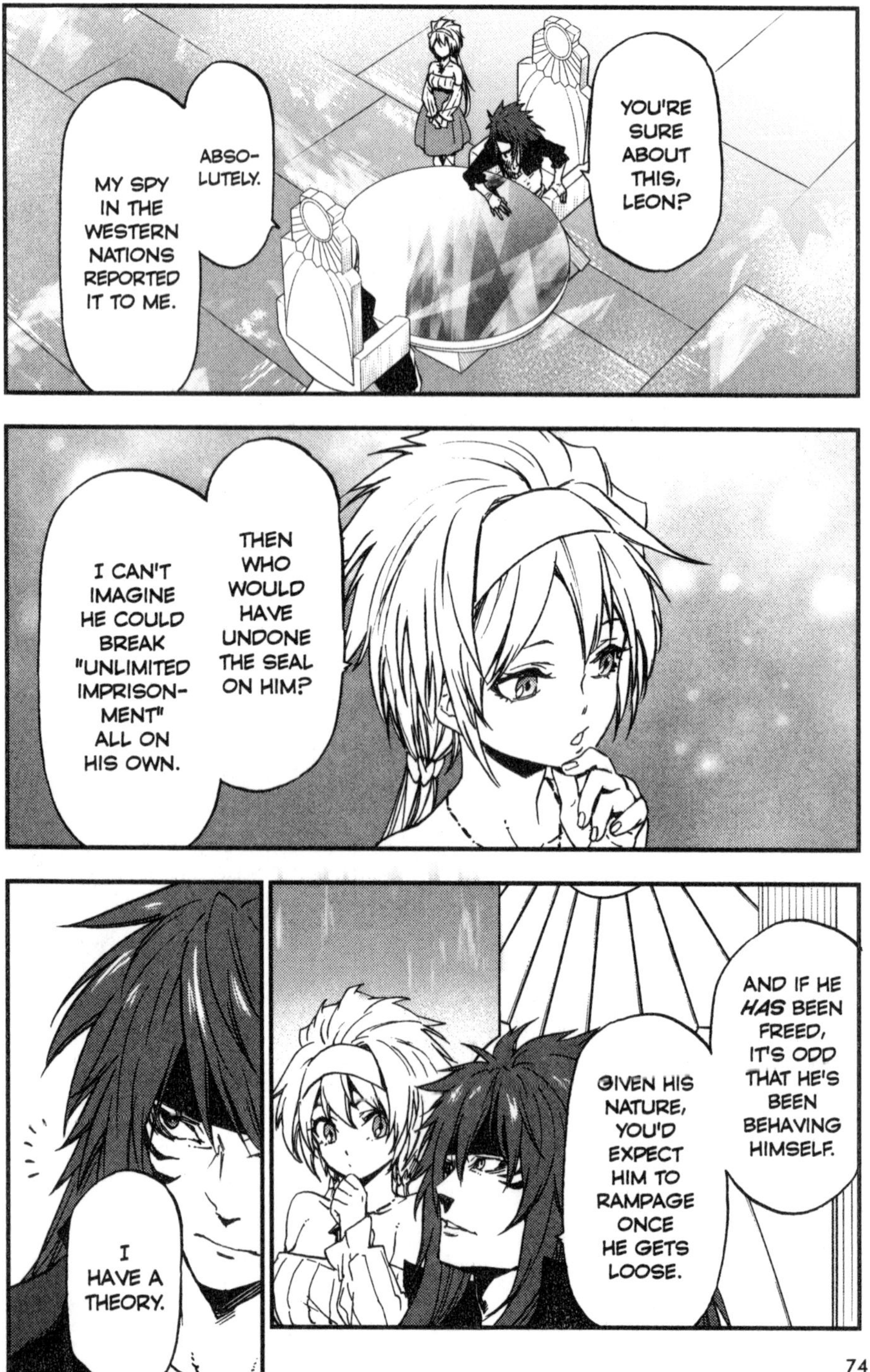
YOU'RE SURE ABOUT THIS, LEON?
ABSO-LUTELY.
MY SPY IN THE WESTERN NATIONS REPORTED IT TO ME.
THEN WHO WOULD HAVE UNDONE THE SEAL ON HIM?
I CAN'T IMAGINE HE COULD BREAK "UNLIMITED IMPRISON-MENT" ALL ON HIS OWN.
AND IF HE *HAS* BEEN FREED, IT'S ODD THAT HE'S BEEN BEHAVING HIMSELF.
GIVEN HIS NATURE, YOU'D EXPECT HIM TO RAMPAGE ONCE HE GETS LOOSE.
I HAVE A THEORY.

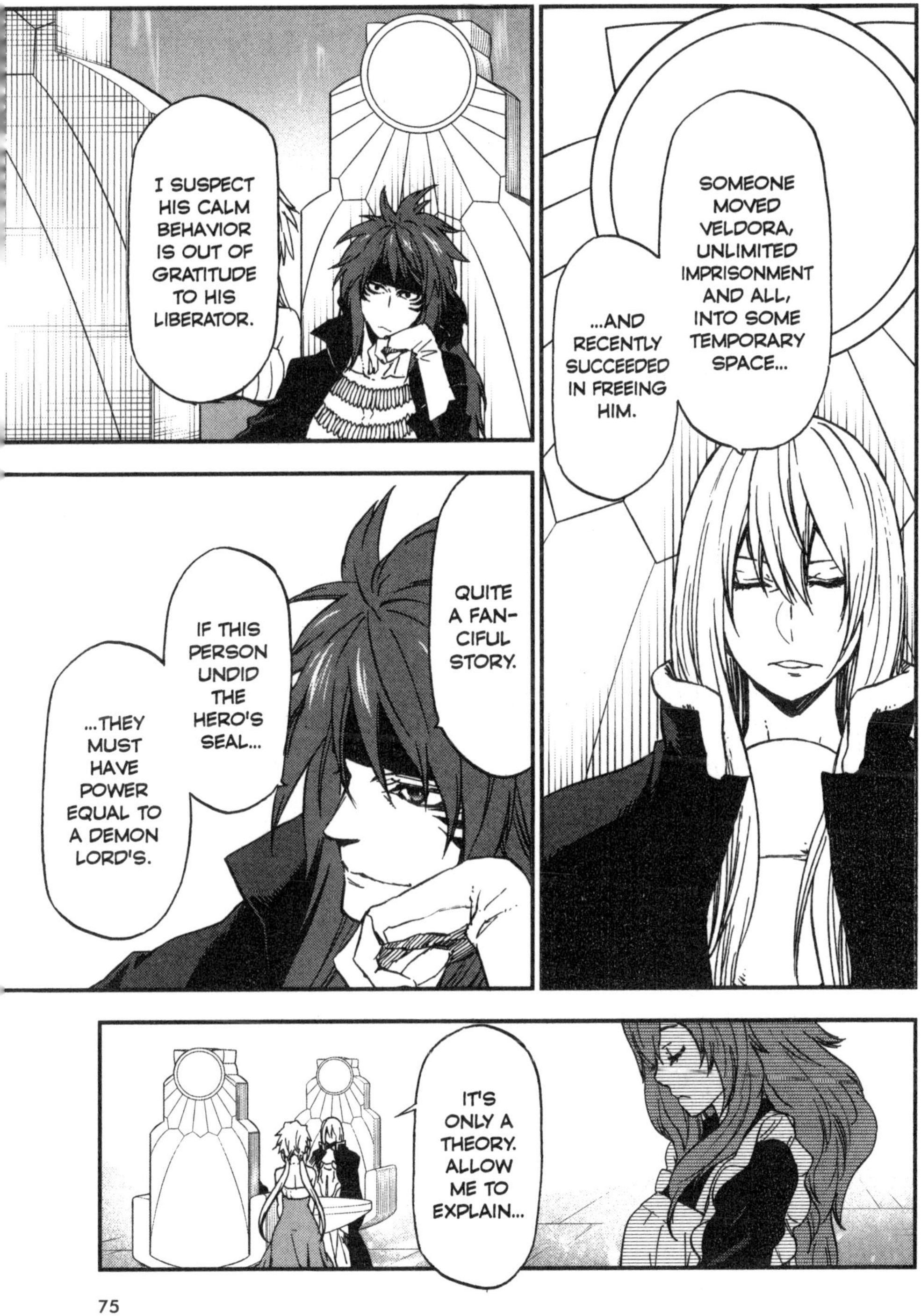
SOMEONE MOVED VELDORA, UNLIMITED IMPRISONMENT AND ALL, INTO SOME TEMPORARY SPACE...
...AND RECENTLY SUCCEEDED IN FREEING HIM.
I SUSPECT HIS CALM BEHAVIOR IS OUT OF GRATITUDE TO HIS LIBERATOR.
QUITE A FAN-CIFUL STORY.
IF THIS PERSON UNDID THE HERO'S SEAL...
...THEY MUST HAVE POWER EQUAL TO A DEMON LORD'S.
IT'S ONLY A THEORY. ALLOW ME TO EXPLAIN...

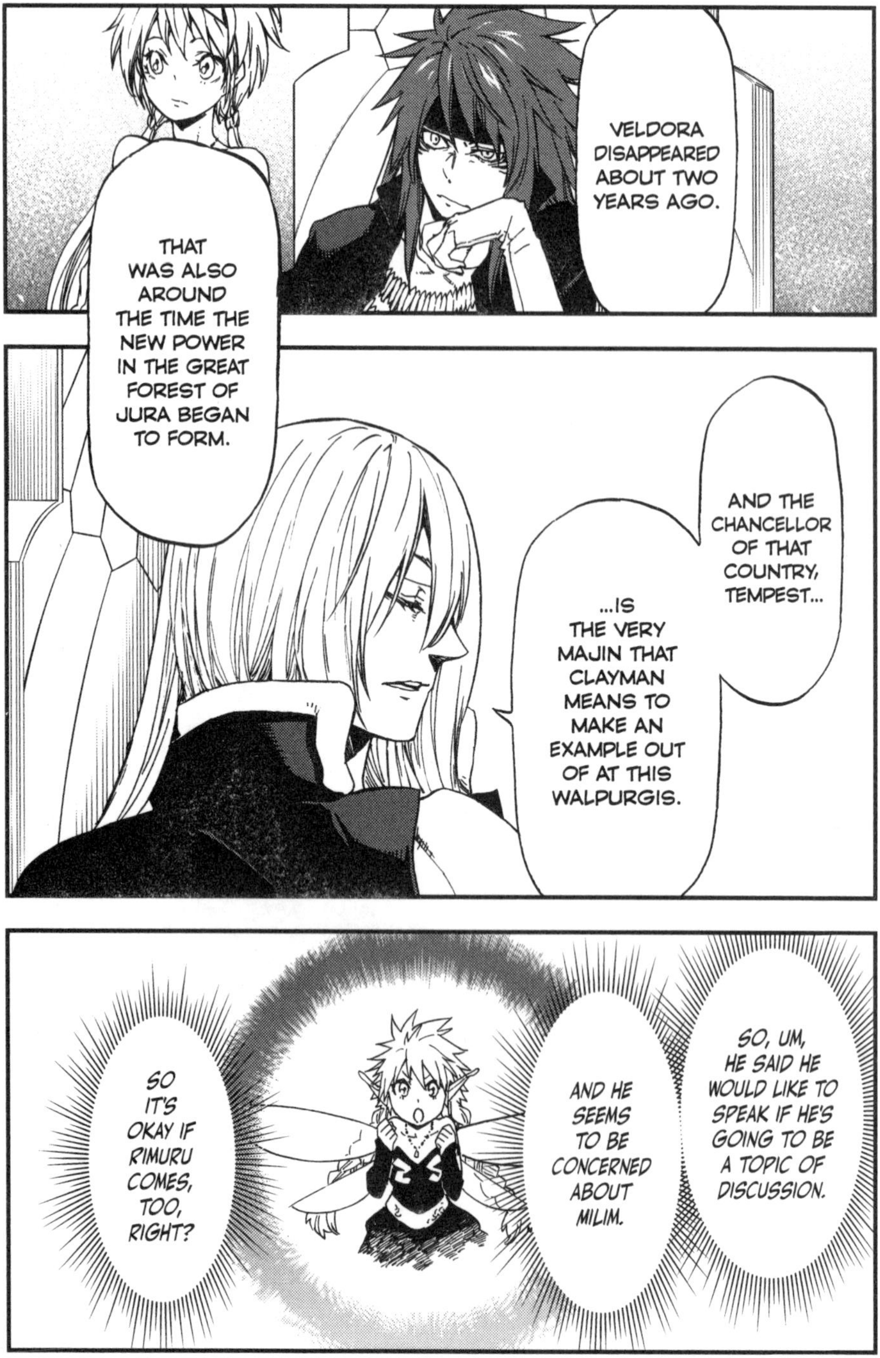
VELDORA DISAPPEARED ABOUT TWO YEARS AGO.
THAT WAS ALSO AROUND THE TIME THE NEW POWER IN THE GREAT FOREST OF JURA BEGAN TO FORM.
AND THE CHANCELLOR OF THAT COUNTRY, TEMPEST...
...IS THE VERY MAJIN THAT CLAYMAN MEANS TO MAKE AN EXAMPLE OUT OF AT THIS WALPURGIS.
SO, UM, HE SAID HE WOULD LIKE TO SPEAK IF HE'S GOING TO BE A TOPIC OF DISCUSSION.
AND HE SEEMS TO BE CONCERNED ABOUT MILIM.
SO IT'S OKAY IF RIMURU COMES, TOO, RIGHT?

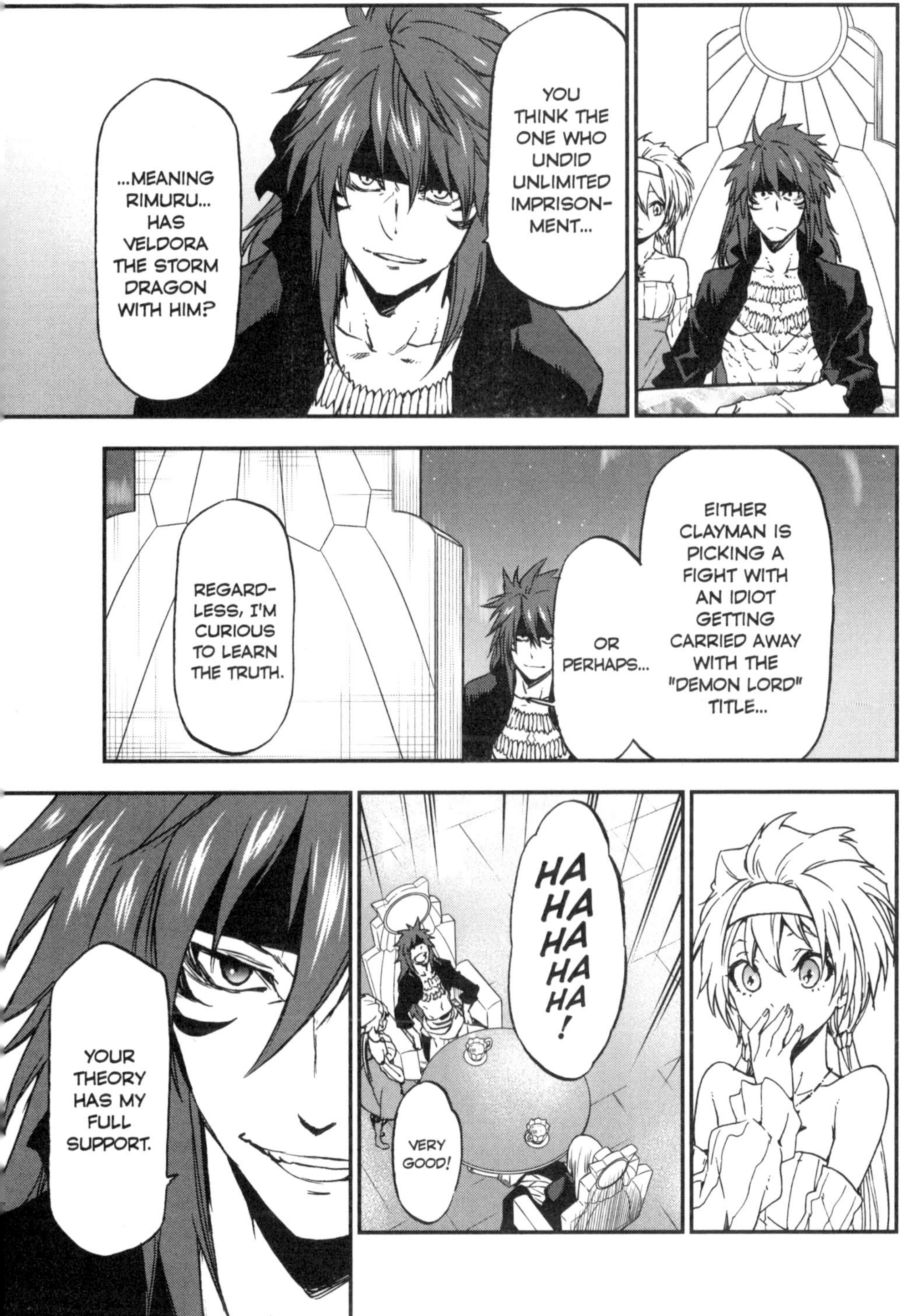
YOU THINK THE ONE WHO UNDID UNLIMITED IMPRISONMENT...
...MEANING RIMURU... HAS VELDORA THE STORM DRAGON WITH HIM?
EITHER CLAYMAN IS PICKING A FIGHT WITH AN IDIOT GETTING CARRIED AWAY WITH THE "DEMON LORD" TITLE...
OR PERHAPS...
REGARDLESS, I'M CURIOUS TO LEARN THE TRUTH.
HAHAHAHAHAHA!
VERY GOOD!
YOUR THEORY HAS MY FULL SUPPORT.

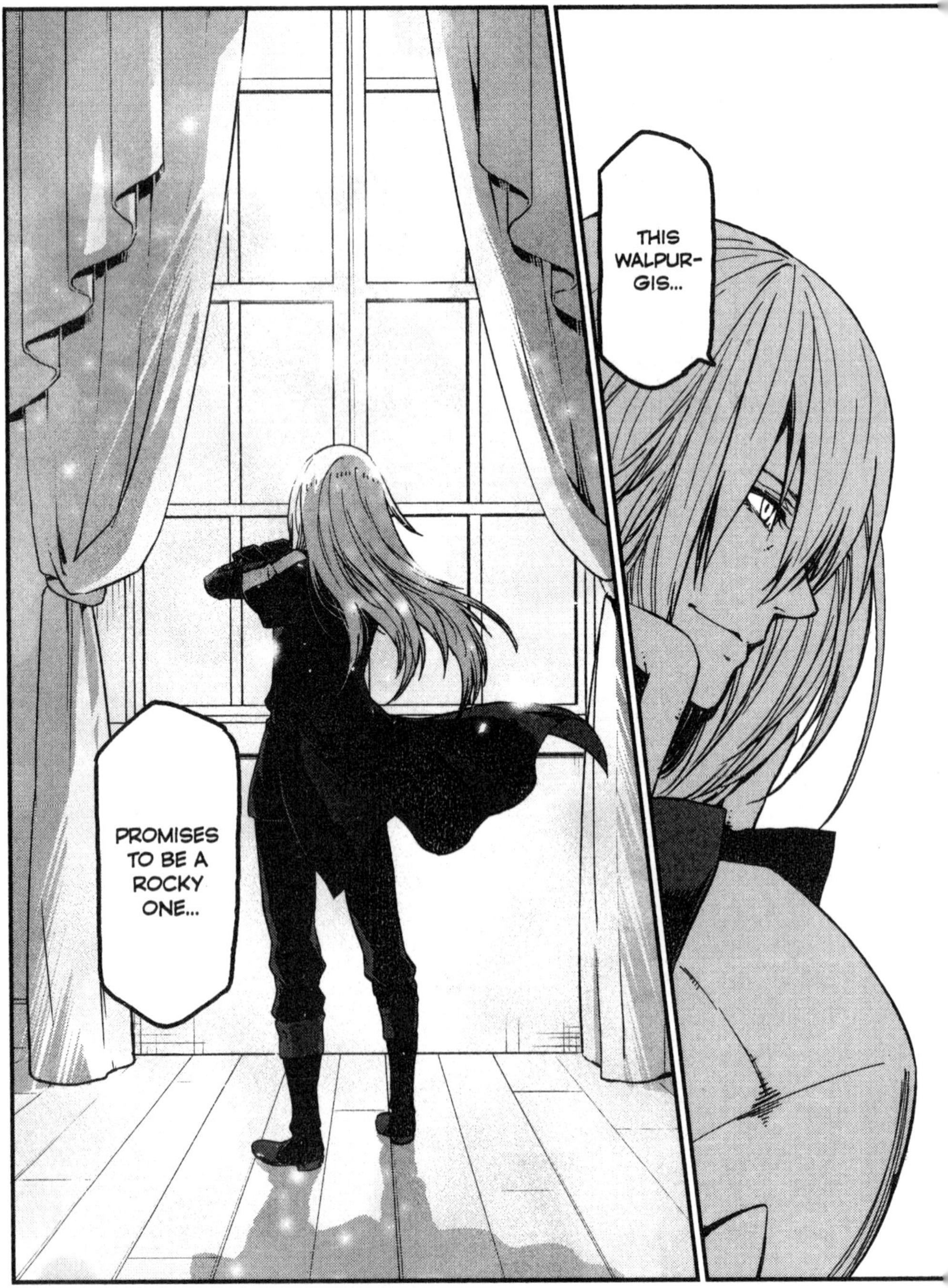
THIS WALPURGIS...
PROMISES TO BE A ROCKY ONE...

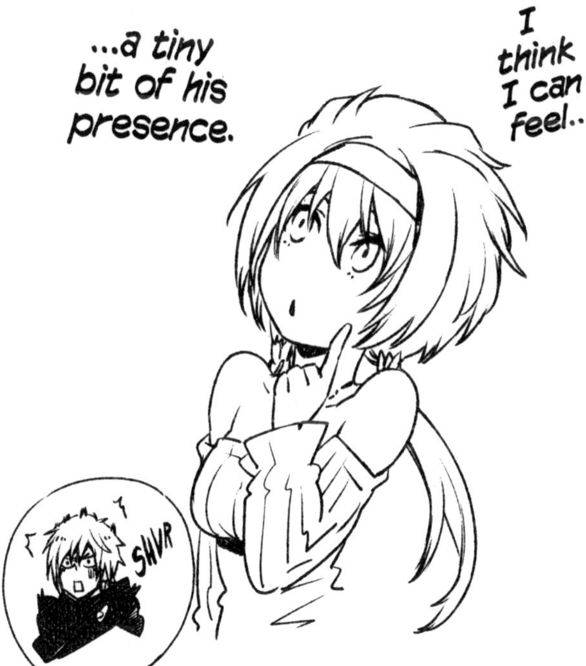
I think I can feel...
...a tiny bit of his presence.
SHVR

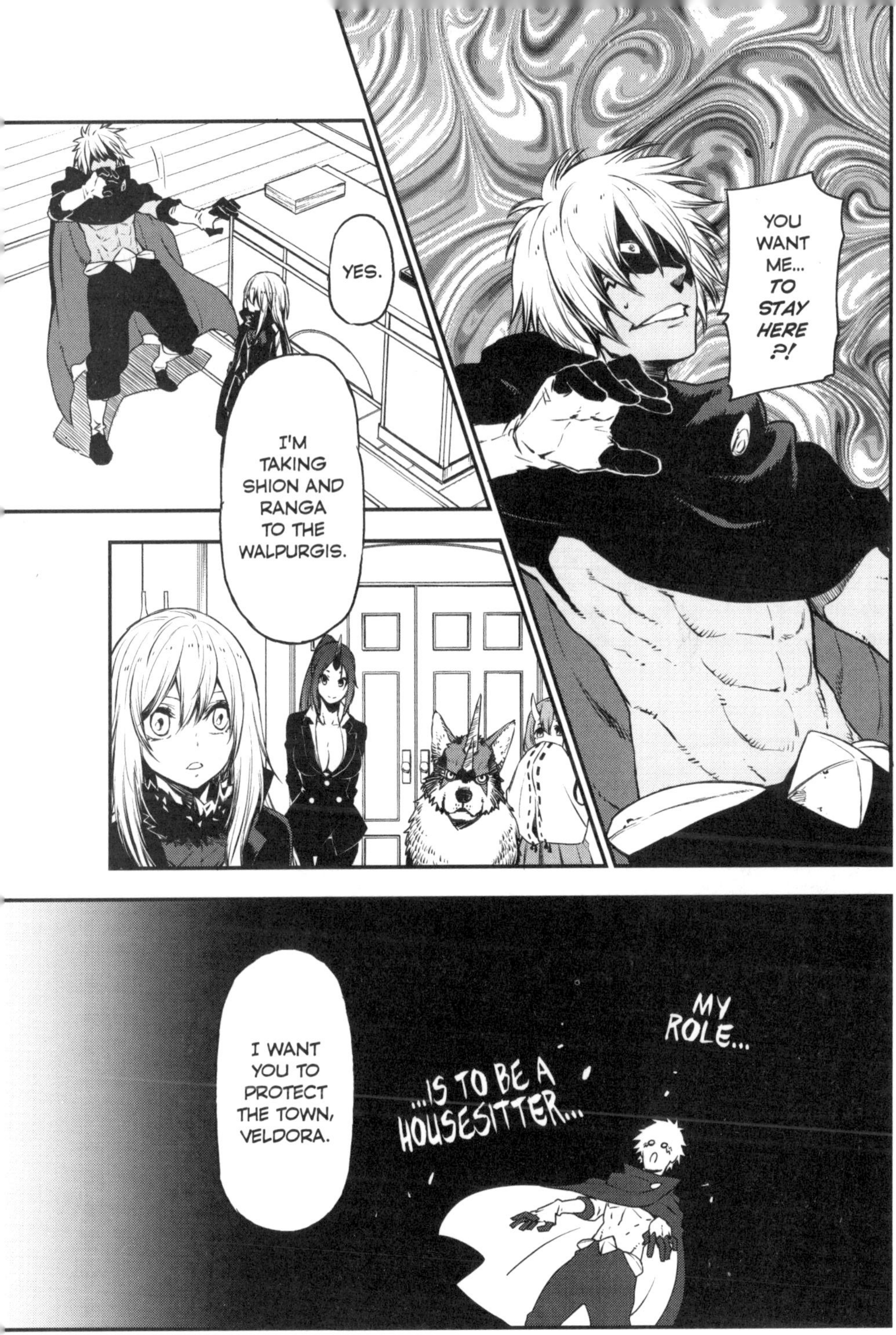
YOU WANT ME... TO STAY HERE?!
YES.
I'M TAKING SHION AND RANGA TO THE WALPURGIS.
I WANT YOU TO PROTECT THE TOWN, VELDORA.
MY ROLE...
...IS TO BE A HOUSESITTER...

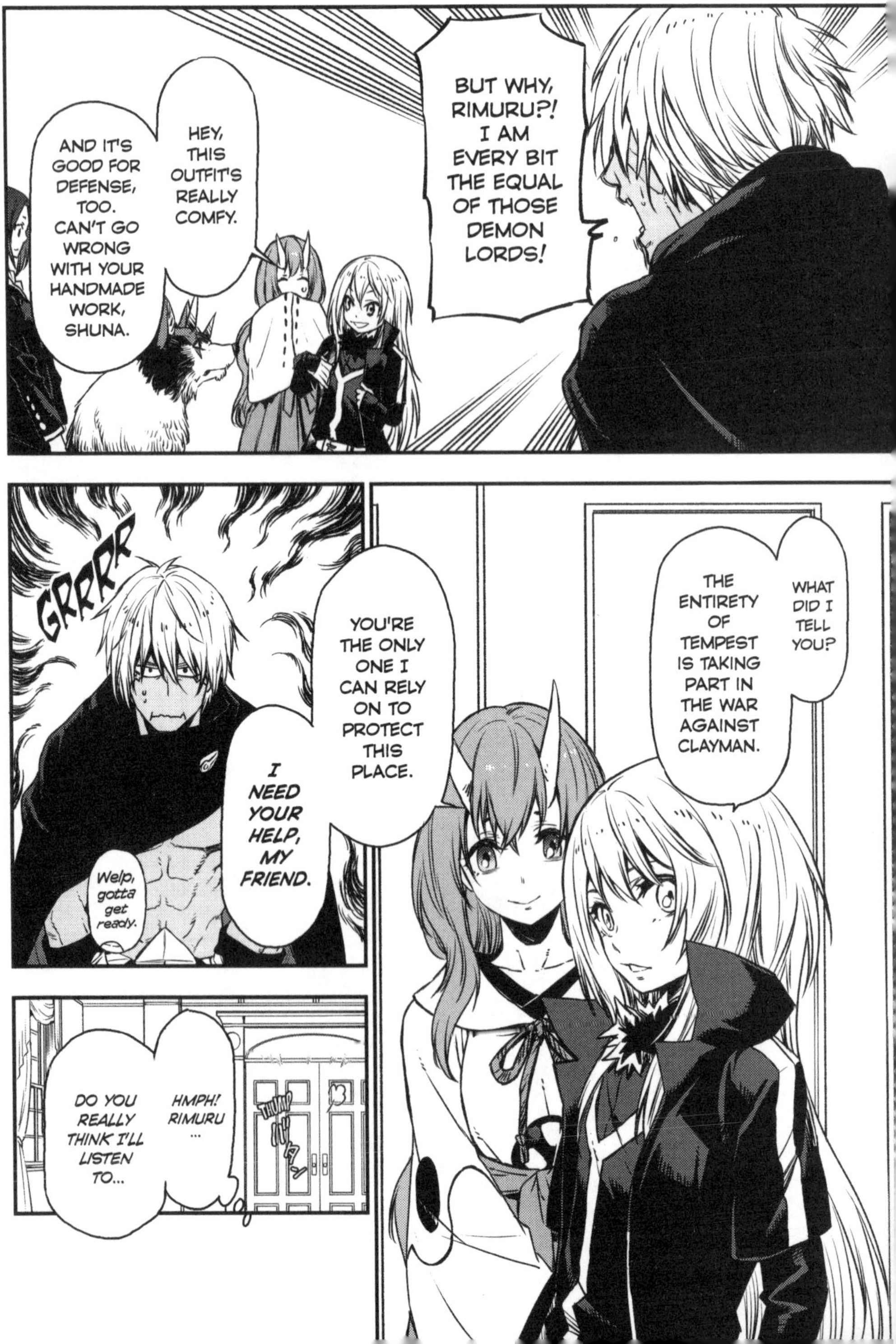
BUT WHY, RIMURU?! I AM EVERY BIT THE EQUAL OF THOSE DEMON LORDS!
HEY, THIS OUTFIT'S REALLY COMFY.
AND IT'S GOOD FOR DEFENSE, TOO. CAN'T GO WRONG WITH YOUR HANDMADE WORK, SHUNA.
WHAT DID I TELL YOU?
THE ENTIRETY OF TEMPEST IS TAKING PART IN THE WAR AGAINST CLAYMAN.
YOU'RE THE ONLY ONE I CAN RELY ON TO PROTECT THIS PLACE.
I NEED YOUR HELP, MY FRIEND.
GRRRR
Welp, gotta get ready.
HMPH! RIMURU...
DO YOU REALLY THINK I'LL LISTEN TO...
THUMP

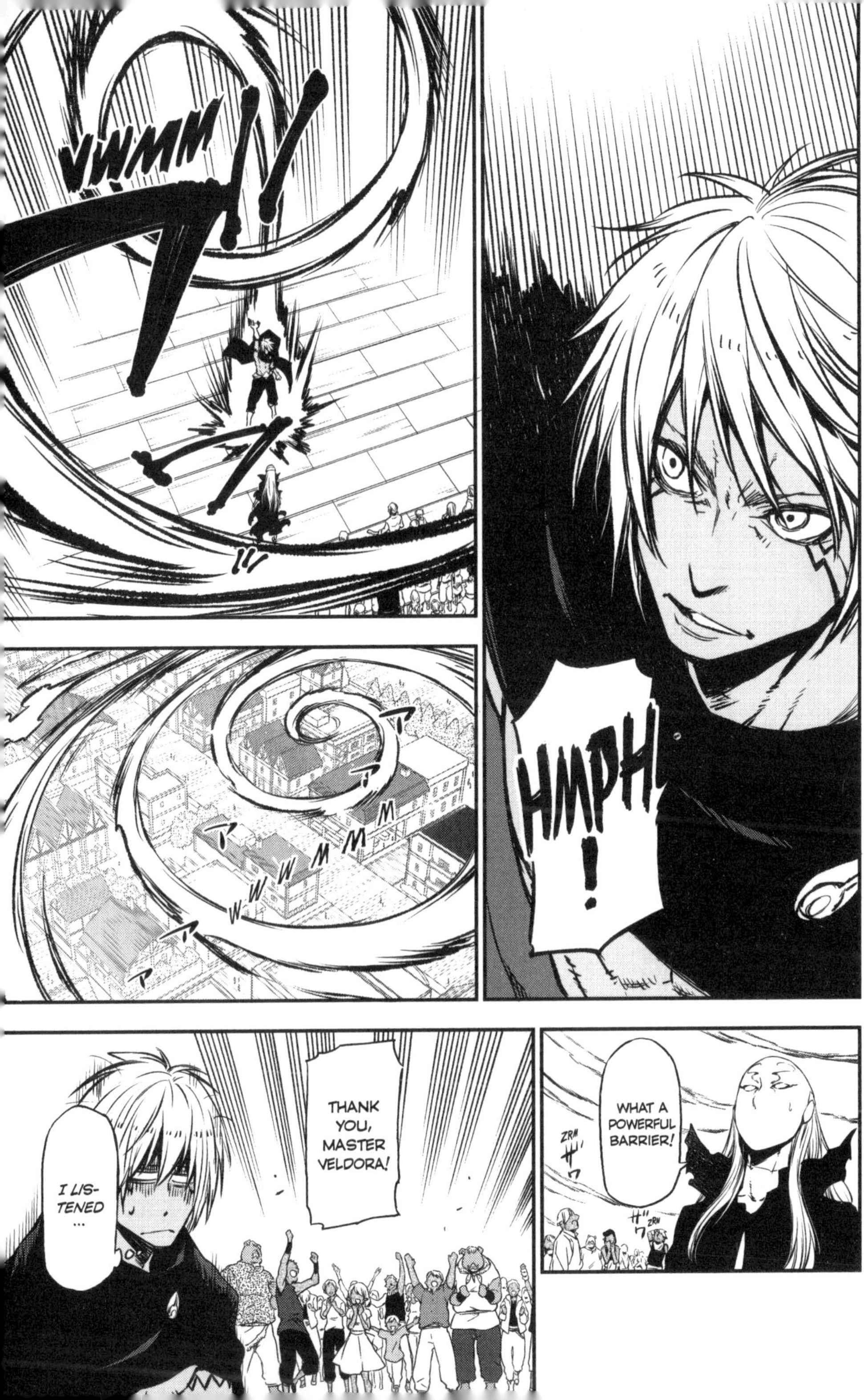
HMPH!
VWMM!!
WWWMMMM
WHAT A POWERFUL BARRIER!
ZRM
ZRM
THANK YOU, MASTER VELDORA!
I LISTENED...

CHAPTER 77 Eve of Battle

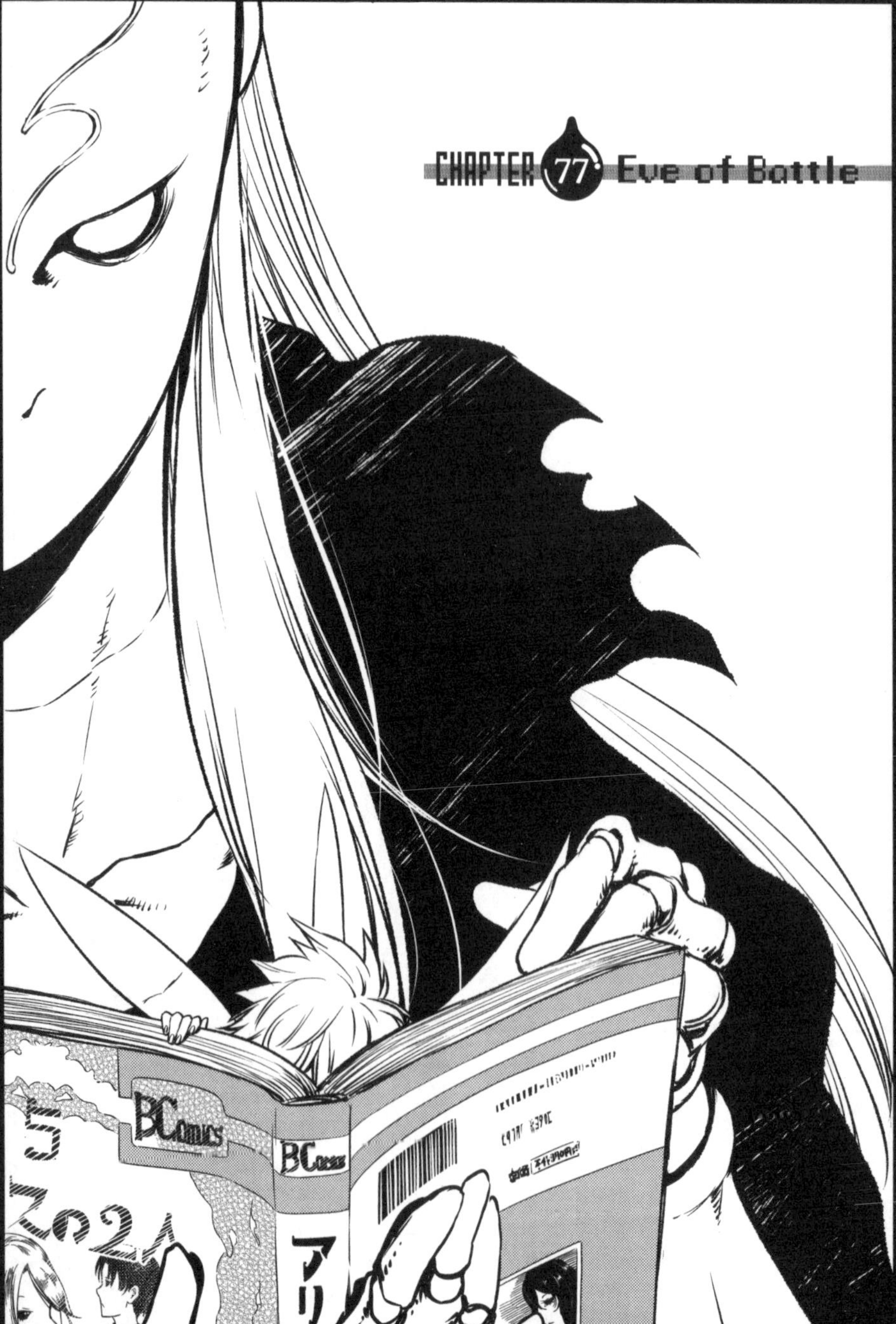
BComics
BComics

BOOK: Aria

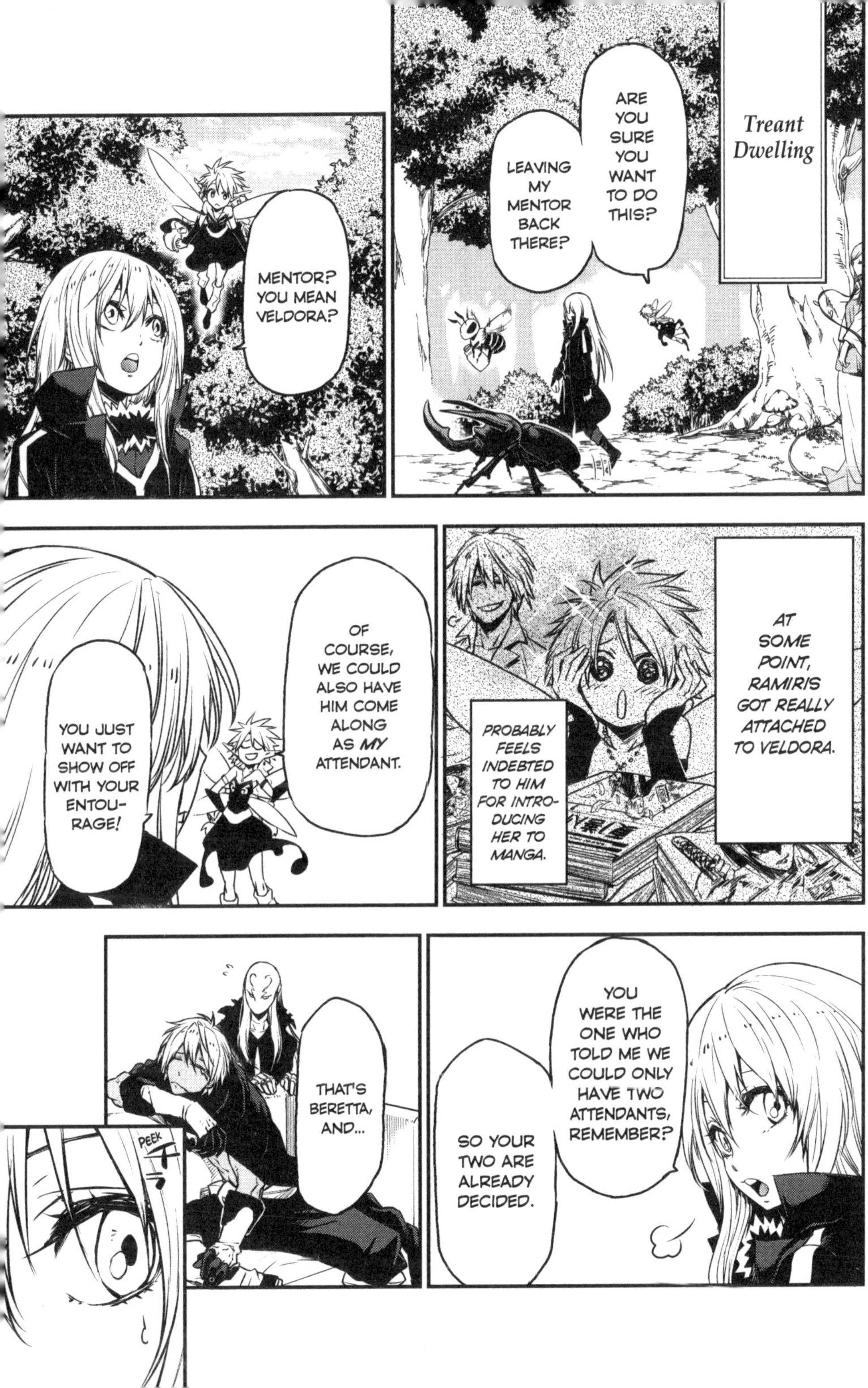
Treant Dwelling
ARE YOU SURE YOU WANT TO DO THIS?
LEAVING MY MENTOR BACK THERE?
MENTOR? YOU MEAN VELDORA?
AT SOME POINT, RAMIRIS GOT REALLY ATTACHED TO VELDORA.
PROBABLY FEELS INDEBTED TO HIM FOR INTRO-DUCING HER TO MANGA.
OF COURSE, WE COULD ALSO HAVE HIM COME ALONG AS MY ATTENDANT.
YOU JUST WANT TO SHOW OFF WITH YOUR ENTOU-RAGE!
YOU WERE THE ONE WHO TOLD ME WE COULD ONLY HAVE TWO ATTENDANTS, REMEMBER?
SO YOUR TWO ARE ALREADY DECIDED.
THAT'S BERETTA, AND...
PEEK

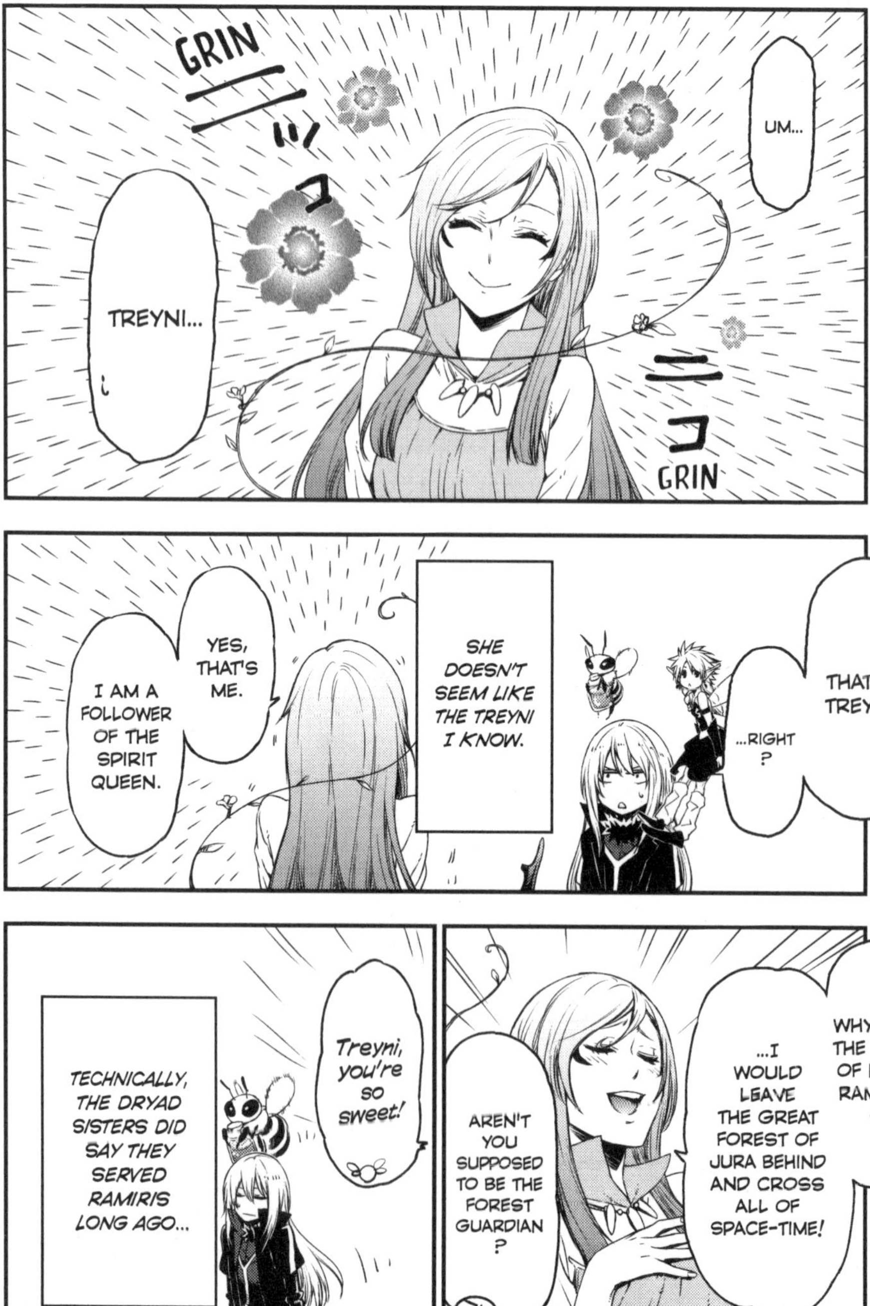
UM...
GRIN
ニッコ
TREYNI... ¿
ニコ
GRIN
THAT *IS* TREYNI...
...RIGHT?
SHE DOESN'T SEEM LIKE THE TREYNI I KNOW.
YES, THAT'S ME.
I AM A FOLLOWER OF THE SPIRIT QUEEN.
WHY, FOR THE SAKE OF LADY RAMIRIS ...
...I WOULD LEAVE THE GREAT FOREST OF JURA BEHIND AND CROSS ALL OF SPACE-TIME!
AREN'T YOU SUPPOSED TO BE THE FOREST GUARDIAN?
Treyni, you're so sweet!
TECHNICALLY, THE DRYAD SISTERS DID SAY THEY SERVED RAMIRIS LONG AGO...

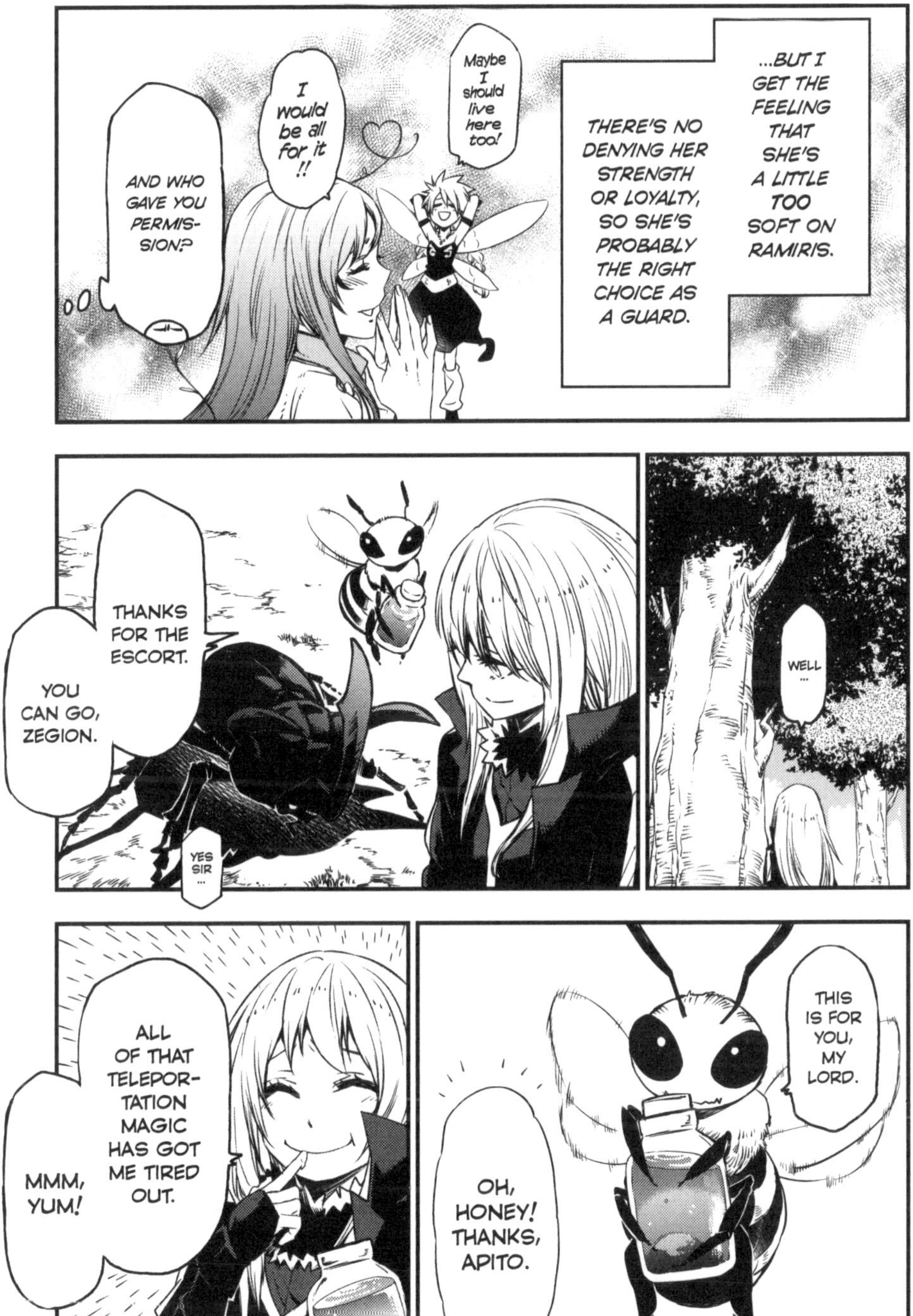
THERE'S NO DENYING HER STRENGTH OR LOYALTY, SO SHE'S PROBABLY THE RIGHT CHOICE AS A GUARD.
...BUT I GET THE FEELING THAT SHE'S A LITTLE TOO SOFT ON RAMIRIS.
Maybe I should live here too!
I would be all for it!!
AND WHO GAVE YOU PERMISSION?
WELL...
THANKS FOR THE ESCORT.
YOU CAN GO, ZEGION.
YES SIR...
THIS IS FOR YOU, MY LORD.
OH, HONEY! THANKS, APITO.
ALL OF THAT TELEPORTATION MAGIC HAS GOT ME TIRED OUT.
MMM, YUM!

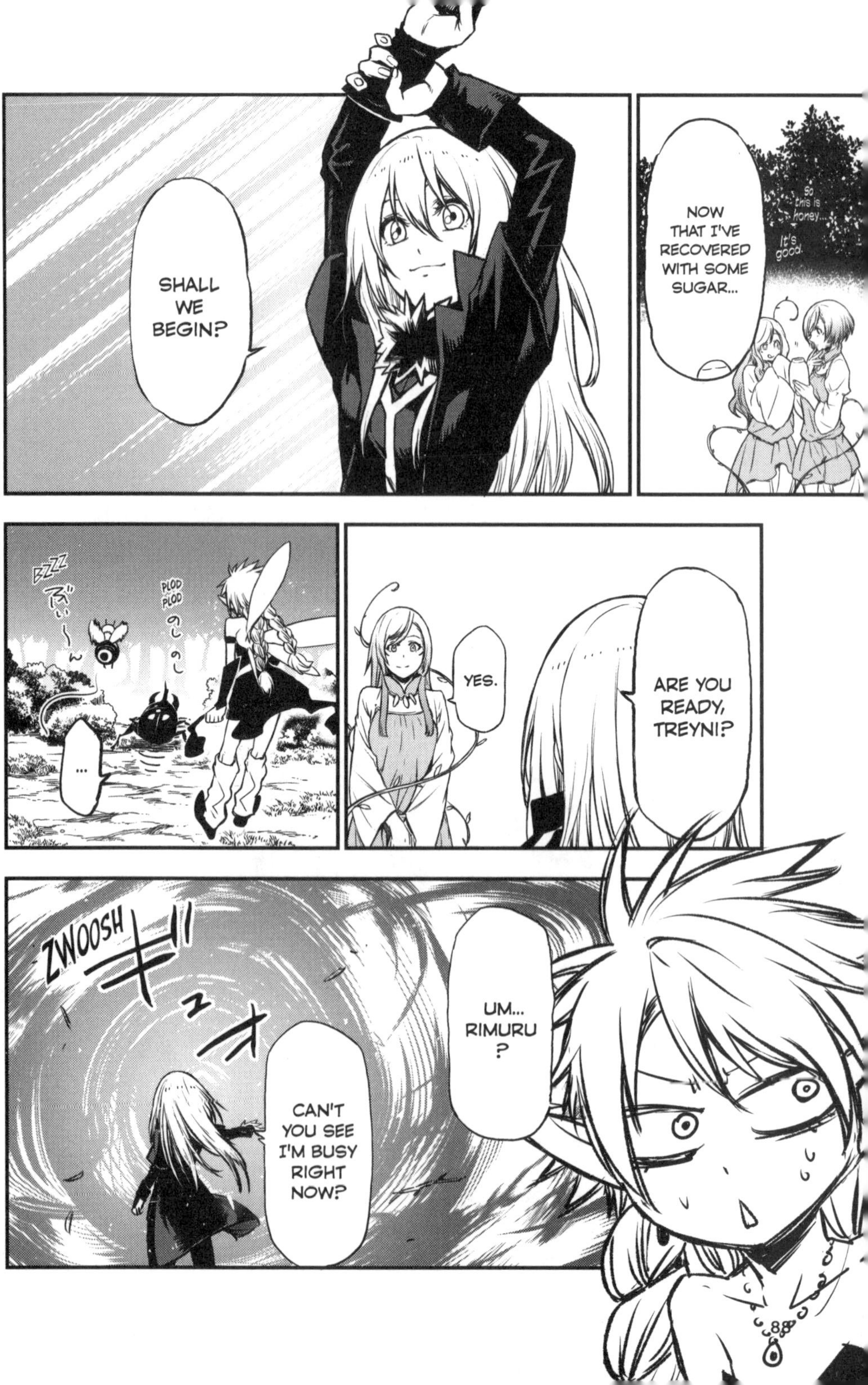

NOW THAT I'VE RECOVERED WITH SOME SUGAR...
So this is honey...
It's good.
SHALL WE BEGIN?
ARE YOU READY, TREYNI?
YES.
PLOD PLOD
のしのし
BZZZ
ぶぃ〜ん
...
UM... RIMURU?
CAN'T YOU SEE I'M BUSY RIGHT NOW?
ZWOOSH
ギュオ

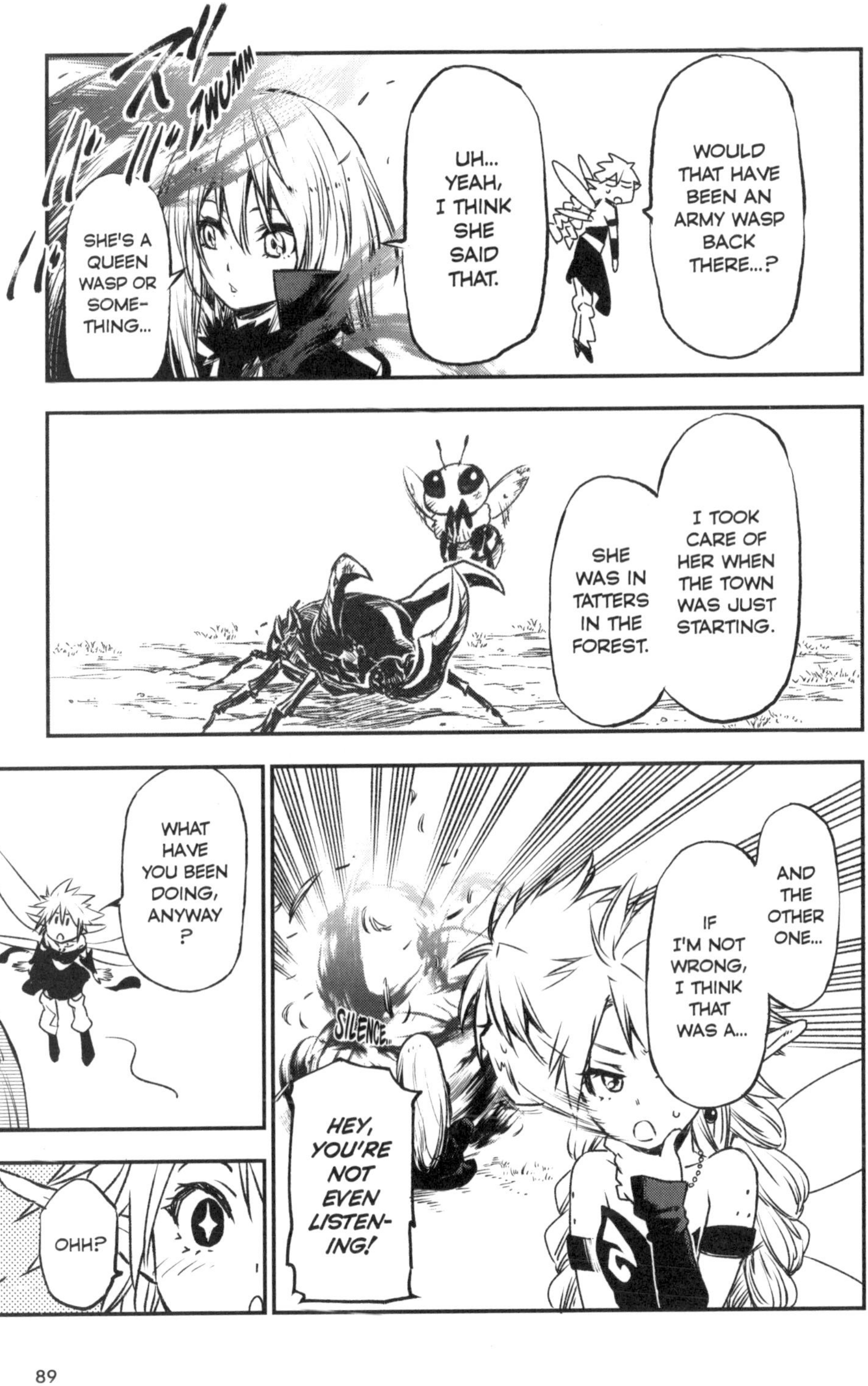
ZWUMM
WOULD THAT HAVE BEEN AN ARMY WASP BACK THERE...?
UH... YEAH, I THINK SHE SAID THAT.
SHE'S A QUEEN WASP OR SOME-THING...
I TOOK CARE OF HER WHEN THE TOWN WAS JUST STARTING.
SHE WAS IN TATTERS IN THE FOREST.
AND THE OTHER ONE...
IF I'M NOT WRONG, I THINK THAT WAS A...
SILENCE...
HEY, YOU'RE NOT EVEN LISTEN-ING!
WHAT HAVE YOU BEEN DOING, ANYWAY?
OHH?

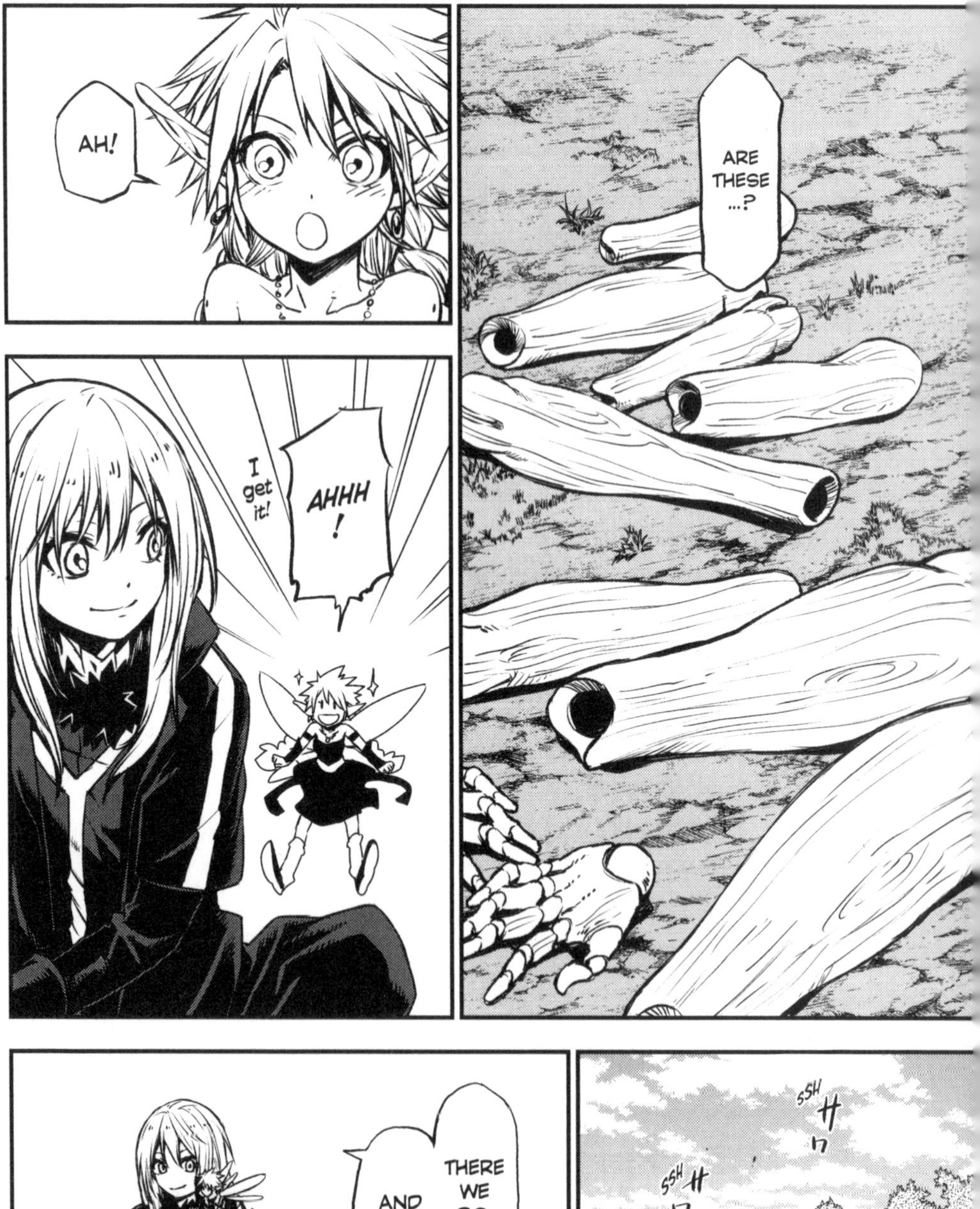
ARE THESE ...?
AH!
AHHH!
I get it!
SSH
SSH
THERE WE GO.
AND NOW...

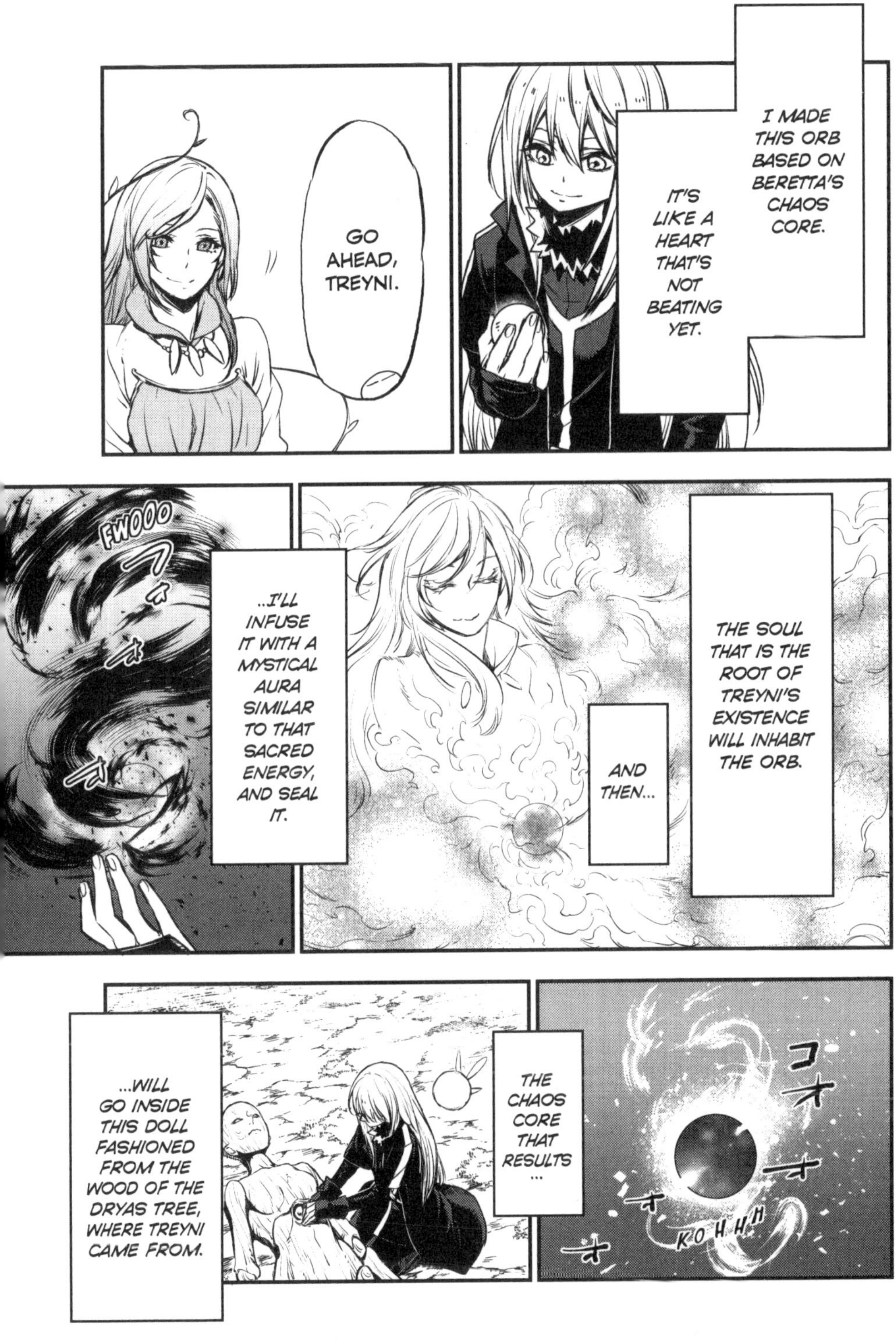
I MADE THIS ORB BASED ON BERETTA'S CHAOS CORE.
IT'S LIKE A HEART THAT'S NOT BEATING YET.
GO AHEAD, TREYNI.
THE SOUL THAT IS THE ROOT OF TREYNI'S EXISTENCE WILL INHABIT THE ORB.
AND THEN...
...I'LL INFUSE IT WITH A MYSTICAL AURA SIMILAR TO THAT SACRED ENERGY, AND SEAL IT.
FWOOO
フォォォ
コオオオ
KOHHH
THE CHAOS CORE THAT RESULTS...
...WILL GO INSIDE THIS DOLL FASHIONED FROM THE WOOD OF THE DRYAS TREE, WHERE TREYNI CAME FROM.

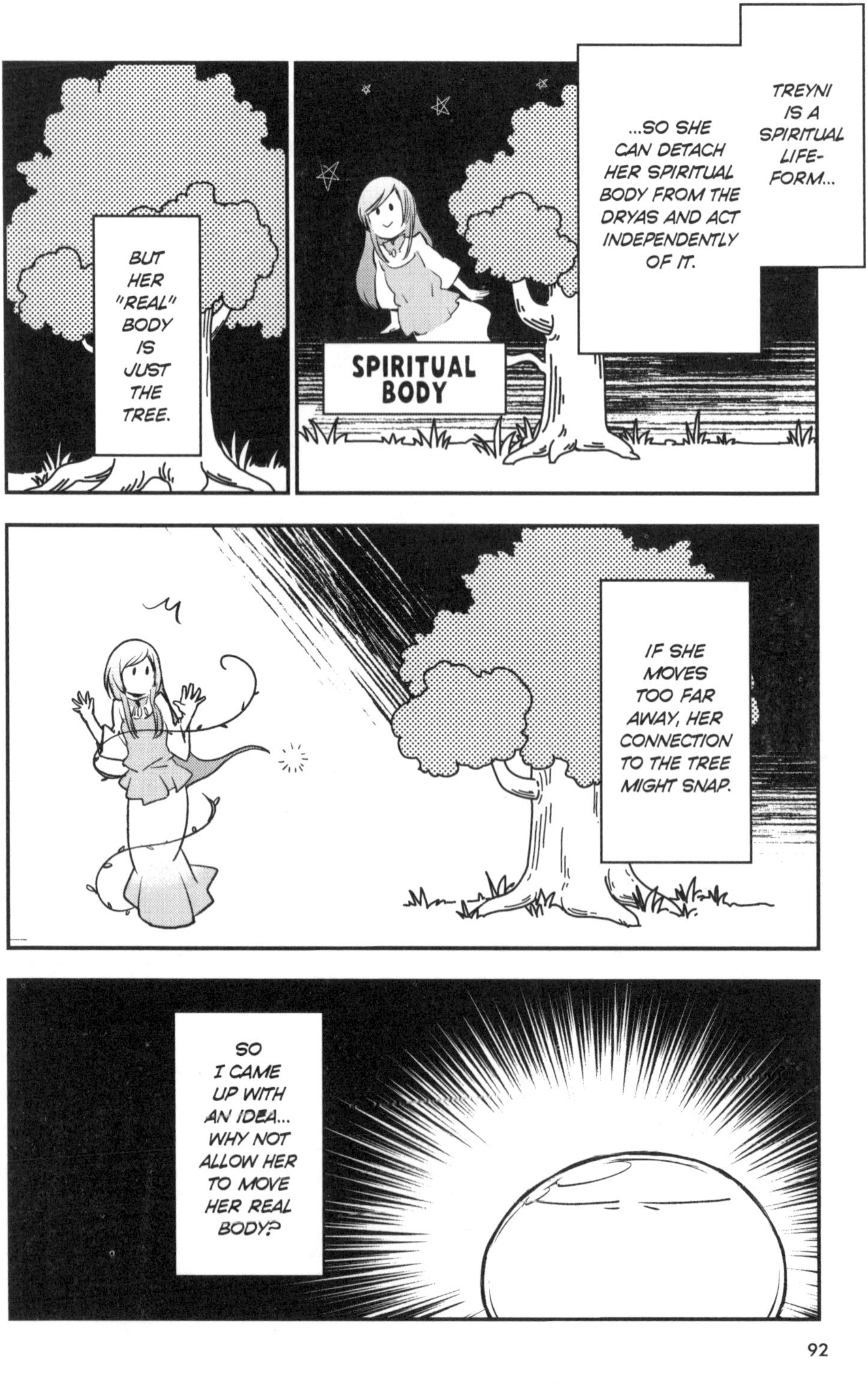
TREYNI IS A SPIRITUAL LIFE-FORM...
...SO SHE CAN DETACH HER SPIRITUAL BODY FROM THE DRYAS AND ACT INDEPENDENTLY OF IT.
SPIRITUAL BODY
BUT HER "REAL" BODY IS JUST THE TREE.
IF SHE MOVES TOO FAR AWAY, HER CONNECTION TO THE TREE MIGHT SNAP.
SO I CAME UP WITH AN IDEA... WHY NOT ALLOW HER TO MOVE HER REAL BODY?

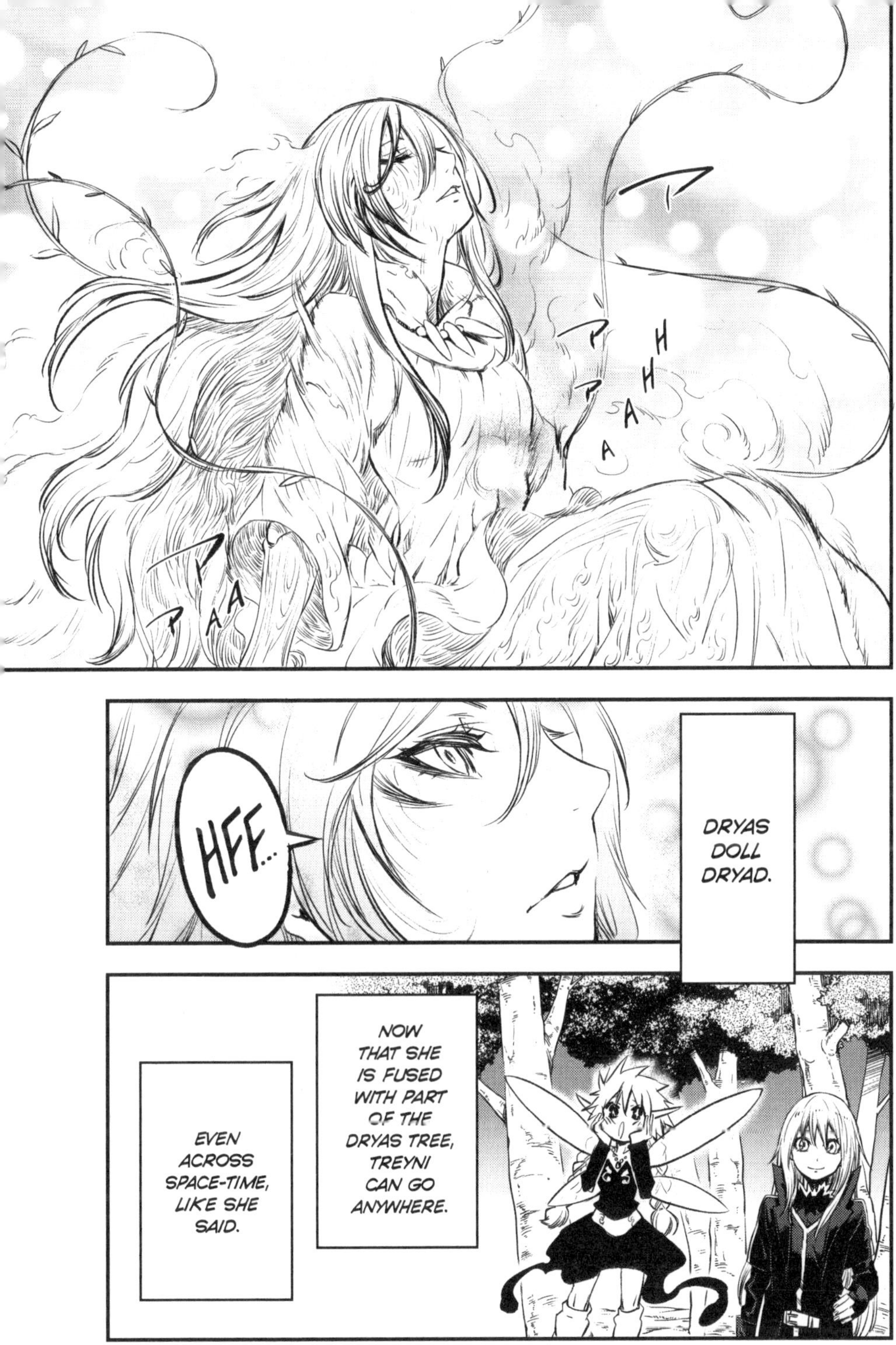
PAA
DRYAS DOLL DRYAD.
HFF...
NOW THAT SHE IS FUSED WITH PART OF THE DRYAS TREE, TREYNI CAN GO ANYWHERE.
EVEN ACROSS SPACE-TIME, LIKE SHE SAID.

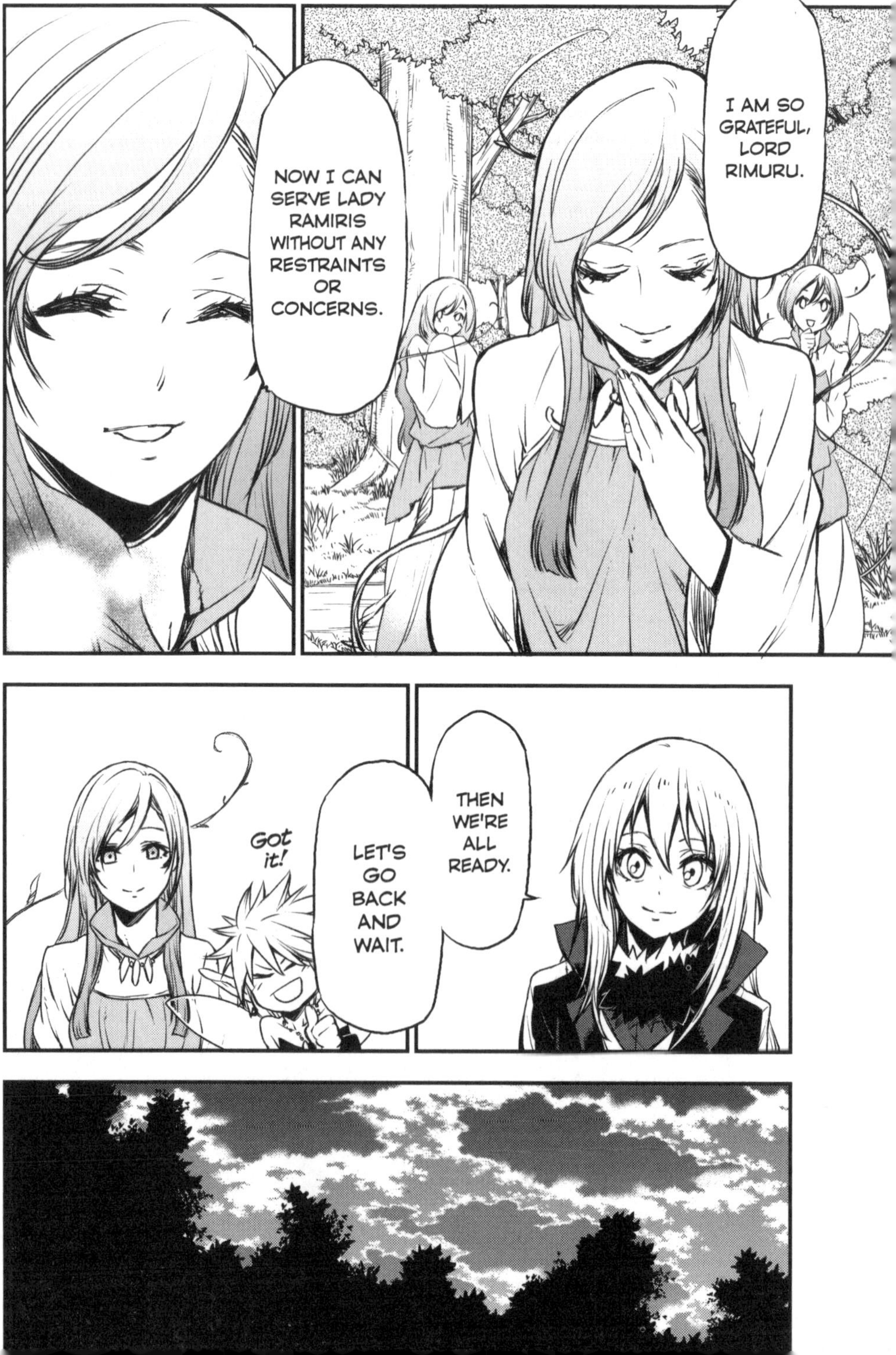
I AM SO GRATEFUL, LORD RIMURU.
NOW I CAN SERVE LADY RAMIRIS WITHOUT ANY RESTRAINTS OR CONCERNS.
THEN WE'RE ALL READY.
LET'S GO BACK AND WAIT.
Got it!

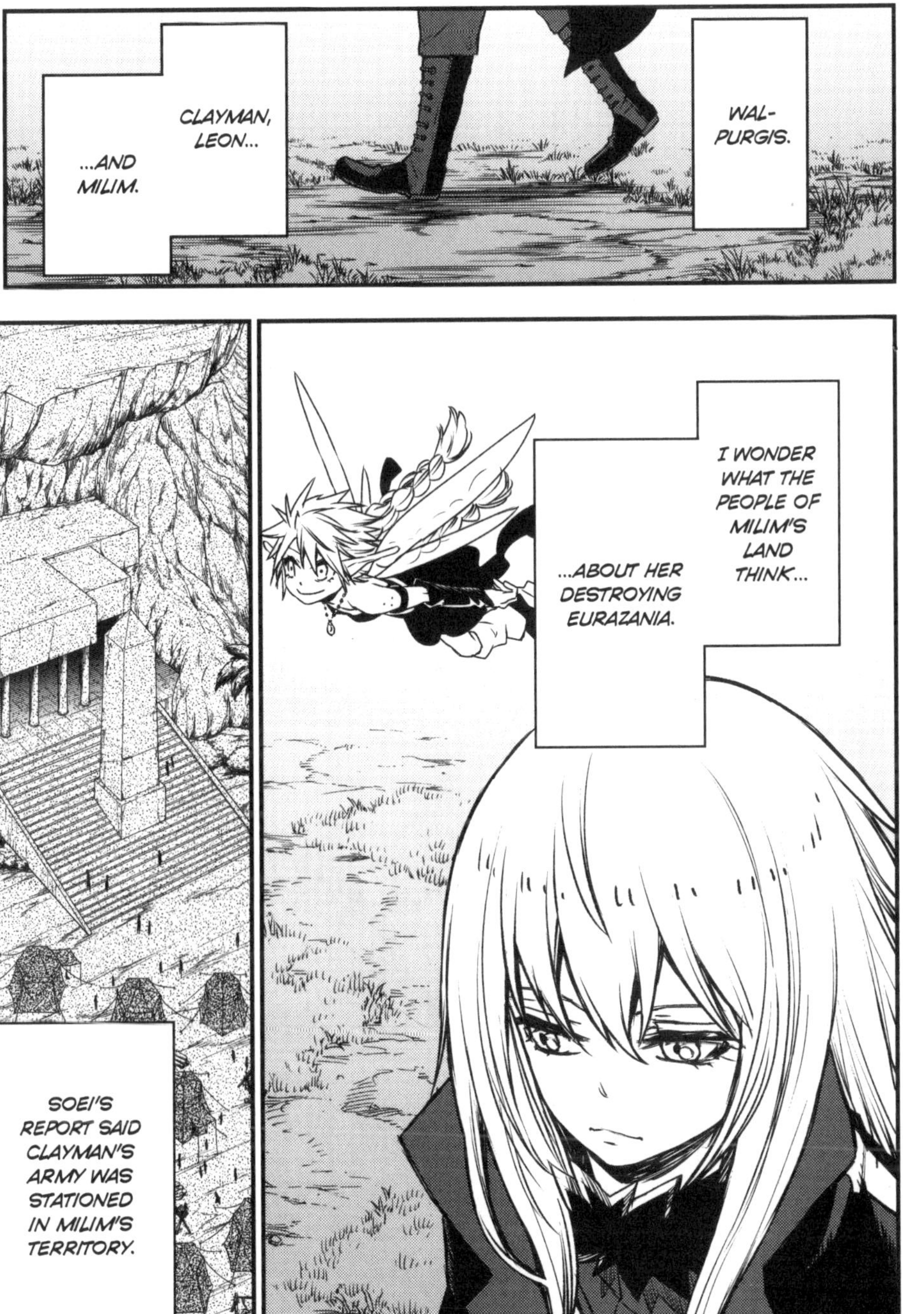
WAL-PURGIS.
CLAYMAN, LEON...
...AND MILIM.
I WONDER WHAT THE PEOPLE OF MILIM'S LAND THINK...
...ABOUT HER DESTROYING EURAZANIA.
SOEI'S REPORT SAID CLAYMAN'S ARMY WAS STATIONED IN MILIM'S TERRITORY.

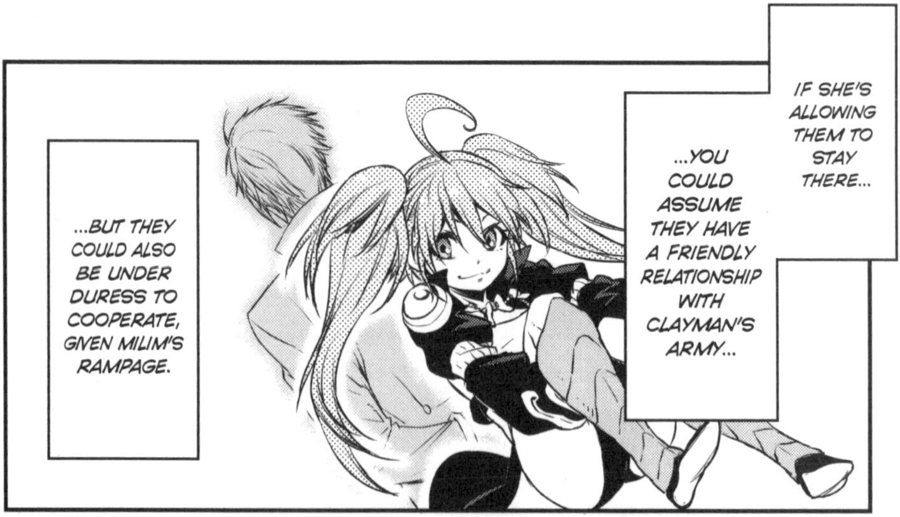
IF SHE'S ALLOWING THEM TO STAY THERE...
...YOU COULD ASSUME THEY HAVE A FRIENDLY RELATIONSHIP WITH CLAYMAN'S ARMY...
...BUT THEY COULD ALSO BE UNDER DURESS TO COOPERATE, GIVEN MILIM'S RAMPAGE.

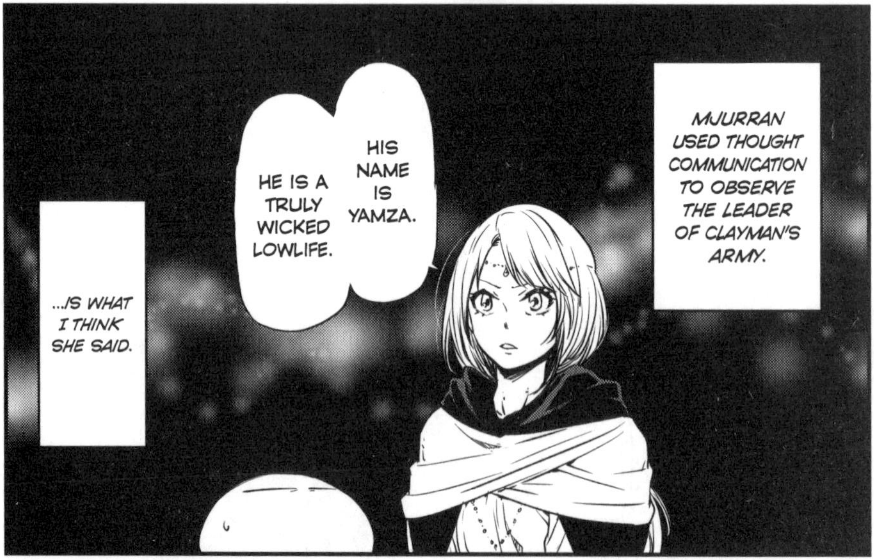
MJURRAN USED THOUGHT COMMUNICATION TO OBSERVE THE LEADER OF CLAYMAN'S ARMY.
HIS NAME IS YAMZA.
HE IS A TRULY WICKED LOWLIFE.
...IS WHAT I THINK SHE SAID.

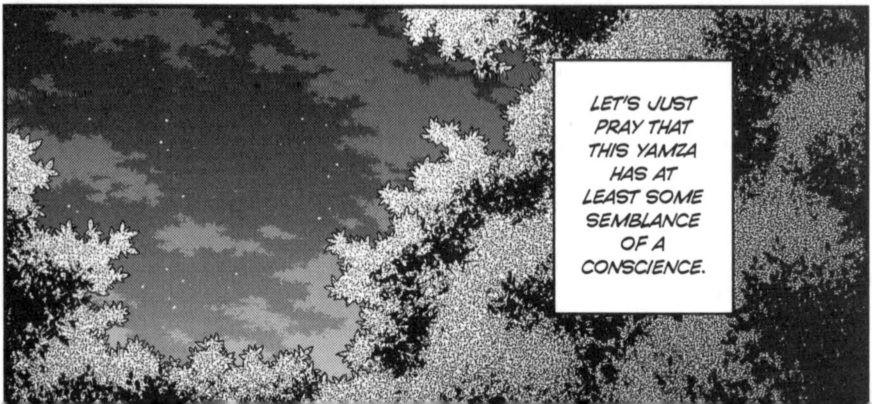
LET'S JUST PRAY THAT THIS YAMZA HAS AT LEAST SOME SEMBLANCE OF A CONSCIENCE.

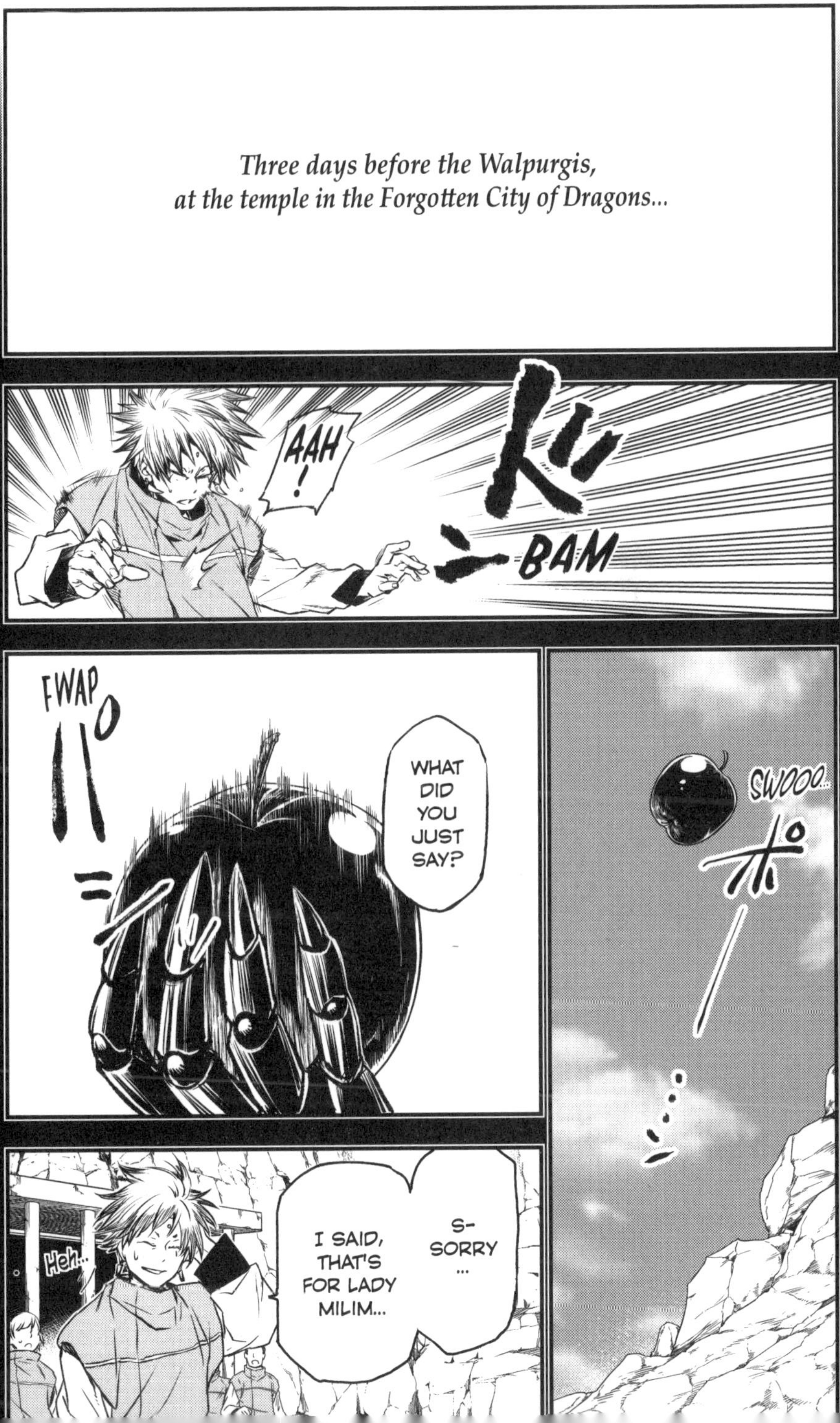
Three days before the Walpurgis, at the temple in the Forgotten City of Dragons...
BAM
AAH!
SWOOO...
FWAP
WHAT DID YOU JUST SAY?
S-SORRY...
I SAID, THAT'S FOR LADY MILIM...
Heh...

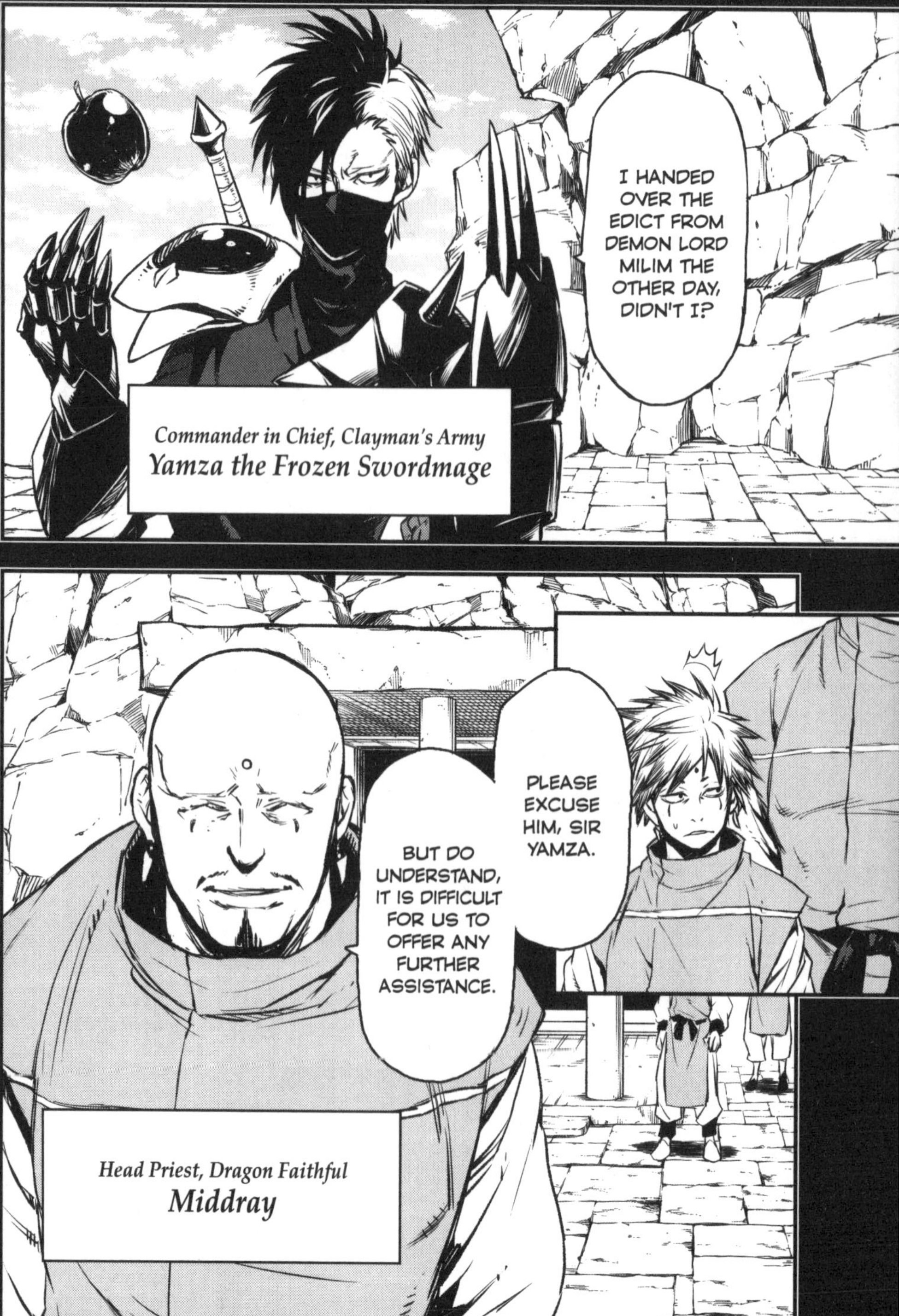
I HANDED OVER THE EDICT FROM DEMON LORD MILIM THE OTHER DAY, DIDN'T I?
Commander in Chief, Clayman's Army
Yamza the Frozen Swordmage
PLEASE EXCUSE HIM, SIR YAMZA.
BUT DO UNDERSTAND, IT IS DIFFICULT FOR US TO OFFER ANY FURTHER ASSISTANCE.
Head Priest, Dragon Faithful
Middray

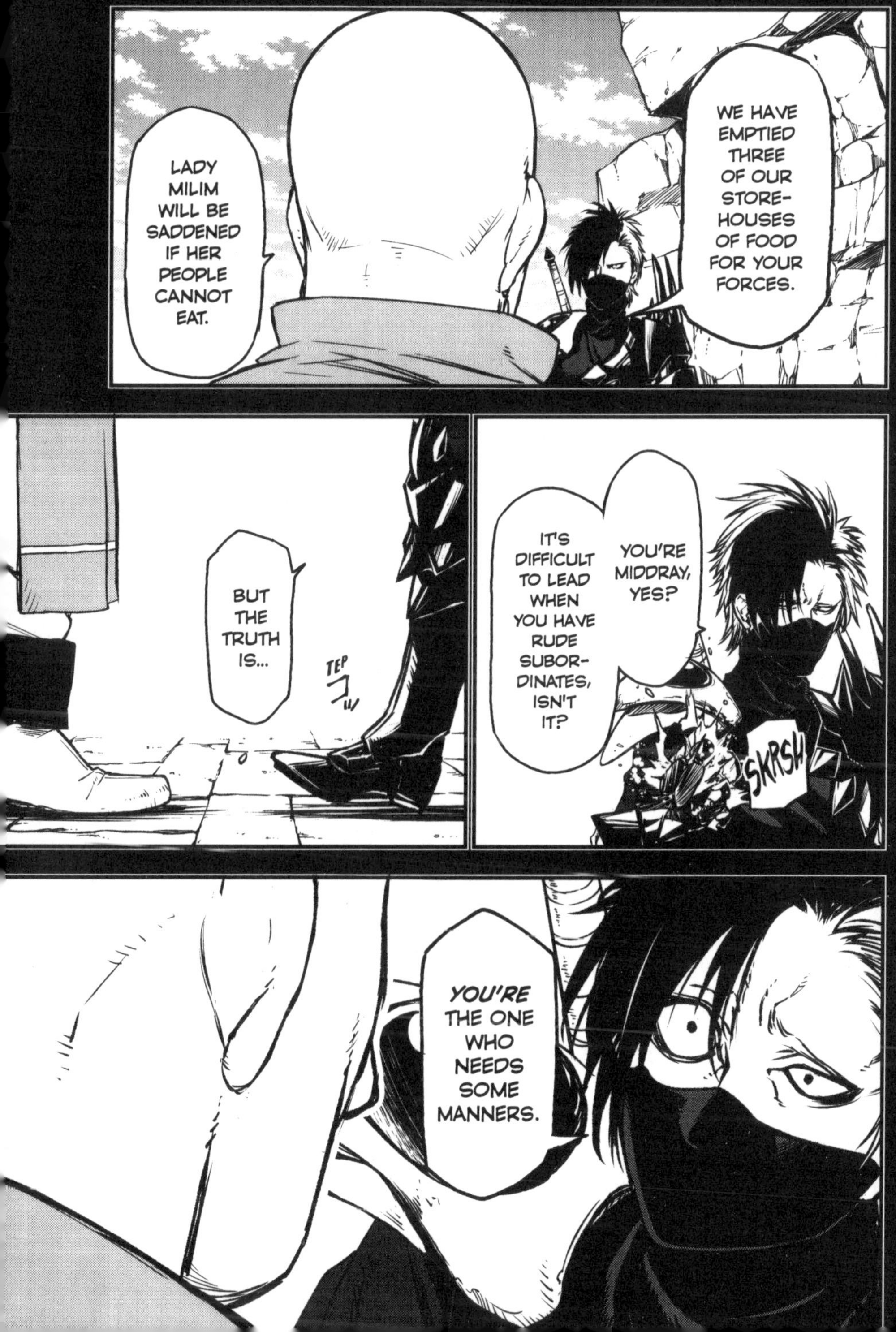
WE HAVE EMPTIED THREE OF OUR STORE-HOUSES OF FOOD FOR YOUR FORCES.
LADY MILIM WILL BE SADDENED IF HER PEOPLE CANNOT EAT.
YOU'RE MIDDRAY, YES?
IT'S DIFFICULT TO LEAD WHEN YOU HAVE RUDE SUBOR-DINATES, ISN'T IT?
SKRSH
BUT THE TRUTH IS...
TEP
YOU'RE THE ONE WHO NEEDS SOME MANNERS.

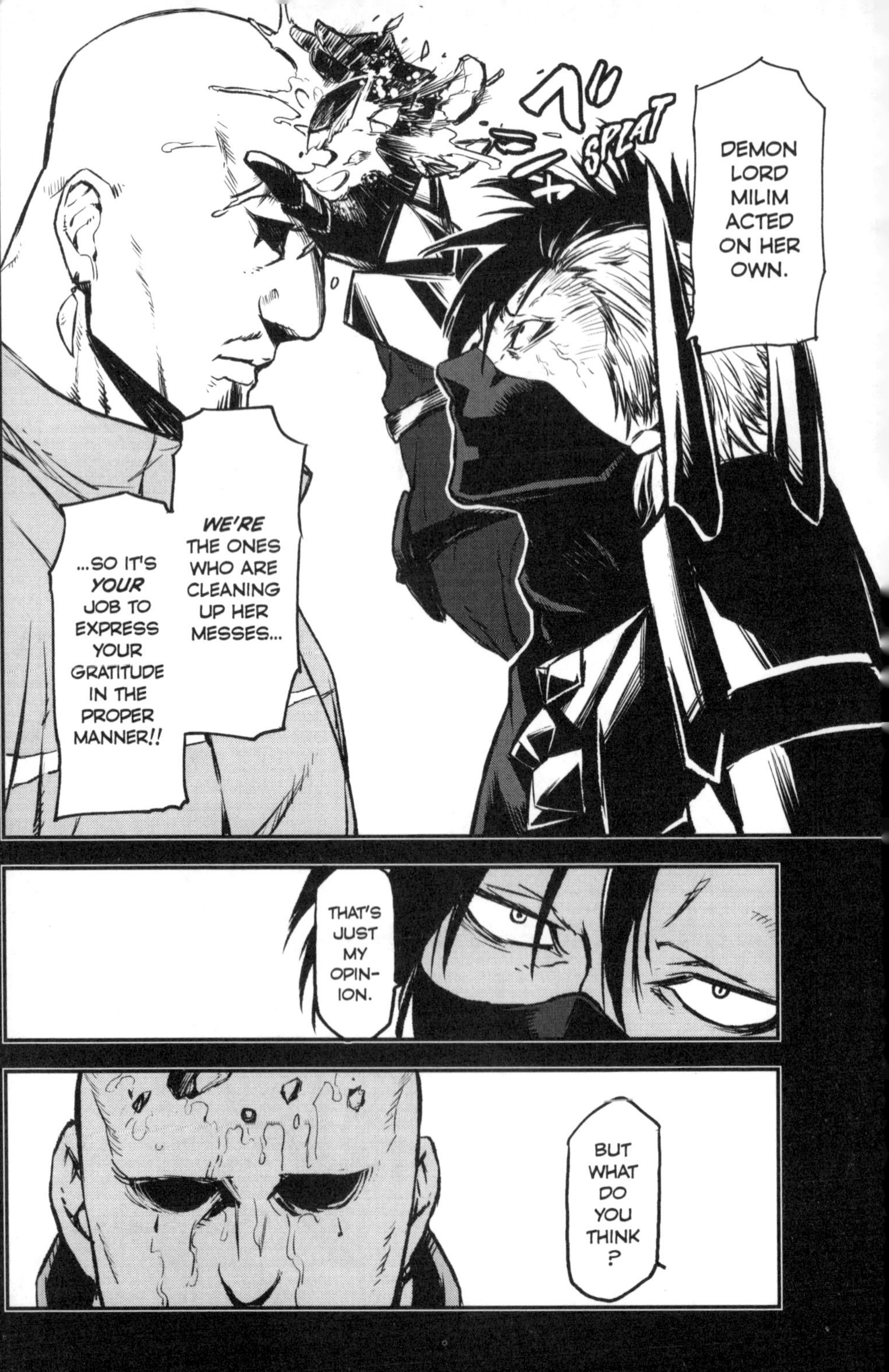
DEMON LORD MILIM ACTED ON HER OWN.
SPLAT
WE'RE THE ONES WHO ARE CLEANING UP HER MESSES...
...SO IT'S *YOUR* JOB TO EXPRESS YOUR GRATITUDE IN THE PROPER MANNER!!
THAT'S JUST MY OPINION.
BUT WHAT DO YOU THINK?

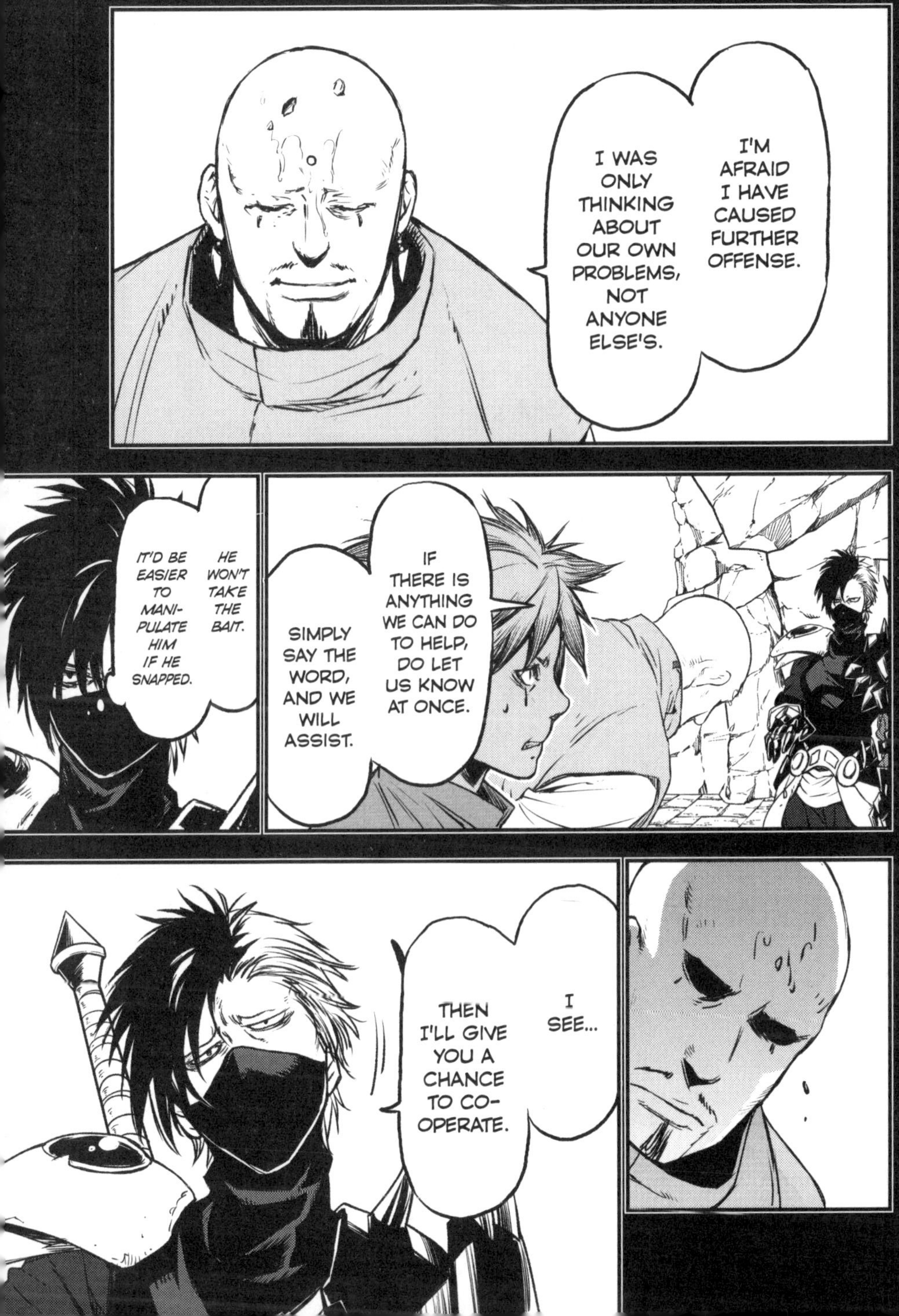
I'M AFRAID I HAVE CAUSED FURTHER OFFENSE.
I WAS ONLY THINKING ABOUT OUR OWN PROBLEMS, NOT ANYONE ELSE'S.
IF THERE IS ANYTHING WE CAN DO TO HELP, DO LET US KNOW AT ONCE.
SIMPLY SAY THE WORD, AND WE WILL ASSIST.
HE WON'T TAKE THE BAIT.
IT'D BE EASIER TO MANI-PULATE HIM IF HE SNAPPED.
I SEE...
THEN I'LL GIVE YOU A CHANCE TO CO-OPERATE.

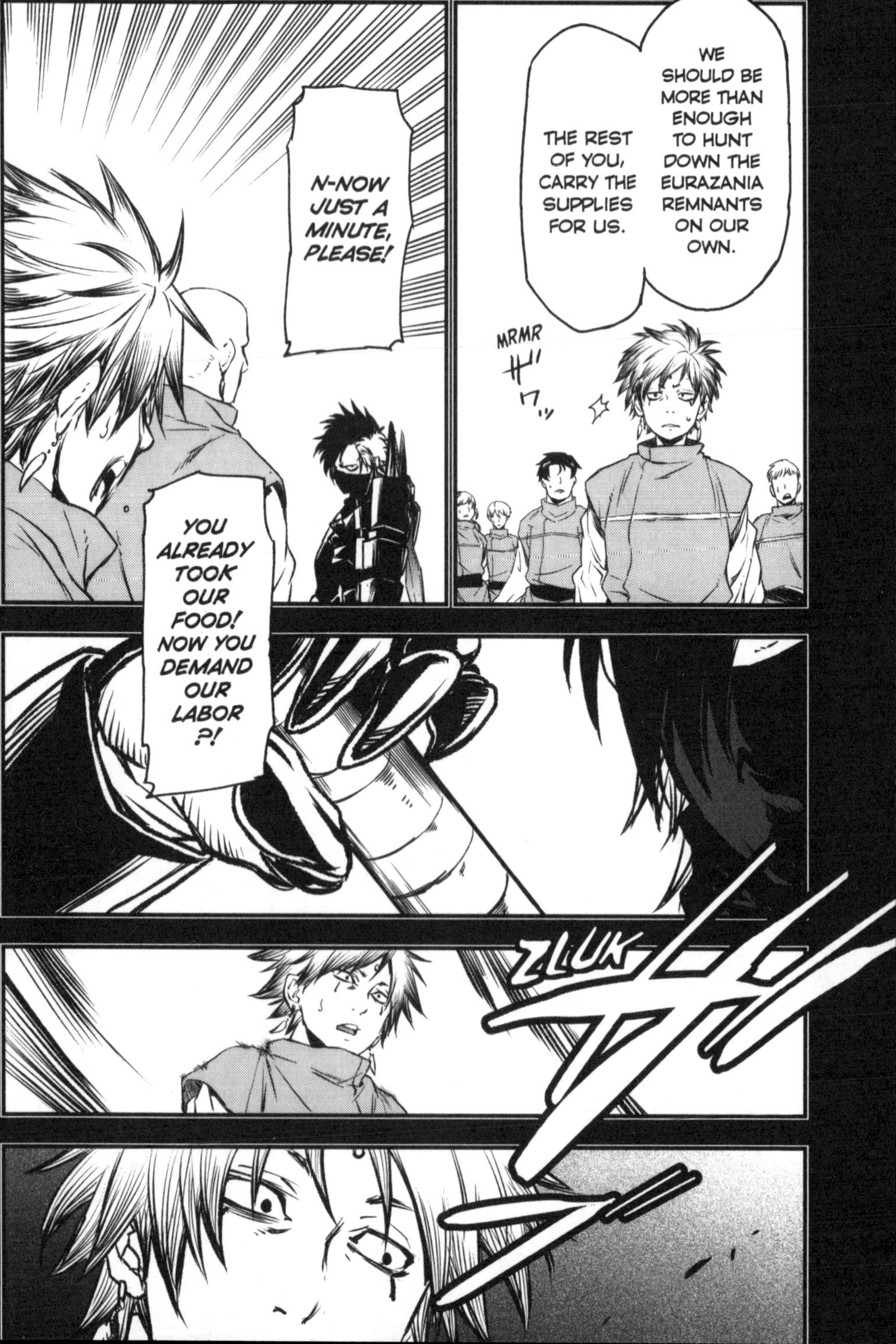
WE SHOULD BE MORE THAN ENOUGH TO HUNT DOWN THE EURAZANIA REMNANTS ON OUR OWN.
THE REST OF YOU, CARRY THE SUPPLIES FOR US.
MRMR
N-NOW JUST A MINUTE, PLEASE!
YOU ALREADY TOOK OUR FOOD! NOW YOU DEMAND OUR LABOR ?!
ZLUK

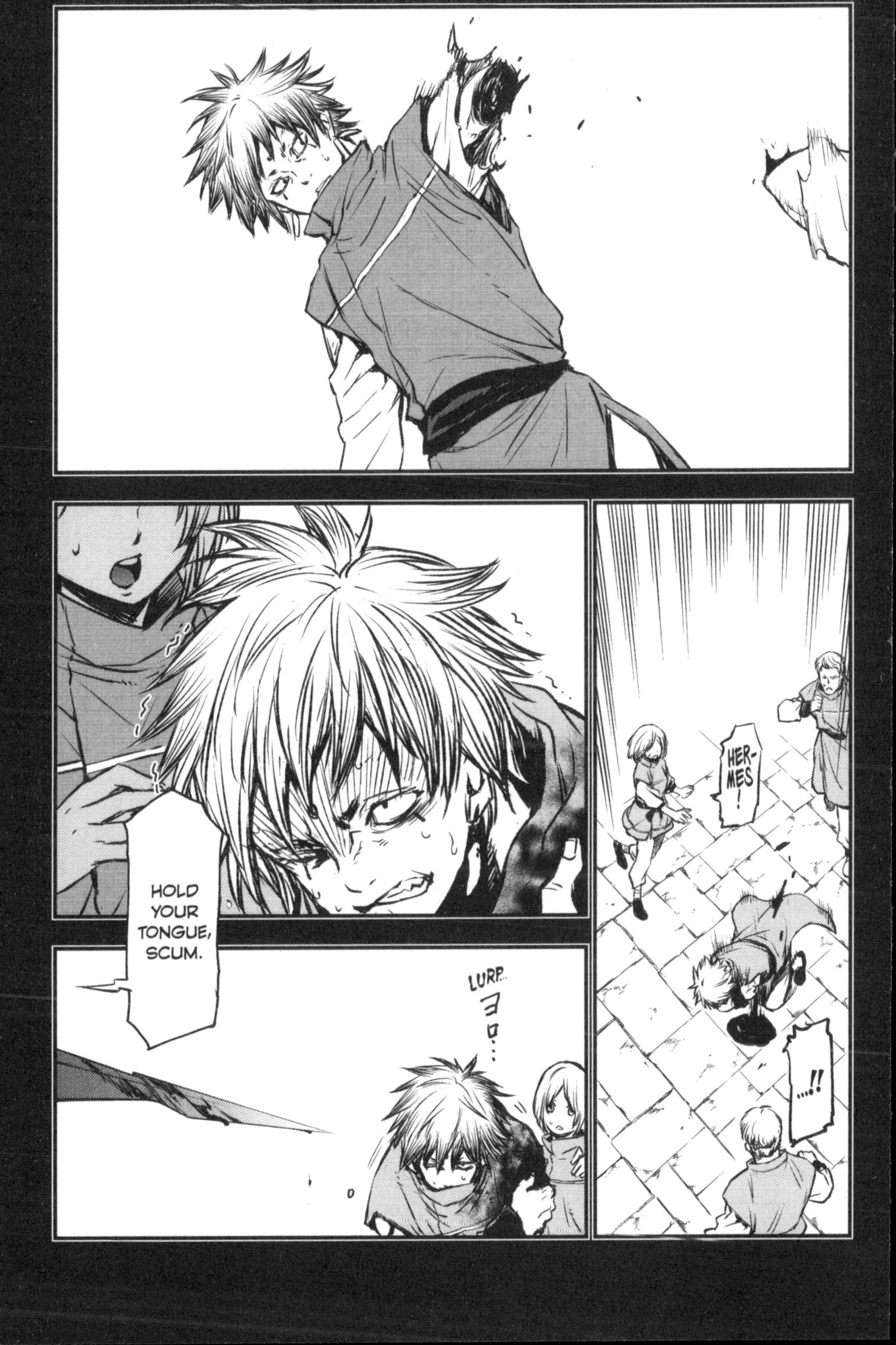
HER-MES!
...!!
HOLD YOUR TONGUE, SCUM.
LURP...
ヨロ…

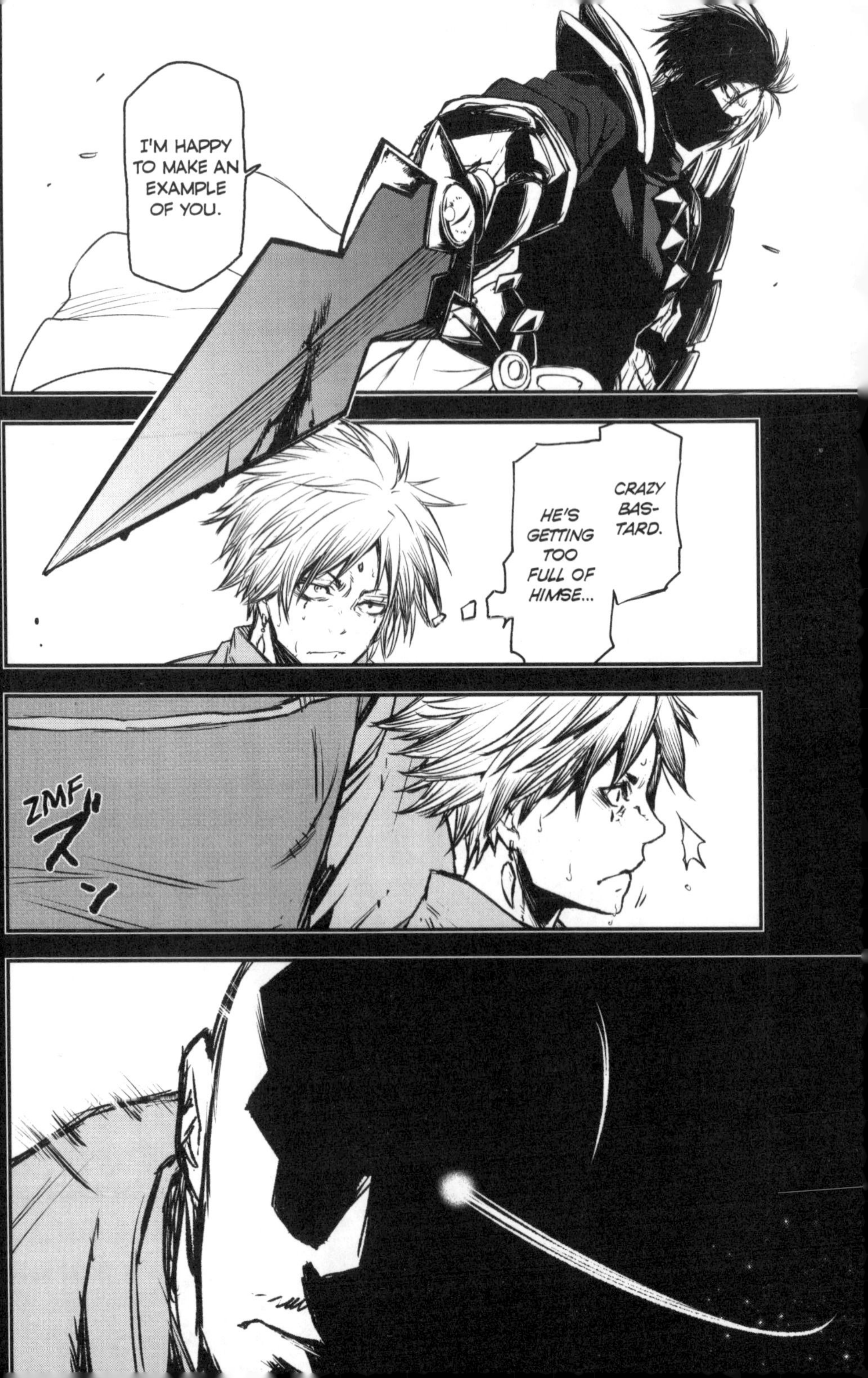
I'M HAPPY TO MAKE AN EXAMPLE OF YOU.
CRAZY BAS-TARD.
HE'S GETTING TOO FULL OF HIMSE...
ZMF

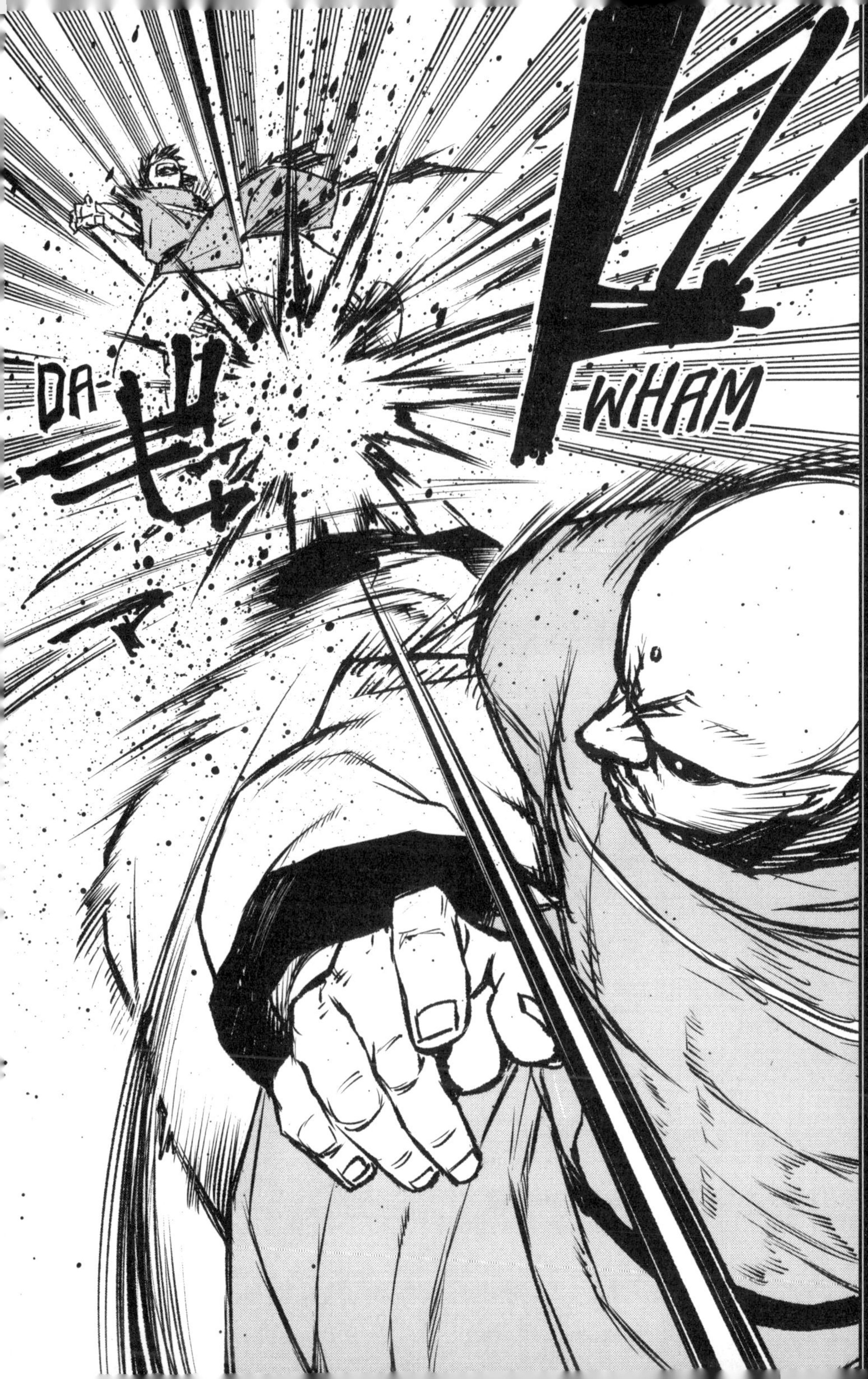
WHAM
DA-

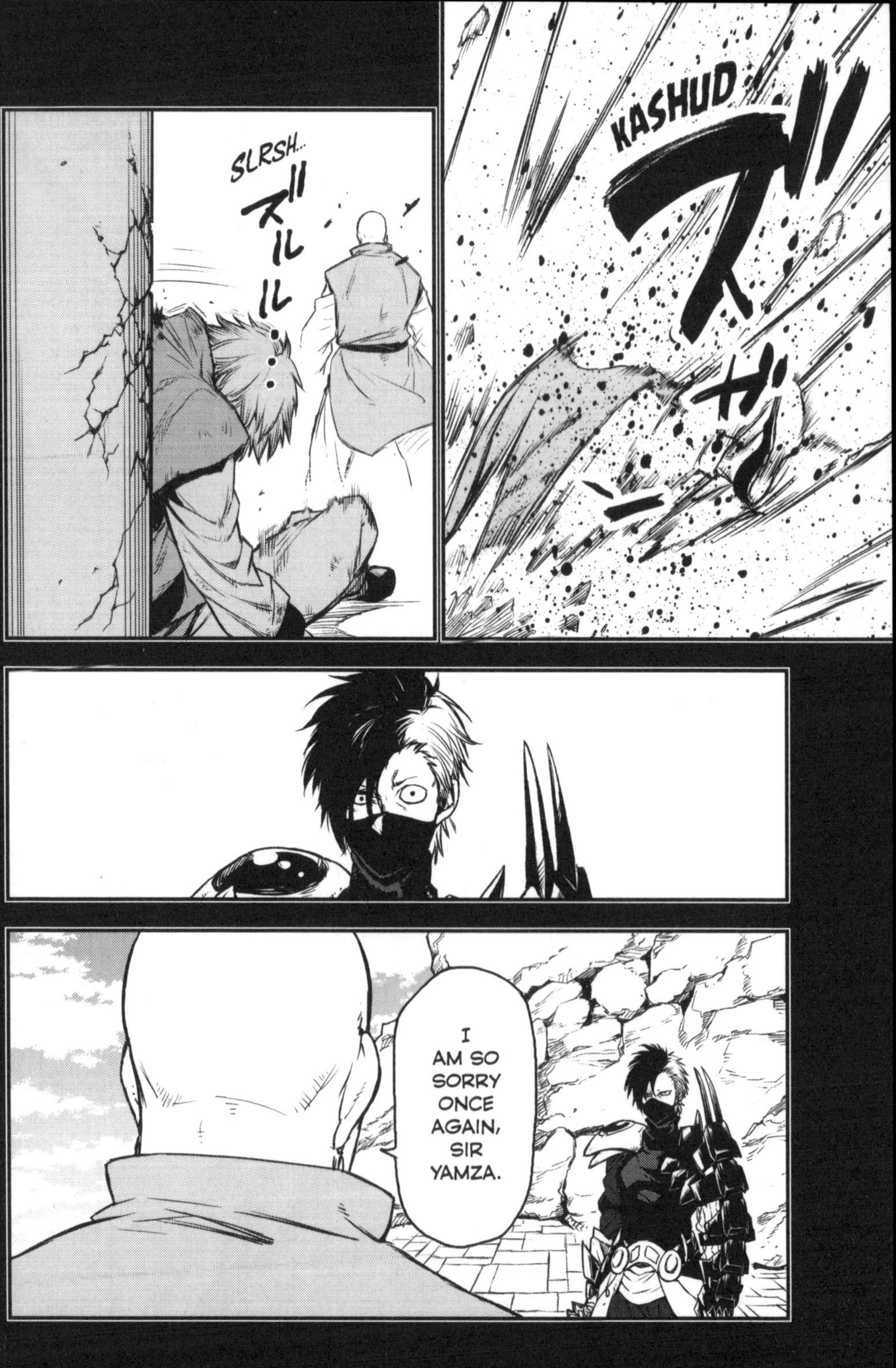
KASHUD
SLRSH..
ズルル
I AM SO SORRY ONCE AGAIN, SIR YAMZA.

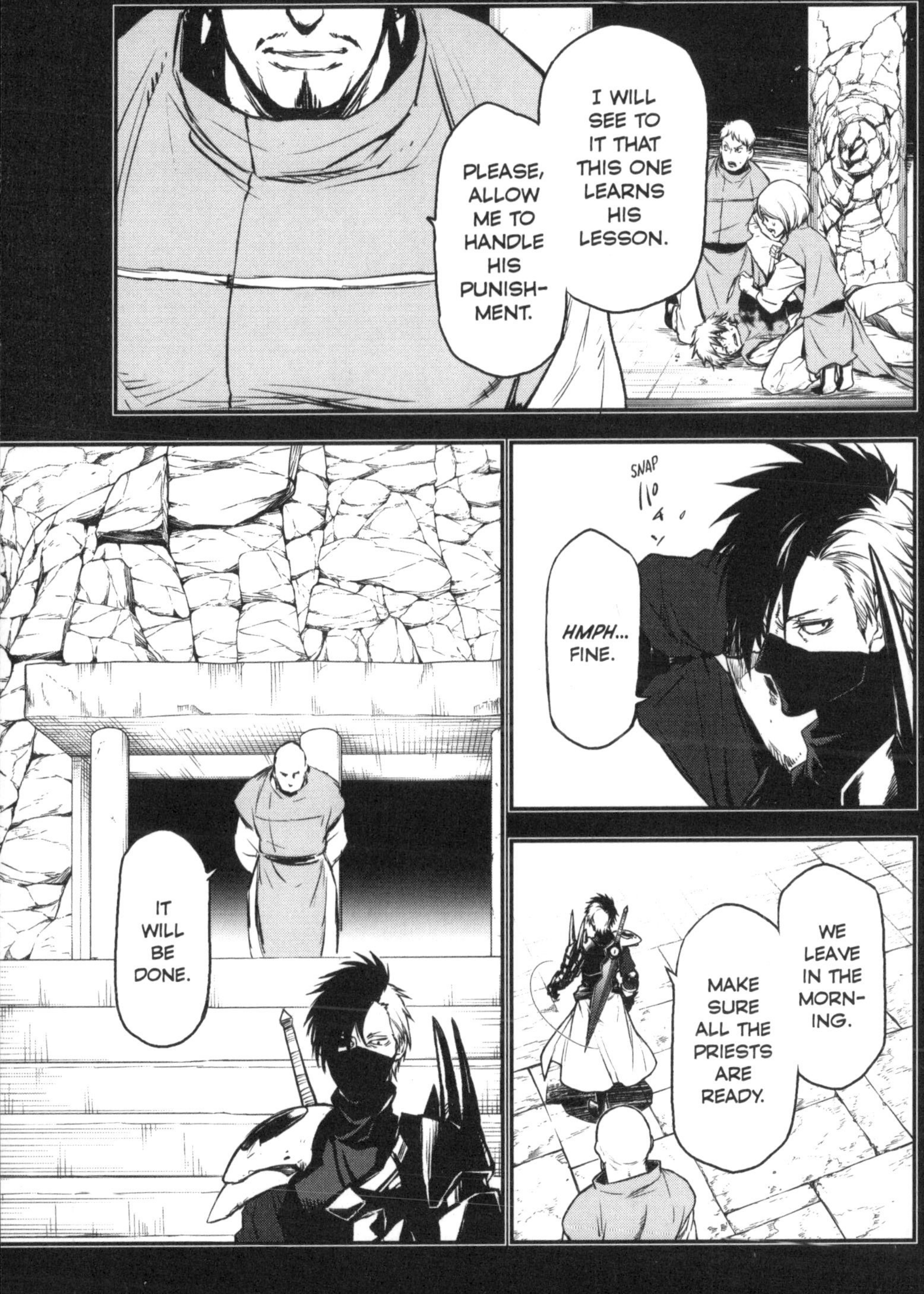
I WILL SEE TO IT THAT THIS ONE LEARNS HIS LESSON.
PLEASE, ALLOW ME TO HANDLE HIS PUNISHMENT.
SNAP
HMPH... FINE.
WE LEAVE IN THE MORNING.
MAKE SURE ALL THE PRIESTS ARE READY.
IT WILL BE DONE.

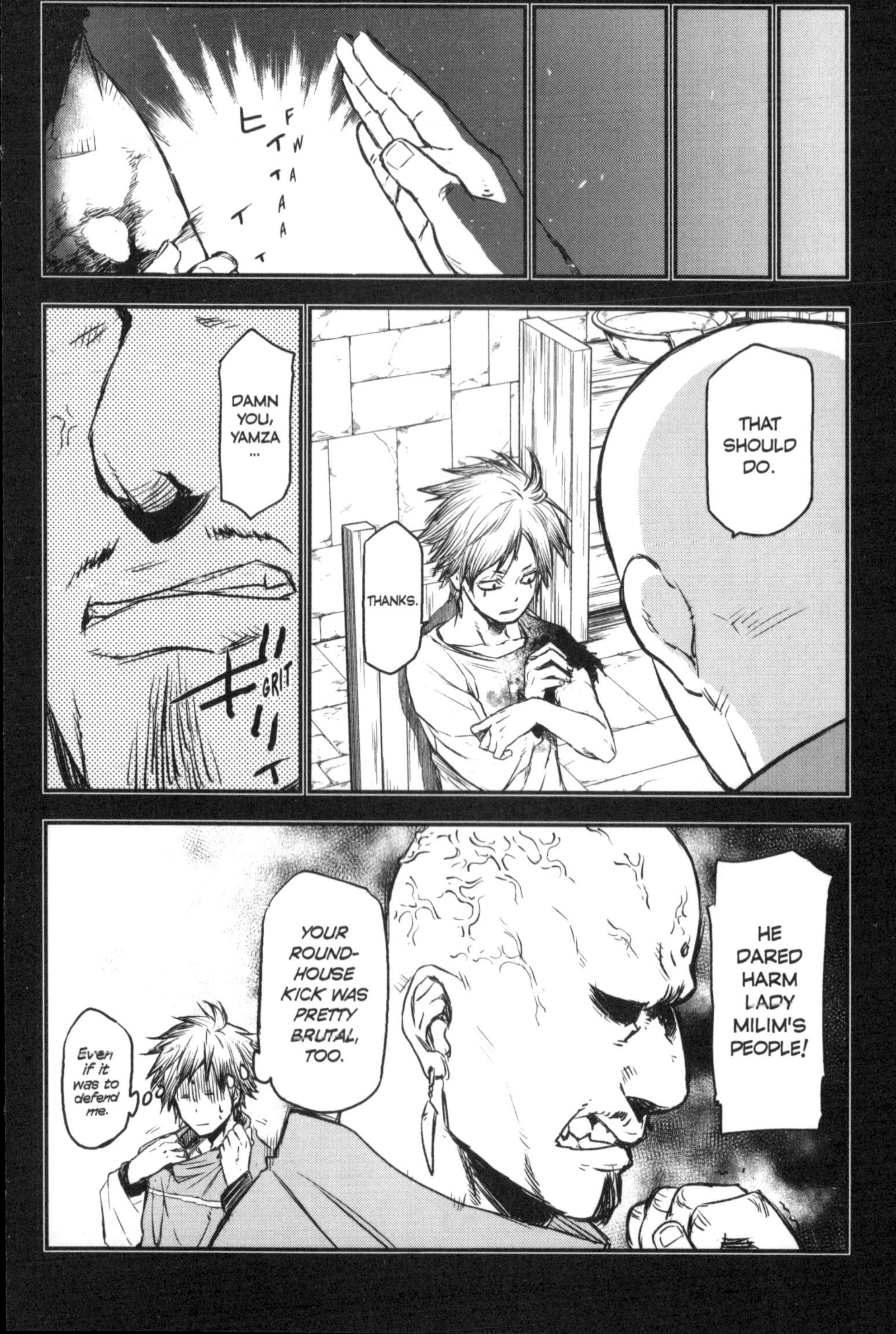
FWAAAA
THAT SHOULD DO.
THANKS.
DAMN YOU, YAMZA...
GRIT
HE DARED HARM LADY MILIM'S PEOPLE!
YOUR ROUNDHOUSE KICK WAS PRETTY BRUTAL, TOO.
Even if it was to defend me.

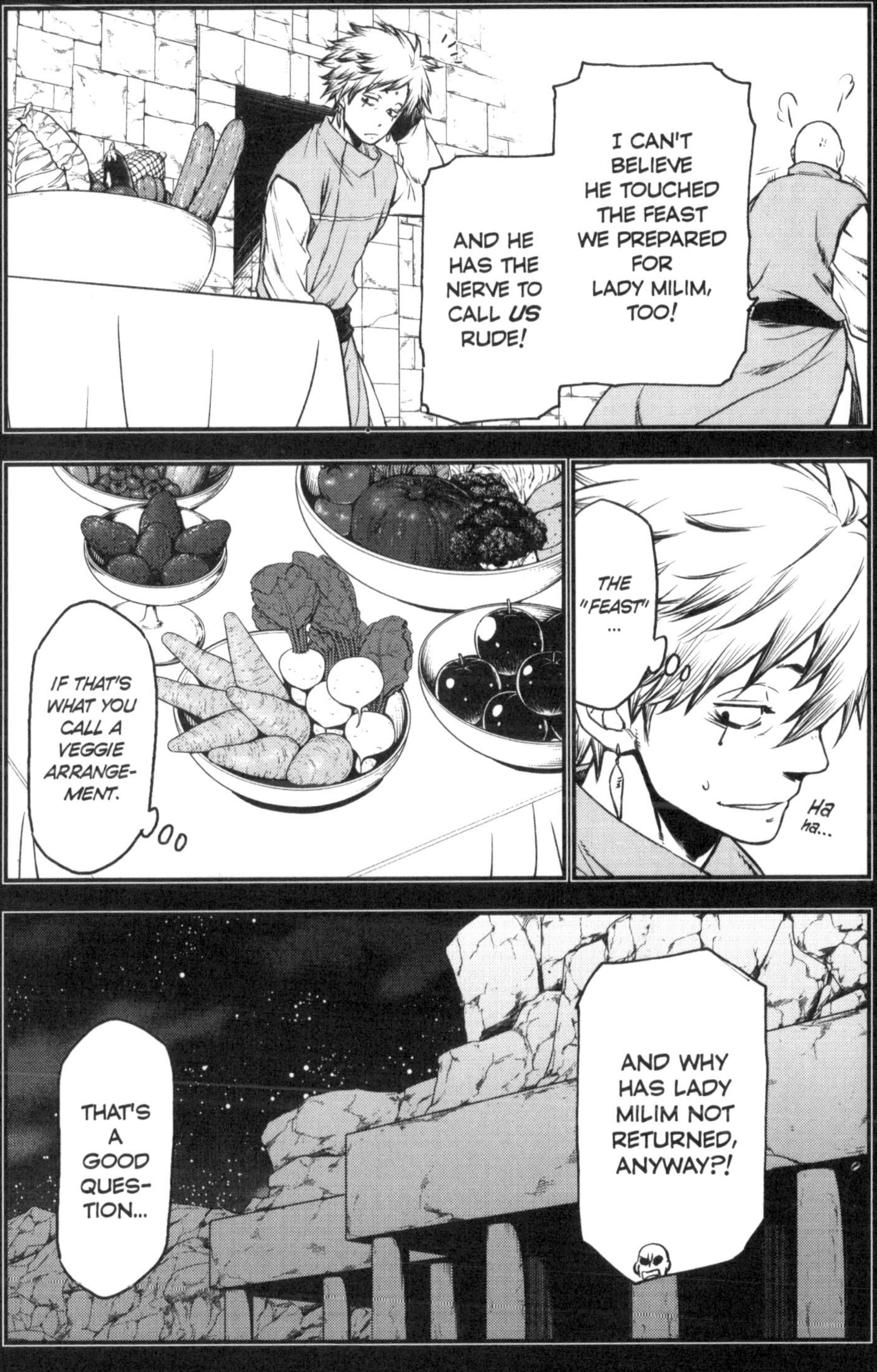
I CAN'T BELIEVE HE TOUCHED THE FEAST WE PREPARED FOR LADY MILIM, TOO!
AND HE HAS THE NERVE TO CALL *US* RUDE!
THE "FEAST"...
Ha ha...
IF THAT'S WHAT YOU CALL A VEGGIE ARRANGE-MENT.
AND WHY HAS LADY MILIM NOT RETURNED, ANYWAY?!
THAT'S A GOOD QUES-TION...

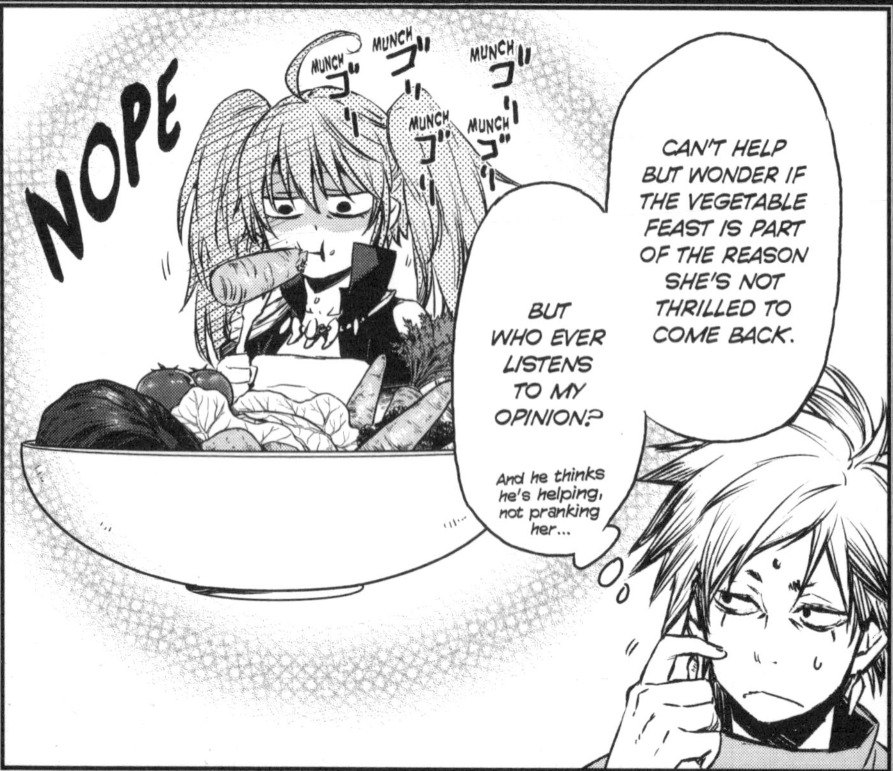
CAN'T HELP BUT WONDER IF THE VEGETABLE FEAST IS PART OF THE REASON SHE'S NOT THRILLED TO COME BACK.
MUNCH
MUNCH
MUNCH
MUNCH
MUNCH
NOPE
BUT WHO EVER LISTENS TO MY OPINION?
And he thinks he's helping, not pranking her...

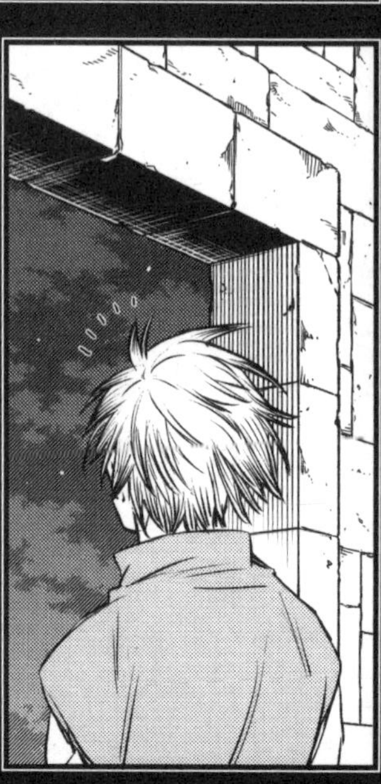

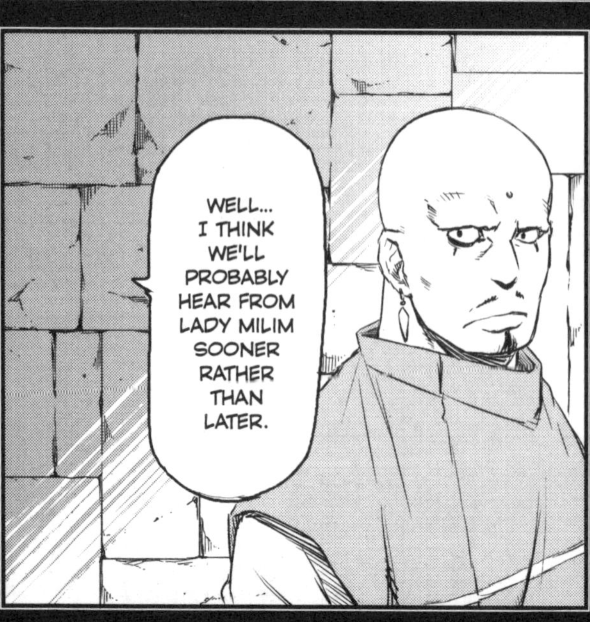
WELL... I THINK WE'LL PROBABLY HEAR FROM LADY MILIM SOONER RATHER THAN LATER.

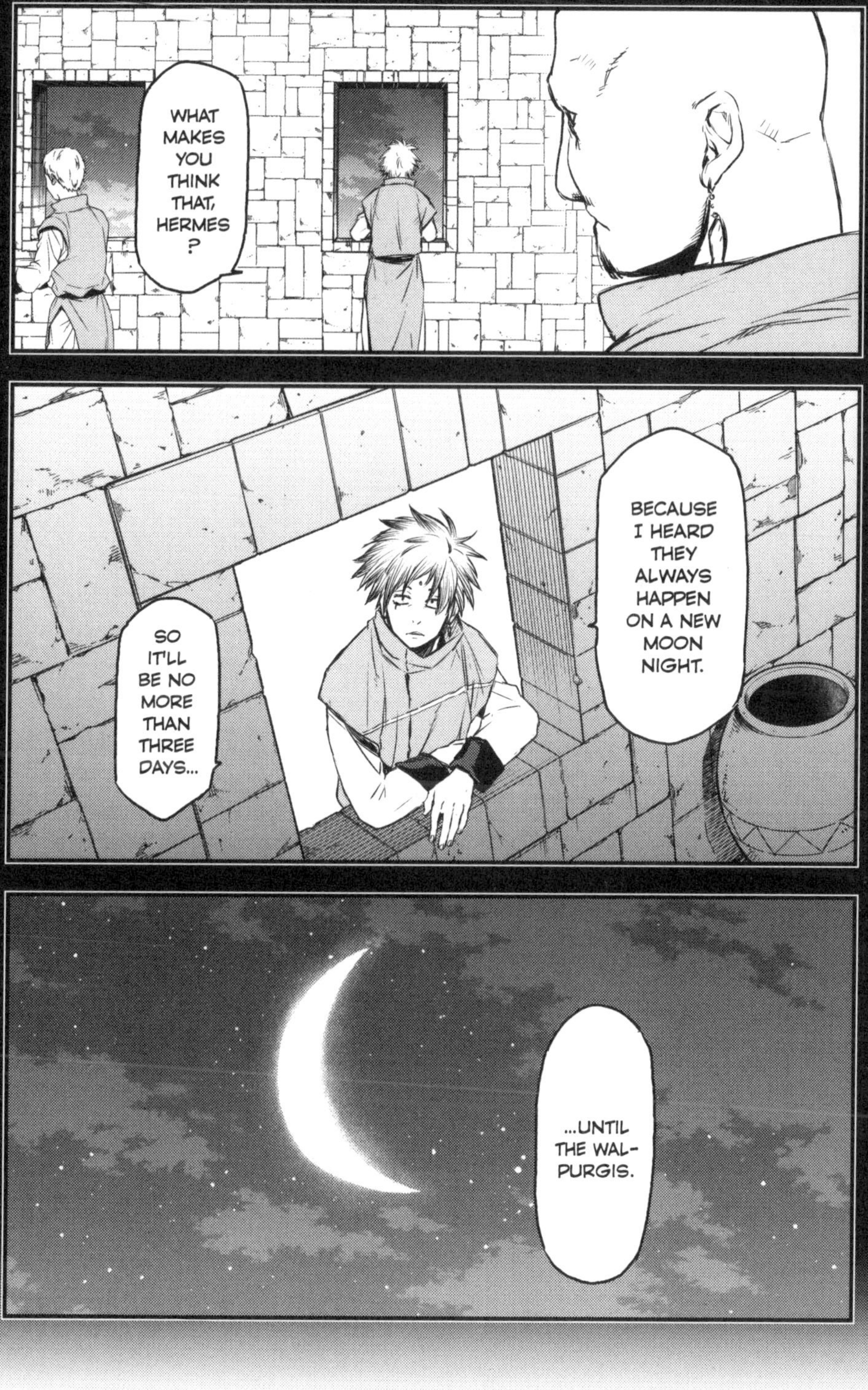
WHAT MAKES YOU THINK THAT, HERMES?
BECAUSE I HEARD THEY ALWAYS HAPPEN ON A NEW MOON NIGHT.
SO IT'LL BE NO MORE THAN THREE DAYS...
...UNTIL THE WAL-PURGIS.

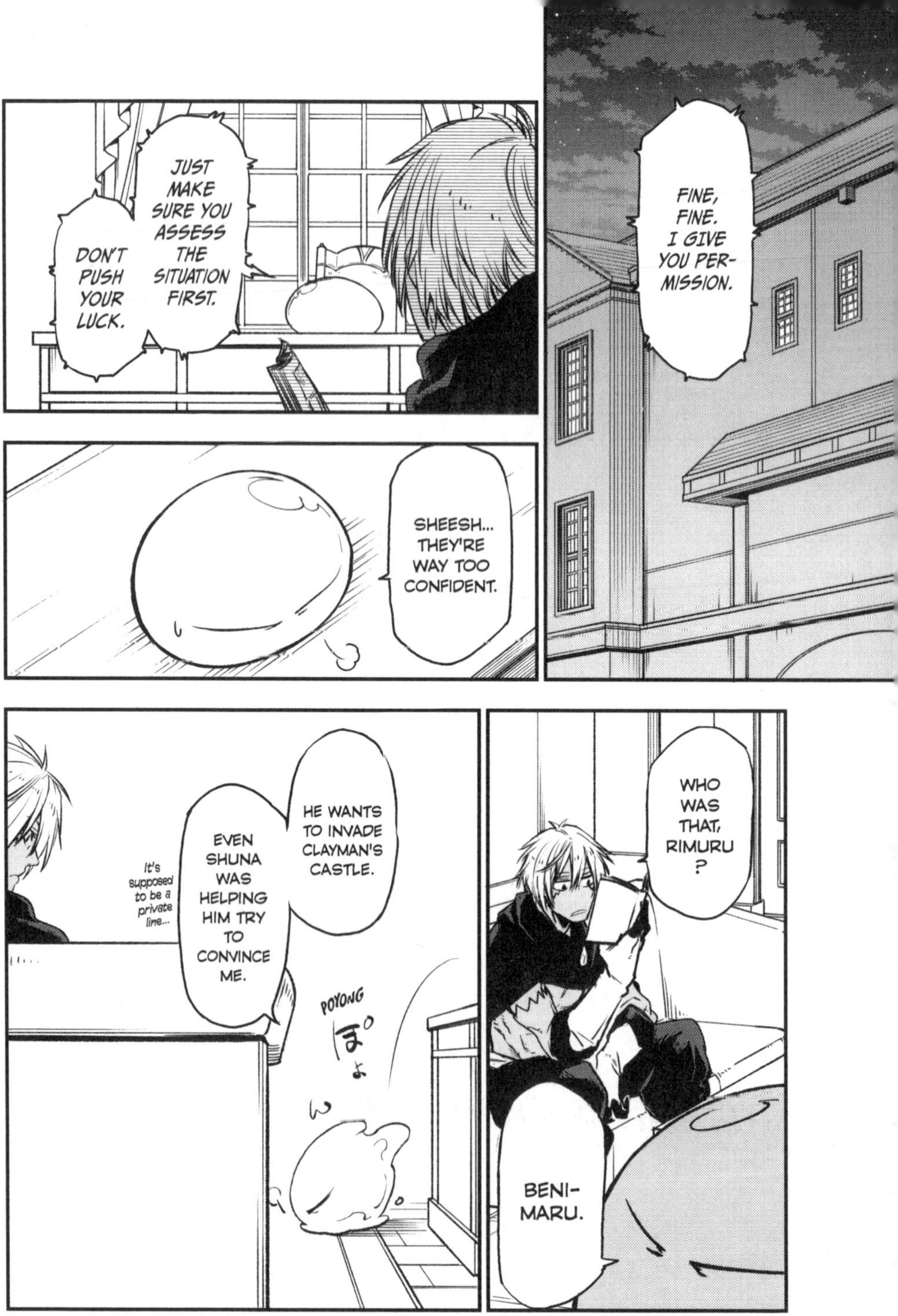
FINE, FINE. I GIVE YOU PER-MISSION.
JUST MAKE SURE YOU ASSESS THE SITUATION FIRST.
DON'T PUSH YOUR LUCK.
SHEESH... THEY'RE WAY TOO CONFIDENT.
WHO WAS THAT, RIMURU?
BENI-MARU.
HE WANTS TO INVADE CLAYMAN'S CASTLE.
EVEN SHUNA WAS HELPING HIM TRY TO CONVINCE ME.
It's supposed to be a private line...
POYONG

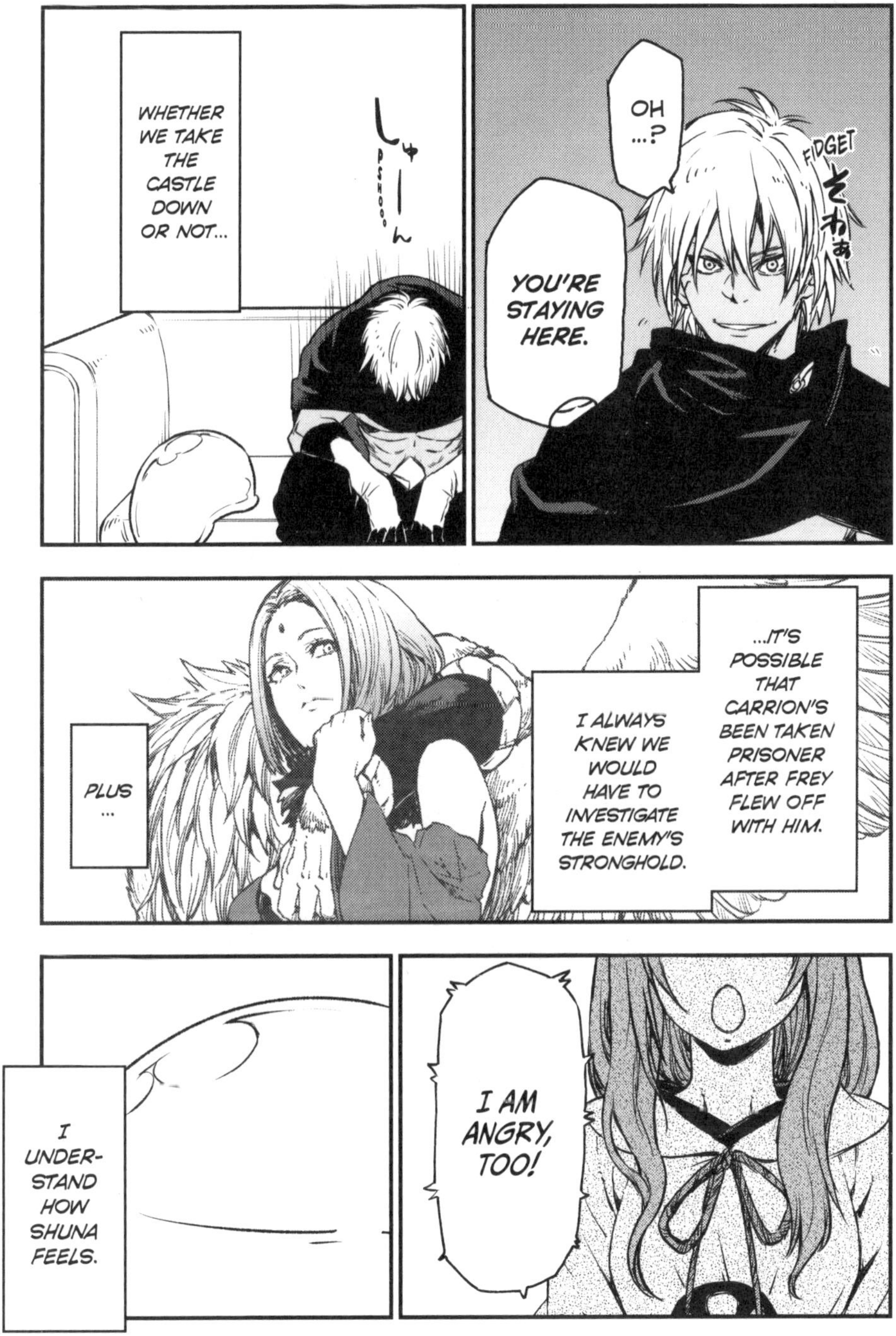
OH ...?
YOU'RE STAYING HERE.
FIDGET
ざわぁ
WHETHER WE TAKE THE CASTLE DOWN OR NOT...
しゅーん
PSHOOO
...IT'S POSSIBLE THAT CARRION'S BEEN TAKEN PRISONER AFTER FREY FLEW OFF WITH HIM.
I ALWAYS KNEW WE WOULD HAVE TO INVESTIGATE THE ENEMY'S STRONGHOLD.
PLUS ...
I AM ANGRY, TOO!
I UNDER-STAND HOW SHUNA FEELS.

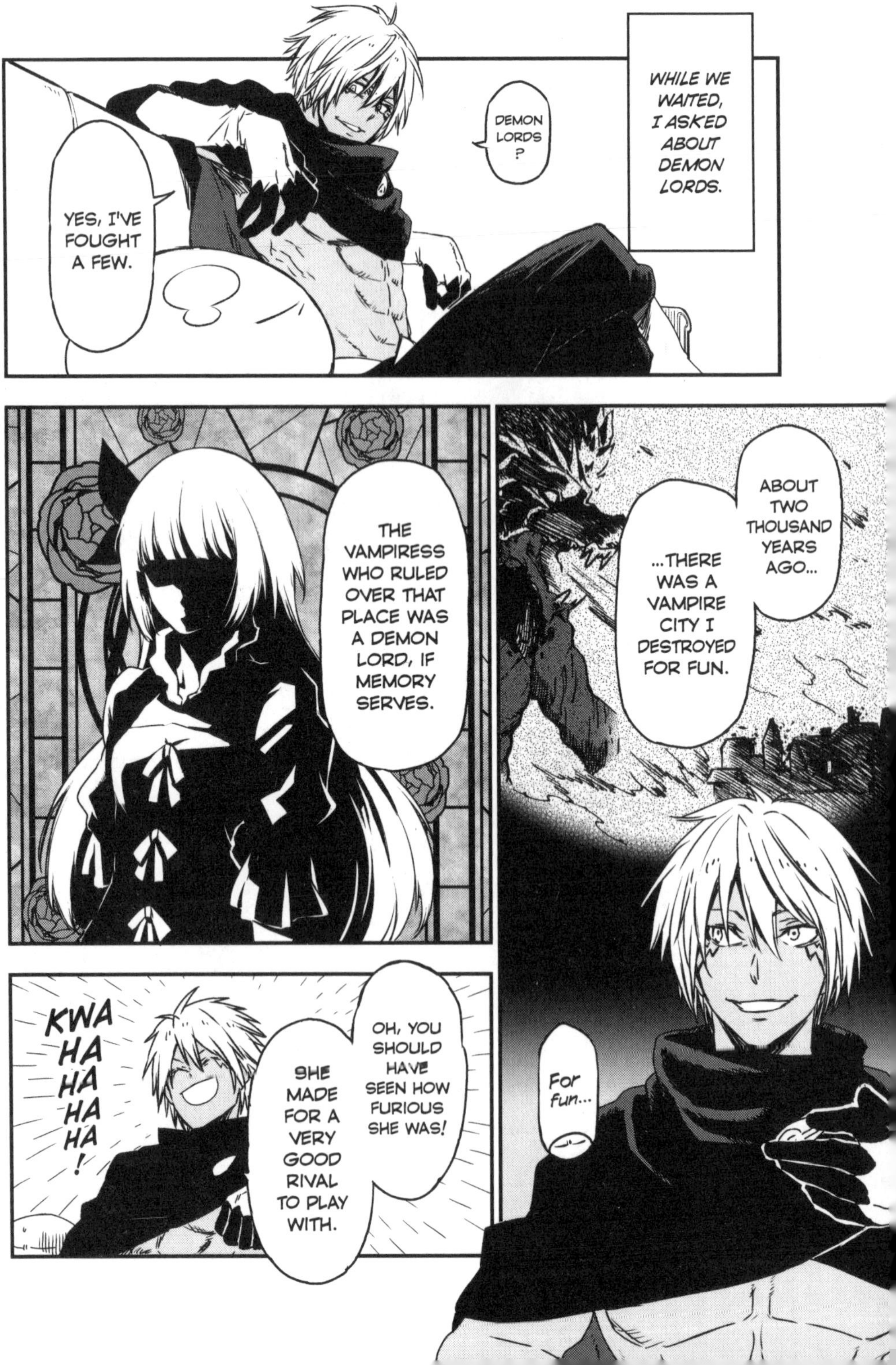
WHILE WE WAITED, I ASKED ABOUT DEMON LORDS.
DEMON LORDS?
YES, I'VE FOUGHT A FEW.
ABOUT TWO THOUSAND YEARS AGO...
...THERE WAS A VAMPIRE CITY I DESTROYED FOR FUN.
For fun...
THE VAMPIRESS WHO RULED OVER THAT PLACE WAS A DEMON LORD, IF MEMORY SERVES.
OH, YOU SHOULD HAVE SEEN HOW FURIOUS SHE WAS!
SHE MADE FOR A VERY GOOD RIVAL TO PLAY WITH.
KWA HA HA HA HA!

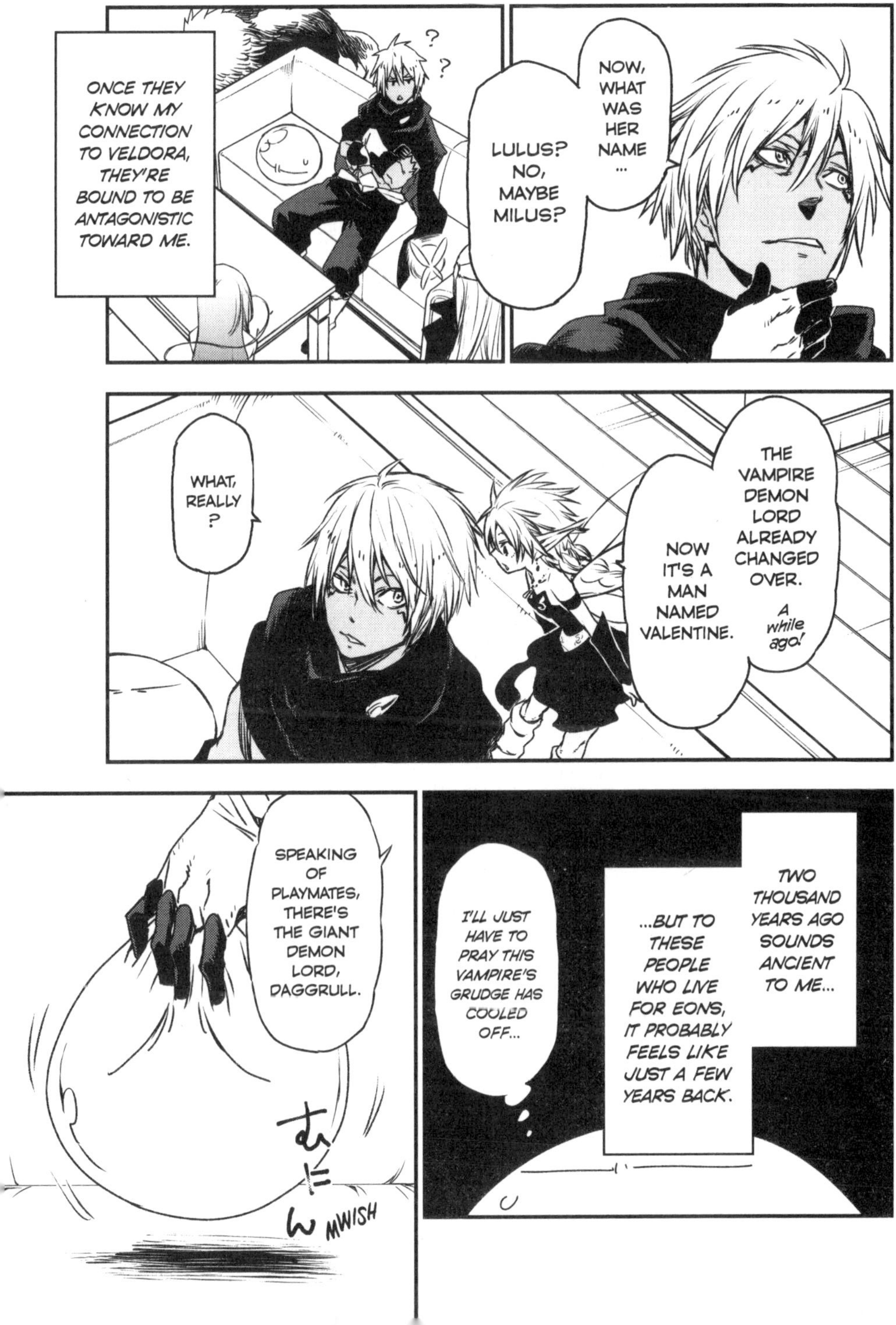
NOW, WHAT WAS HER NAME ...
LULUS? NO, MAYBE MILUS?
? ?
ONCE THEY KNOW MY CONNECTION TO VELDORA, THEY'RE BOUND TO BE ANTAGONISTIC TOWARD ME.
THE VAMPIRE DEMON LORD ALREADY CHANGED OVER.
A while ago!
NOW IT'S A MAN NAMED VALENTINE.
WHAT, REALLY?
TWO THOUSAND YEARS AGO SOUNDS ANCIENT TO ME...
...BUT TO THESE PEOPLE WHO LIVE FOR EONS, IT PROBABLY FEELS LIKE JUST A FEW YEARS BACK.
I'LL JUST HAVE TO PRAY THIS VAMPIRE'S GRUDGE HAS COOLED OFF...
SPEAKING OF PLAYMATES, THERE'S THE GIANT DEMON LORD, DAGGRULL.
むにん
MWISH

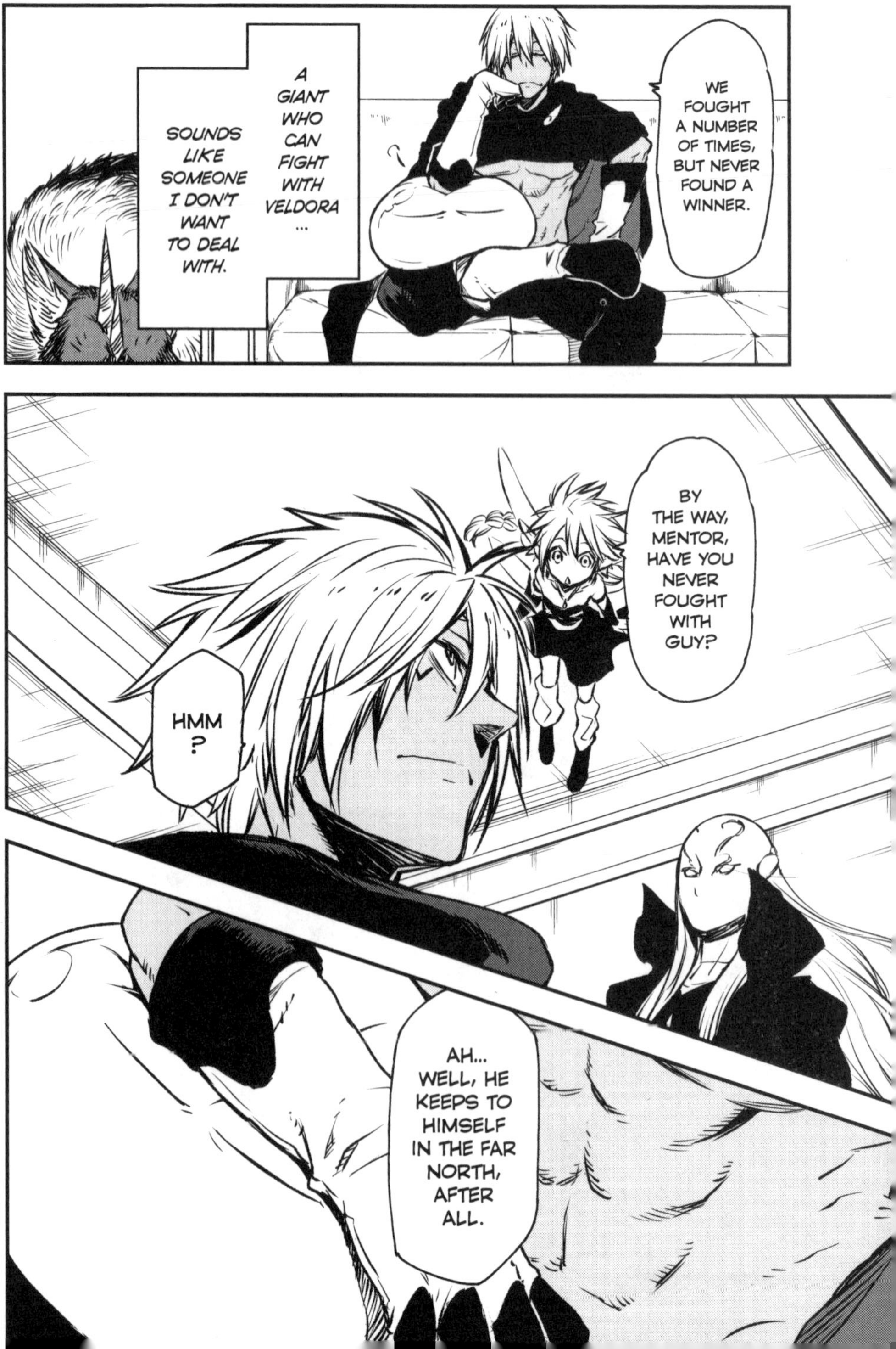
WE FOUGHT A NUMBER OF TIMES, BUT NEVER FOUND A WINNER.
A GIANT WHO CAN FIGHT WITH VELDORA...
SOUNDS LIKE SOMEONE I DON'T WANT TO DEAL WITH.
BY THE WAY, MENTOR, HAVE YOU NEVER FOUGHT WITH GUY?
HMM?
AH... WELL, HE KEEPS TO HIMSELF IN THE FAR NORTH, AFTER ALL.

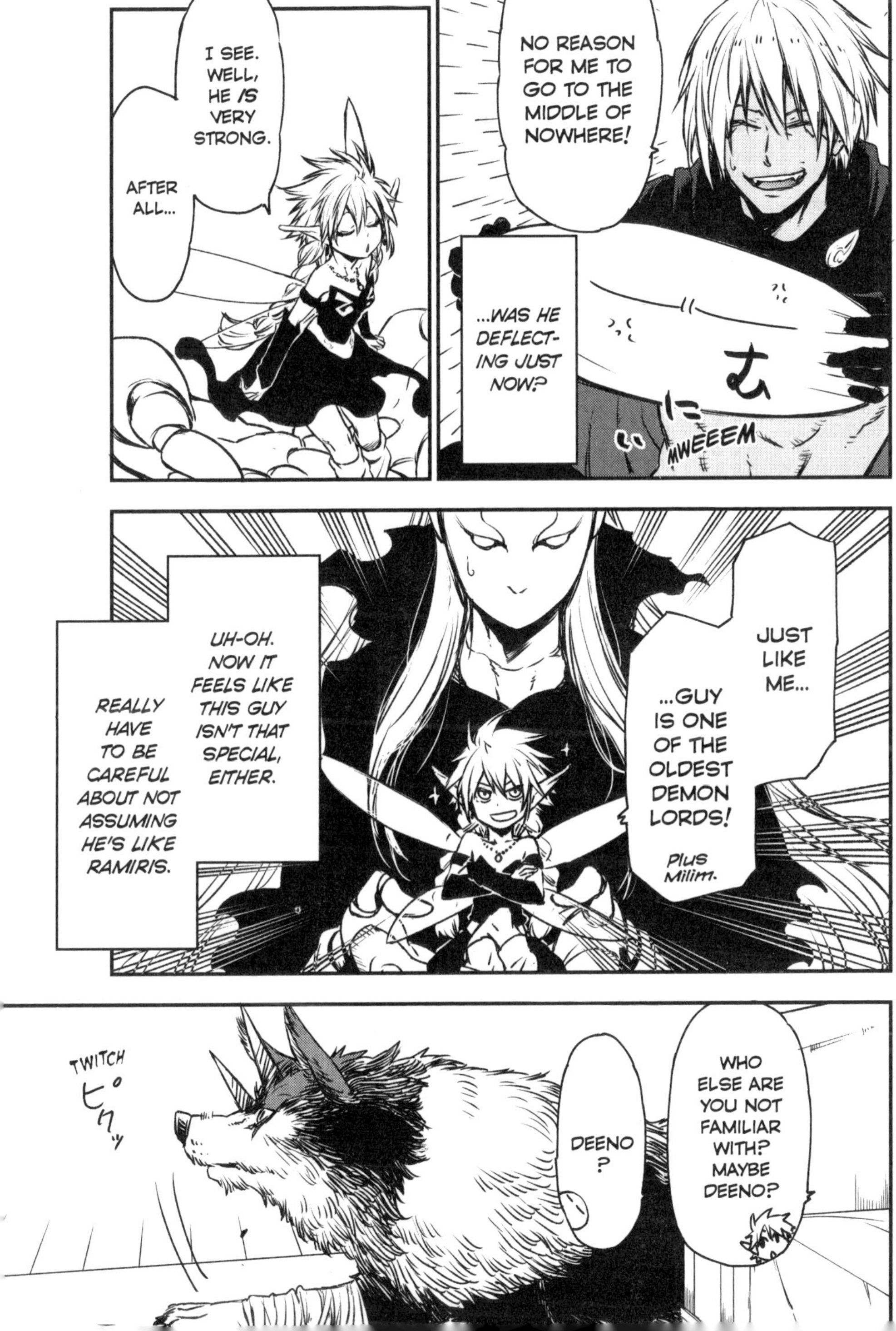
NO REASON FOR ME TO GO TO THE MIDDLE OF NOWHERE!
...WAS HE DEFLECTING JUST NOW?
むにぃ
MWEEEM
I SEE. WELL, HE IS VERY STRONG.
AFTER ALL...
JUST LIKE ME...
...GUY IS ONE OF THE OLDEST DEMON LORDS!
Plus Milim.
UH-OH. NOW IT FEELS LIKE THIS GUY ISN'T THAT SPECIAL, EITHER.
REALLY HAVE TO BE CAREFUL ABOUT NOT ASSUMING HE'S LIKE RAMIRIS.
WHO ELSE ARE YOU NOT FAMILIAR WITH? MAYBE DEENO?
DEENO?
TWITCH
ピクッ

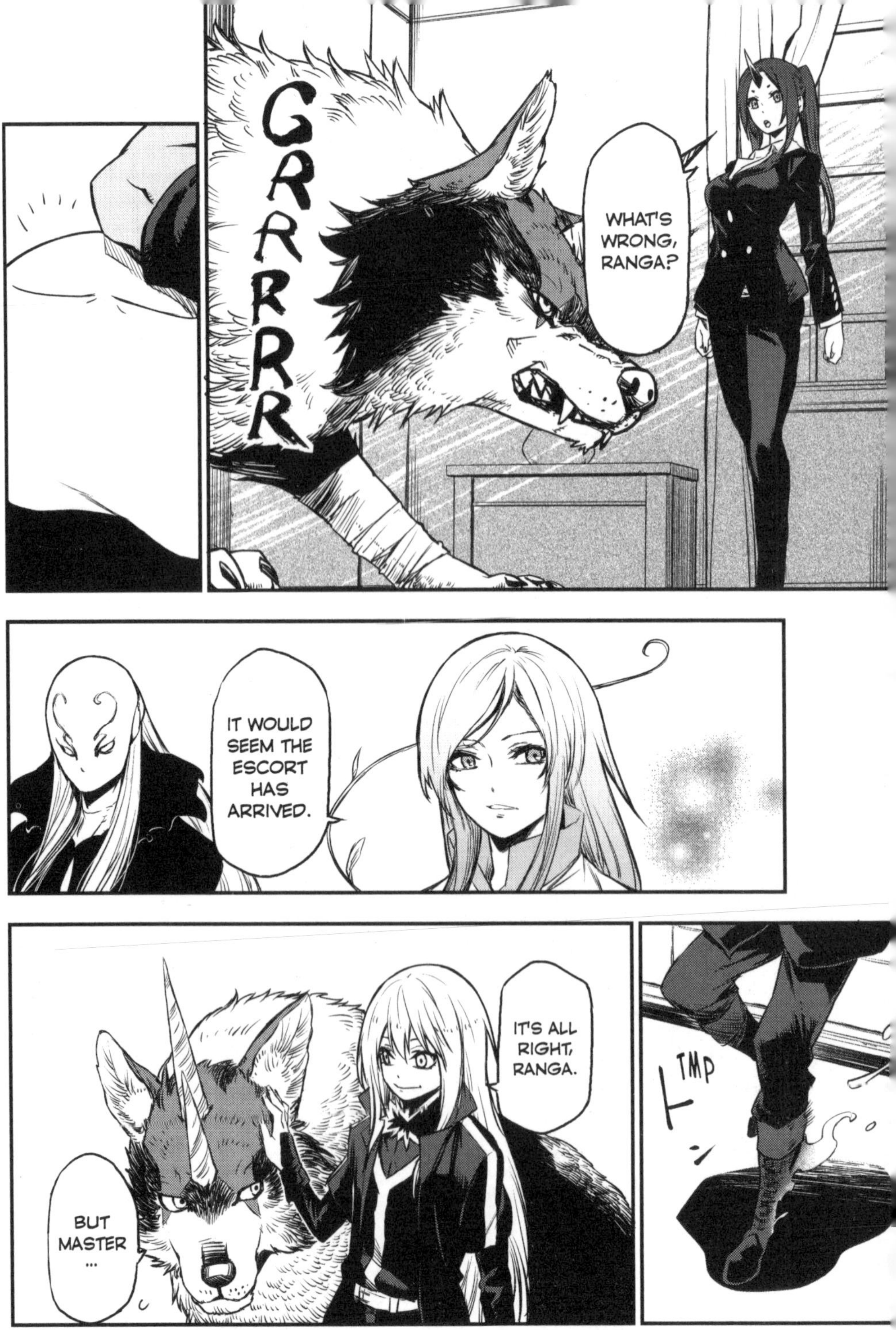
WHAT'S WRONG, RANGA?
GRRRR
IT WOULD SEEM THE ESCORT HAS ARRIVED.
TMP
IT'S ALL RIGHT, RANGA.
BUT MASTER ...

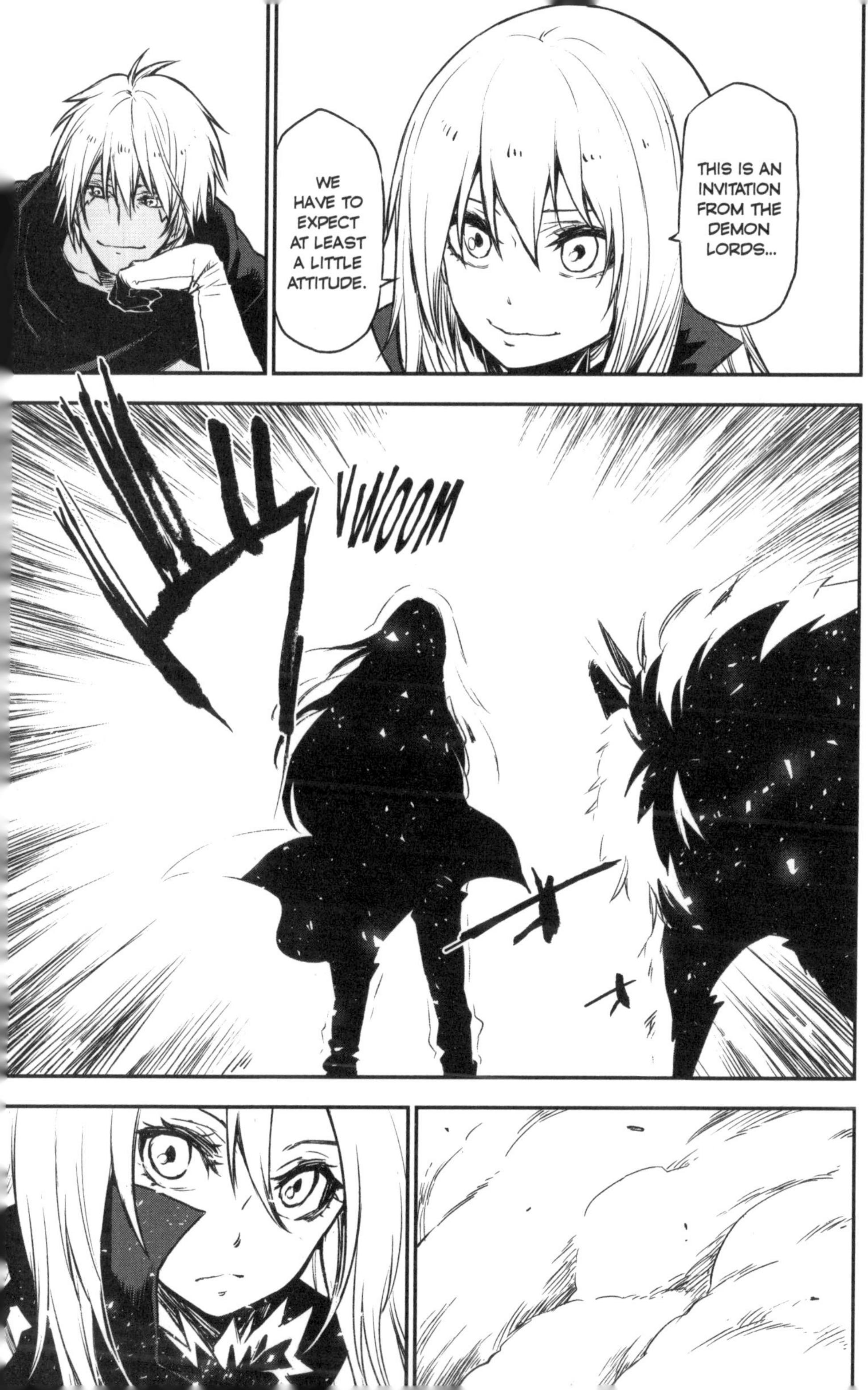
THIS IS AN INVITATION FROM THE DEMON LORDS...
WE HAVE TO EXPECT AT LEAST A LITTLE ATTITUDE.
VWOOM

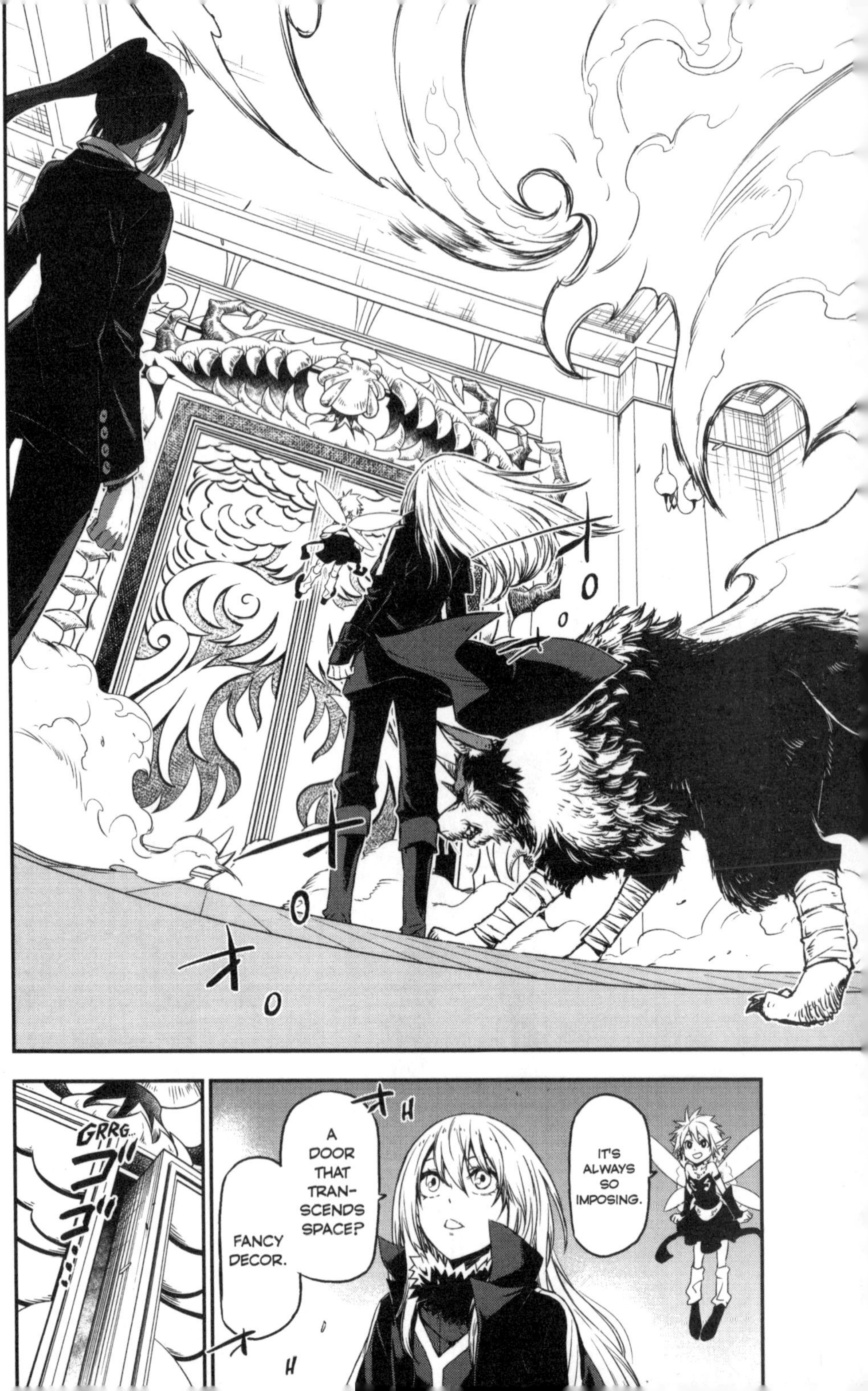

IT'S ALWAYS SO IMPOSING.
A DOOR THAT TRAN-SCENDS SPACE?
FANCY DECOR.
GRRG..

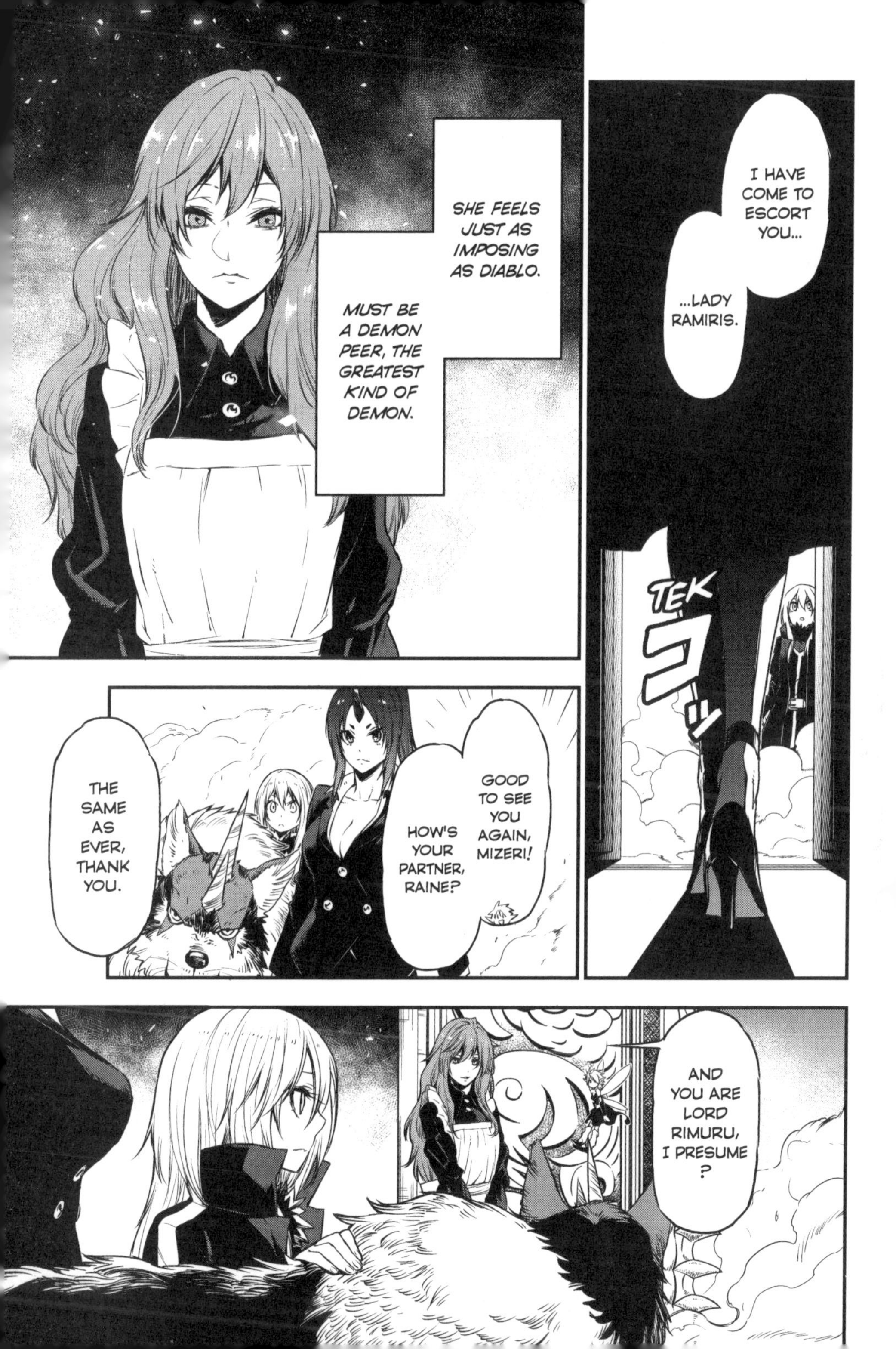
I HAVE COME TO ESCORT YOU...
...LADY RAMIRIS.
TEK
SHE FEELS JUST AS IMPOSING AS DIABLO.
MUST BE A DEMON PEER, THE GREATEST KIND OF DEMON.
GOOD TO SEE YOU AGAIN, MIZERI!
HOW'S YOUR PARTNER, RAINE?
THE SAME AS EVER, THANK YOU.
AND YOU ARE LORD RIMURU, I PRESUME?

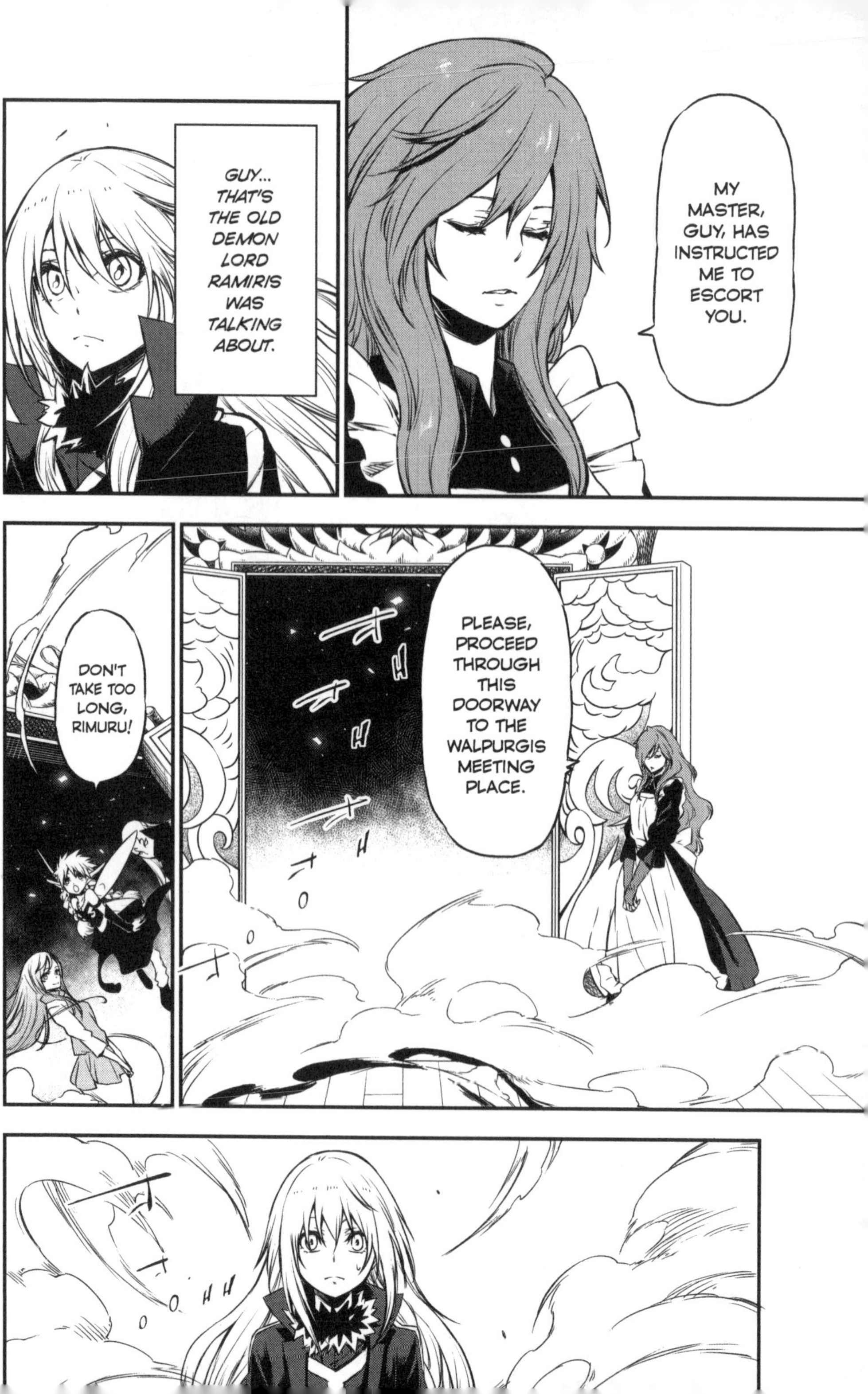
MY MASTER, GUY, HAS INSTRUCTED ME TO ESCORT YOU.
GUY... THAT'S THE OLD DEMON LORD RAMIRIS WAS TALKING ABOUT.
PLEASE, PROCEED THROUGH THIS DOORWAY TO THE WALPURGIS MEETING PLACE.
DON'T TAKE TOO LONG, RIMURU!

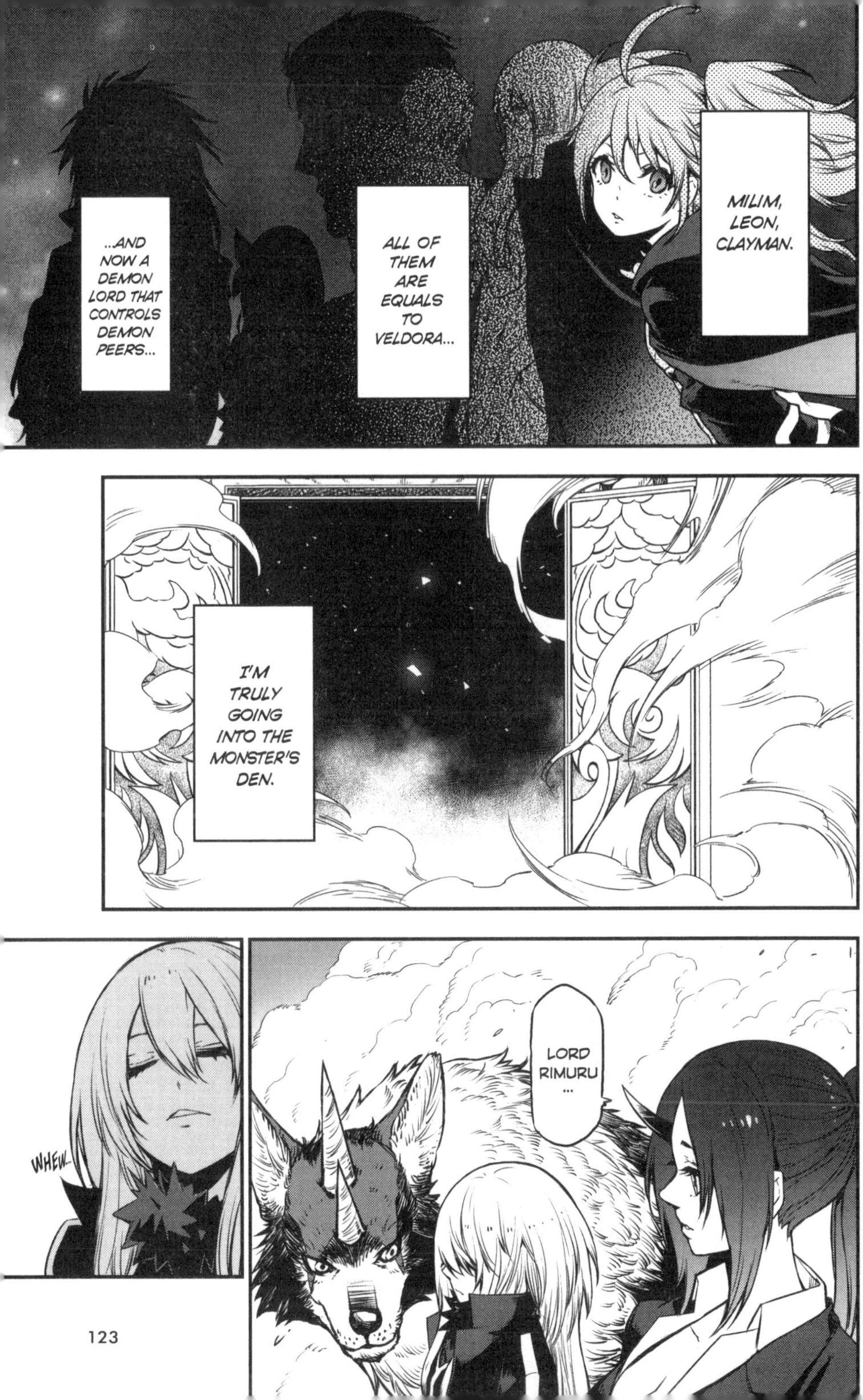
MILIM, LEON, CLAYMAN.
ALL OF THEM ARE EQUALS TO VELDORA...
...AND NOW A DEMON LORD THAT CONTROLS DEMON PEERS...
I'M TRULY GOING INTO THE MONSTER'S DEN.
LORD RIMURU ...
WHEW...

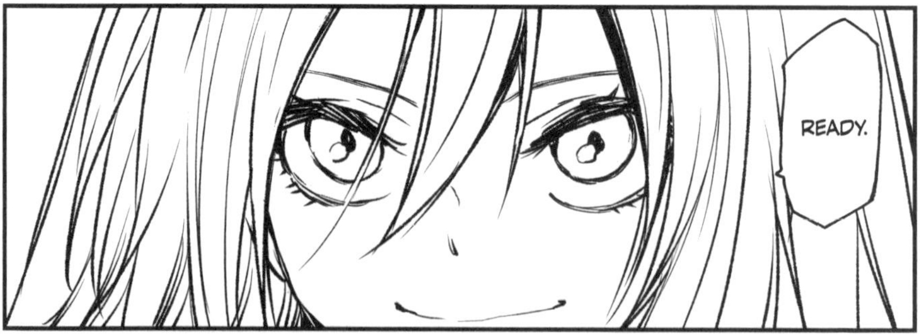
READY.
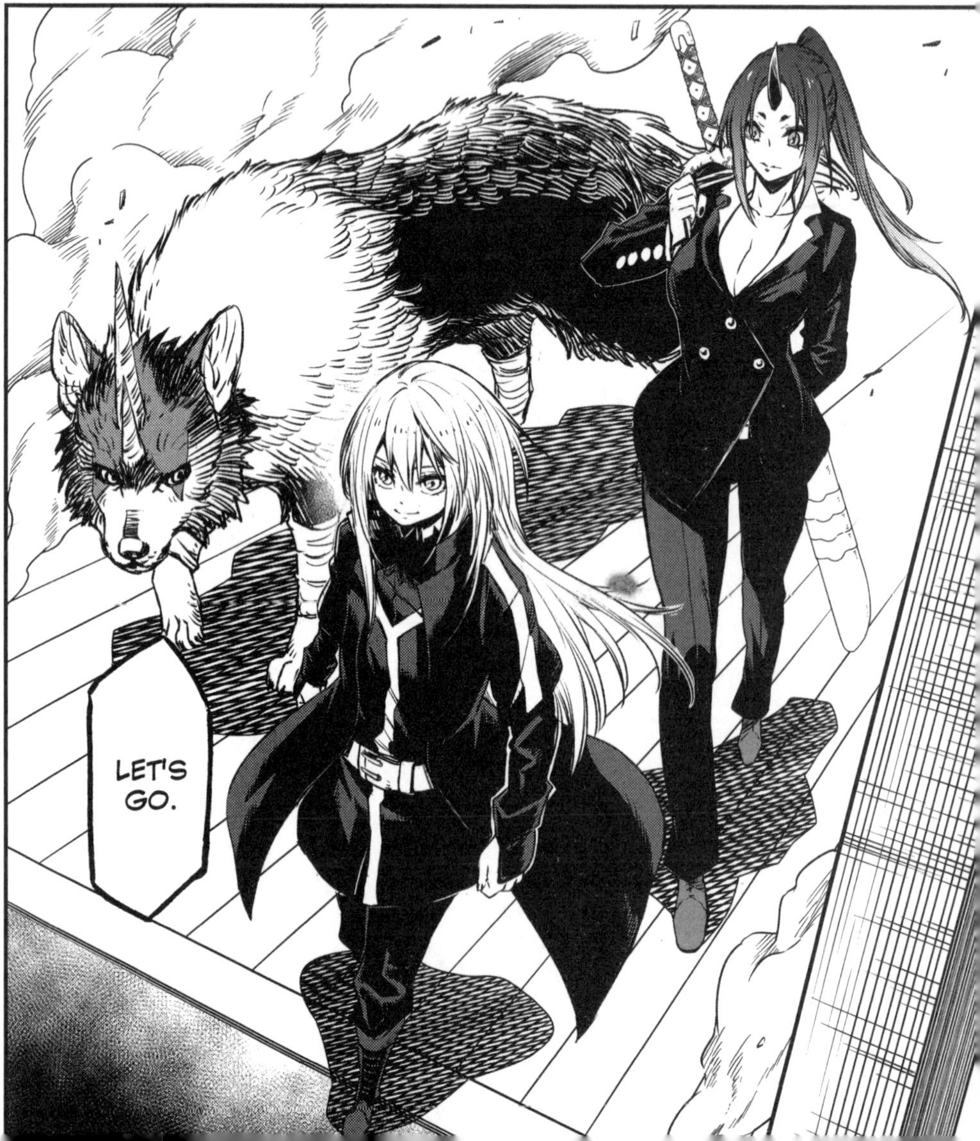
LET'S GO.

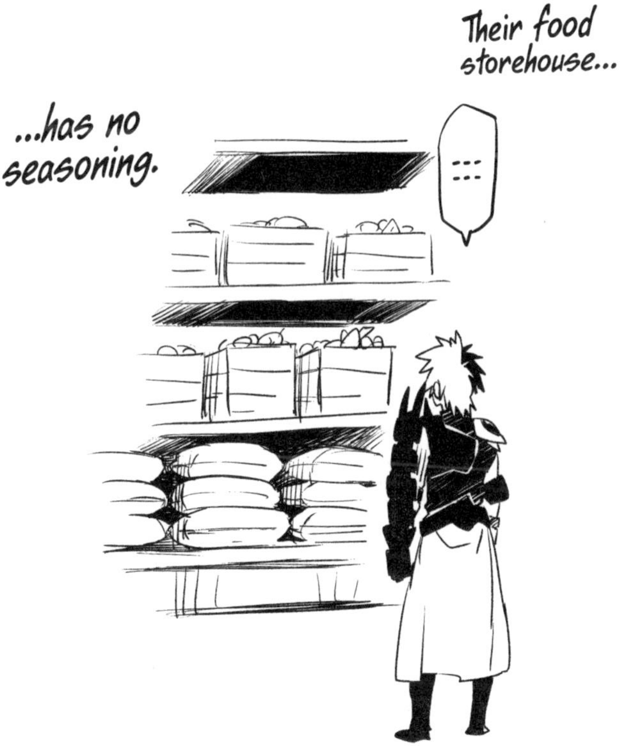
Their food storehouse...
......
...has no seasoning.

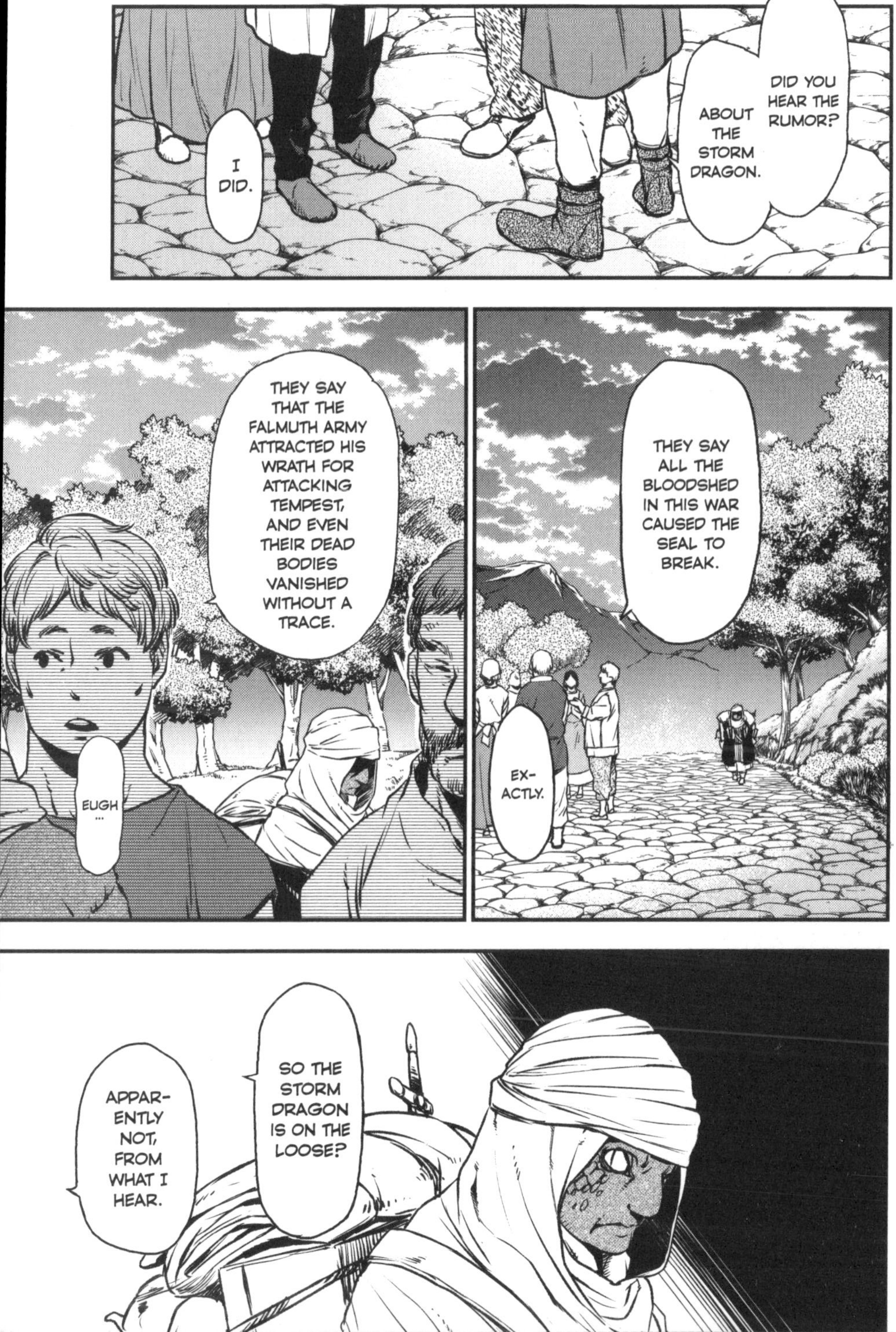
DID YOU HEAR THE RUMOR?
ABOUT THE STORM DRAGON.
I DID.
THEY SAY ALL THE BLOODSHED IN THIS WAR CAUSED THE SEAL TO BREAK.
EX-ACTLY.
THEY SAY THAT THE FALMUTH ARMY ATTRACTED HIS WRATH FOR ATTACKING TEMPEST, AND EVEN THEIR DEAD BODIES VANISHED WITHOUT A TRACE.
EUGH...
SO THE STORM DRAGON IS ON THE LOOSE?
APPAR-ENTLY NOT, FROM WHAT I HEAR.

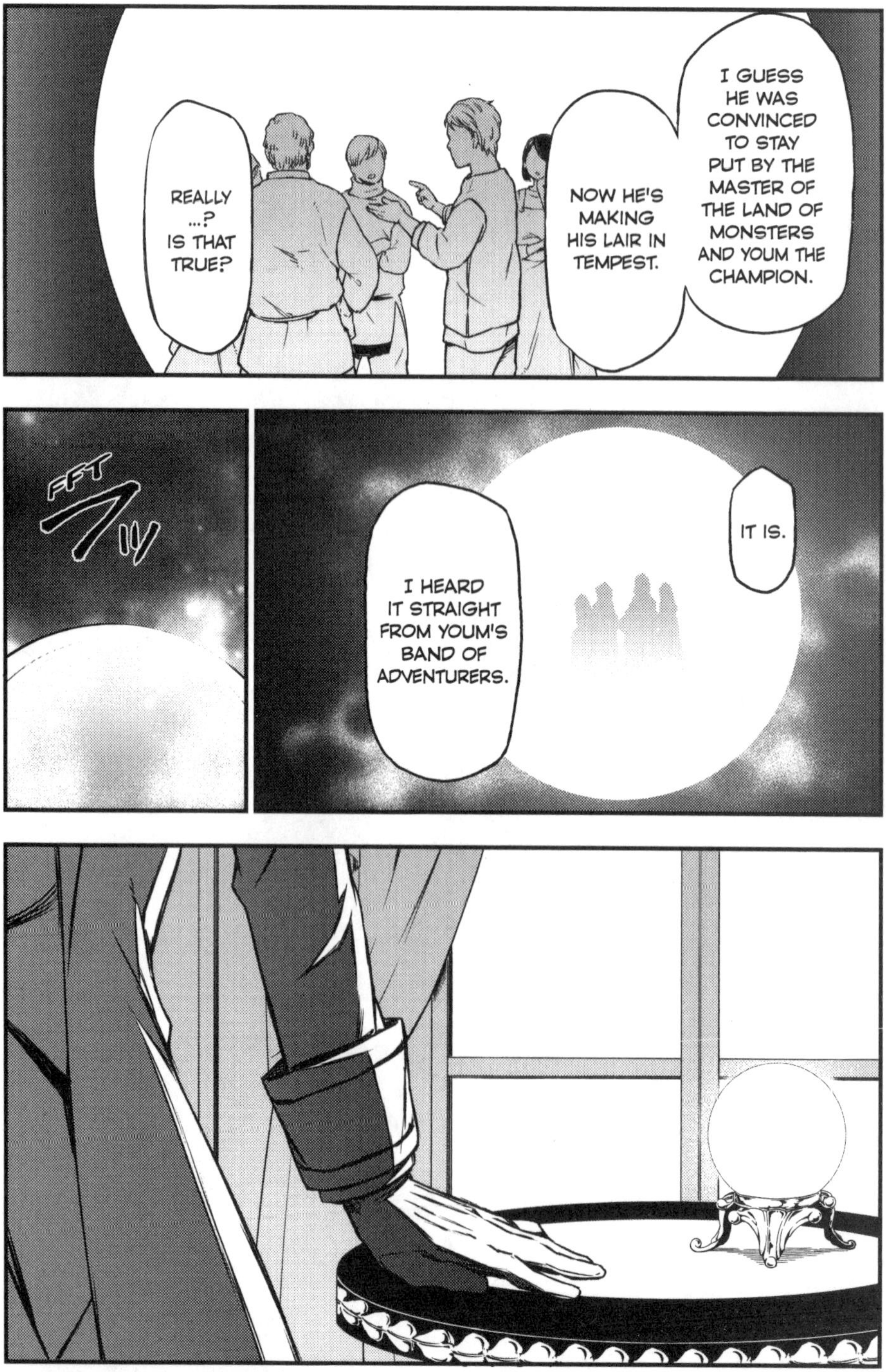
I GUESS HE WAS CONVINCED TO STAY PUT BY THE MASTER OF THE LAND OF MONSTERS AND YOUM THE CHAMPION.
NOW HE'S MAKING HIS LAIR IN TEMPEST.
REALLY ...? IS THAT TRUE?
IT IS.
I HEARD IT STRAIGHT FROM YOUM'S BAND OF ADVENTURERS.
FFT
フッ

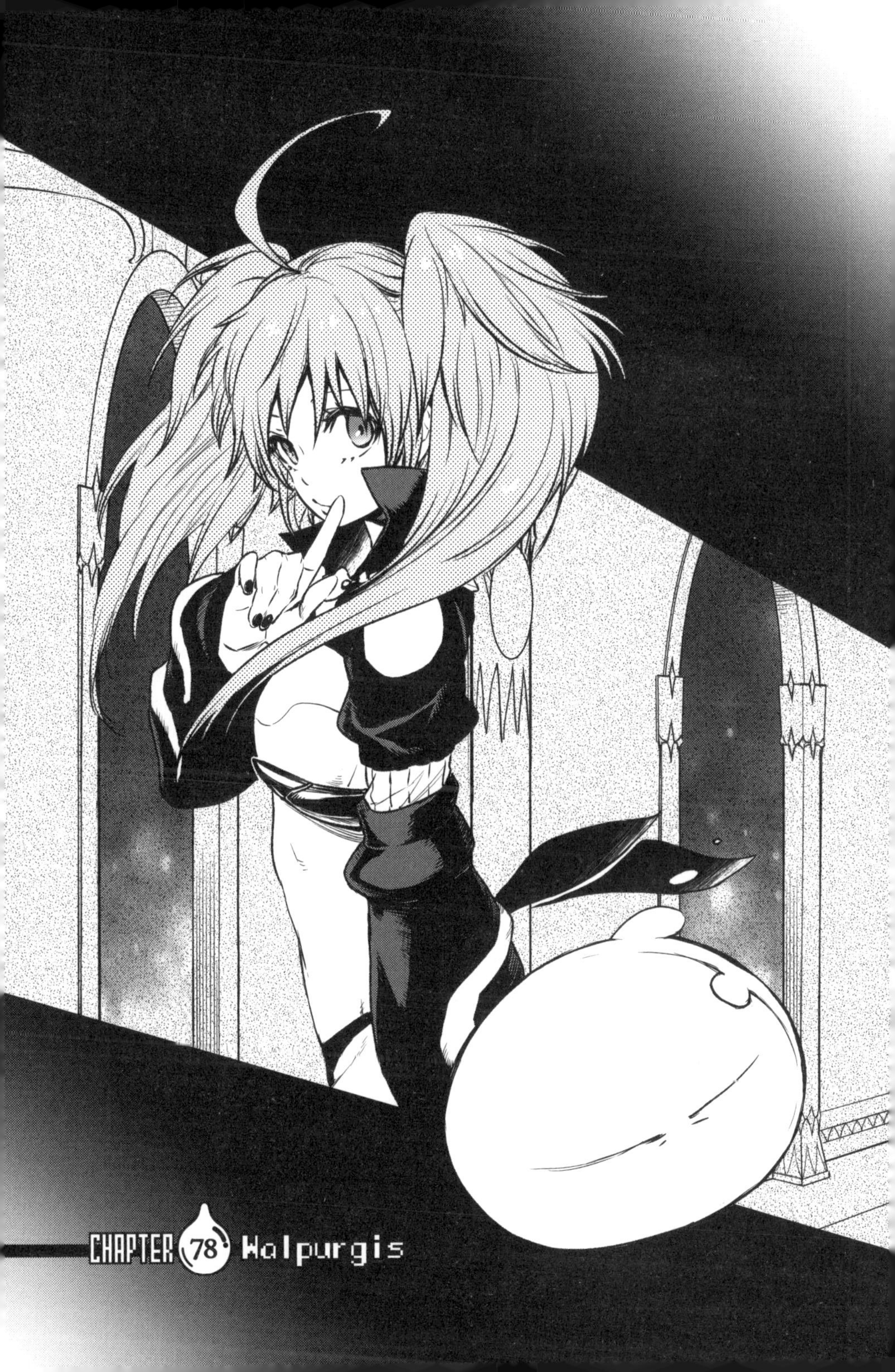
CHAPTER 78 Walpurgis

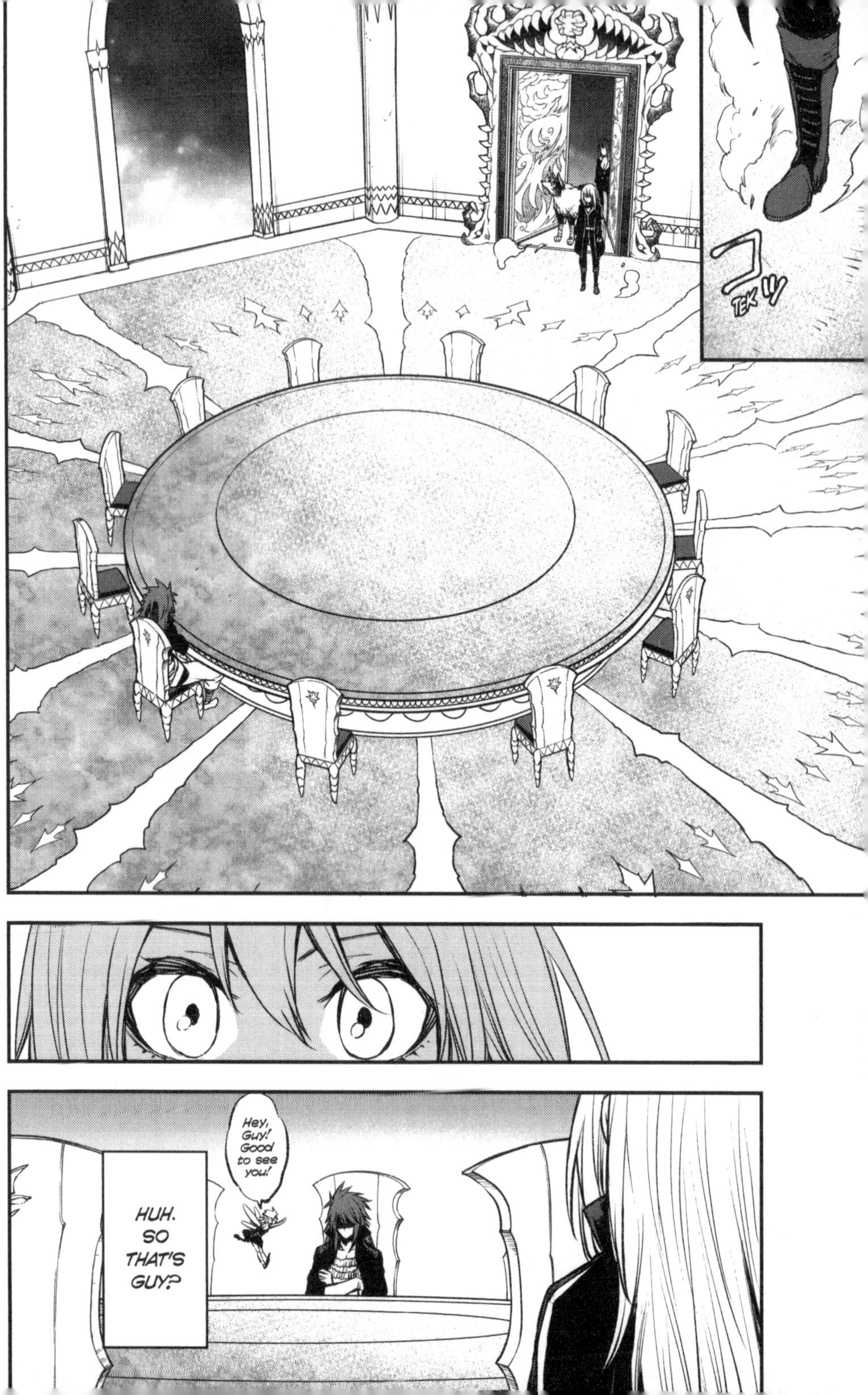

コッ
TEK
Hey, Guy! Good to see you!
HUH. SO THAT'S GUY?

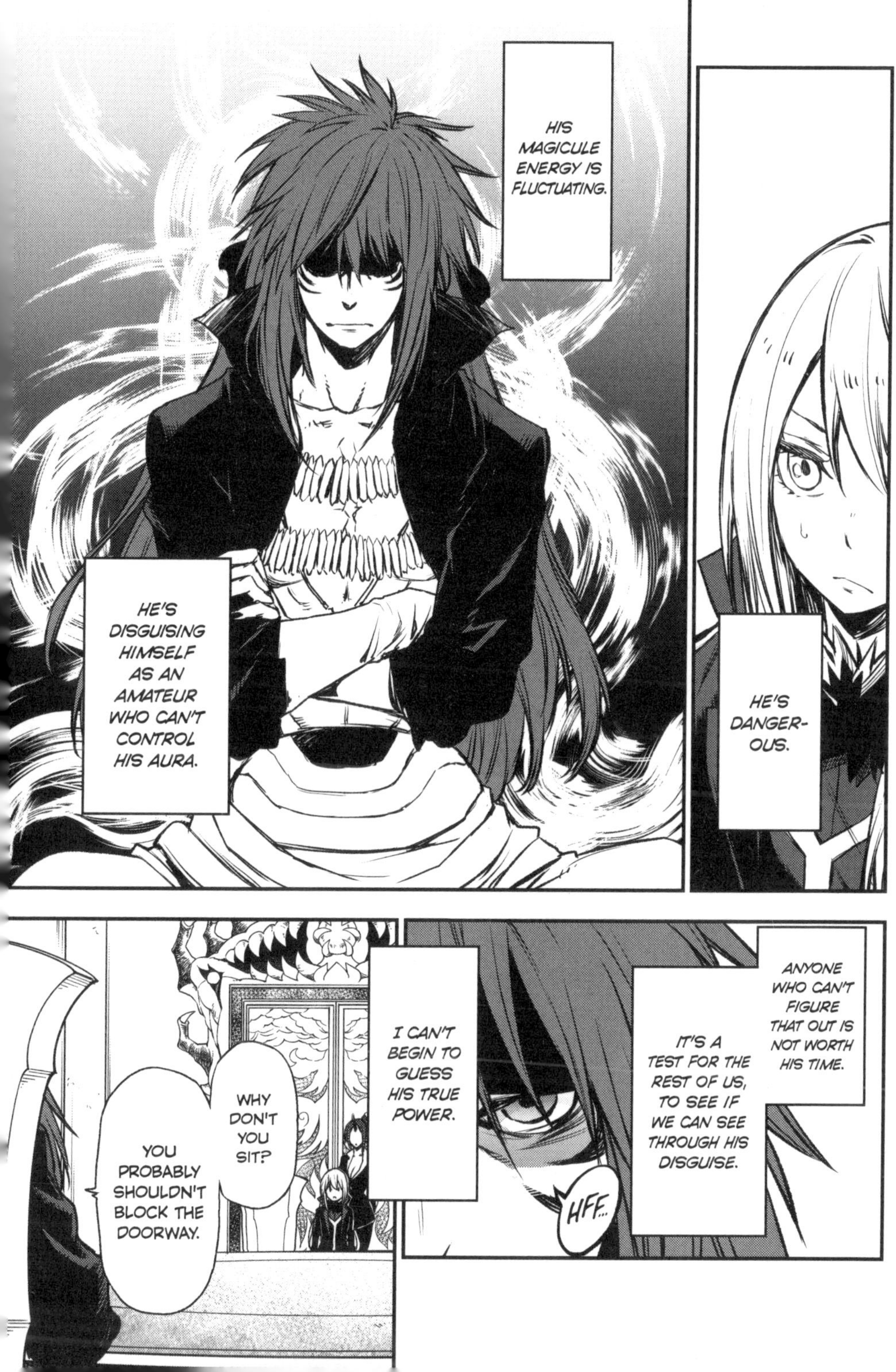
HE'S DANGER-OUS.
HIS MAGICULE ENERGY IS FLUCTUATING.
HE'S DISGUISING HIMSELF AS AN AMATEUR WHO CAN'T CONTROL HIS AURA.
ANYONE WHO CAN'T FIGURE THAT OUT IS NOT WORTH HIS TIME.
IT'S A TEST FOR THE REST OF US, TO SEE IF WE CAN SEE THROUGH HIS DISGUISE.
HFF...
I CAN'T BEGIN TO GUESS HIS TRUE POWER.
WHY DON'T YOU SIT?
YOU PROBABLY SHOULDN'T BLOCK THE DOORWAY.

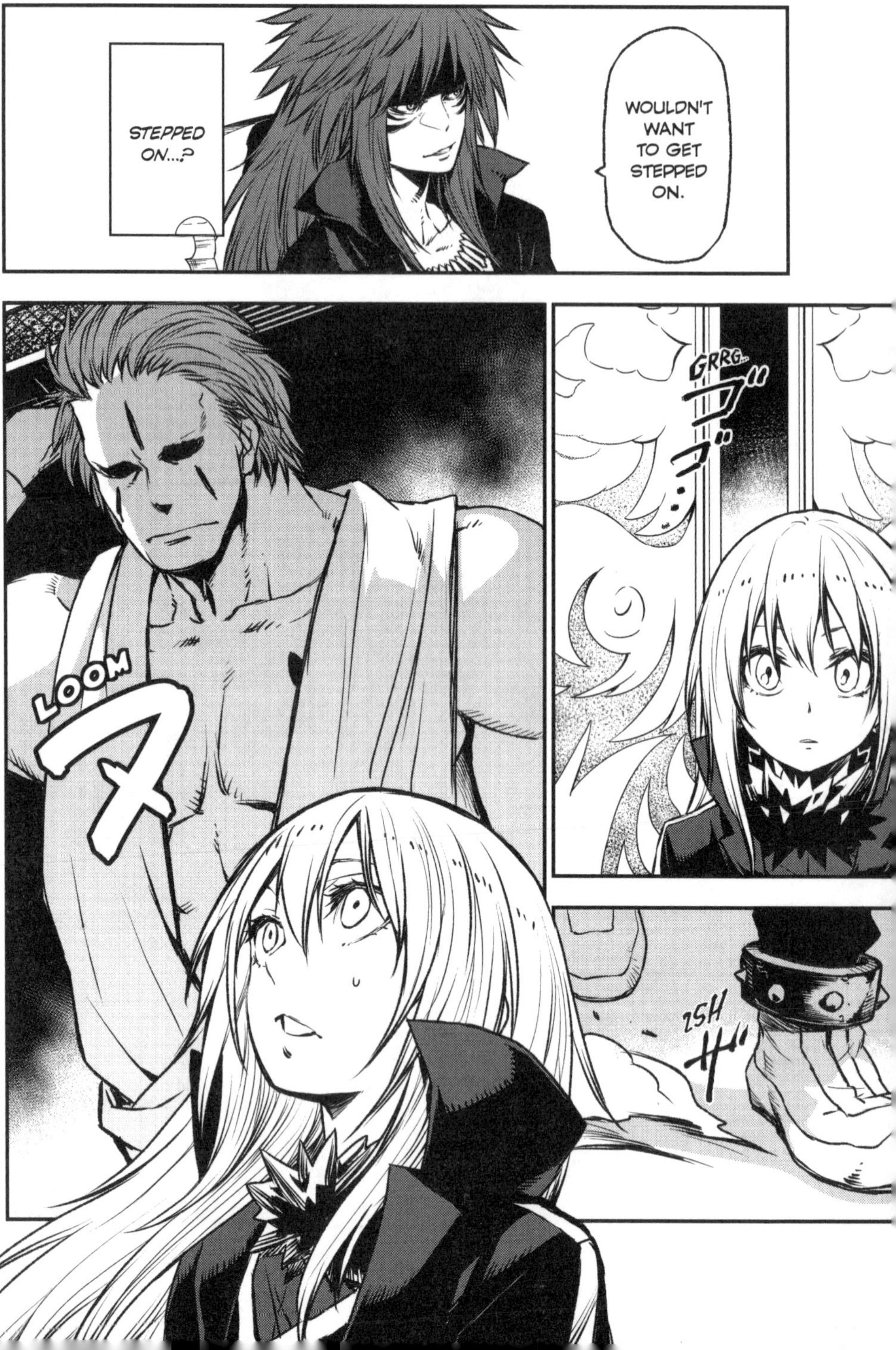
WOULDN'T WANT TO GET STEPPED ON.
STEPPED ON...?
GRRG..
ZSH
LOOM

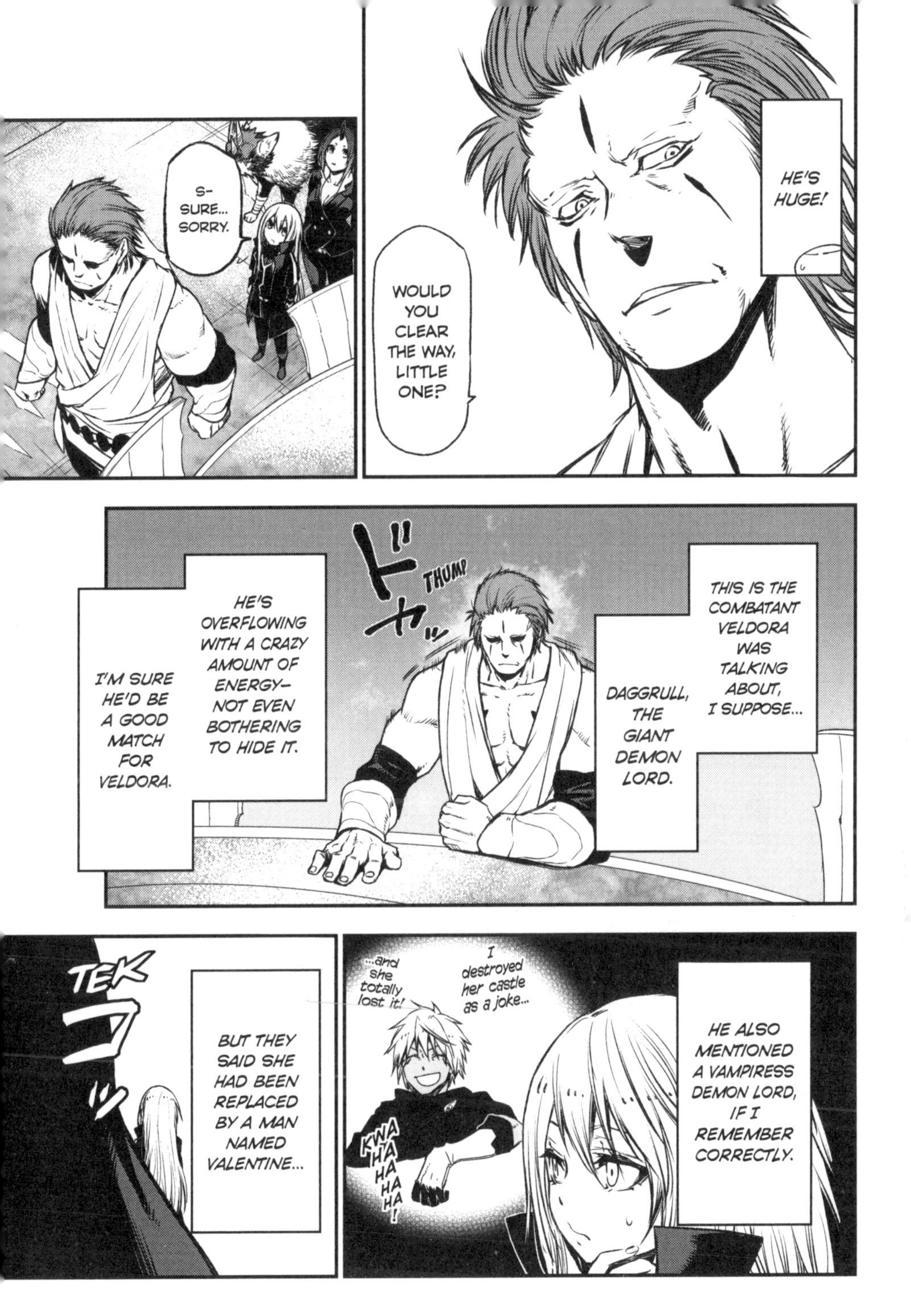
HE'S HUGE!
WOULD YOU CLEAR THE WAY, LITTLE ONE?
S-SURE... SORRY.
THIS IS THE COMBATANT VELDORA WAS TALKING ABOUT, I SUPPOSE...
DAGGRULL, THE GIANT DEMON LORD.
THUMP
HE'S OVERFLOWING WITH A CRAZY AMOUNT OF ENERGY—NOT EVEN BOTHERING TO HIDE IT.
I'M SURE HE'D BE A GOOD MATCH FOR VELDORA.
HE ALSO MENTIONED A VAMPIRESS DEMON LORD, IF I REMEMBER CORRECTLY.
I destroyed her castle as a joke...
...and she totally lost it!
KWAHAHAHAHA!
BUT THEY SAID SHE HAD BEEN REPLACED BY A MAN NAMED VALENTINE...
TEK

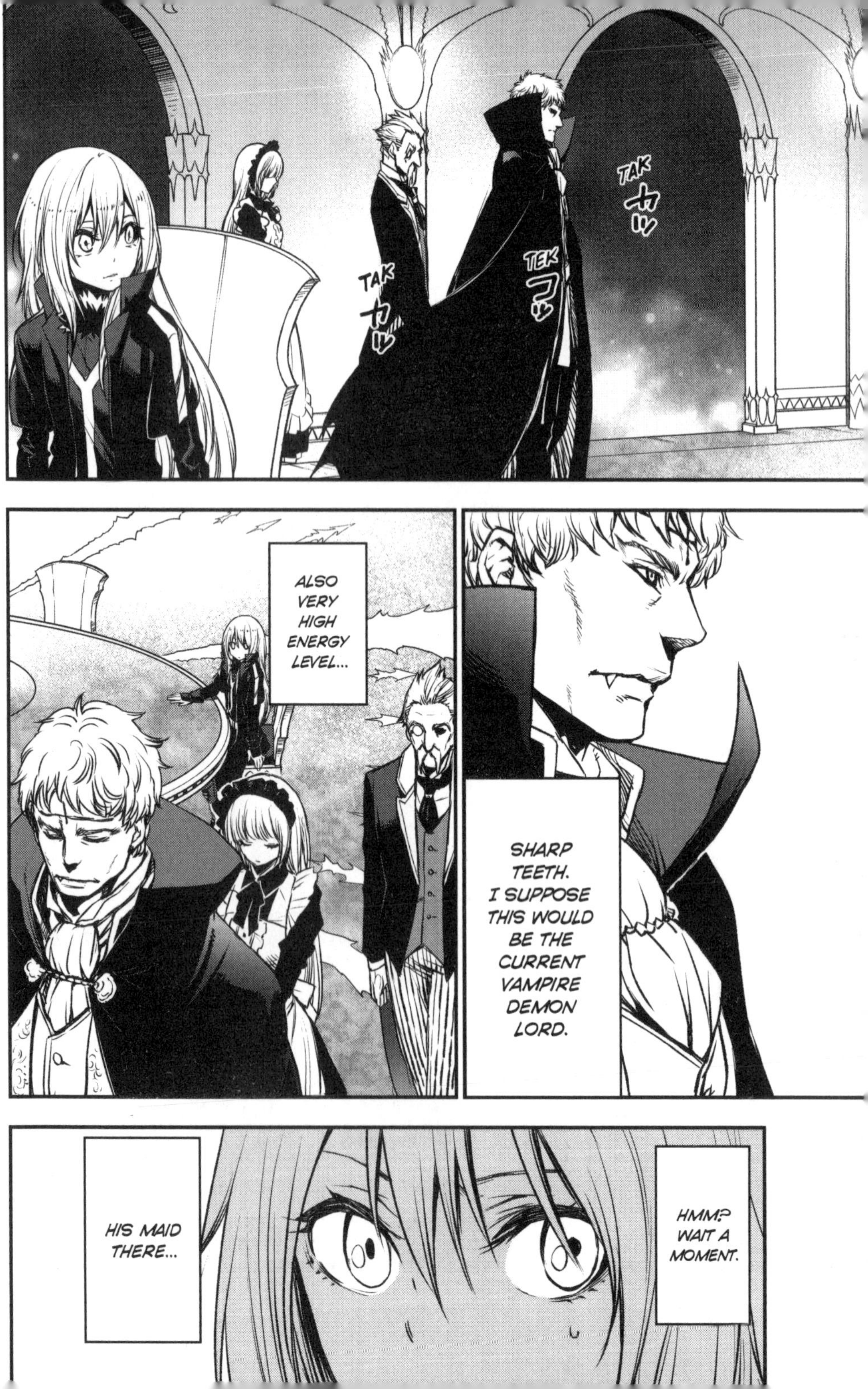
TAK
カッ
TEK
コッ
TAK
カッ
SHARP TEETH. I SUPPOSE THIS WOULD BE THE CURRENT VAMPIRE DEMON LORD.
ALSO VERY HIGH ENERGY LEVEL...
HMM? WAIT A MOMENT.
HIS MAID THERE...

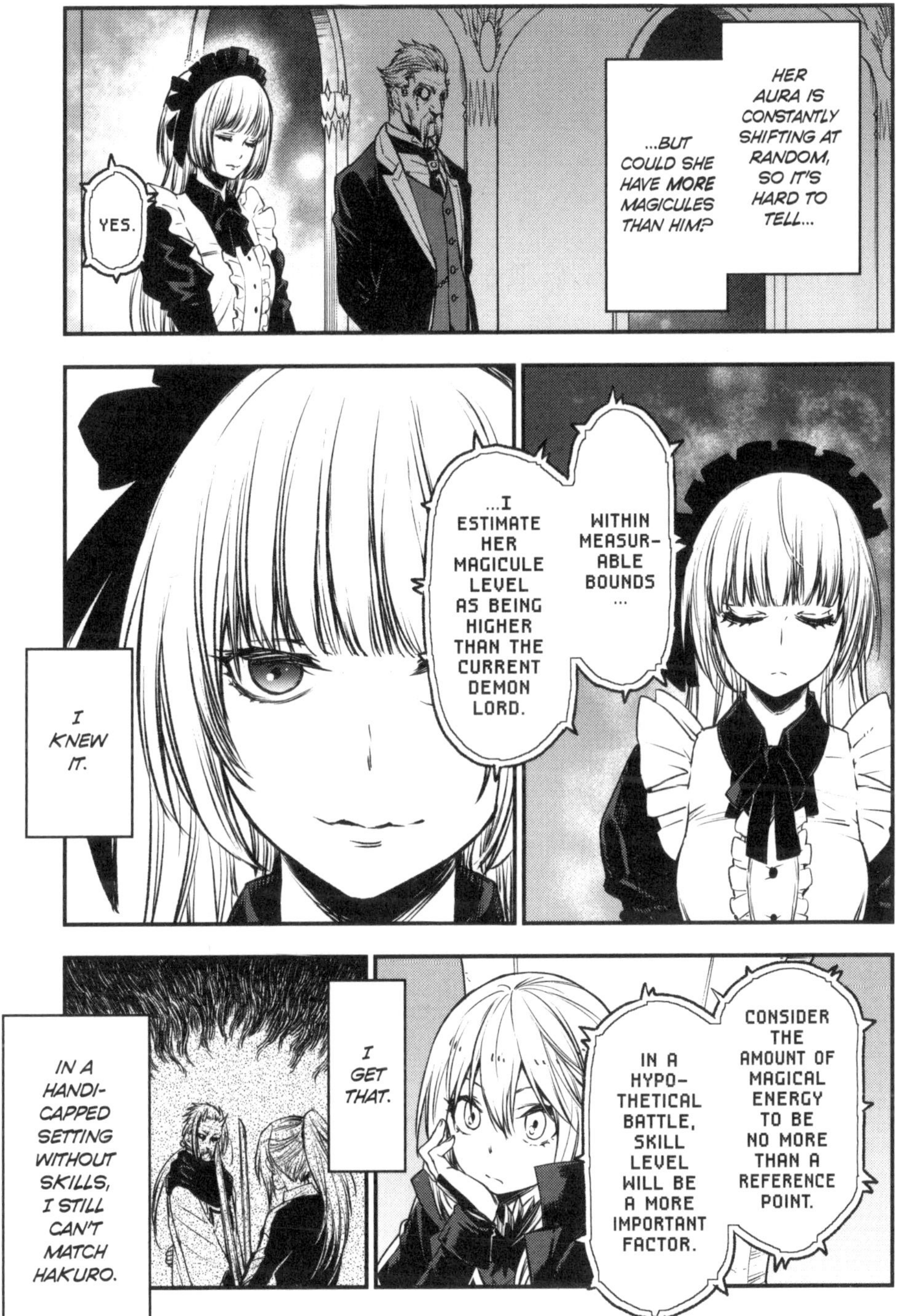
HER AURA IS CONSTANTLY SHIFTING AT RANDOM, SO IT'S HARD TO TELL...
...BUT COULD SHE HAVE MORE MAGICULES THAN HIM?
YES.
WITHIN MEASURABLE BOUNDS...
...I ESTIMATE HER MAGICULE LEVEL AS BEING HIGHER THAN THE CURRENT DEMON LORD.
I KNEW IT.
CONSIDER THE AMOUNT OF MAGICAL ENERGY TO BE NO MORE THAN A REFERENCE POINT.
IN A HYPOTHETICAL BATTLE, SKILL LEVEL WILL BE A MORE IMPORTANT FACTOR.
I GET THAT.
IN A HANDICAPPED SETTING WITHOUT SKILLS, I STILL CAN'T MATCH HAKURO.

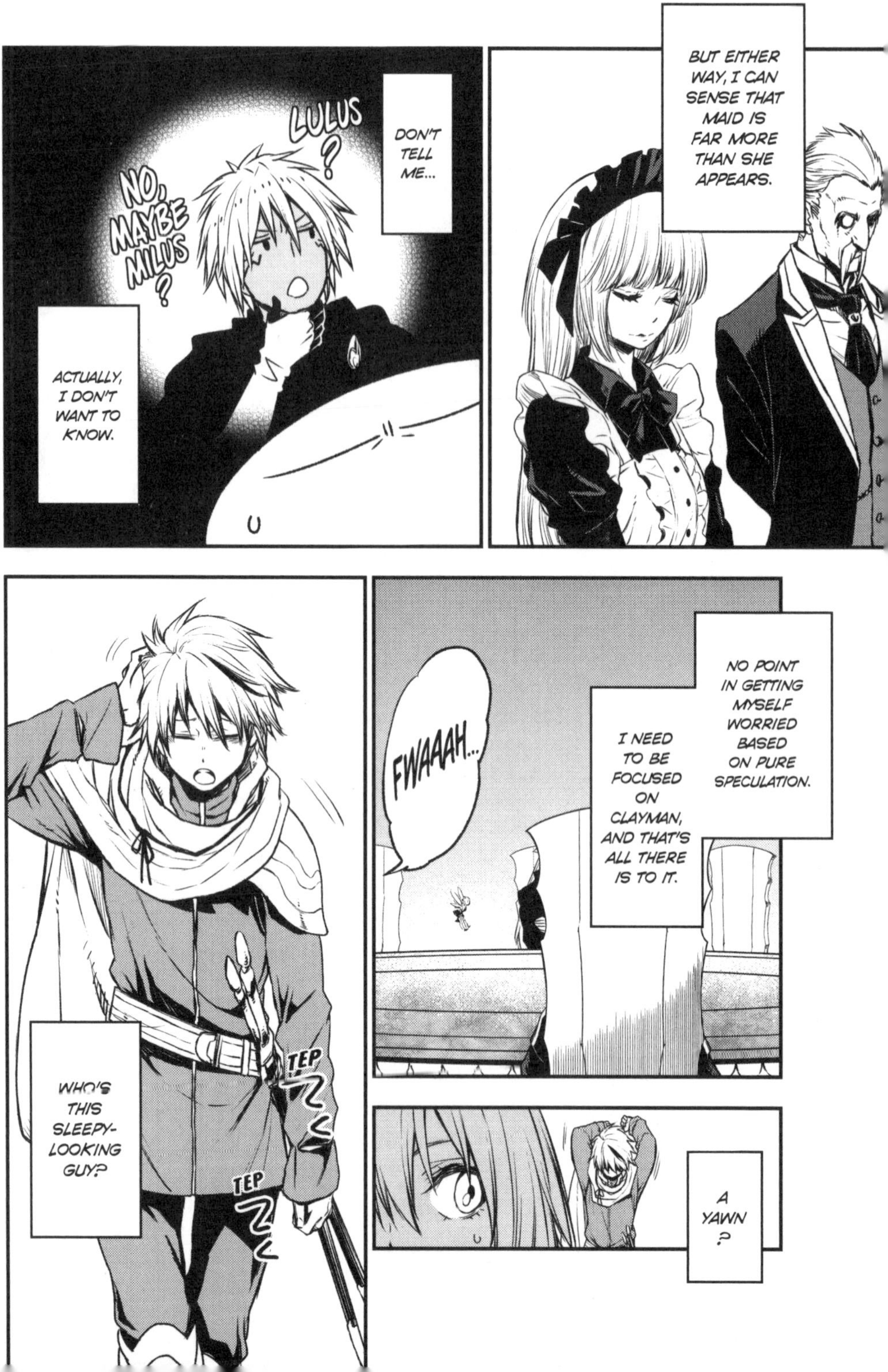
BUT EITHER WAY, I CAN SENSE THAT MAID IS FAR MORE THAN SHE APPEARS.
DON'T TELL ME...
LULUS?
NO, MAYBE MILUS?
ACTUALLY, I DON'T WANT TO KNOW.
NO POINT IN GETTING MYSELF WORRIED BASED ON PURE SPECULATION.
I NEED TO BE FOCUSED ON CLAYMAN, AND THAT'S ALL THERE IS TO IT.
FWAAAH...
A YAWN?
WHO'S THIS SLEEPY-LOOKING GUY?
TEP
TEP

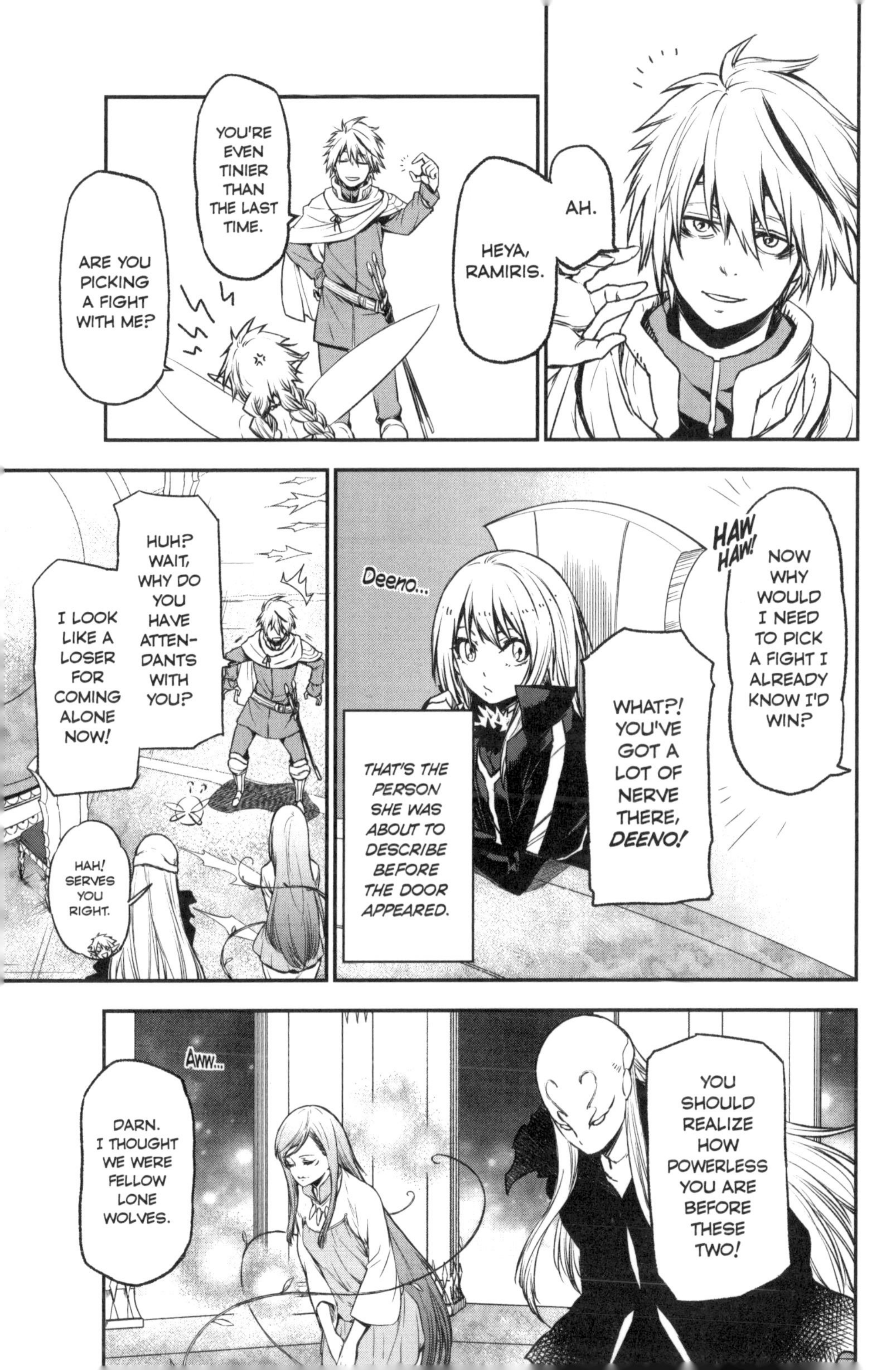
AH.
HEYA, RAMIRIS.
YOU'RE EVEN TINIER THAN THE LAST TIME.
ARE YOU PICKING A FIGHT WITH ME?
HAW HAW!
NOW WHY WOULD I NEED TO PICK A FIGHT I ALREADY KNOW I'D WIN?
WHAT?! YOU'VE GOT A LOT OF NERVE THERE, DEENO!
Deeno...
THAT'S THE PERSON SHE WAS ABOUT TO DESCRIBE BEFORE THE DOOR APPEARED.
HUH? WAIT, WHY DO YOU HAVE ATTEN-DANTS WITH YOU?
I LOOK LIKE A LOSER FOR COMING ALONE NOW!
HAH! SERVES YOU RIGHT.
YOU SHOULD REALIZE HOW POWERLESS YOU ARE BEFORE THESE TWO!
Aww...
DARN. I THOUGHT WE WERE FELLOW LONE WOLVES.

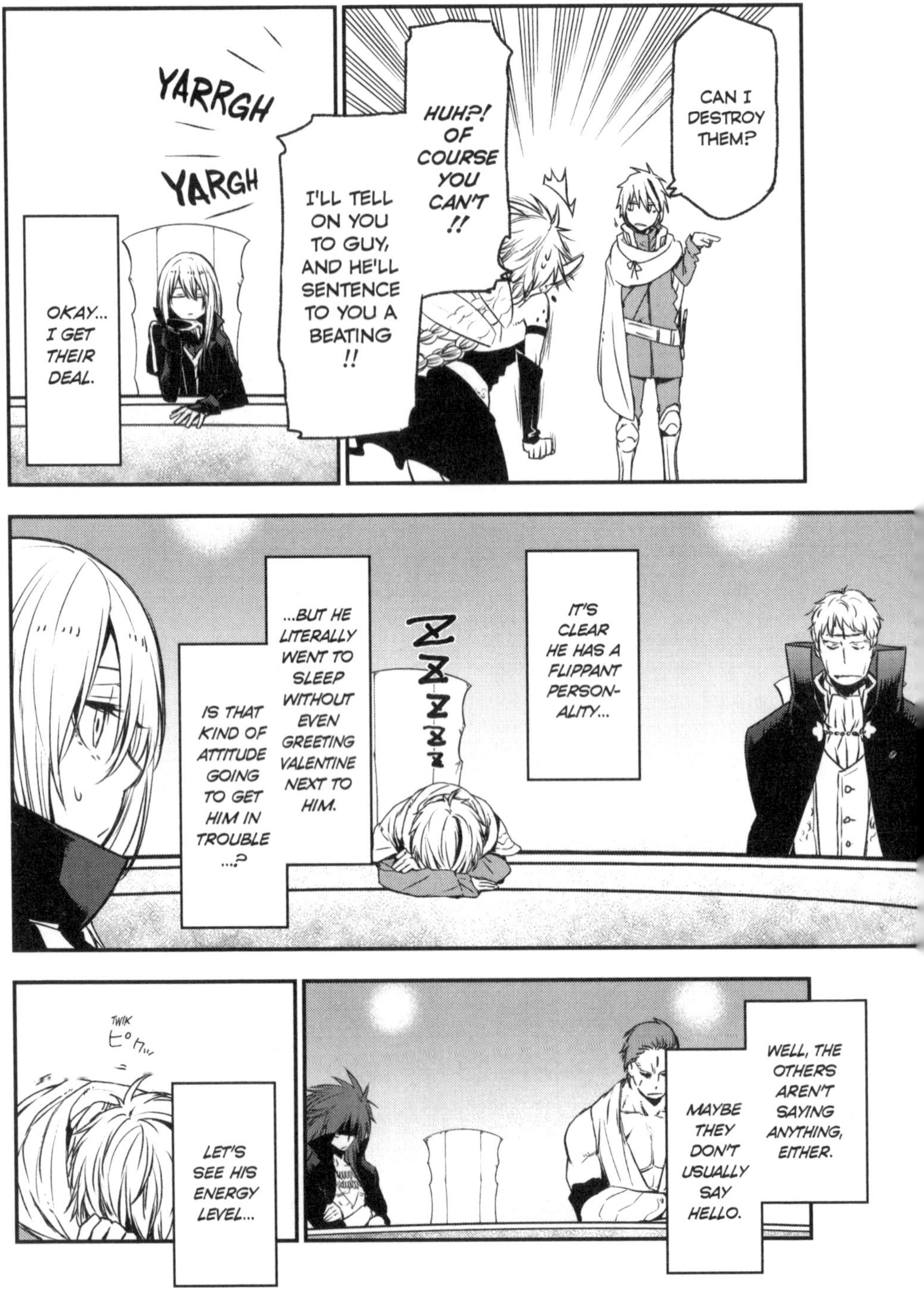
CAN I DESTROY THEM?
HUH?! OF COURSE YOU CAN'T !!
I'LL TELL ON YOU TO GUY, AND HE'LL SENTENCE TO YOU A BEATING !!
YARRGH
YARGH
OKAY... I GET THEIR DEAL.
IT'S CLEAR HE HAS A FLIPPANT PERSON-ALITY...
...BUT HE LITERALLY WENT TO SLEEP WITHOUT EVEN GREETING VALENTINE NEXT TO HIM.
ZZZZ
IS THAT KIND OF ATTITUDE GOING TO GET HIM IN TROUBLE ...?
WELL, THE OTHERS AREN'T SAYING ANYTHING, EITHER.
MAYBE THEY DON'T USUALLY SAY HELLO.
TWIK
LET'S SEE HIS ENERGY LEVEL...

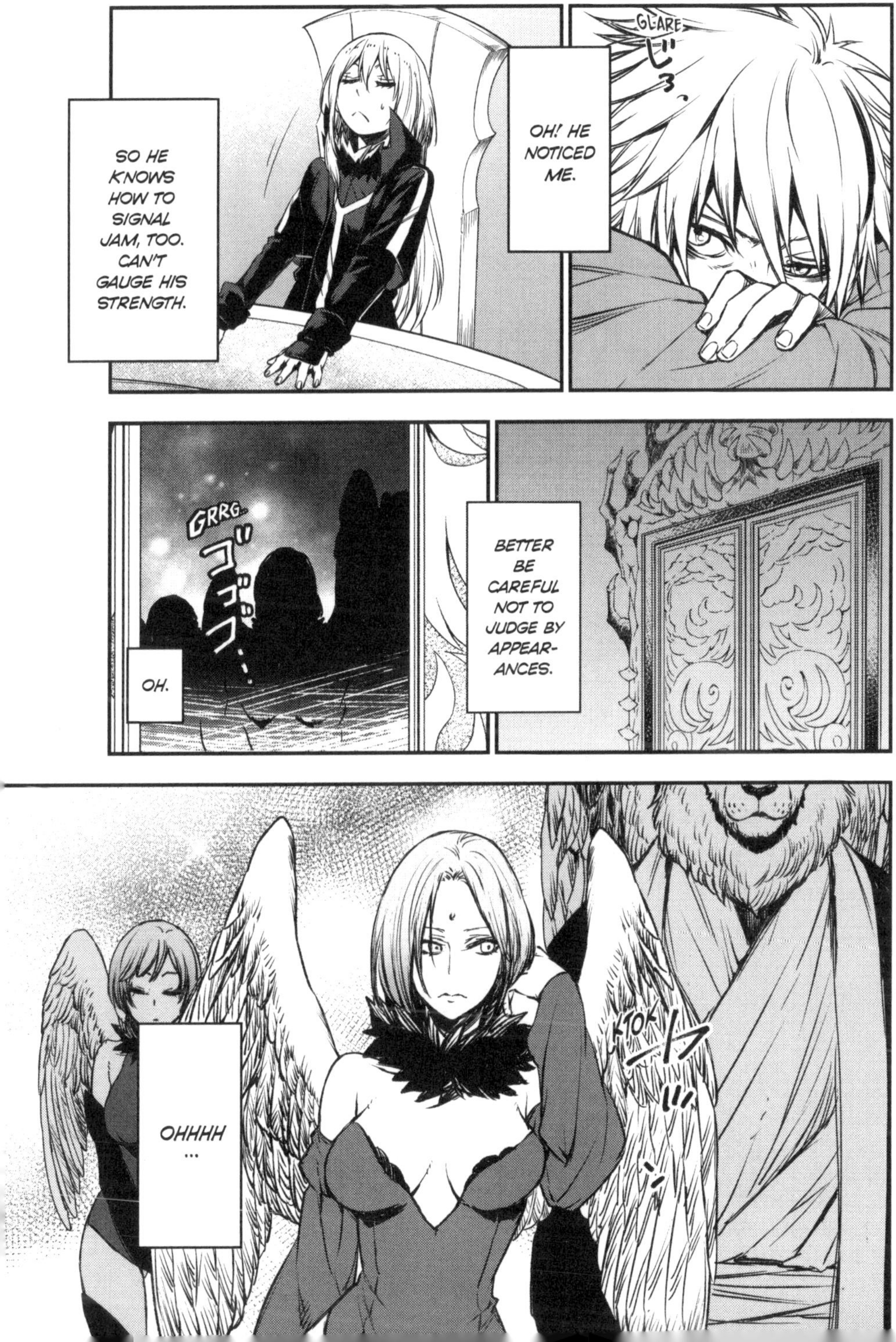
GLARE
OH! HE NOTICED ME.
SO HE KNOWS HOW TO SIGNAL JAM, TOO. CAN'T GAUGE HIS STRENGTH.
BETTER BE CAREFUL NOT TO JUDGE BY APPEARANCES.
GRRG...
OH.
KTOK
OHHHH...

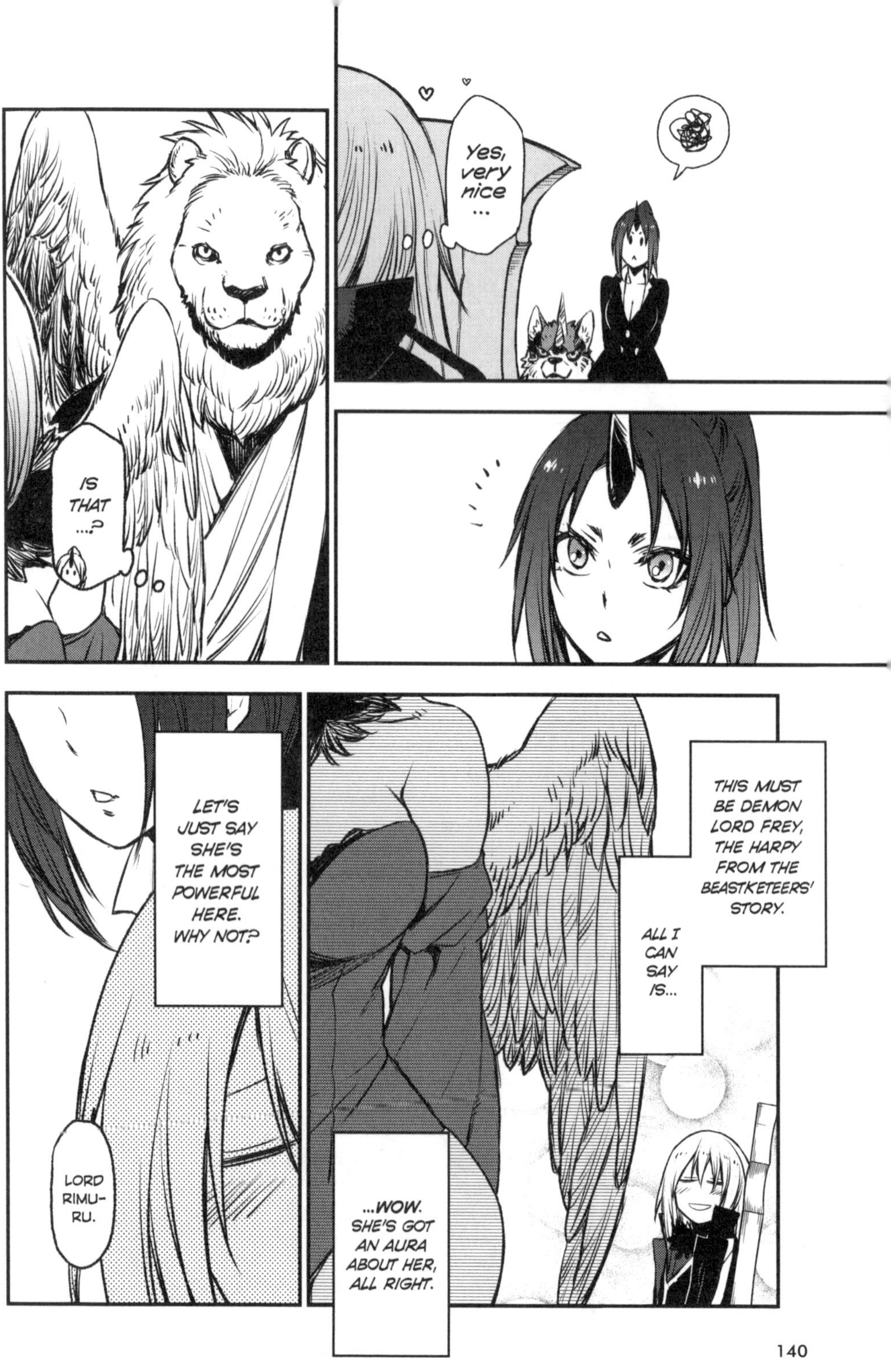
Yes, very nice...
IS THAT ...?
THIS MUST BE DEMON LORD FREY, THE HARPY FROM THE BEASTKETEERS' STORY.
ALL I CAN SAY IS...
...WOW. SHE'S GOT AN AURA ABOUT HER, ALL RIGHT.
LET'S JUST SAY SHE'S THE MOST POWERFUL HERE. WHY NOT?
LORD RIMURU.

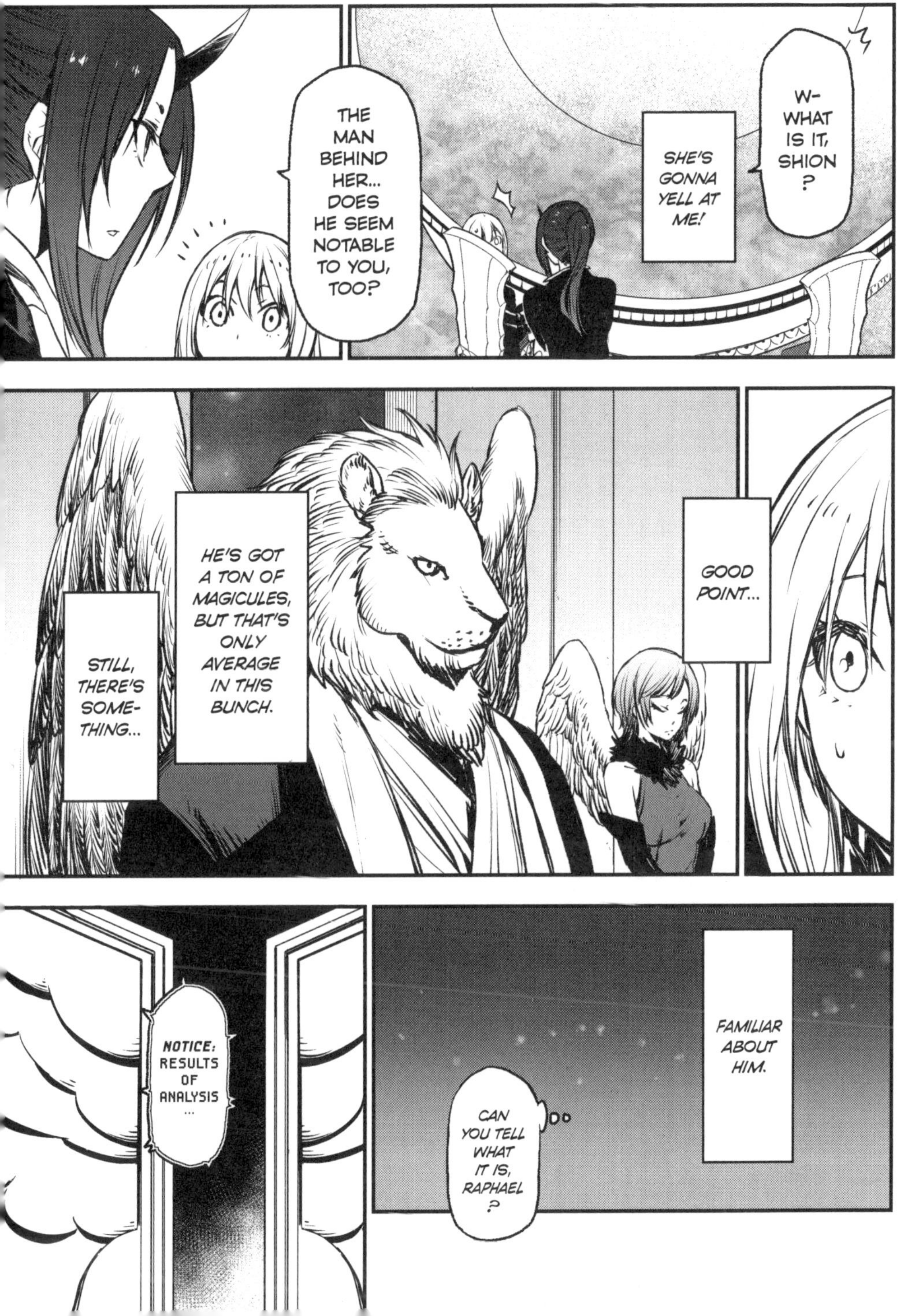
W-WHAT IS IT, SHION?
SHE'S GONNA YELL AT ME!
THE MAN BEHIND HER... DOES HE SEEM NOTABLE TO YOU, TOO?
GOOD POINT...
HE'S GOT A TON OF MAGICULES, BUT THAT'S ONLY AVERAGE IN THIS BUNCH.
STILL, THERE'S SOME-THING...
FAMILIAR ABOUT HIM.
CAN YOU TELL WHAT IT IS, RAPHAEL?
NOTICE: RESULTS OF ANALYSIS...

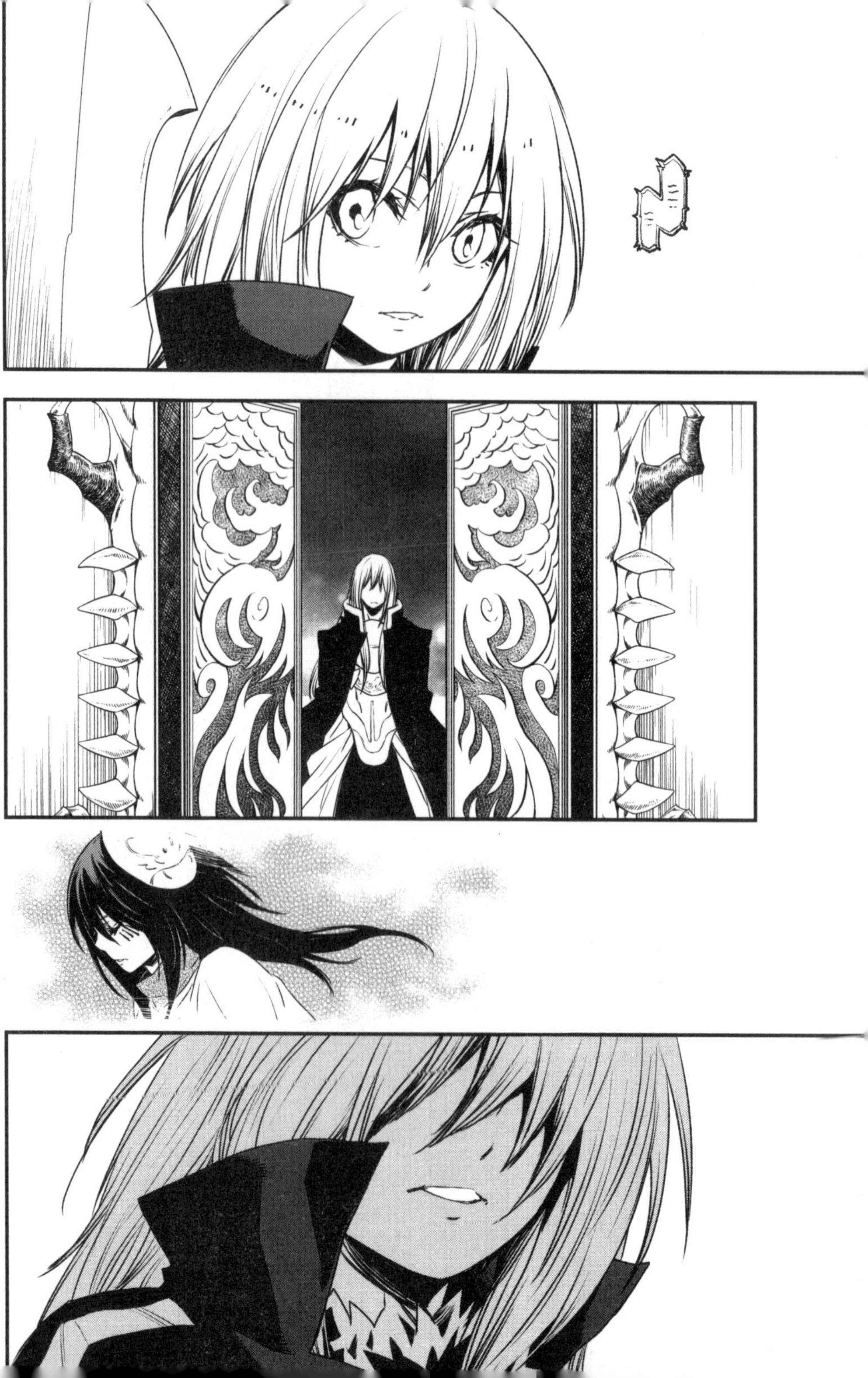

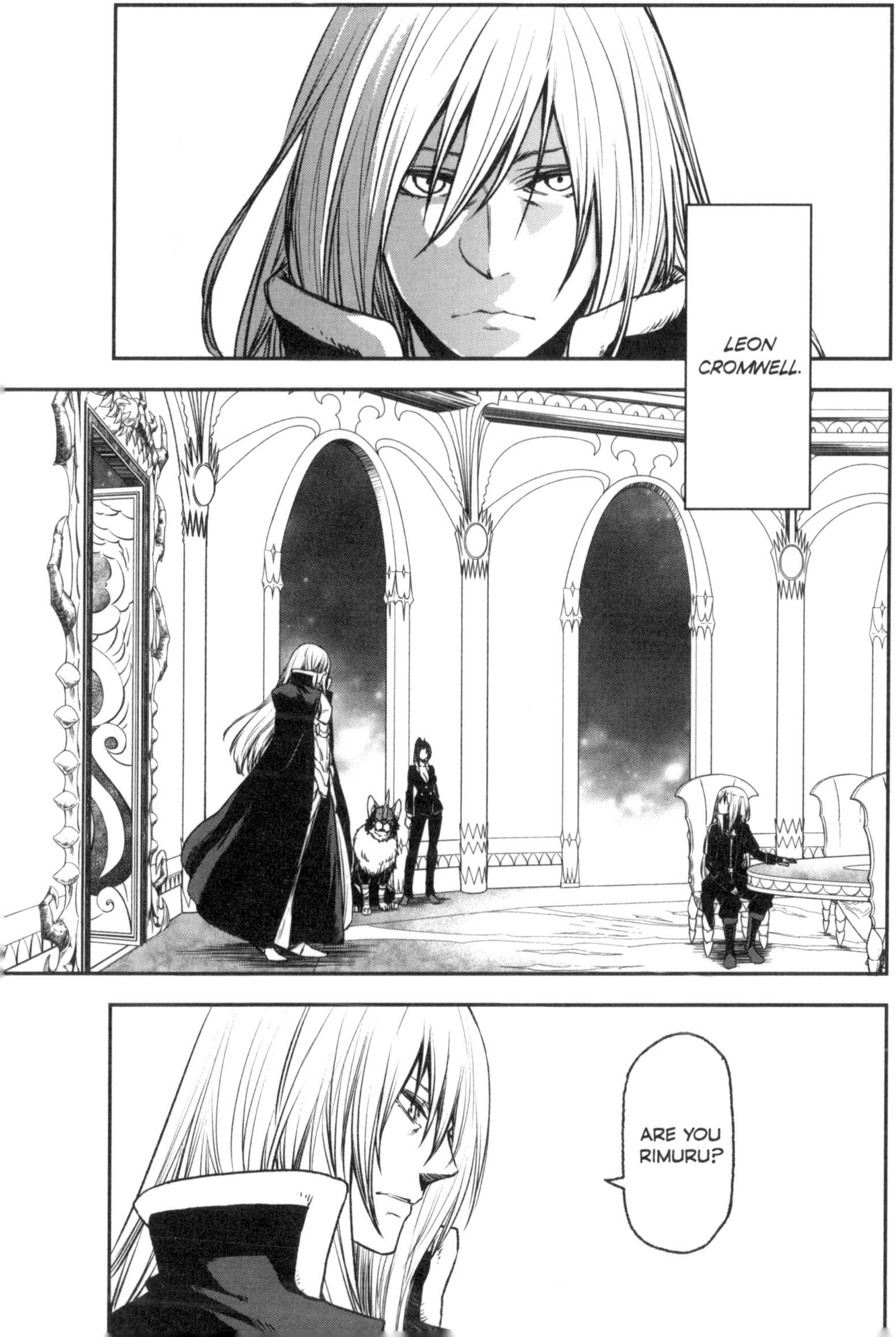
LEON
CROMWELL.
ARE YOU
RIMURU?

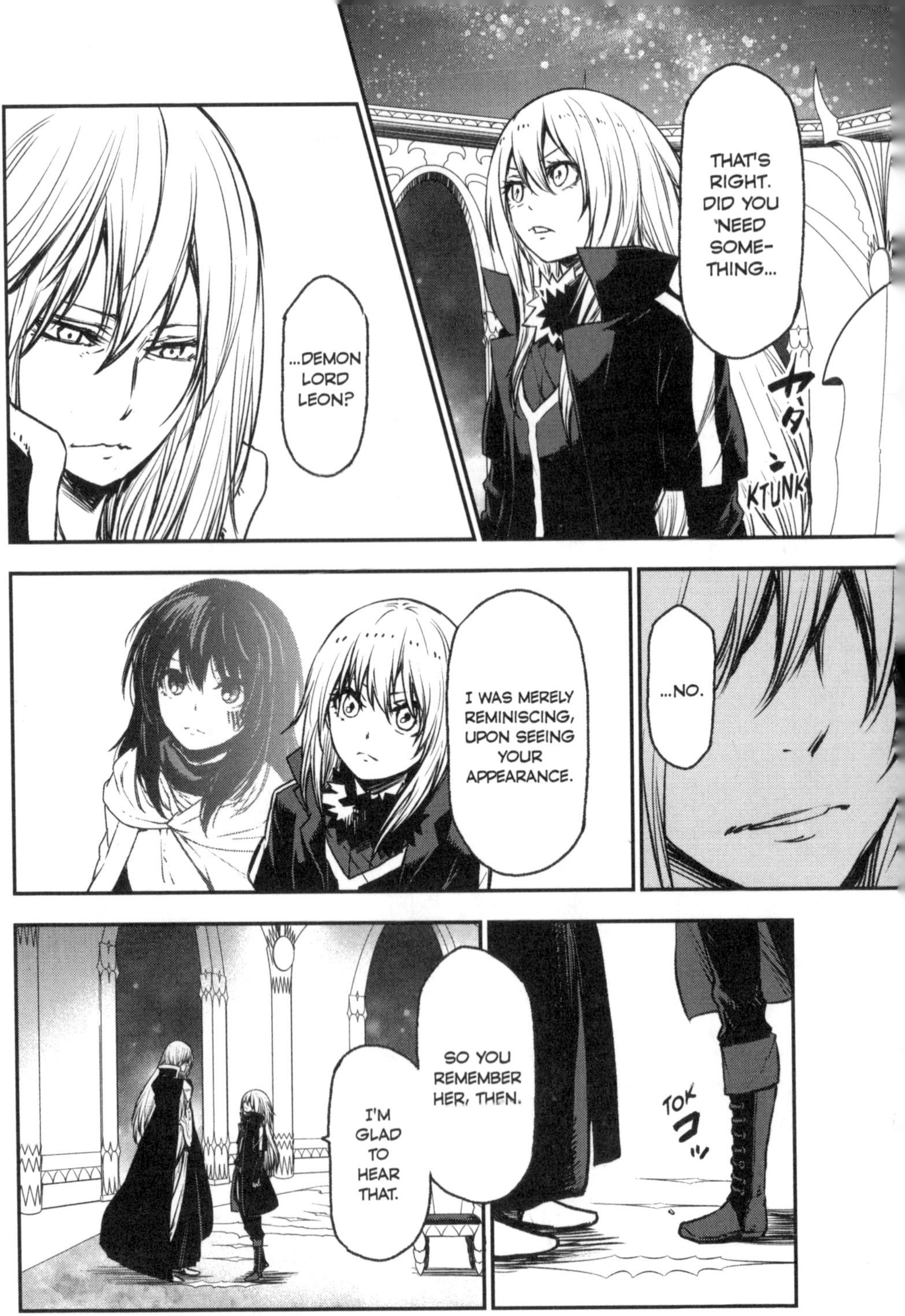
THAT'S RIGHT. DID YOU NEED SOMETHING...
KTUNK
...DEMON LORD LEON?
...NO.
I WAS MERELY REMINISCING, UPON SEEING YOUR APPEARANCE.
TOK
SO YOU REMEMBER HER, THEN.
I'M GLAD TO HEAR THAT.

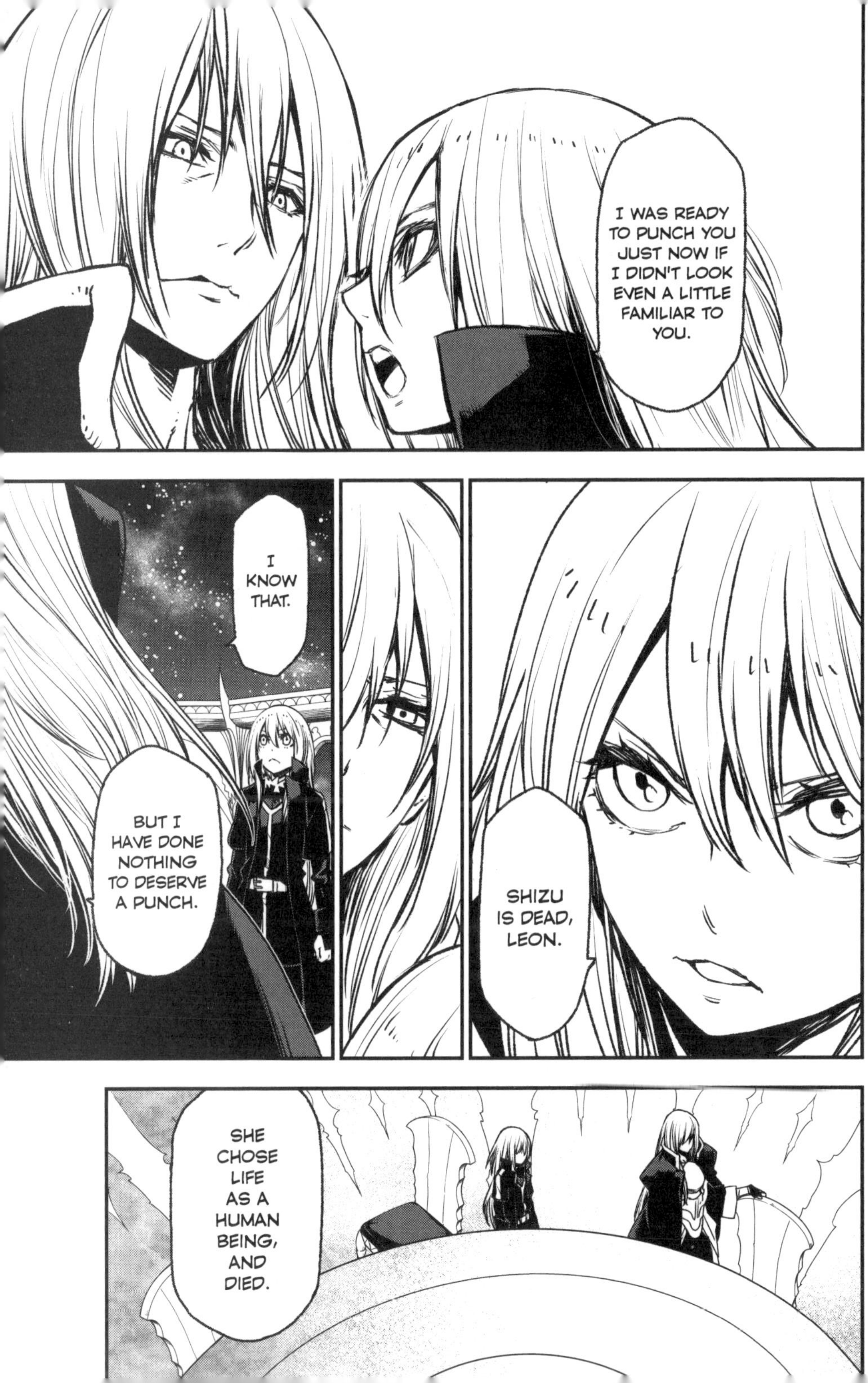
I WAS READY TO PUNCH YOU JUST NOW IF I DIDN'T LOOK EVEN A LITTLE FAMILIAR TO YOU.
SHIZU IS DEAD, LEON.
I KNOW THAT.
BUT I HAVE DONE NOTHING TO DESERVE A PUNCH.
SHE CHOSE LIFE AS A HUMAN BEING, AND DIED.

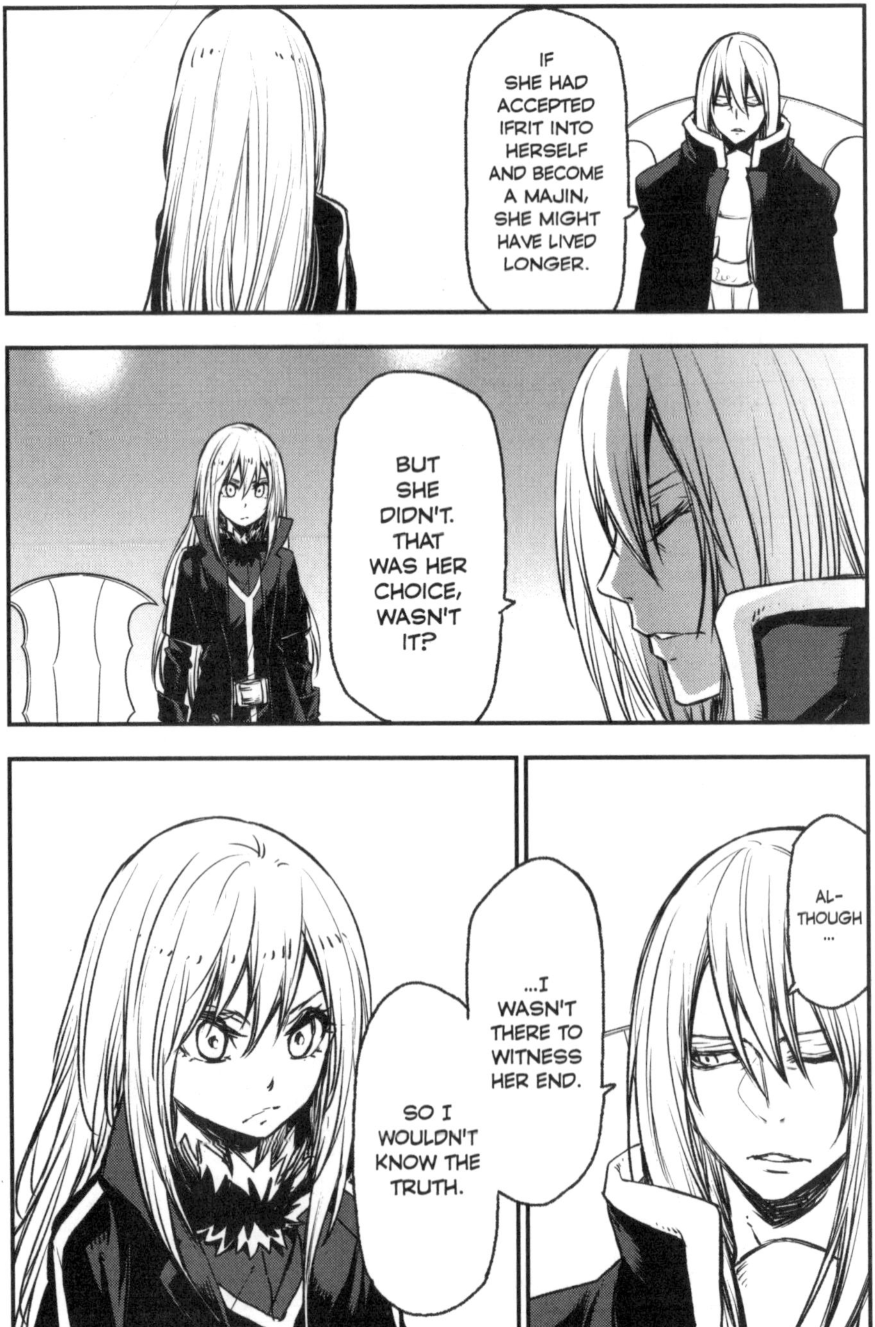
IF SHE HAD ACCEPTED IFRIT INTO HERSELF AND BECOME A MAJIN, SHE MIGHT HAVE LIVED LONGER.
BUT SHE DIDN'T. THAT WAS HER CHOICE, WASN'T IT?
AL-THOUGH...
...I WASN'T THERE TO WITNESS HER END.
SO I WOULDN'T KNOW THE TRUTH.

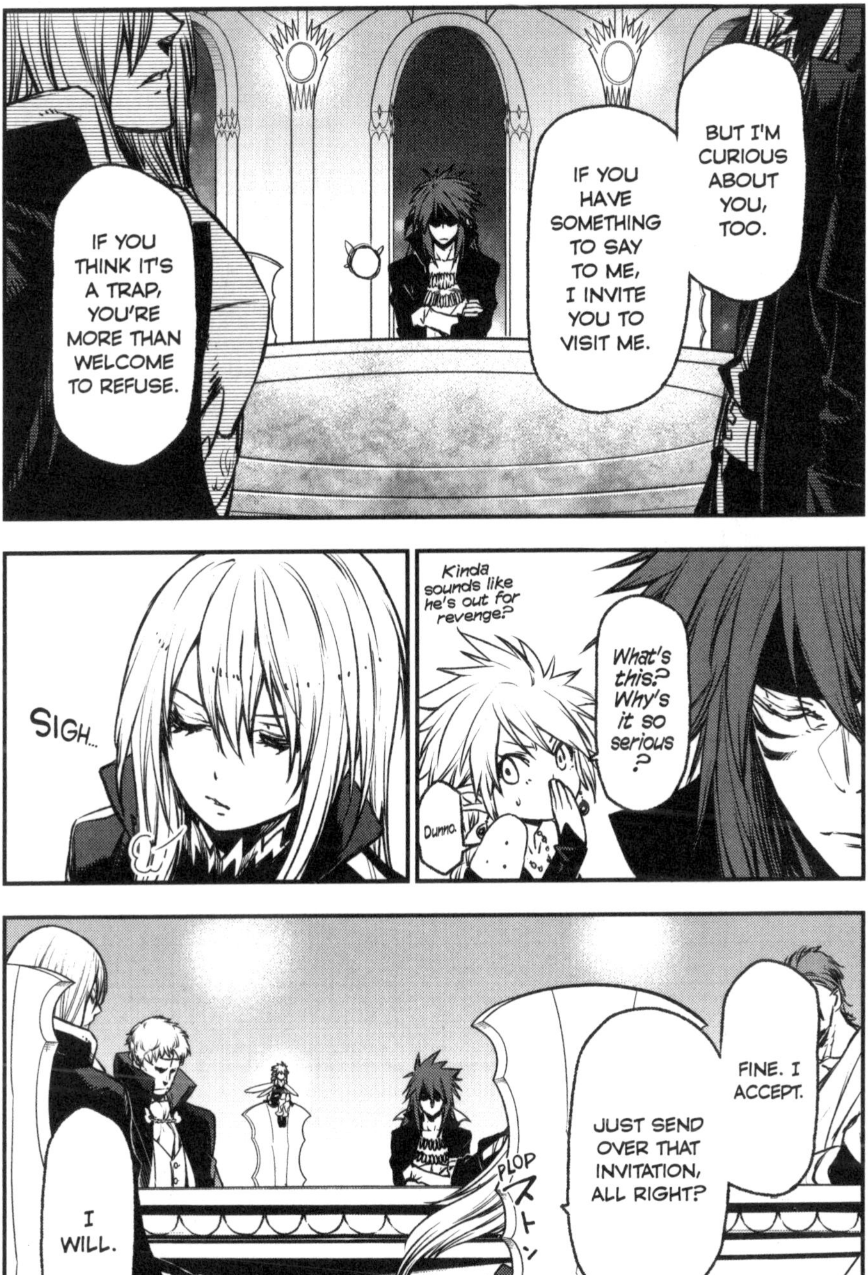
BUT I'M CURIOUS ABOUT YOU, TOO.
IF YOU HAVE SOMETHING TO SAY TO ME, I INVITE YOU TO VISIT ME.
IF YOU THINK IT'S A TRAP, YOU'RE MORE THAN WELCOME TO REFUSE.
What's this? Why's it so serious?
Kinda sounds like he's out for revenge?
Dunno.
SIGH...
FINE. I ACCEPT.
JUST SEND OVER THAT INVITATION, ALL RIGHT?
PLOP
ストン
I WILL.

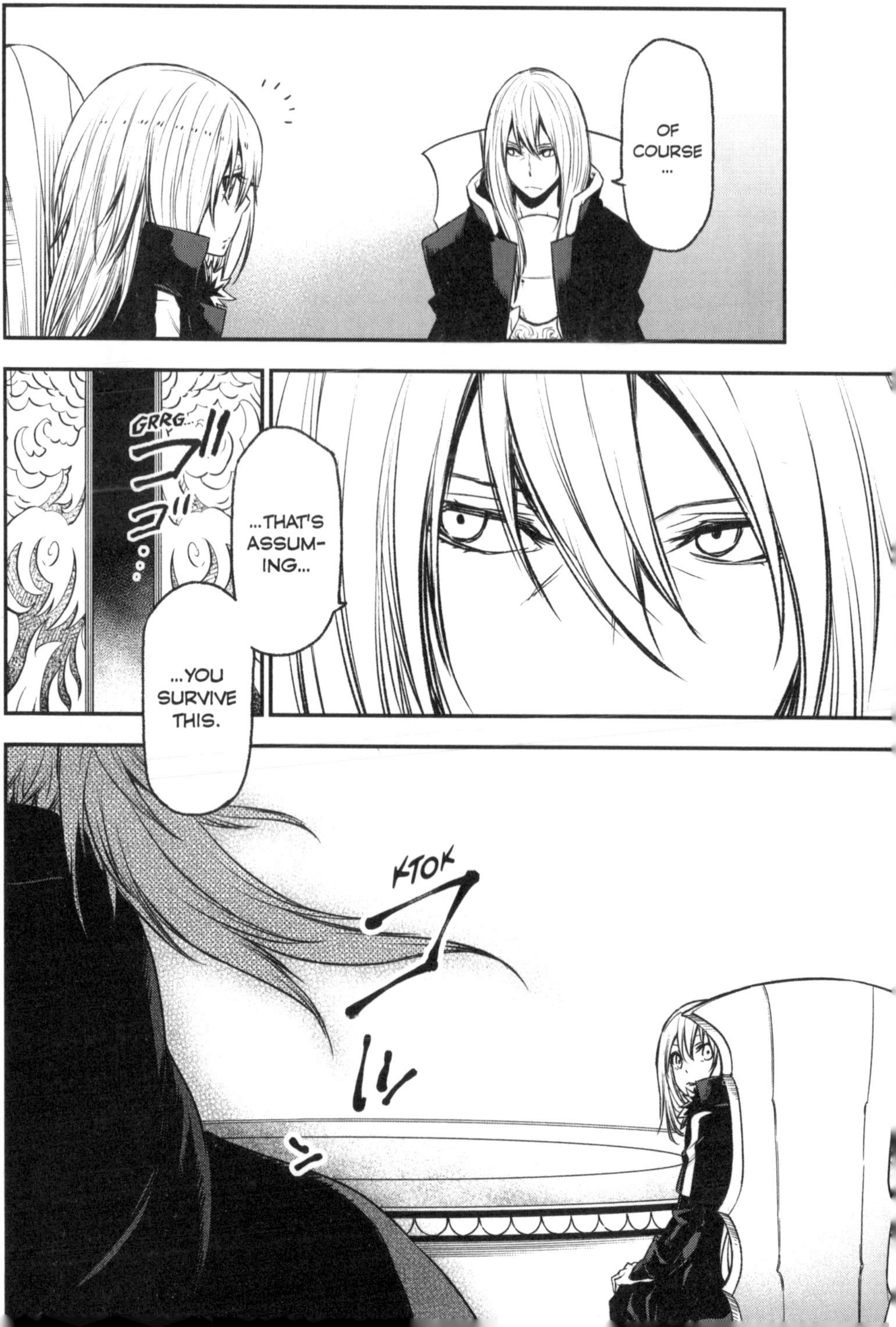
OF COURSE ...
...THAT'S ASSUM-ING...
...YOU SURVIVE THIS.
GRRG...
KTOK

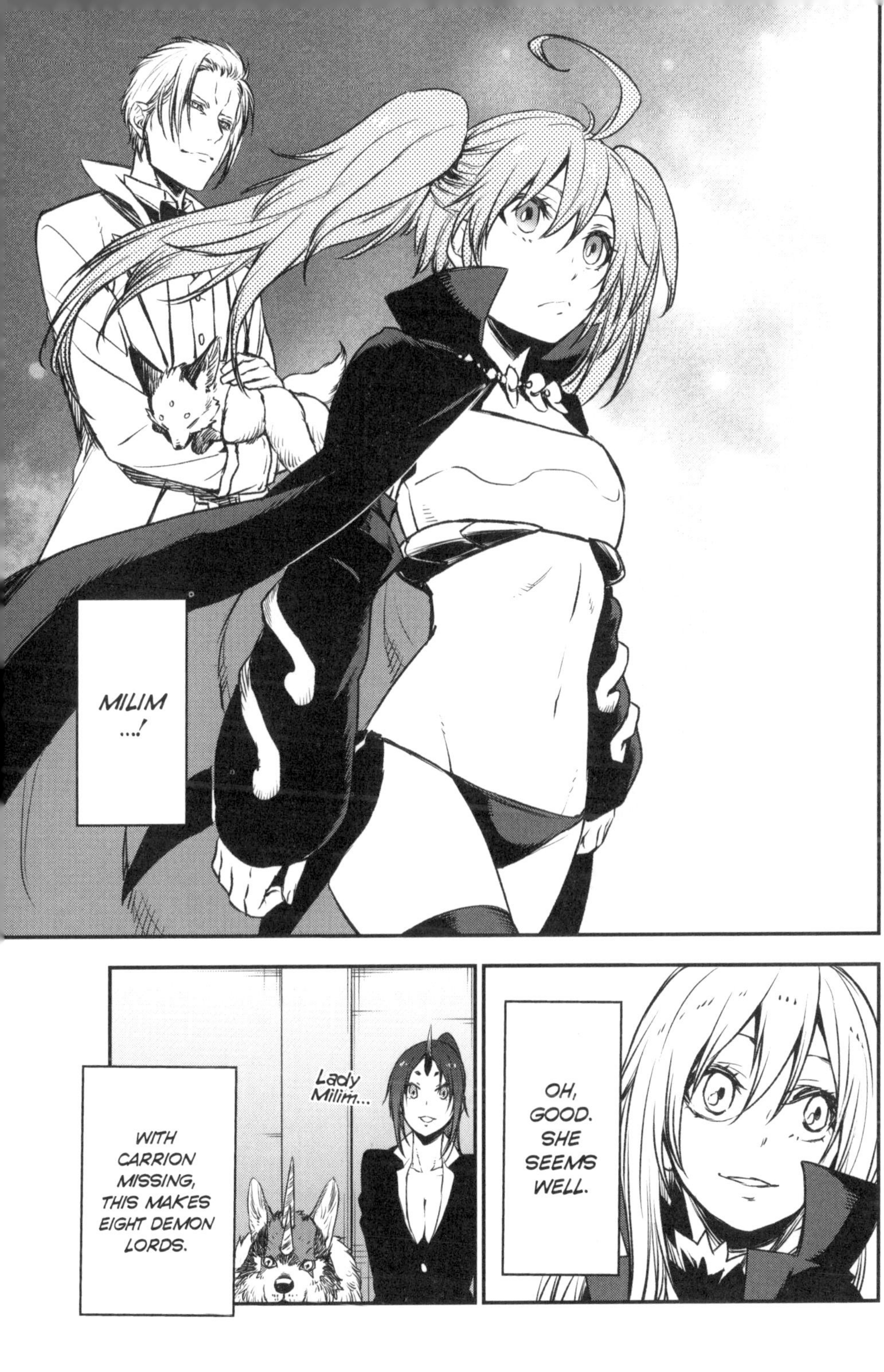
MILIM ...!
OH, GOOD. SHE SEEMS WELL.
Lady Milim...
WITH CARRION MISSING, THIS MAKES EIGHT DEMON LORDS.

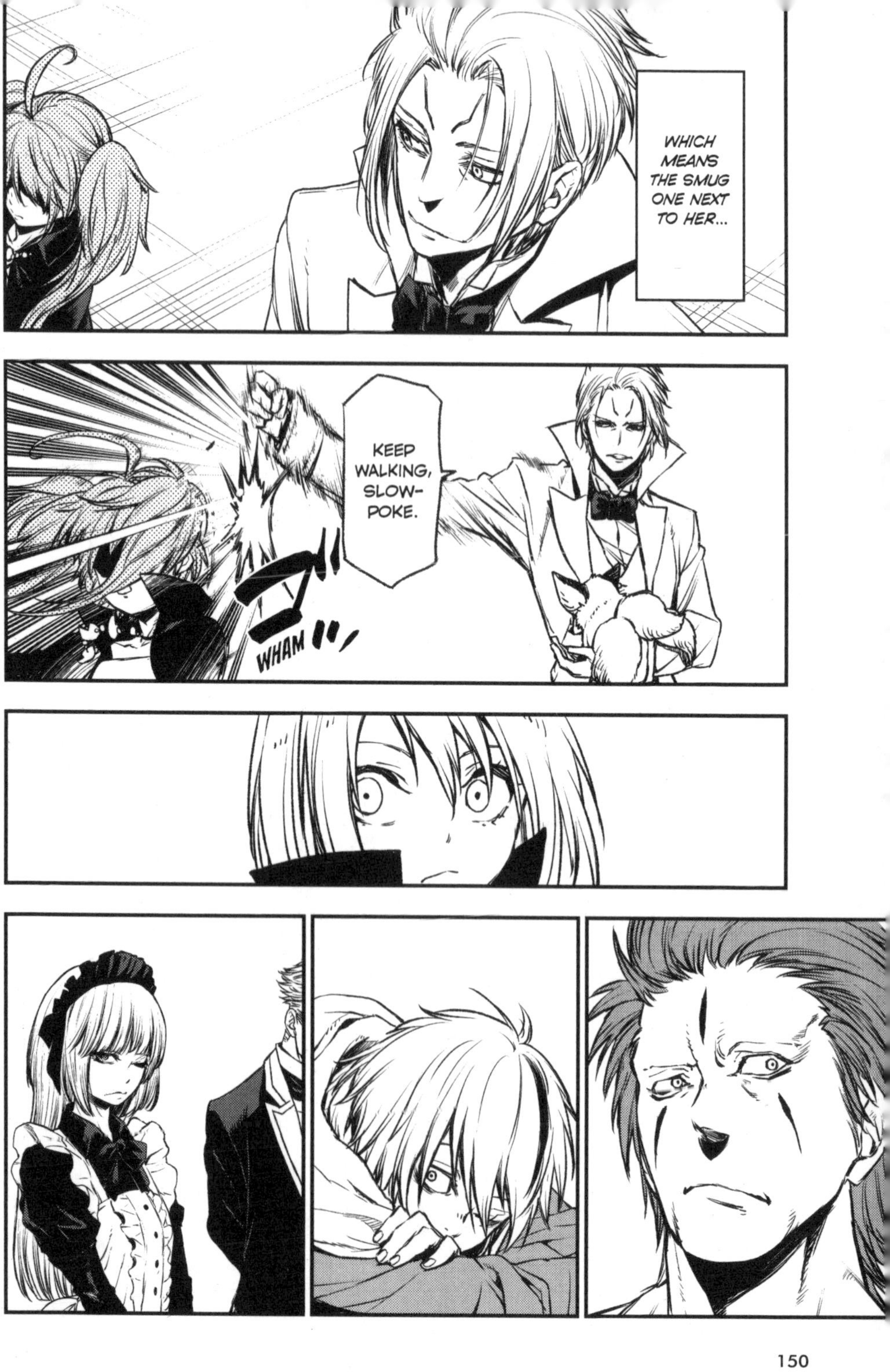
WHICH MEANS THE SMUG ONE NEXT TO HER...
KEEP WALKING, SLOW-POKE.
WHAM

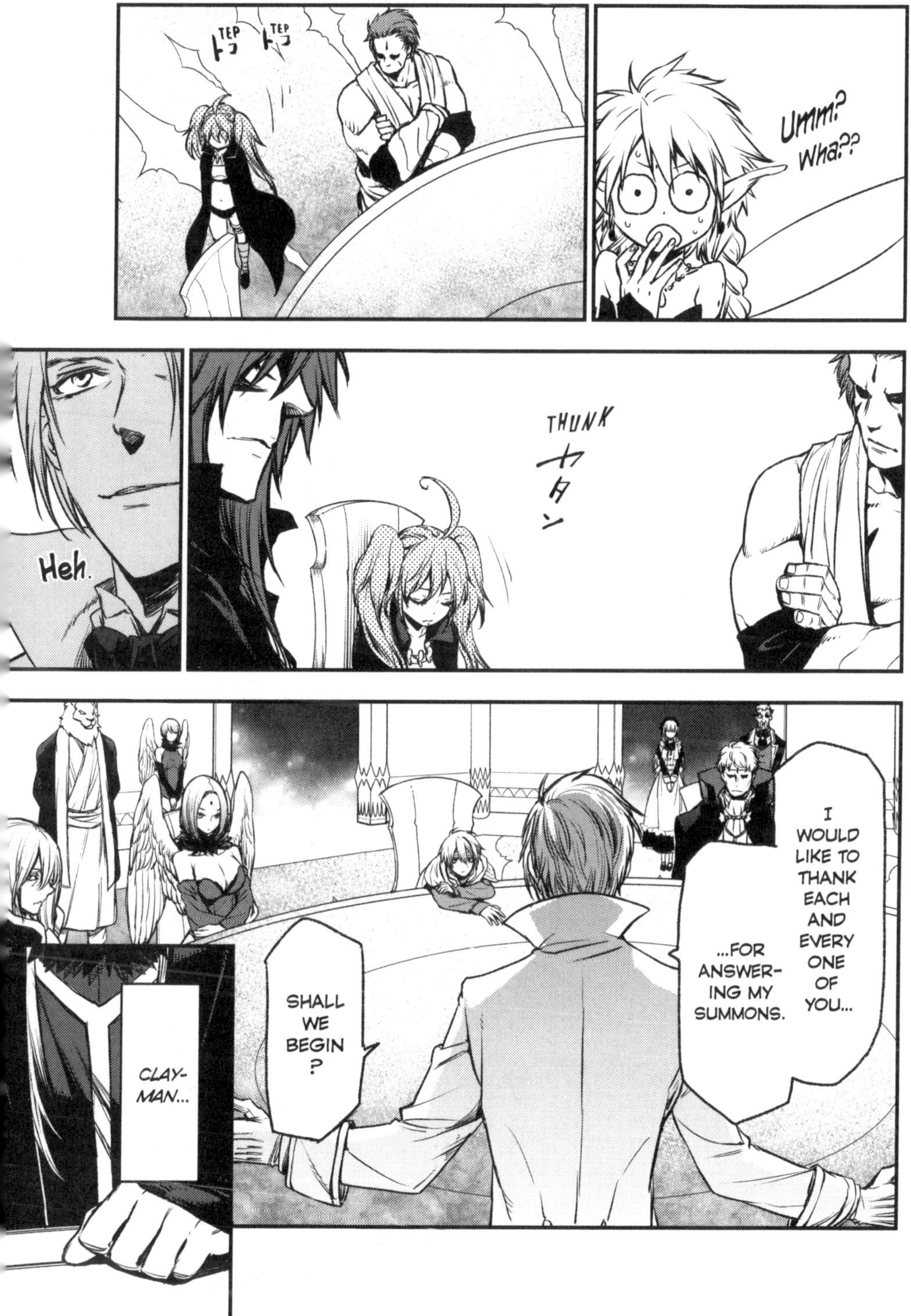
Umm? Wha??
TEP TEP
THUNK
Heh.
I WOULD LIKE TO THANK EACH AND EVERY ONE OF YOU...
...FOR ANSWERING MY SUMMONS.
SHALL WE BEGIN?
CLAY-MAN...

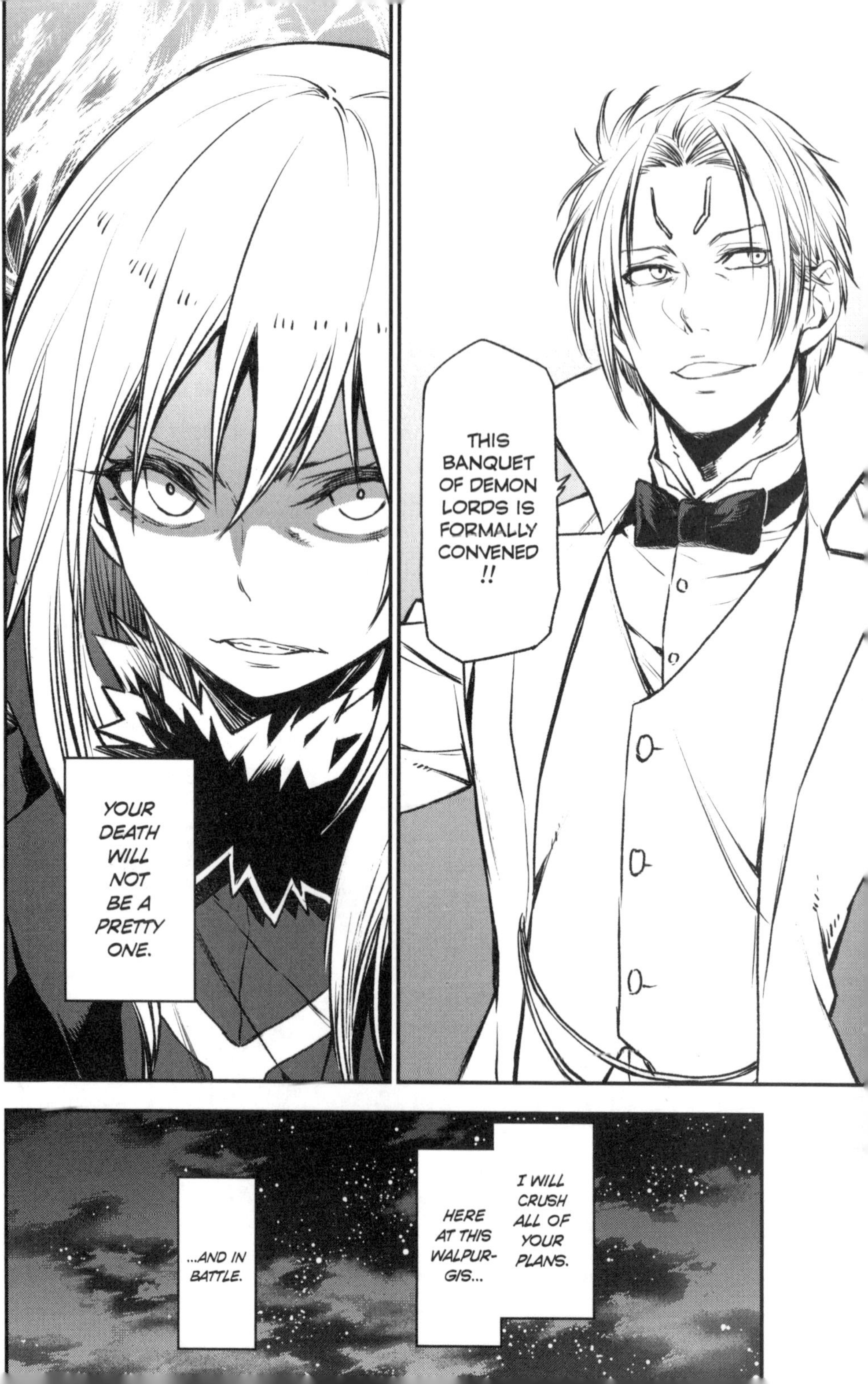
THIS BANQUET OF DEMON LORDS IS FORMALLY CONVENED !!
YOUR DEATH WILL NOT BE A PRETTY ONE.
I WILL CRUSH ALL OF YOUR PLANS.
HERE AT THIS WALPUR-GIS...
...AND IN BATTLE.

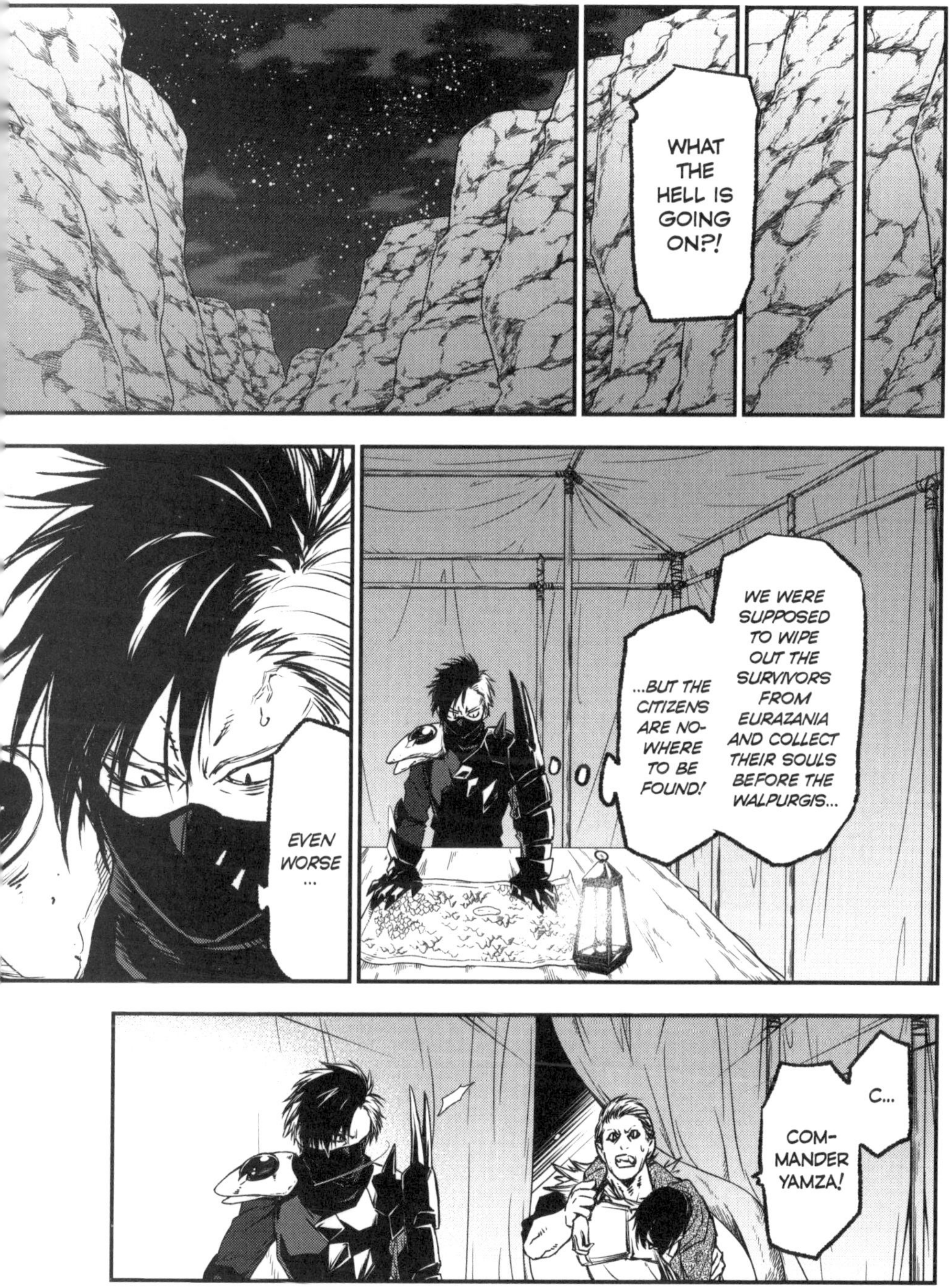
WHAT THE HELL IS GOING ON?!
WE WERE SUPPOSED TO WIPE OUT THE SURVIVORS FROM EURAZANIA AND COLLECT THEIR SOULS BEFORE THE WALPURGIS...
...BUT THE CITIZENS ARE NO-WHERE TO BE FOUND!
EVEN WORSE...
C...
COM-MANDER YAMZA!

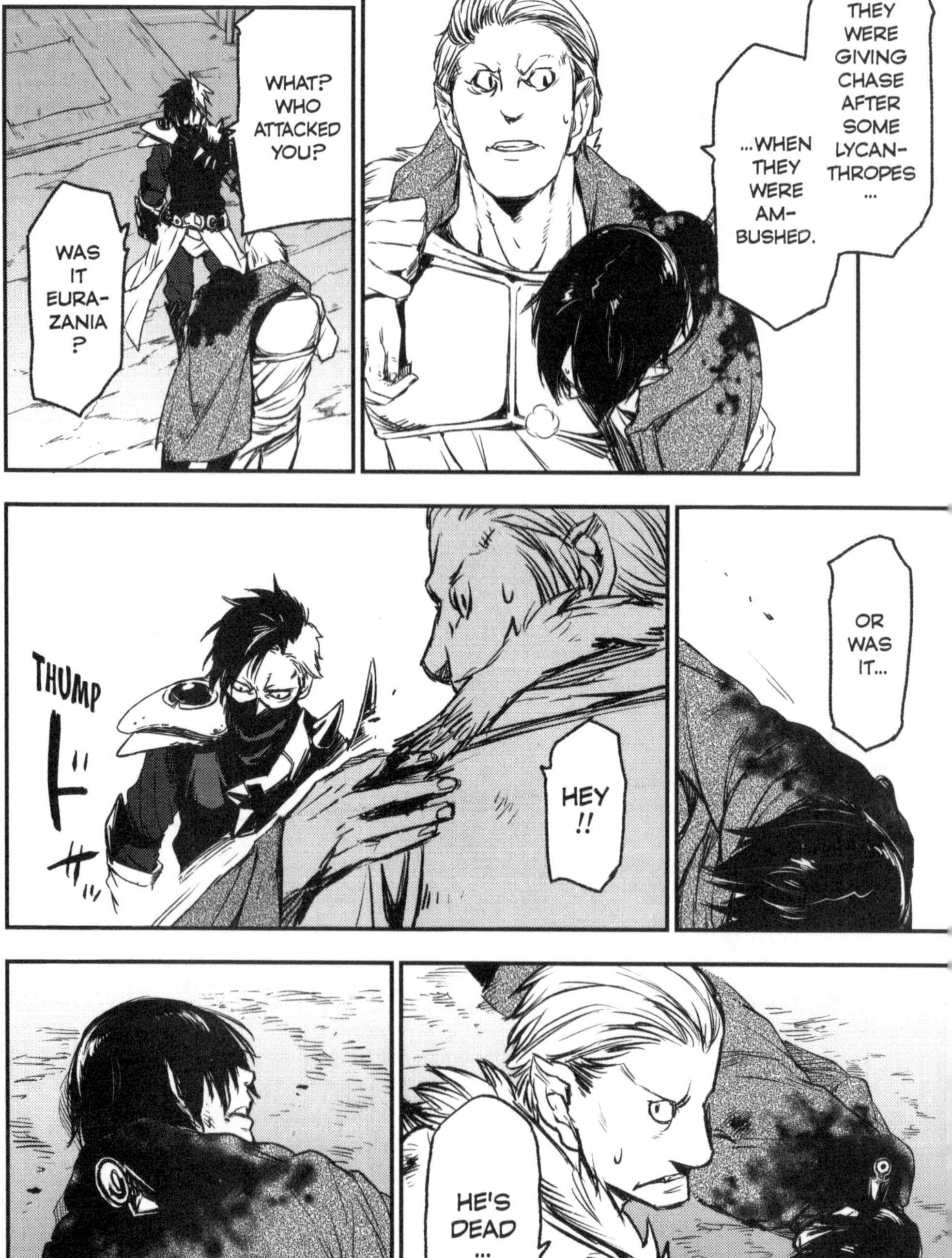

THEY WERE GIVING CHASE AFTER SOME LYCAN-THROPES...
...WHEN THEY WERE AM-BUSHED.
WHAT? WHO ATTACKED YOU?
WAS IT EURA-ZANIA?
OR WAS IT...
THUMP
HEY!!
HE'S DEAD...

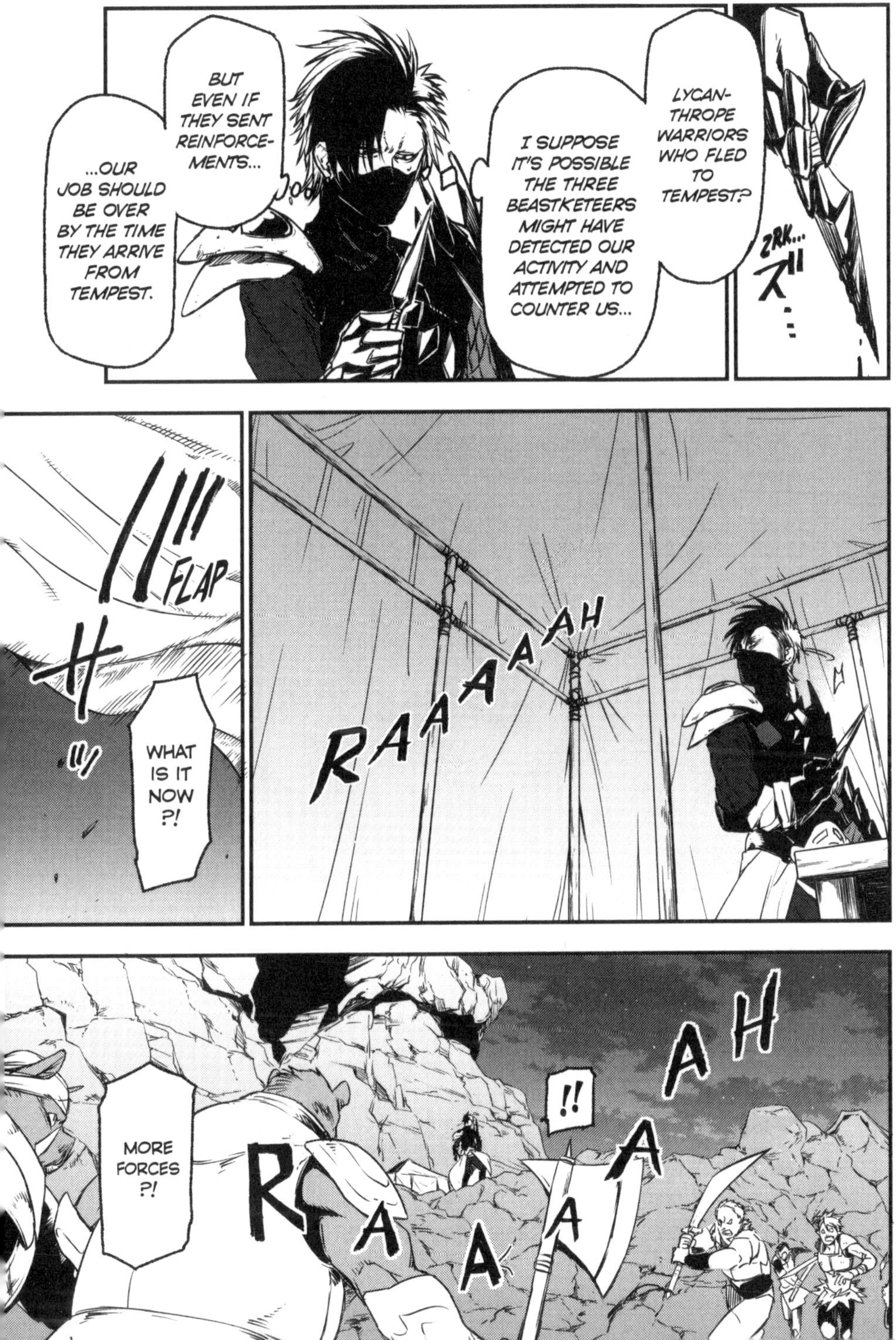
ZRK...
ズ...
LYCAN-THROPE WARRIORS WHO FLED TO TEMPEST?
I SUPPOSE IT'S POSSIBLE THE THREE BEASTKETEERS MIGHT HAVE DETECTED OUR ACTIVITY AND ATTEMPTED TO COUNTER US...
BUT EVEN IF THEY SENT REINFORCE-MENTS...
...OUR JOB SHOULD BE OVER BY THE TIME THEY ARRIVE FROM TEMPEST.
RAAAAAAH
FLAP
WHAT IS IT NOW?!
!!
RAAAAAAAH
MORE FORCES?!

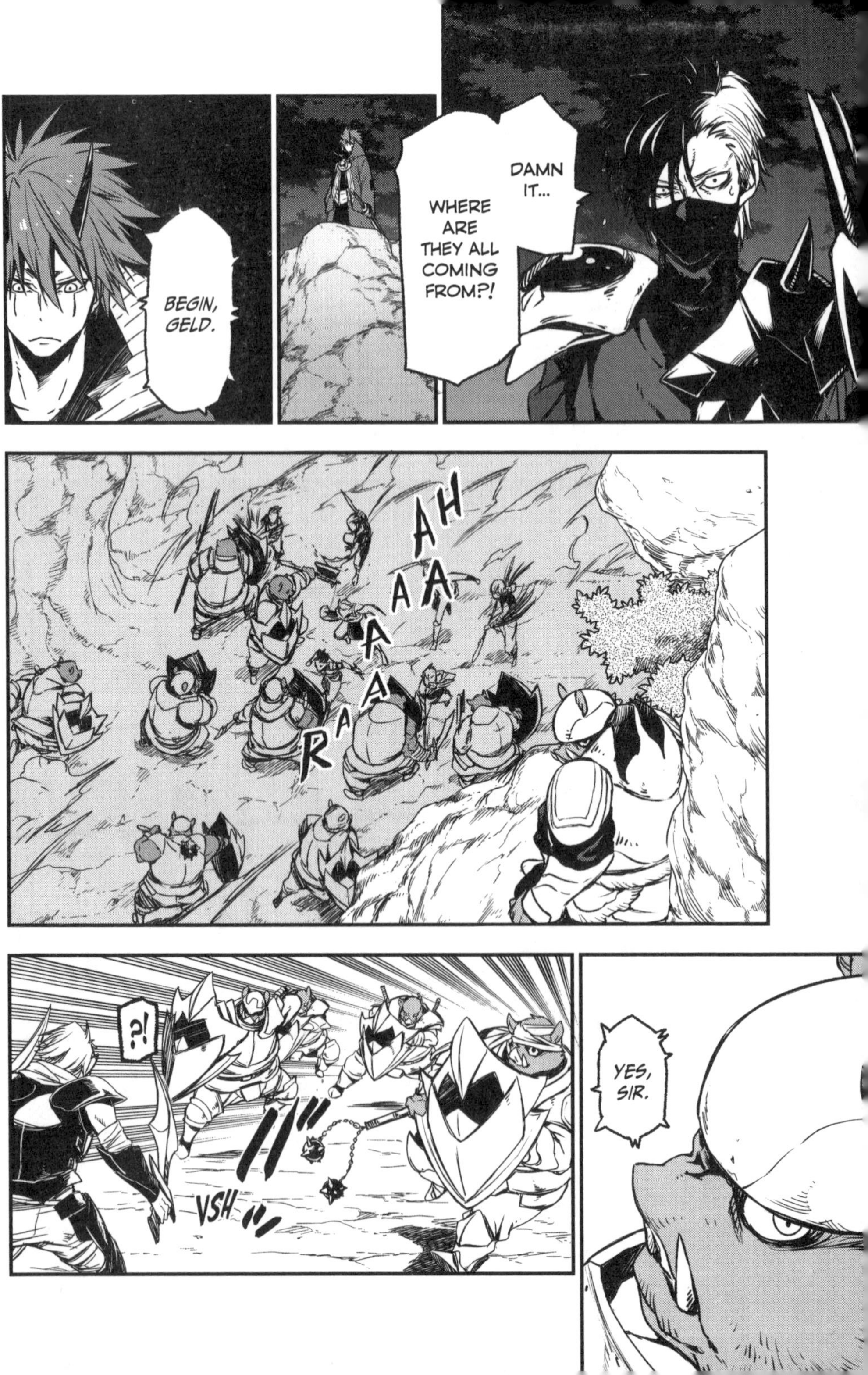
DAMN IT...
WHERE ARE THEY ALL COMING FROM?!
BEGIN, GELD.
RAAAAAAH
YES, SIR.
?!
VSH

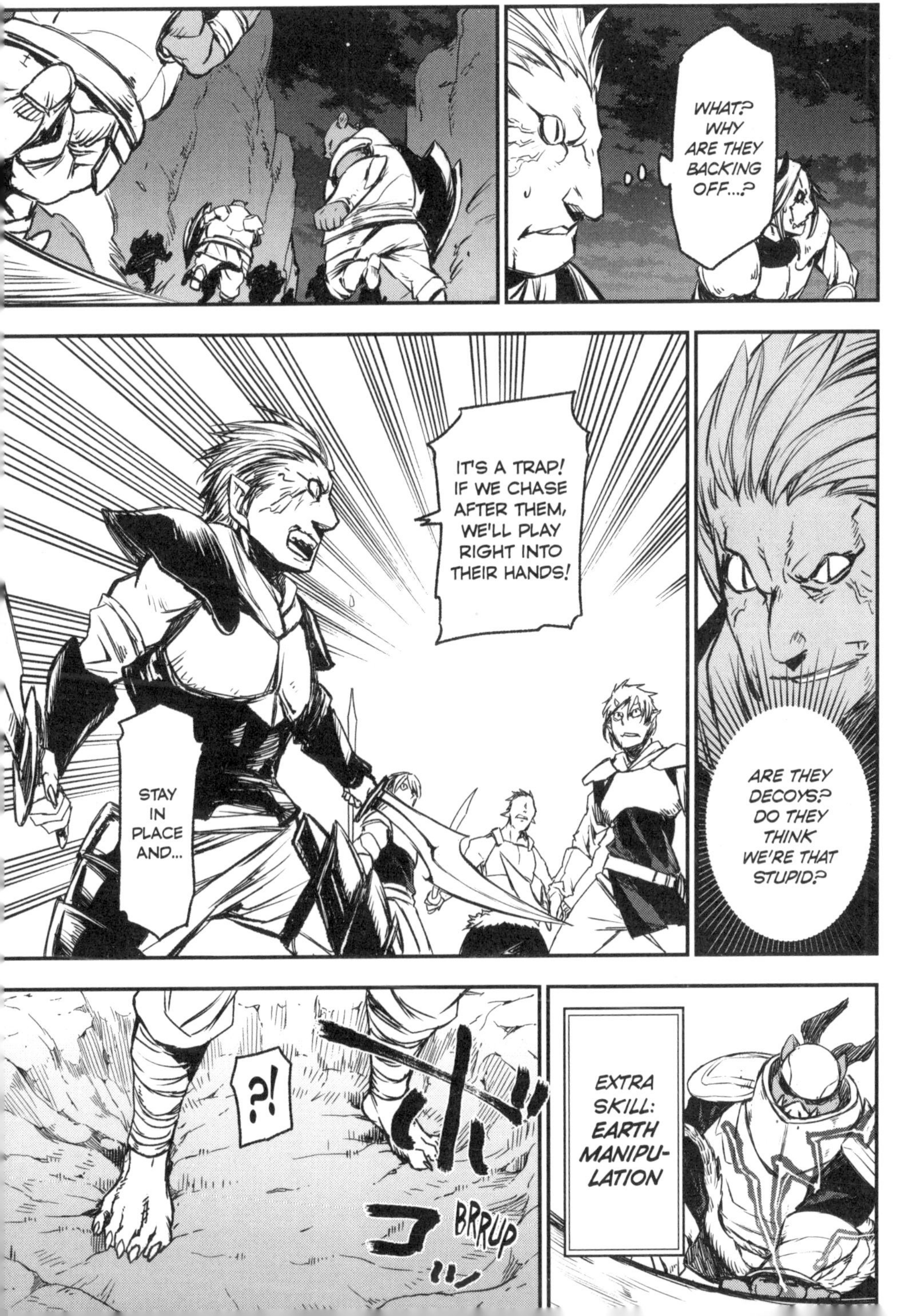
WHAT? WHY ARE THEY BACKING OFF...?
ARE THEY DECOYS? DO THEY THINK WE'RE THAT STUPID?
IT'S A TRAP! IF WE CHASE AFTER THEM, WE'LL PLAY RIGHT INTO THEIR HANDS!
STAY IN PLACE AND...
EXTRA SKILL: EARTH MANIPULATION
?!
BRRUP

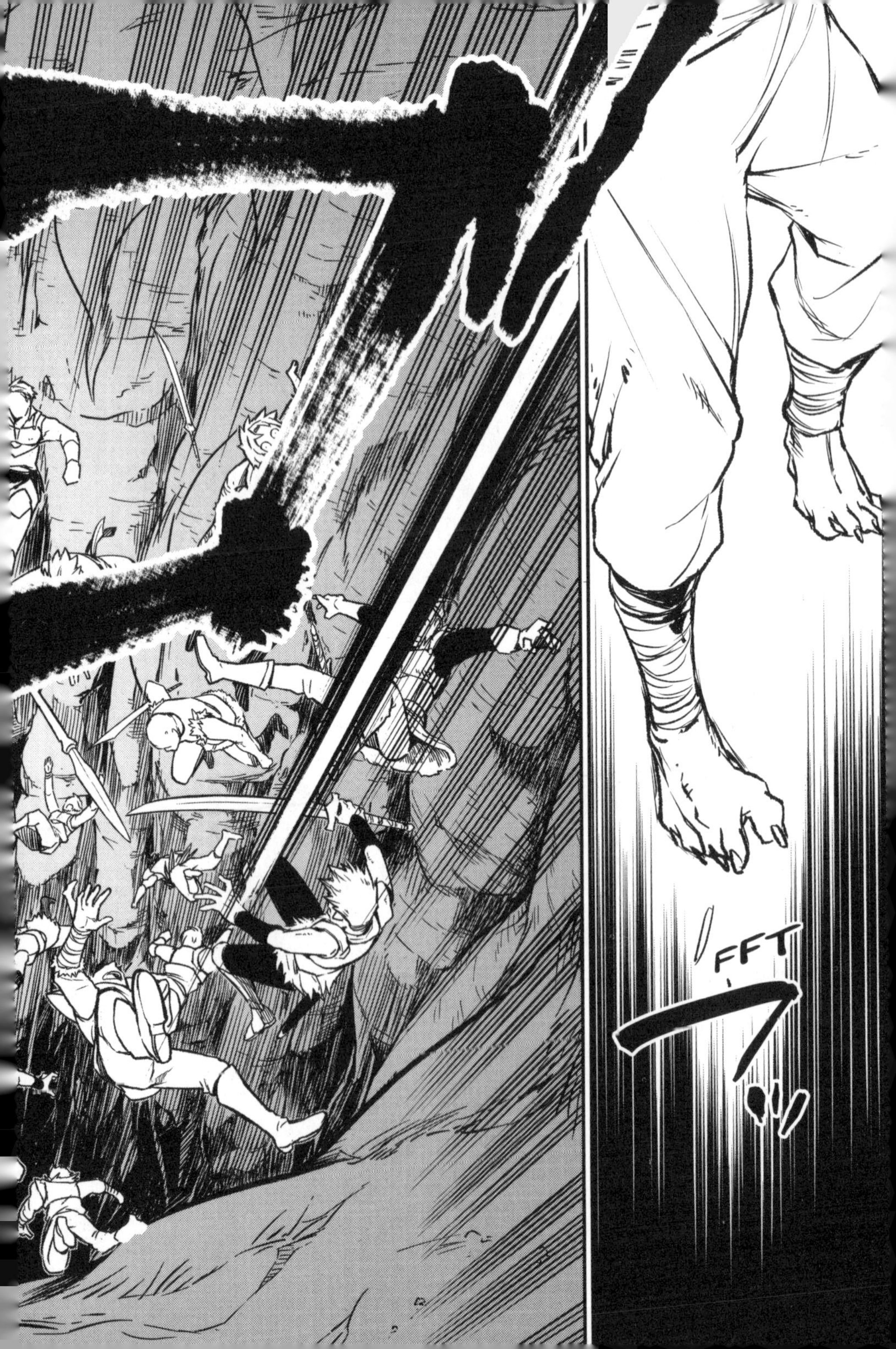
FFT

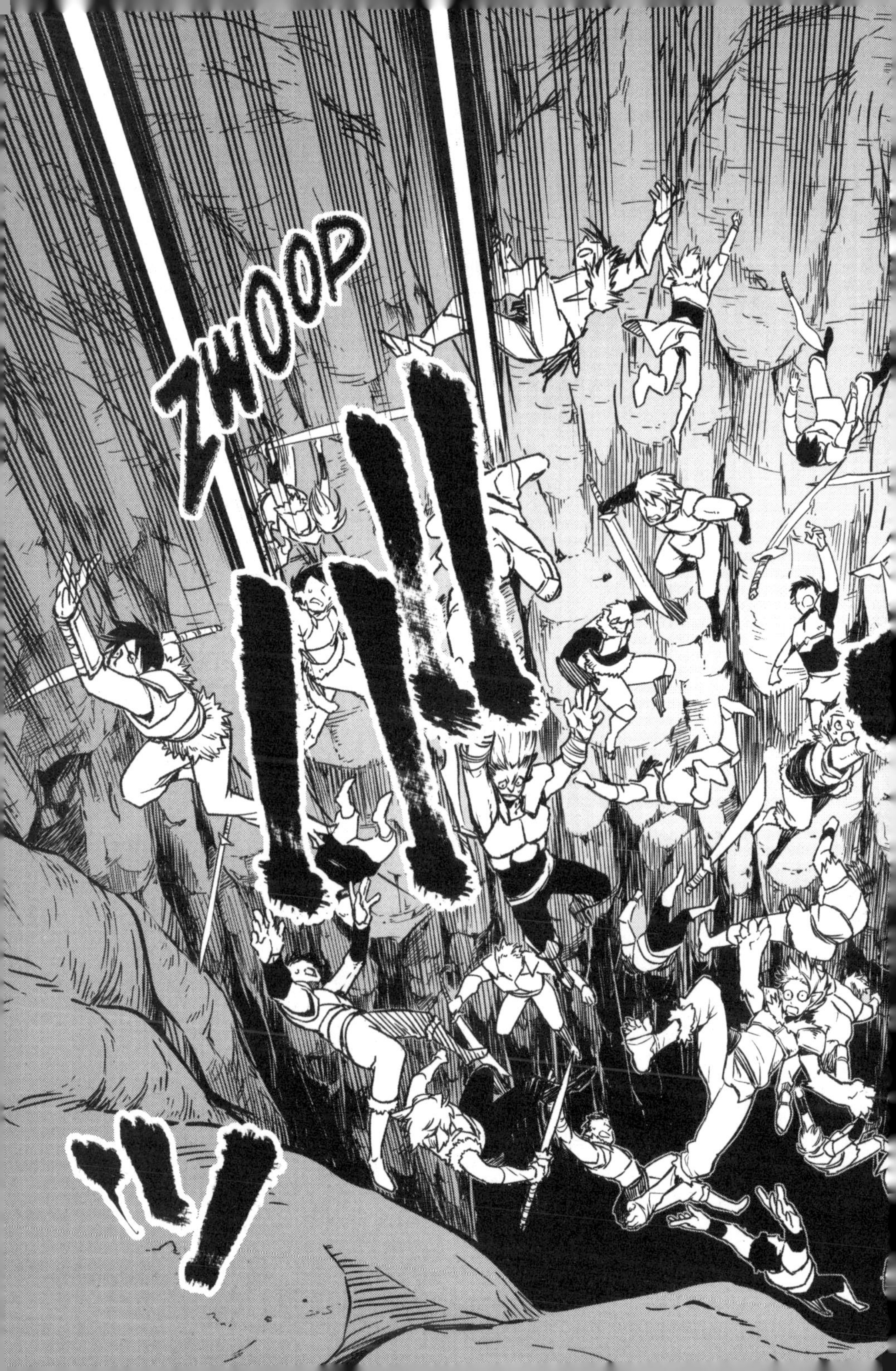
ZWOOP

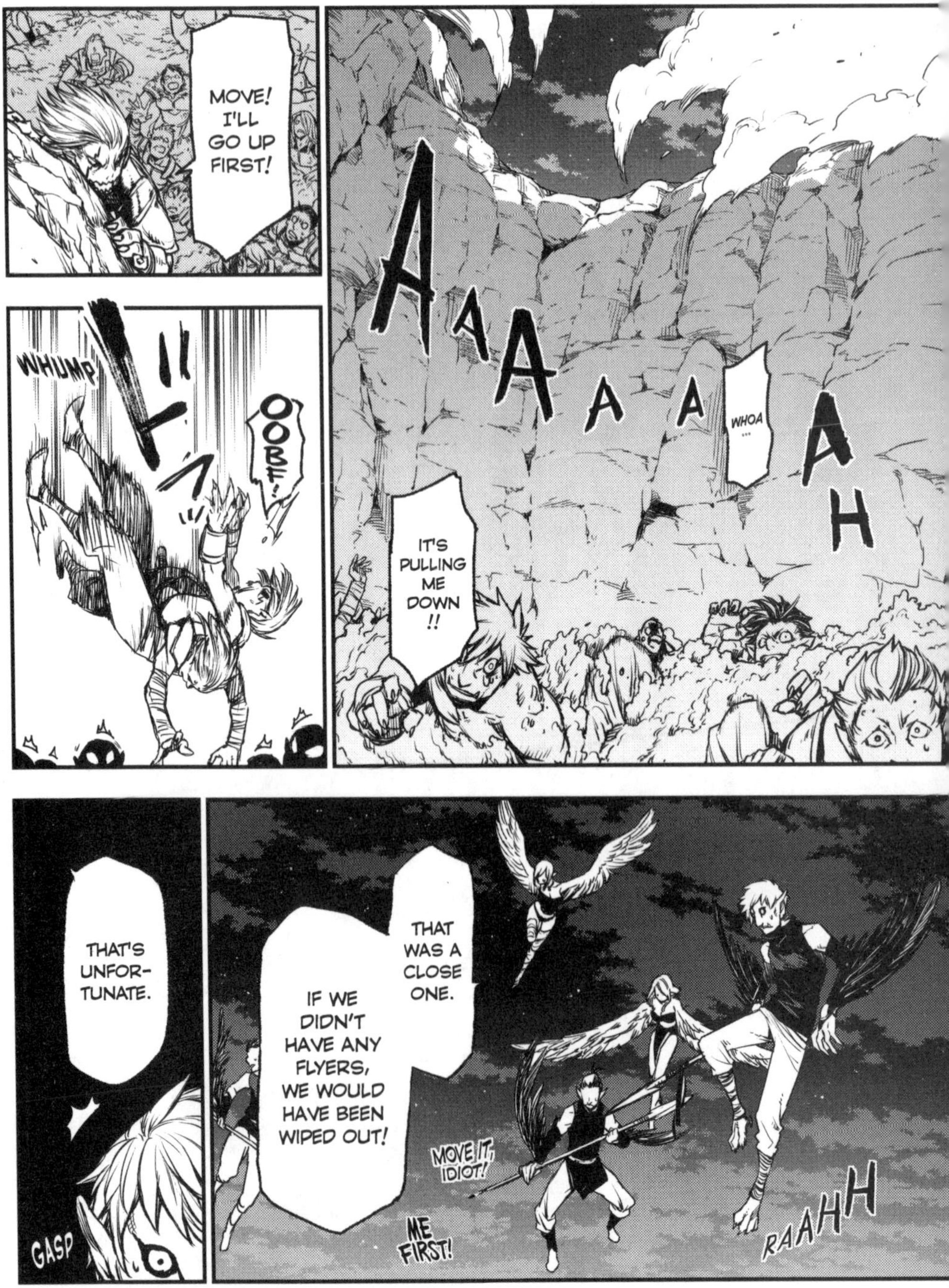
AAAAAAH
WHOA...
IT'S PULLING ME DOWN!!
MOVE! I'LL GO UP FIRST!
WHUMP
OOBF!
THAT WAS A CLOSE ONE.
IF WE DIDN'T HAVE ANY FLYERS, WE WOULD HAVE BEEN WIPED OUT!
MOVE IT, IDIOT!
RAAHH
ME FIRST!
THAT'S UNFOR-TUNATE.
GASP

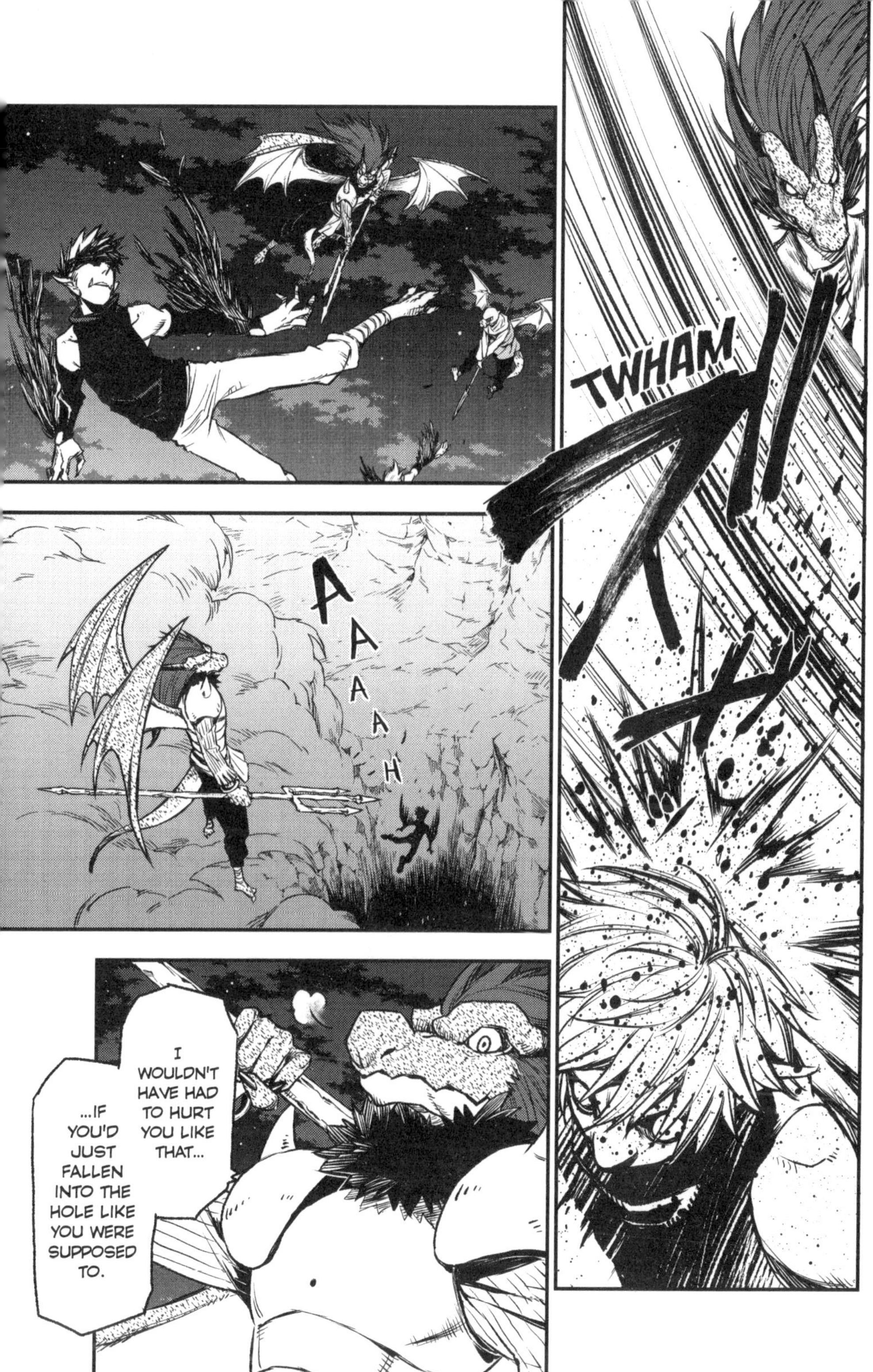
TWHAM
AAAAAH
I WOULDN'T HAVE HAD TO HURT YOU LIKE THAT...
...IF YOU'D JUST FALLEN INTO THE HOLE LIKE YOU WERE SUPPOSED TO.

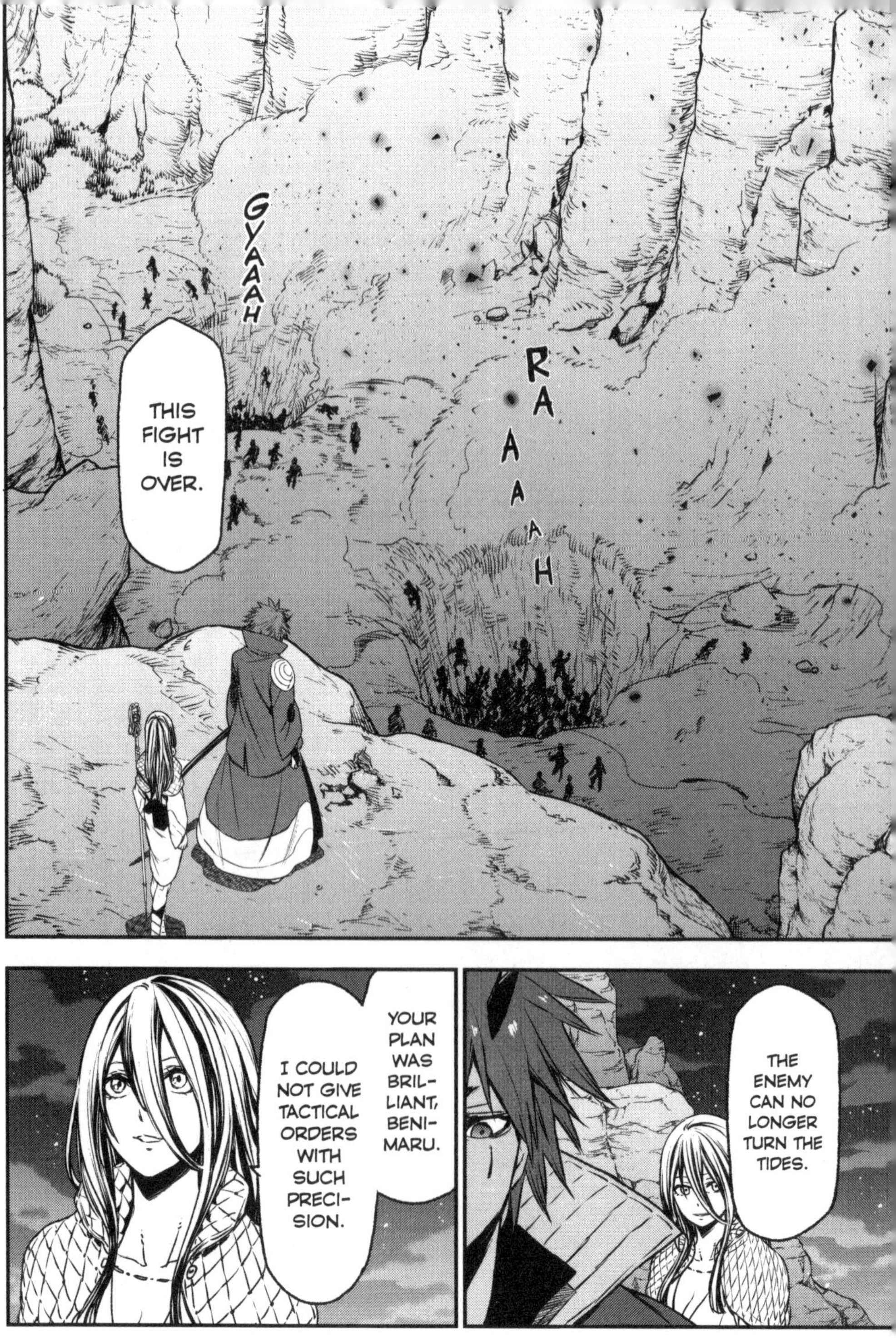
GYAAAH
RAAAAAH
THIS FIGHT IS OVER.
THE ENEMY CAN NO LONGER TURN THE TIDES.
YOUR PLAN WAS BRIL-LIANT, BENI-MARU.
I COULD NOT GIVE TACTICAL ORDERS WITH SUCH PRECI-SION.

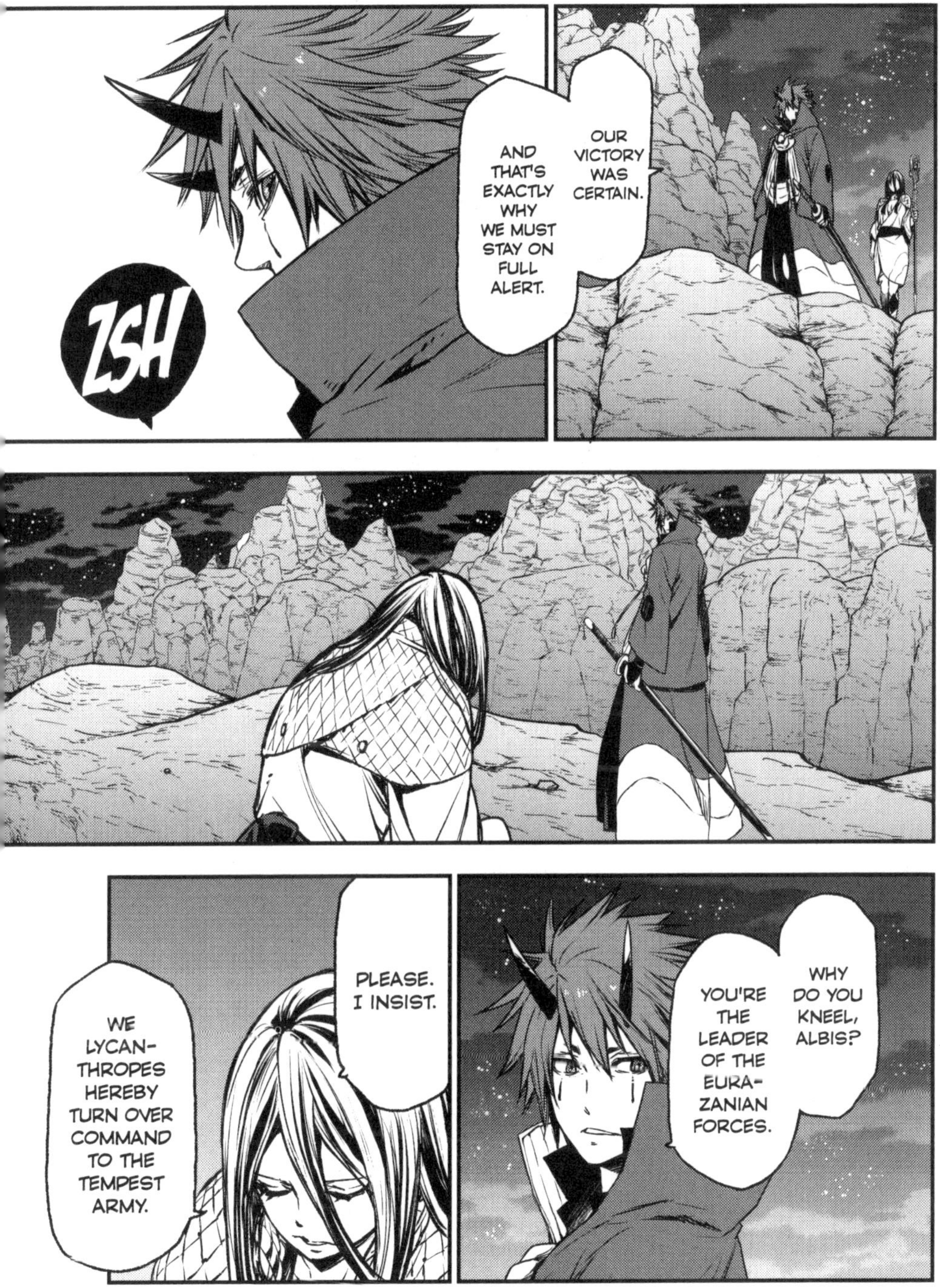
OUR VICTORY WAS CERTAIN.
AND THAT'S EXACTLY WHY WE MUST STAY ON FULL ALERT.
ZSH
WHY DO YOU KNEEL, ALBIS?
YOU'RE THE LEADER OF THE EURA-ZANIAN FORCES.
PLEASE. I INSIST.
WE LYCAN-THROPES HEREBY TURN OVER COMMAND TO THE TEMPEST ARMY.

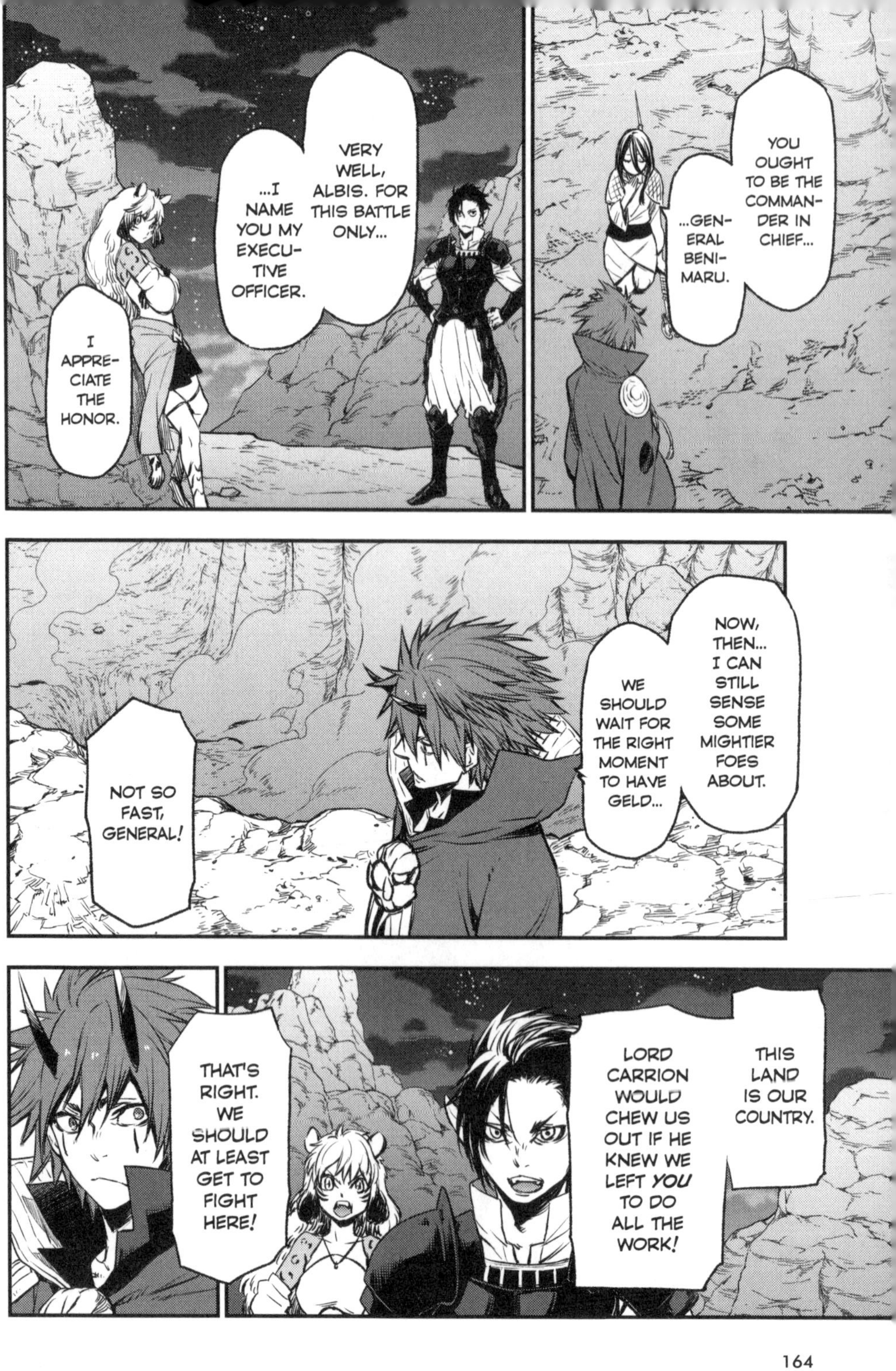
YOU OUGHT TO BE THE COMMANDER IN CHIEF...
...GENERAL BENIMARU.
VERY WELL, ALBIS. FOR THIS BATTLE ONLY...
...I NAME YOU MY EXECUTIVE OFFICER.
I APPRECIATE THE HONOR.
NOW, THEN... I CAN STILL SENSE SOME MIGHTIER FOES ABOUT.
WE SHOULD WAIT FOR THE RIGHT MOMENT TO HAVE GELD...
NOT SO FAST, GENERAL!
THIS LAND IS OUR COUNTRY.
LORD CARRION WOULD CHEW US OUT IF HE KNEW WE LEFT *YOU* TO DO ALL THE WORK!
THAT'S RIGHT. WE SHOULD AT LEAST GET TO FIGHT HERE!

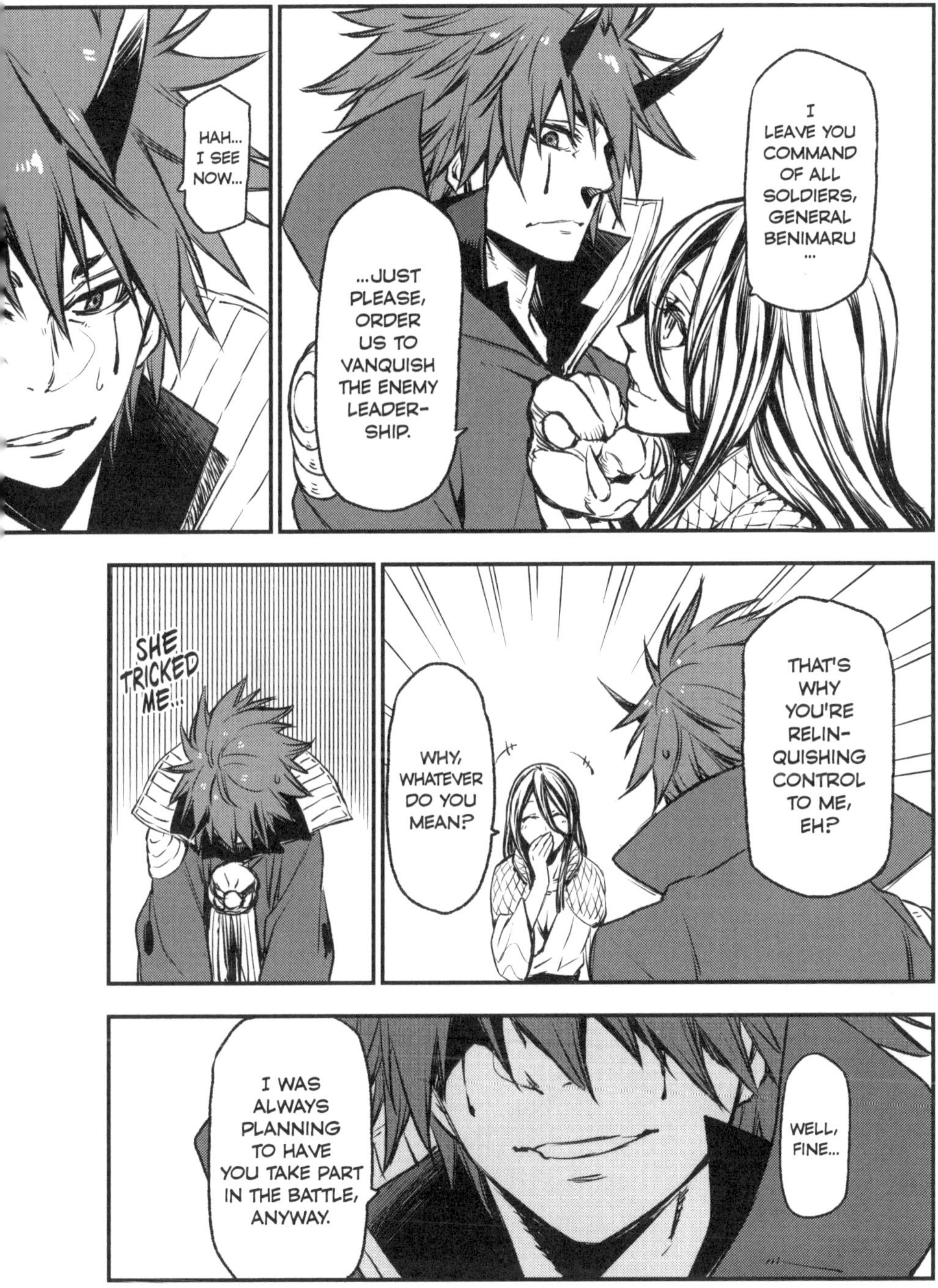
I LEAVE YOU COMMAND OF ALL SOLDIERS, GENERAL BENIMARU...
...JUST PLEASE, ORDER US TO VANQUISH THE ENEMY LEADERSHIP.
HAH... I SEE NOW...
THAT'S WHY YOU'RE RELINQUISHING CONTROL TO ME, EH?
WHY, WHATEVER DO YOU MEAN?
SHE TRICKED ME...
WELL, FINE...
I WAS ALWAYS PLANNING TO HAVE YOU TAKE PART IN THE BATTLE, ANYWAY.

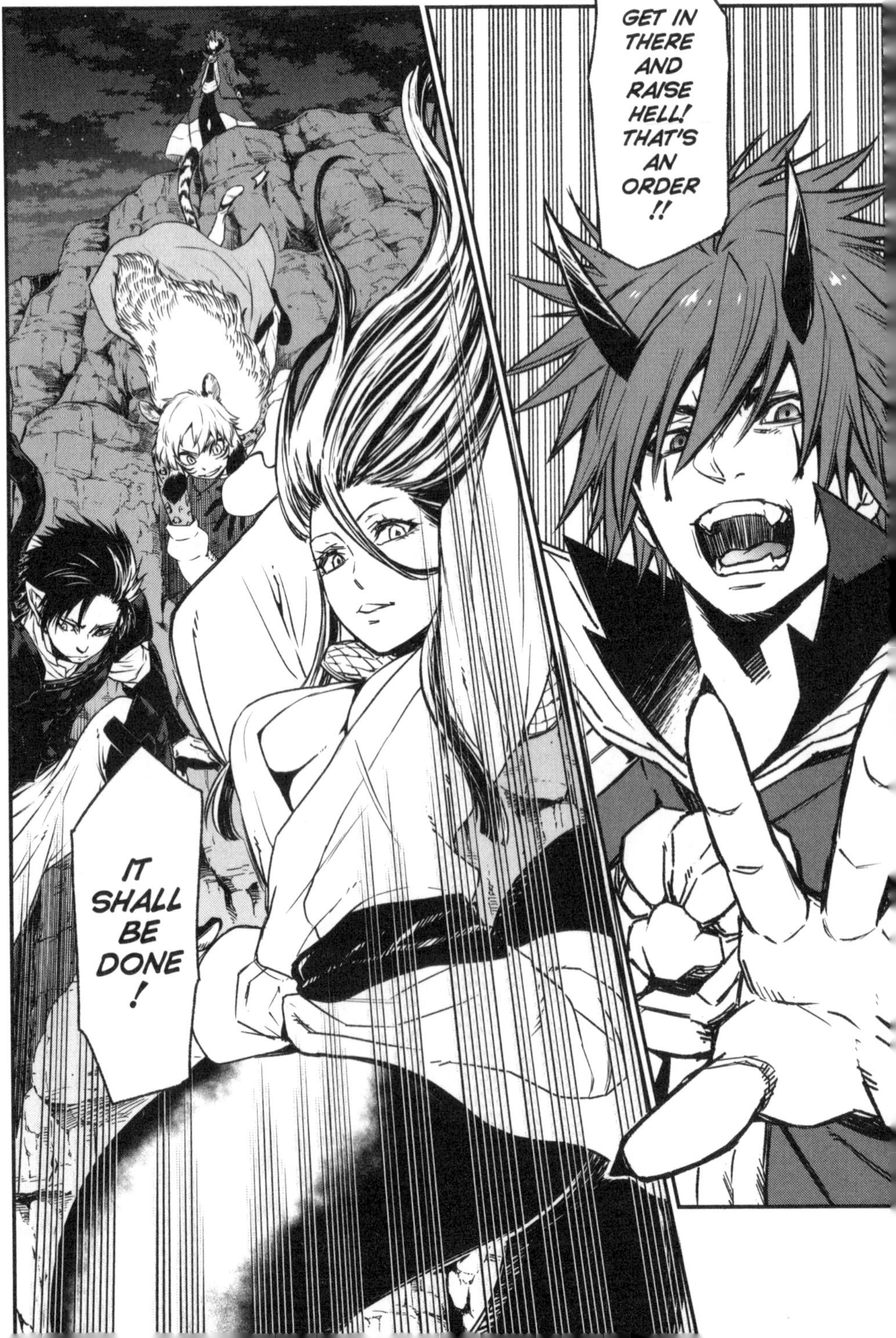
GET IN THERE AND RAISE HELL! THAT'S AN ORDER!!
IT SHALL BE DONE!

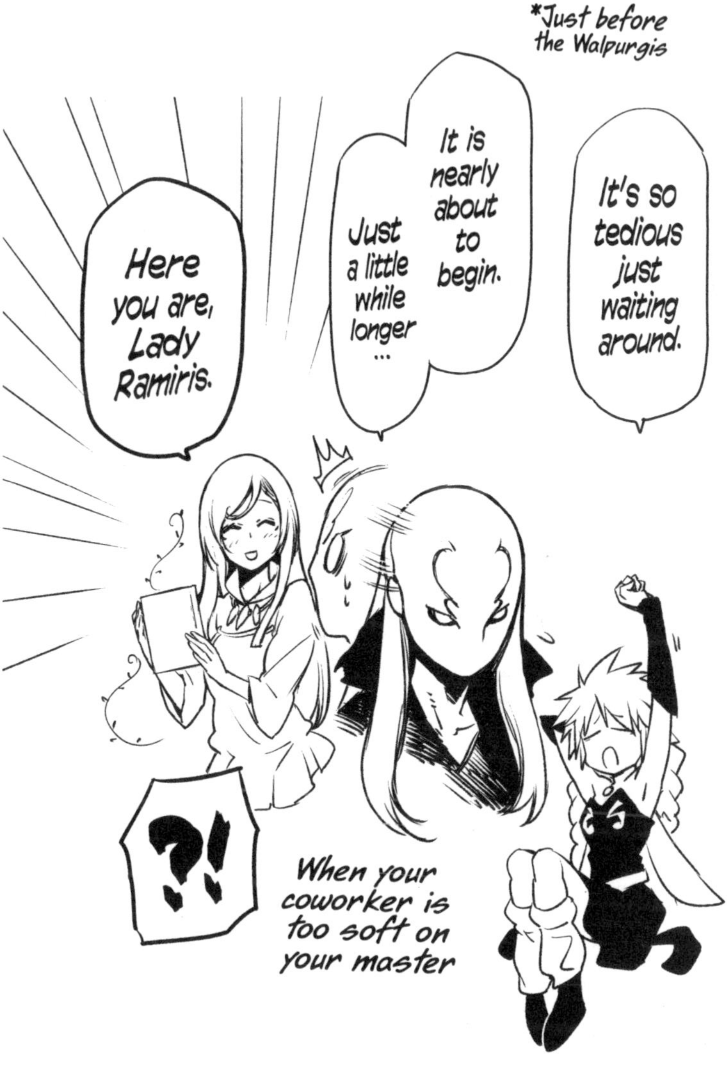
*Just before the Walpurgis
It's so tedious just waiting around.
It is nearly about to begin.
Just a little while longer...
Here you are, Lady Ramiris.
?!
When your coworker is too soft on your master

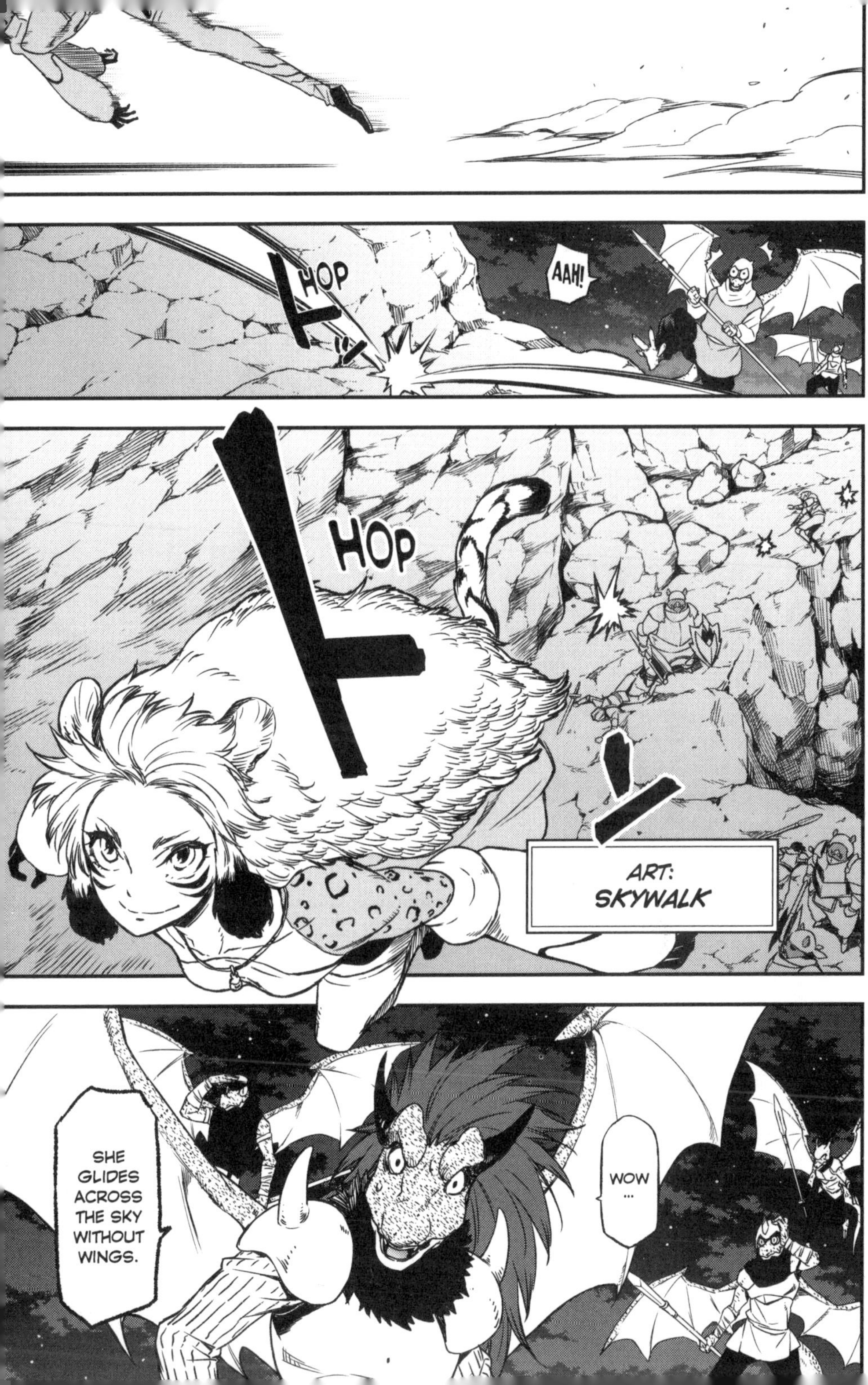

AAH!
HOP
HOP
ART:
SKYWALK
WOW ...
SHE GLIDES ACROSS THE SKY WITHOUT WINGS.

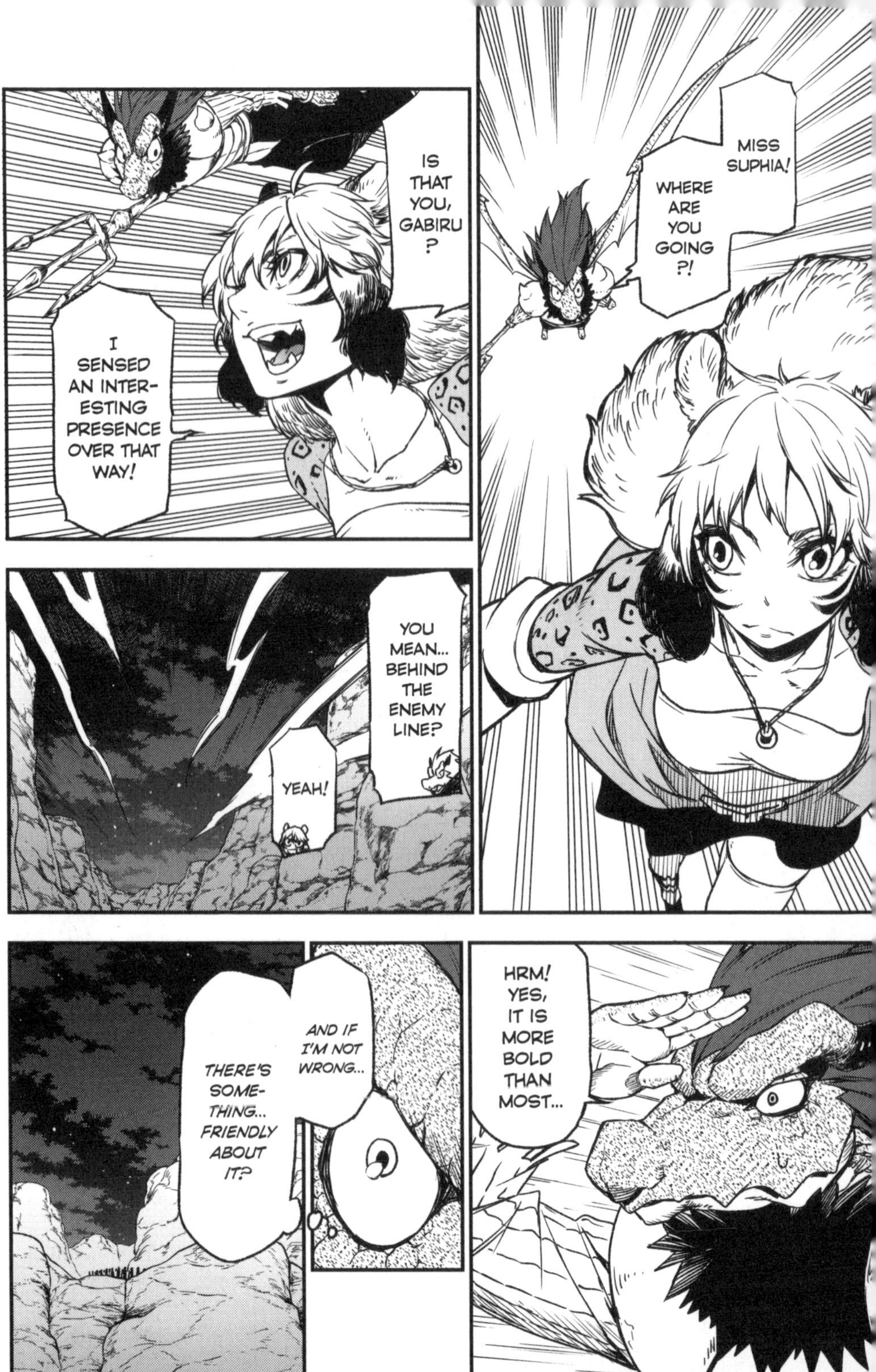
MISS SUPHIA!
WHERE ARE YOU GOING?!
IS THAT YOU, GABIRU?
I SENSED AN INTER-ESTING PRESENCE OVER THAT WAY!
YOU MEAN... BEHIND THE ENEMY LINE?
YEAH!
HRM! YES, IT IS MORE BOLD THAN MOST...
AND IF I'M NOT WRONG...
THERE'S SOME-THING... FRIENDLY ABOUT IT?

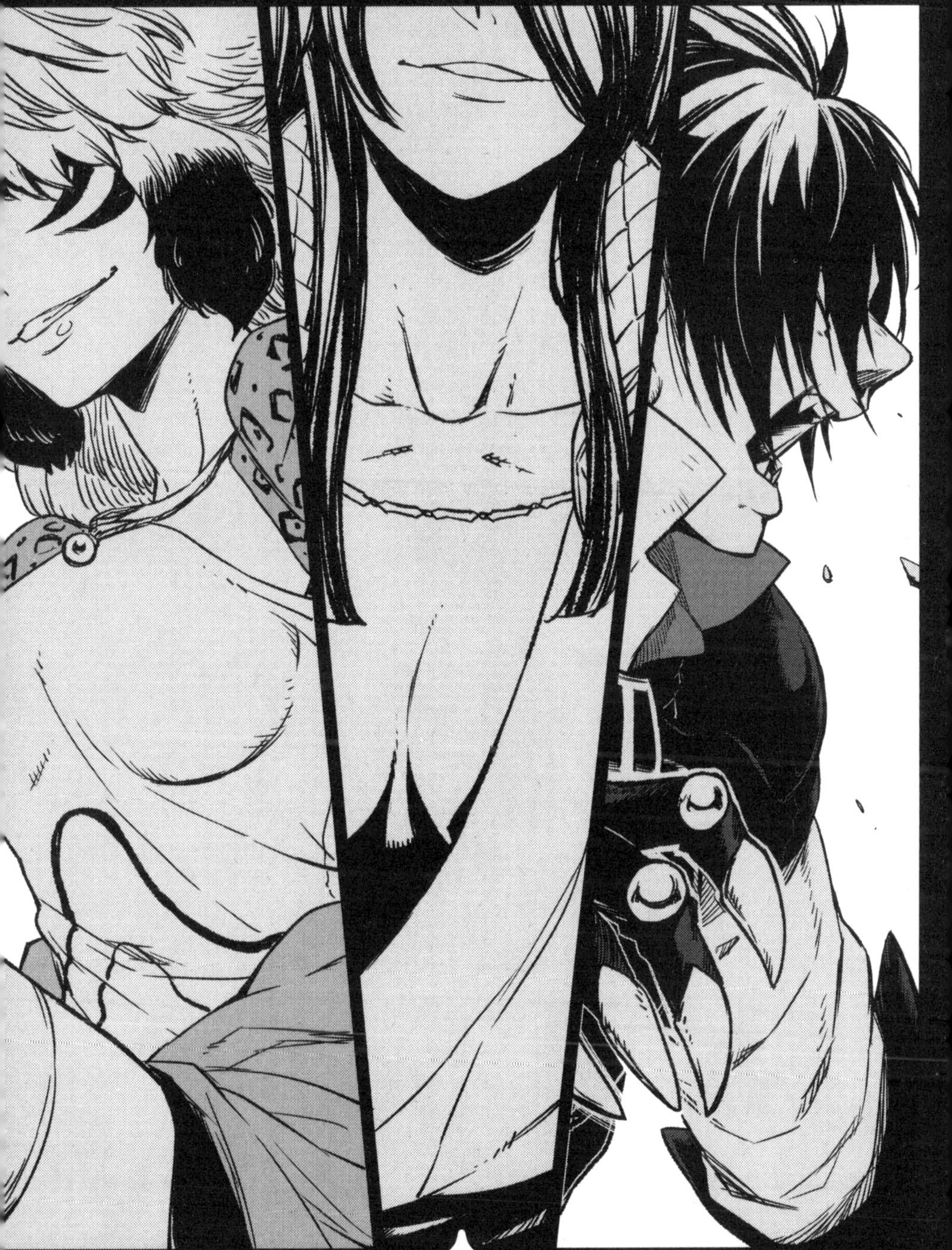

CHAPTER 79 Battle

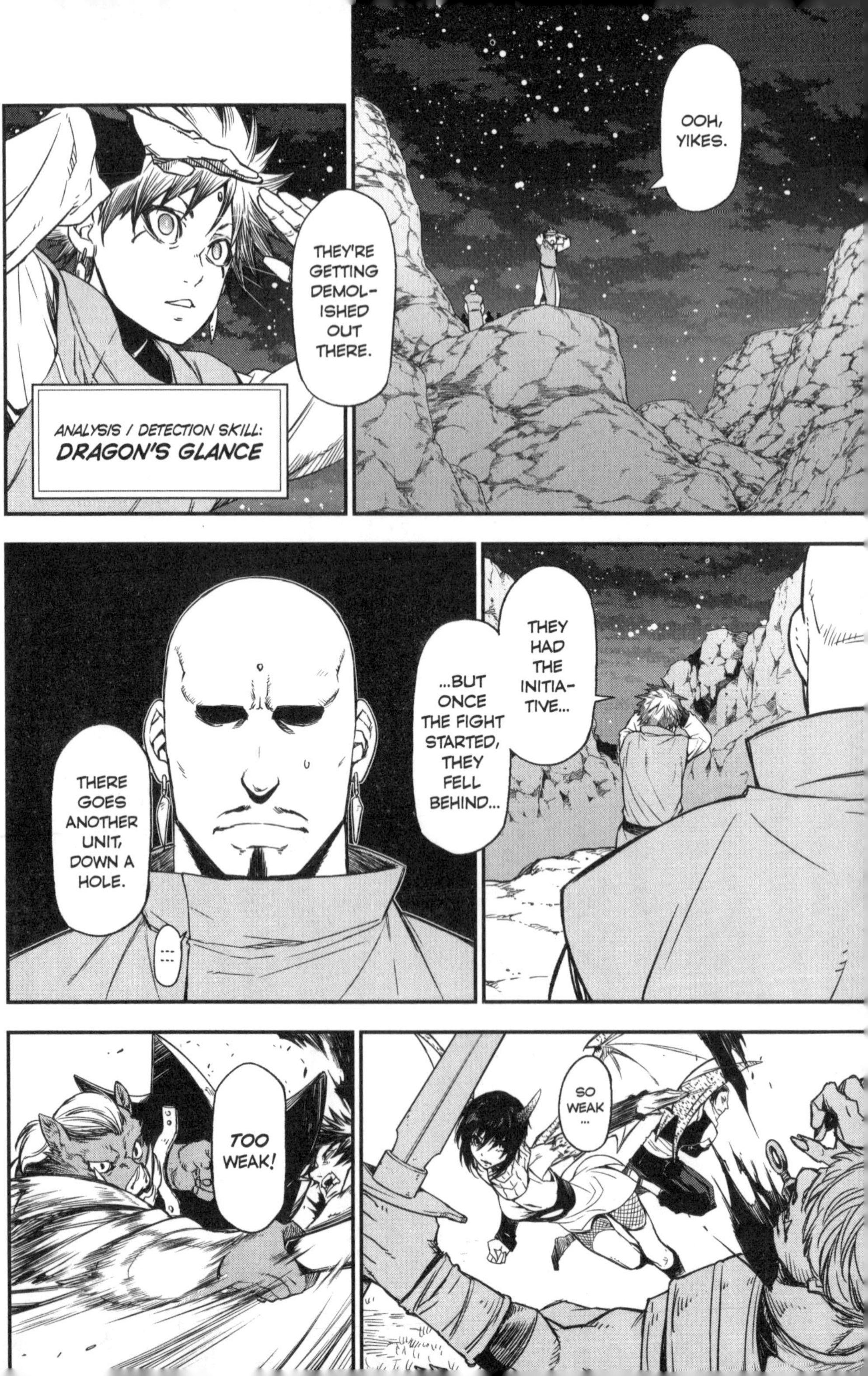
OOH, YIKES.
THEY'RE GETTING DEMOL-ISHED OUT THERE.
ANALYSIS / DETECTION SKILL: DRAGON'S GLANCE
THEY HAD THE INITIA-TIVE...
...BUT ONCE THE FIGHT STARTED, THEY FELL BEHIND...
THERE GOES ANOTHER UNIT, DOWN A HOLE.
......
SO WEAK...
TOO WEAK!

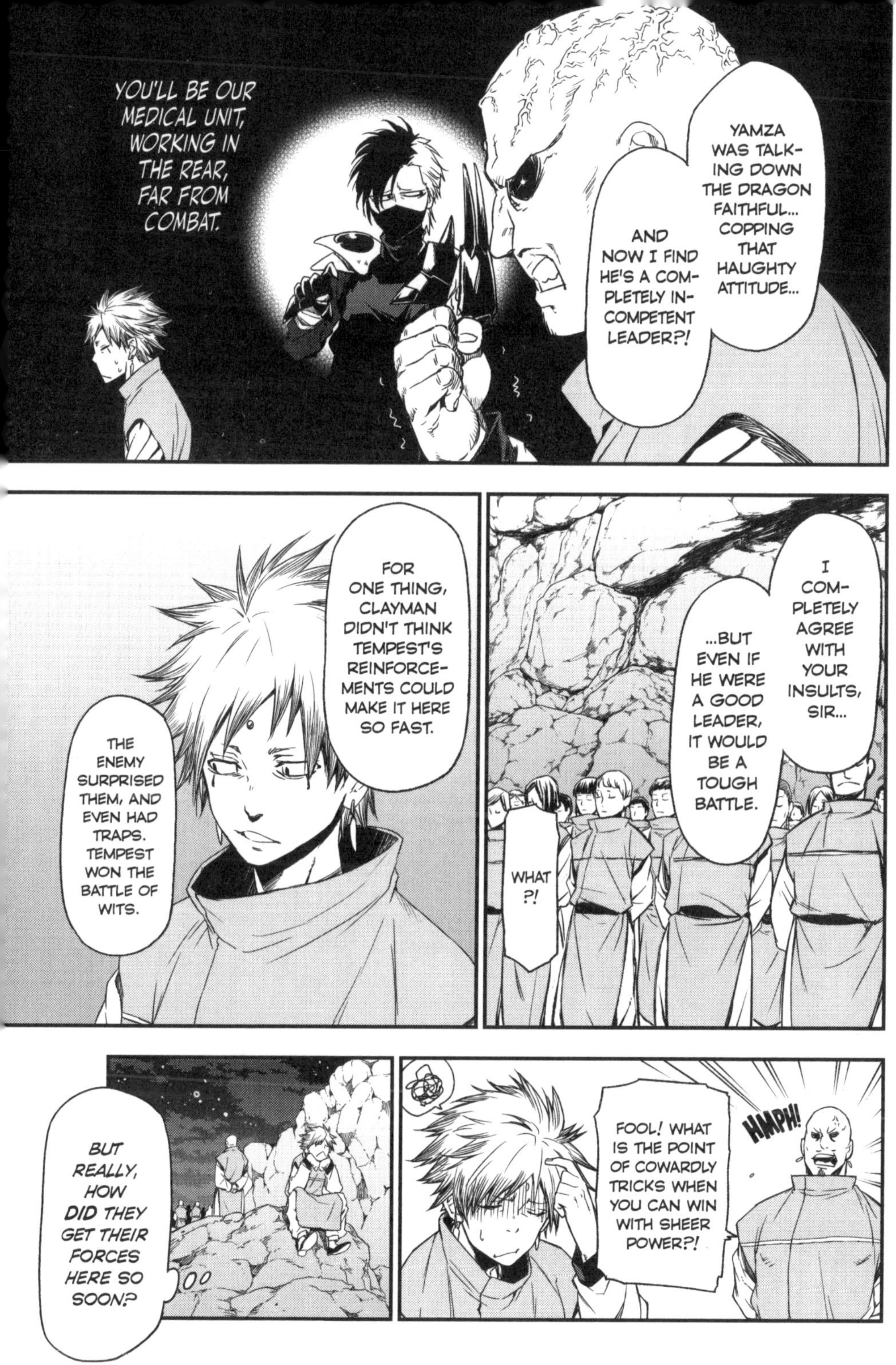
YAMZA WAS TALKING DOWN THE DRAGON FAITHFUL... COPPING THAT HAUGHTY ATTITUDE...
AND NOW I FIND HE'S A COMPLETELY INCOMPETENT LEADER?!
YOU'LL BE OUR MEDICAL UNIT, WORKING IN THE REAR, FAR FROM COMBAT.
I COMPLETELY AGREE WITH YOUR INSULTS, SIR...
...BUT EVEN IF HE WERE A GOOD LEADER, IT WOULD BE A TOUGH BATTLE.
WHAT?!
FOR ONE THING, CLAYMAN DIDN'T THINK TEMPEST'S REINFORCEMENTS COULD MAKE IT HERE SO FAST.
THE ENEMY SURPRISED THEM, AND EVEN HAD TRAPS. TEMPEST WON THE BATTLE OF WITS.
HMPH!
FOOL! WHAT IS THE POINT OF COWARDLY TRICKS WHEN YOU CAN WIN WITH SHEER POWER?!
BUT REALLY, HOW DID THEY GET THEIR FORCES HERE SO SOON?

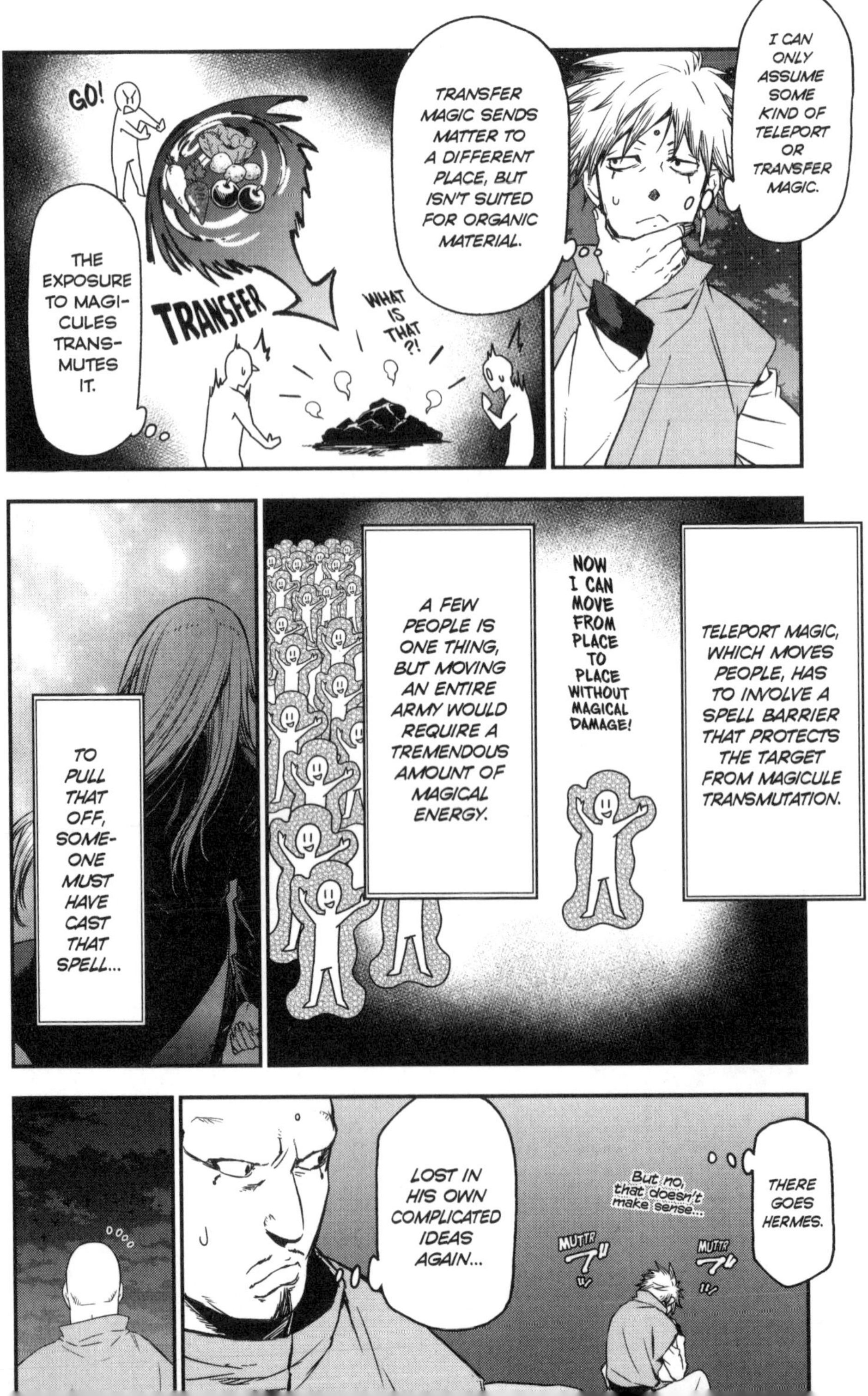
I CAN ONLY ASSUME SOME KIND OF TELEPORT OR TRANSFER MAGIC.
TRANSFER MAGIC SENDS MATTER TO A DIFFERENT PLACE, BUT ISN'T SUITED FOR ORGANIC MATERIAL.
GO!
WHAT IS THAT?!
TRANSFER
THE EXPOSURE TO MAGI-CULES TRANS-MUTES IT.
TELEPORT MAGIC, WHICH MOVES PEOPLE, HAS TO INVOLVE A SPELL BARRIER THAT PROTECTS THE TARGET FROM MAGICULE TRANSMUTATION.
NOW I CAN MOVE FROM PLACE TO PLACE WITHOUT MAGICAL DAMAGE!
A FEW PEOPLE IS ONE THING, BUT MOVING AN ENTIRE ARMY WOULD REQUIRE A TREMENDOUS AMOUNT OF MAGICAL ENERGY.
TO PULL THAT OFF, SOME-ONE MUST HAVE CAST THAT SPELL...
THERE GOES HERMES.
But no, that doesn't make sense...
MUTTR
MUTTR
LOST IN HIS OWN COMPLICATED IDEAS AGAIN...

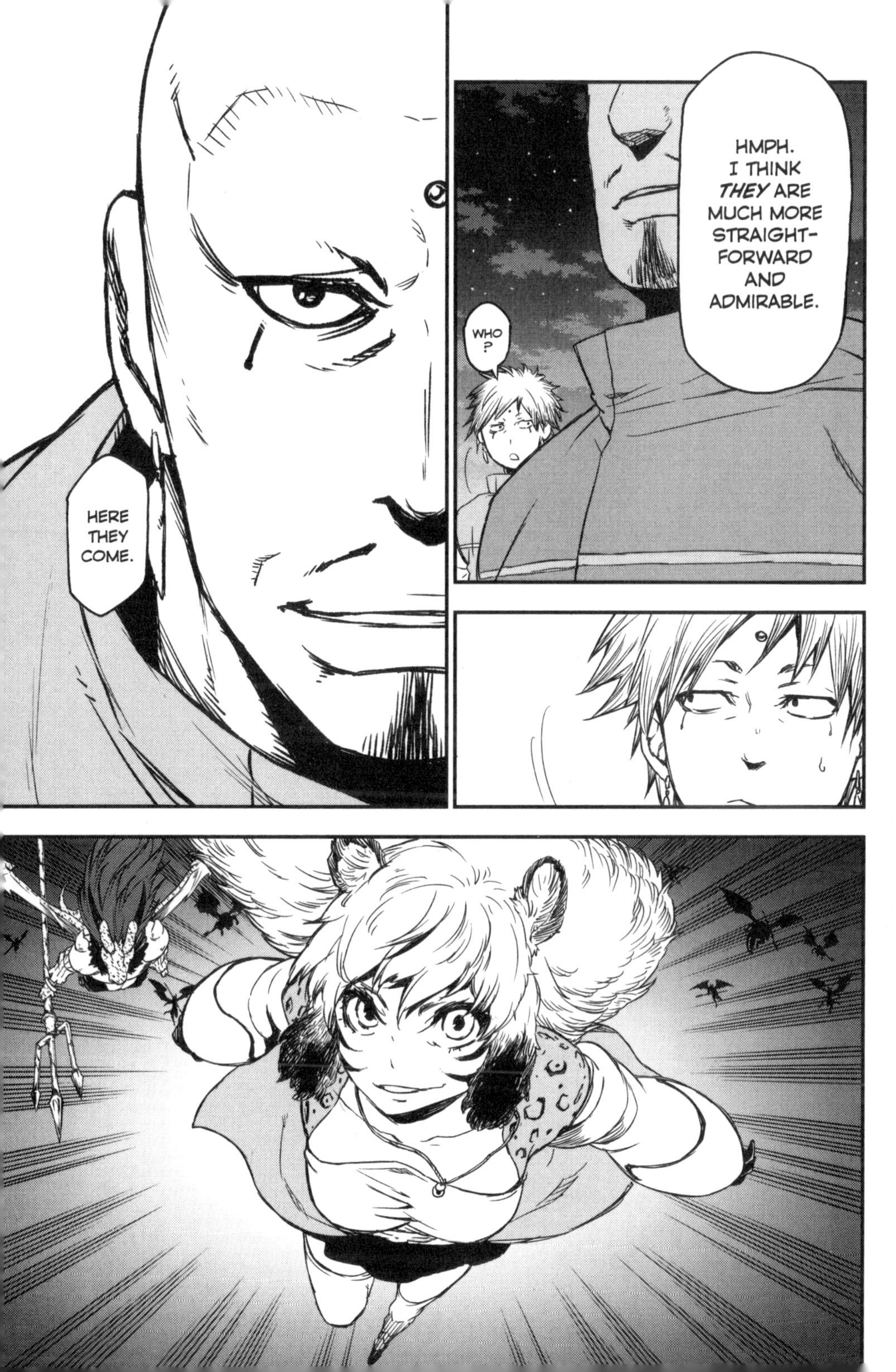
HMPH. I THINK *THEY* ARE MUCH MORE STRAIGHT-FORWARD AND ADMIRABLE.
WHO?
HERE THEY COME.

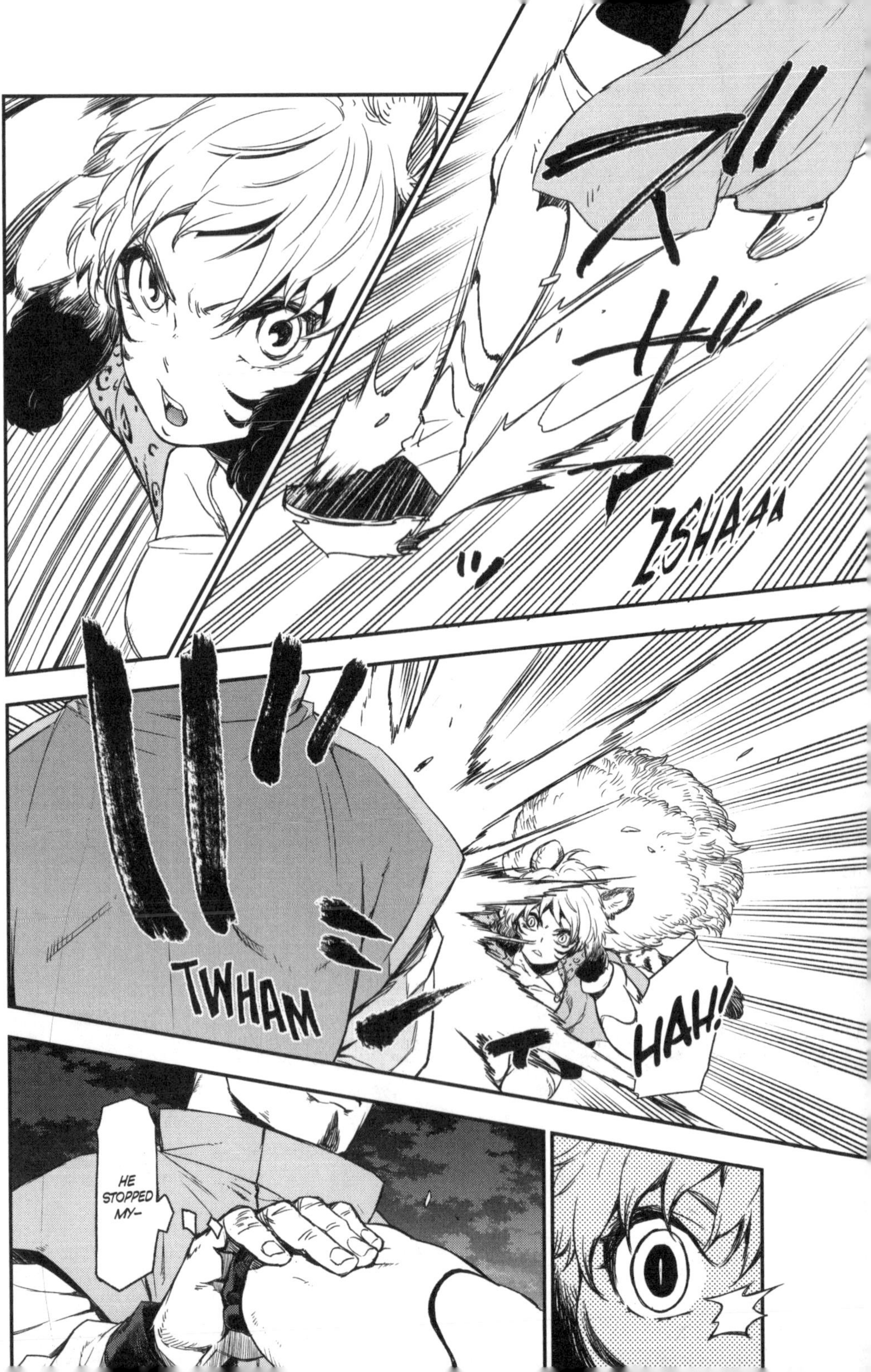
ZSHAAA
HAH!
TWHAM
HE STOPPED MY–

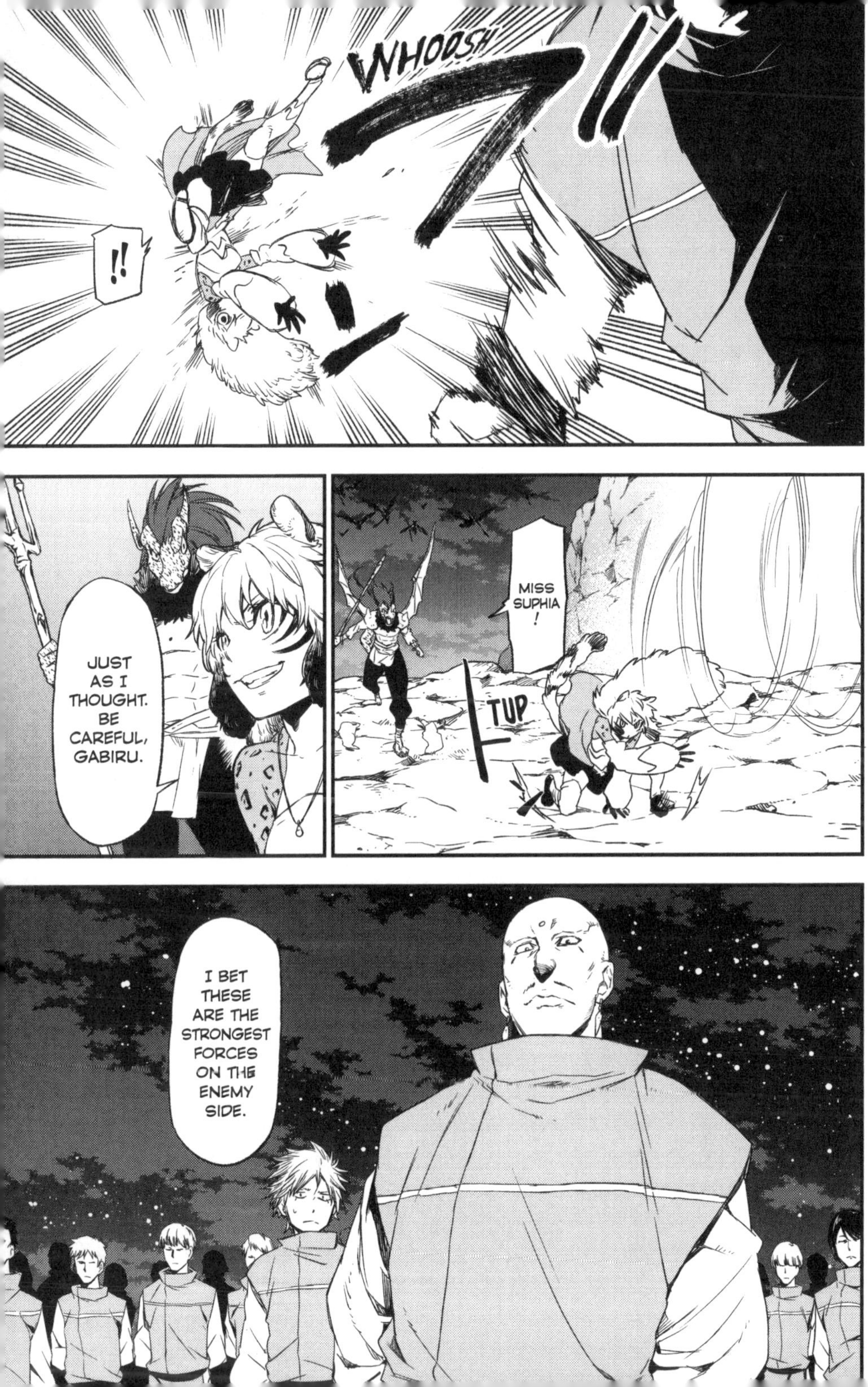
WHOOSH
!!
MISS SUPHIA!
TUP
JUST AS I THOUGHT. BE CAREFUL, GABIRU.
I BET THESE ARE THE STRONGEST FORCES ON THE ENEMY SIDE.

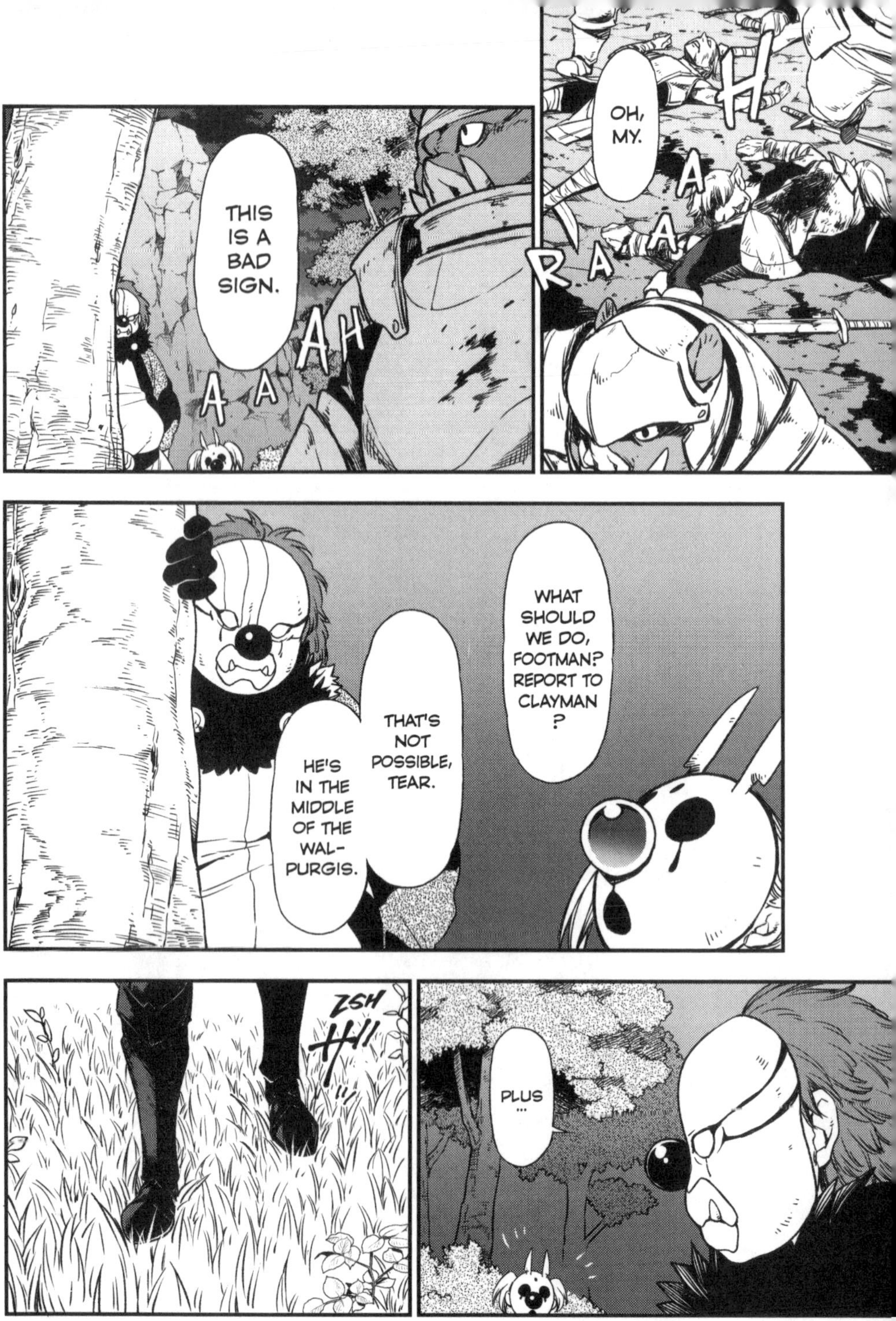
OH, MY.
RAAAAH
THIS IS A BAD SIGN.
AAAH
WHAT SHOULD WE DO, FOOTMAN? REPORT TO CLAYMAN?
THAT'S NOT POSSIBLE, TEAR.
HE'S IN THE MIDDLE OF THE WAL-PURGIS.
PLUS...
ZSHH!!

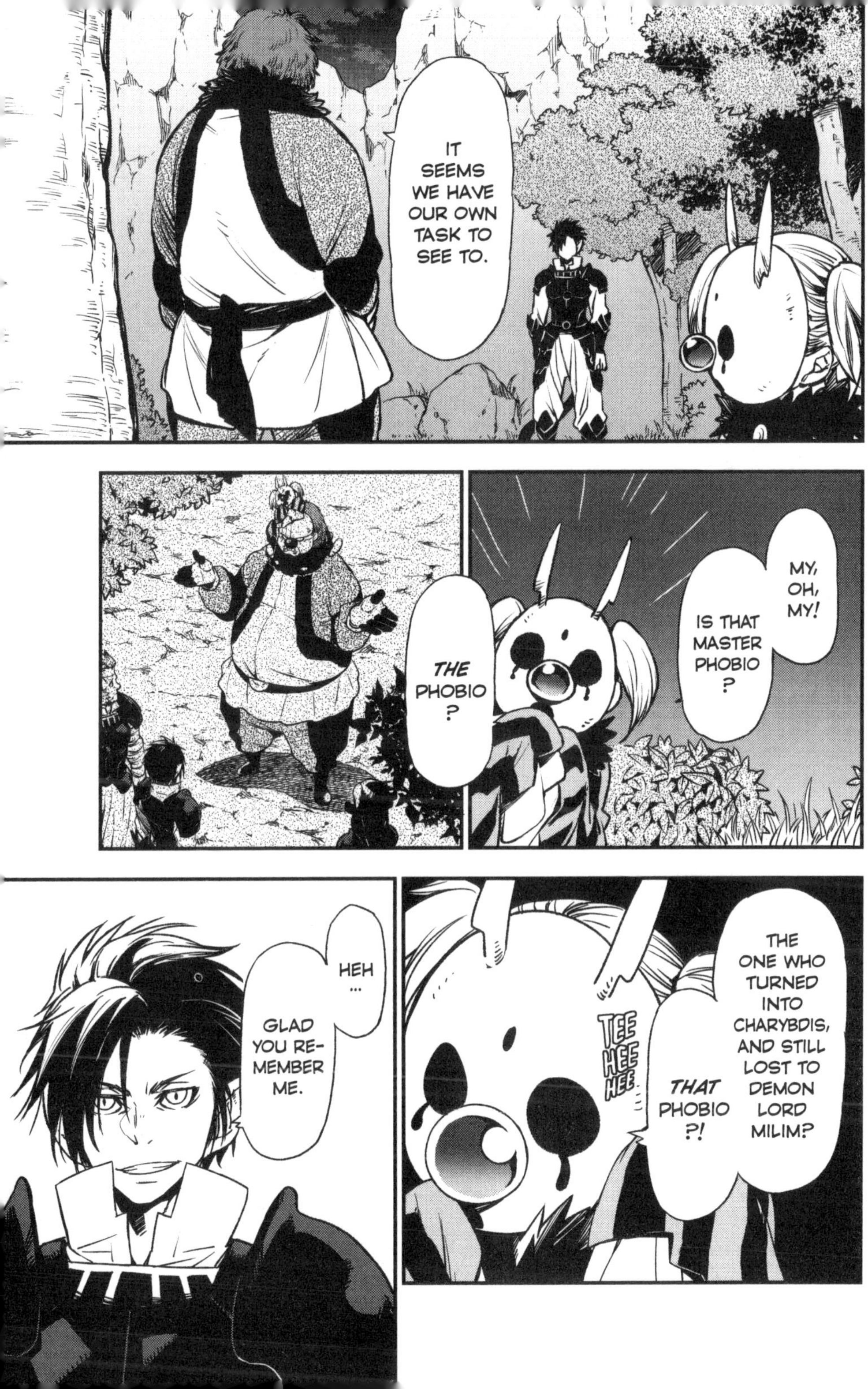
IT SEEMS WE HAVE OUR OWN TASK TO SEE TO.
MY, OH, MY! IS THAT MASTER PHOBIO?
THE PHOBIO?
THE ONE WHO TURNED INTO CHARYBDIS, AND STILL LOST TO DEMON LORD MILIM?
TEE HEE HEE
THAT PHOBIO?!
HEH...
GLAD YOU REMEMBER ME.

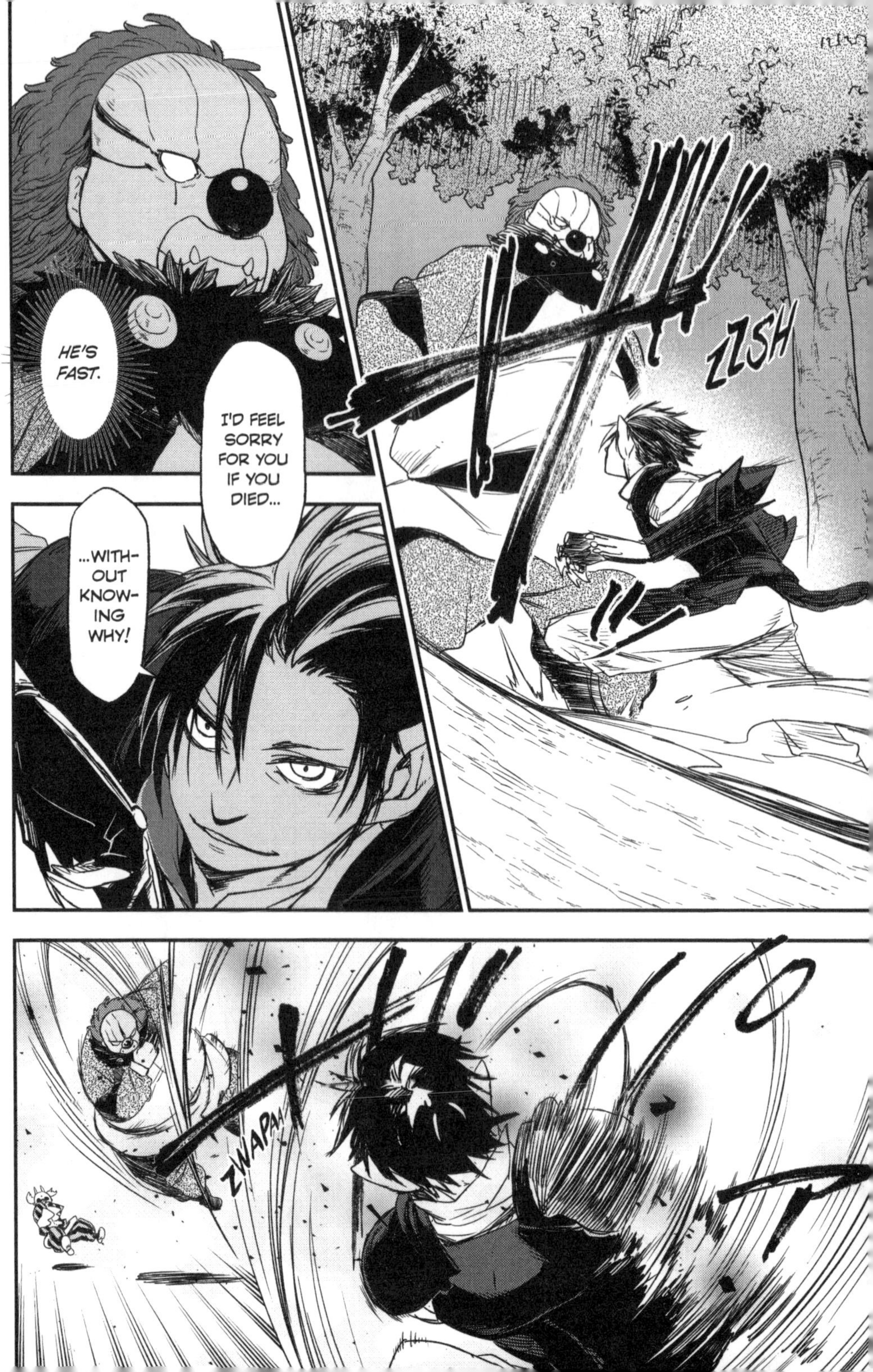
ZZSH
HE'S FAST.
I'D FEEL SORRY FOR YOU IF YOU DIED...
...WITH-OUT KNOWING WHY!
ZWAPAA

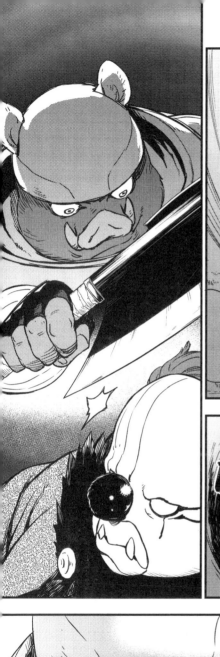

HO HO!

I SEE YOU'VE BUILT UP A RESISTANCE TO TAUNTS...

HELLO AGAIN, FOOT-MAN.

RE-MEMBER ME?

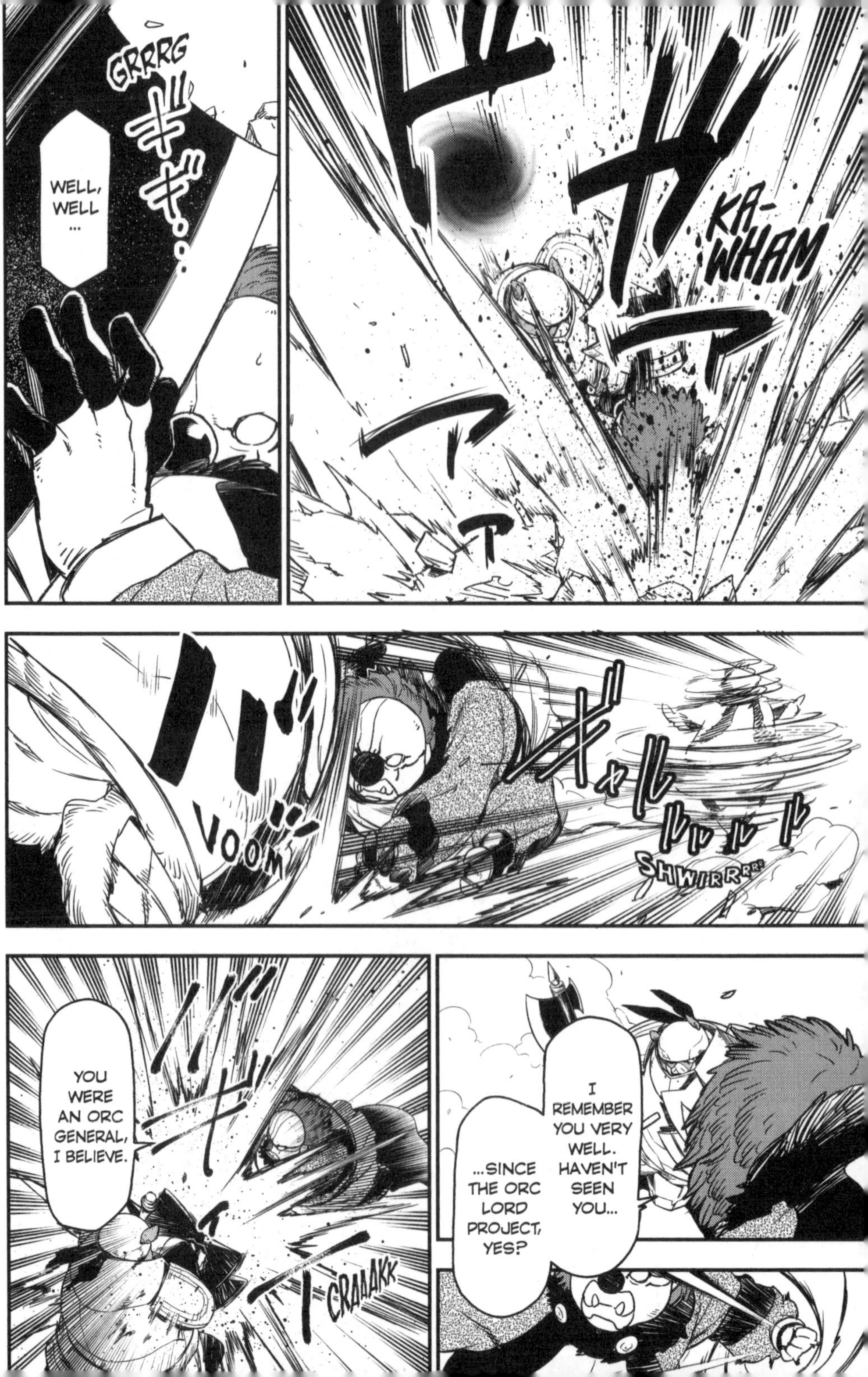
KA-WHAM
GRRRG
WELL, WELL ...
VOOM
SHWIRRRRR
I REMEMBER YOU VERY WELL. HAVEN'T SEEN YOU...
...SINCE THE ORC LORD PROJECT, YES?
YOU WERE AN ORC GENERAL, I BELIEVE.
CRAAAKK

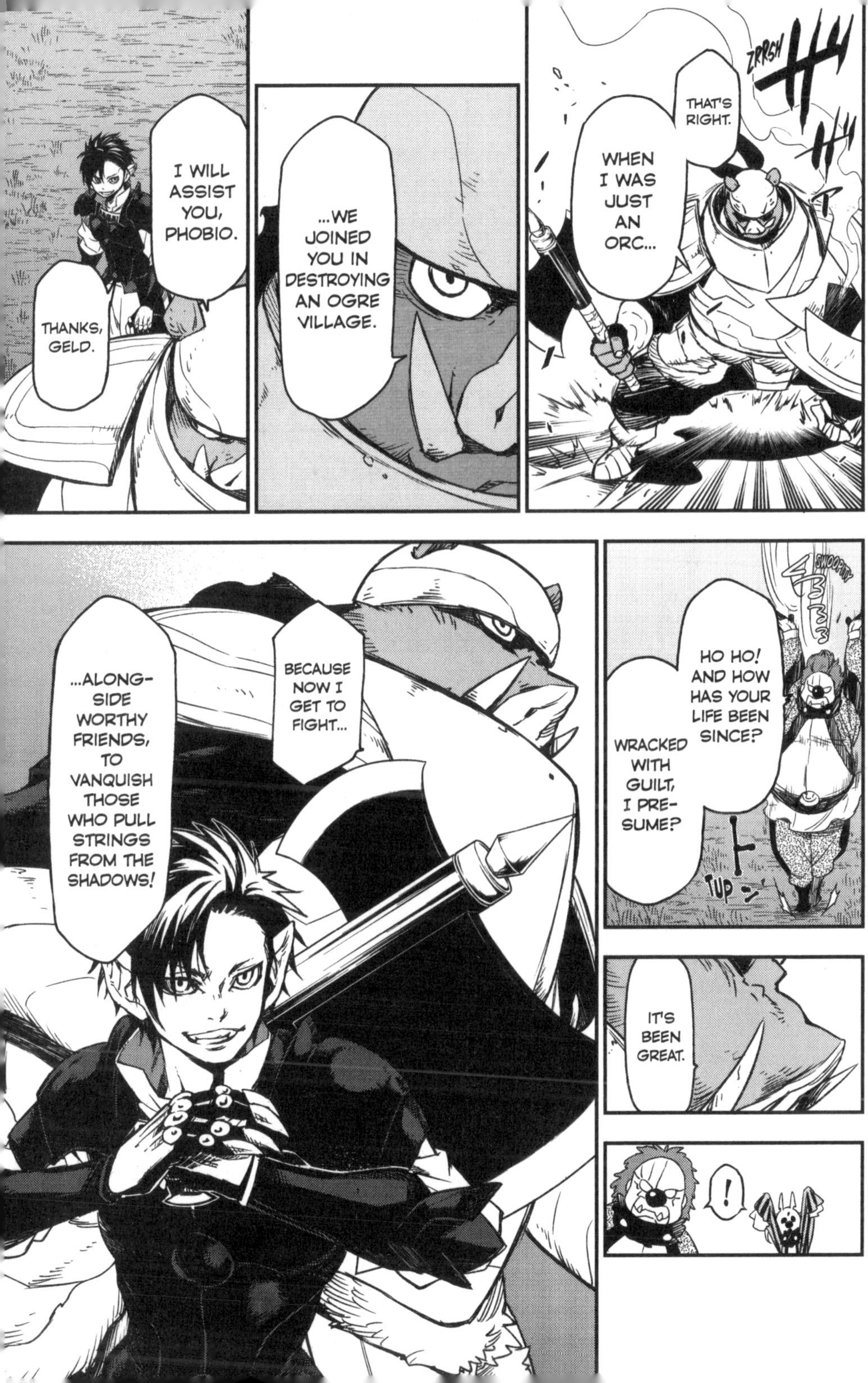
ZRRSH
THAT'S RIGHT.
WHEN I WAS JUST AN ORC...
...WE JOINED YOU IN DESTROYING AN OGRE VILLAGE.
I WILL ASSIST YOU, PHOBIO.
THANKS, GELD.
SWOOPITY
HO HO! AND HOW HAS YOUR LIFE BEEN SINCE?
WRACKED WITH GUILT, I PRESUME?
TUP
IT'S BEEN GREAT.
!
BECAUSE NOW I GET TO FIGHT...
...ALONG-SIDE WORTHY FRIENDS, TO VANQUISH THOSE WHO PULL STRINGS FROM THE SHADOWS!

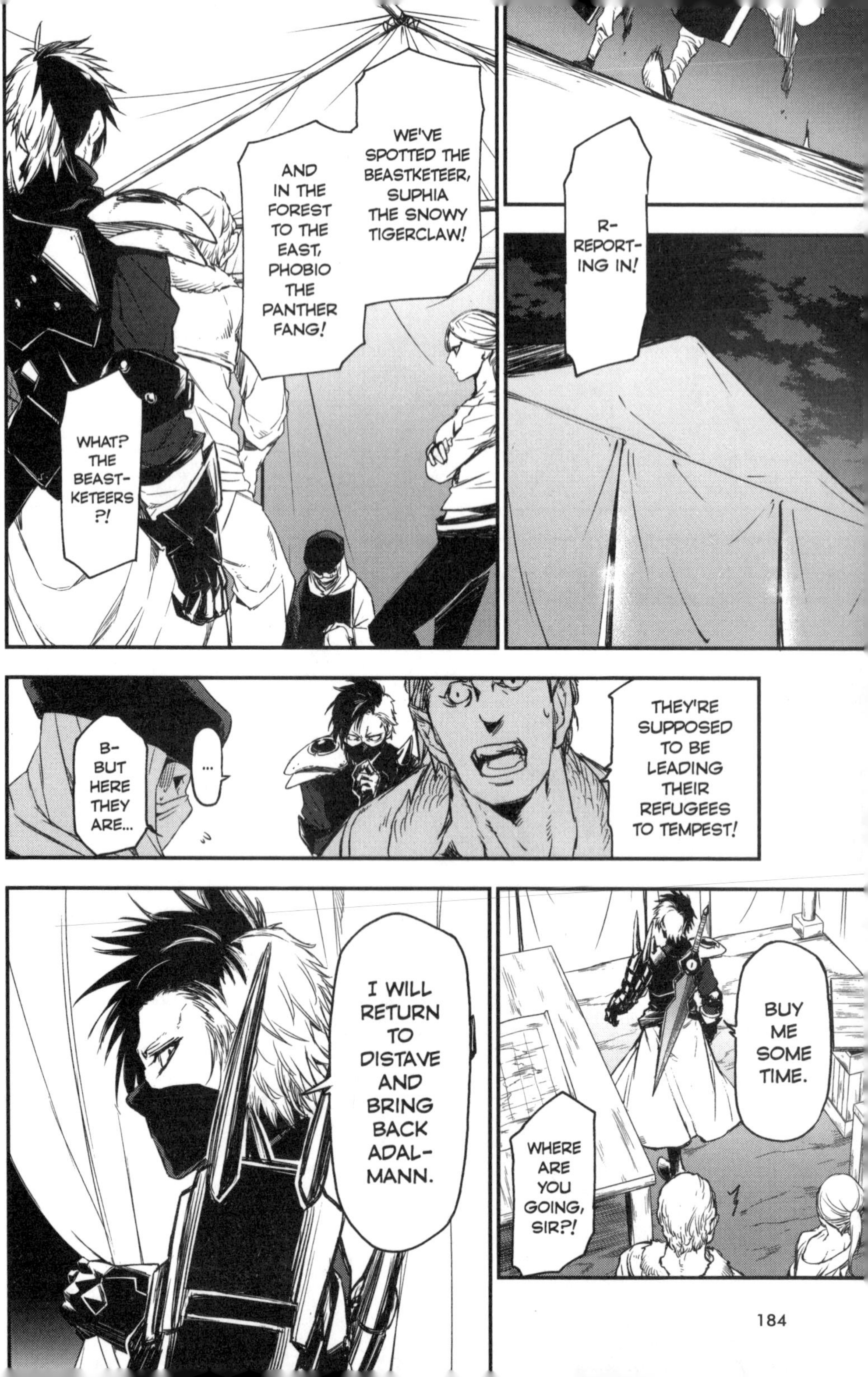
R-REPORTING IN!
WE'VE SPOTTED THE BEASTKETEER, SUPHIA THE SNOWY TIGERCLAW!
AND IN THE FOREST TO THE EAST, PHOBIO THE PANTHER FANG!
WHAT? THE BEASTKETEERS?!
THEY'RE SUPPOSED TO BE LEADING THEIR REFUGEES TO TEMPEST!
...
B-BUT HERE THEY ARE...
BUY ME SOME TIME.
WHERE ARE YOU GOING, SIR?!
I WILL RETURN TO DISTAVE AND BRING BACK ADALMANN.

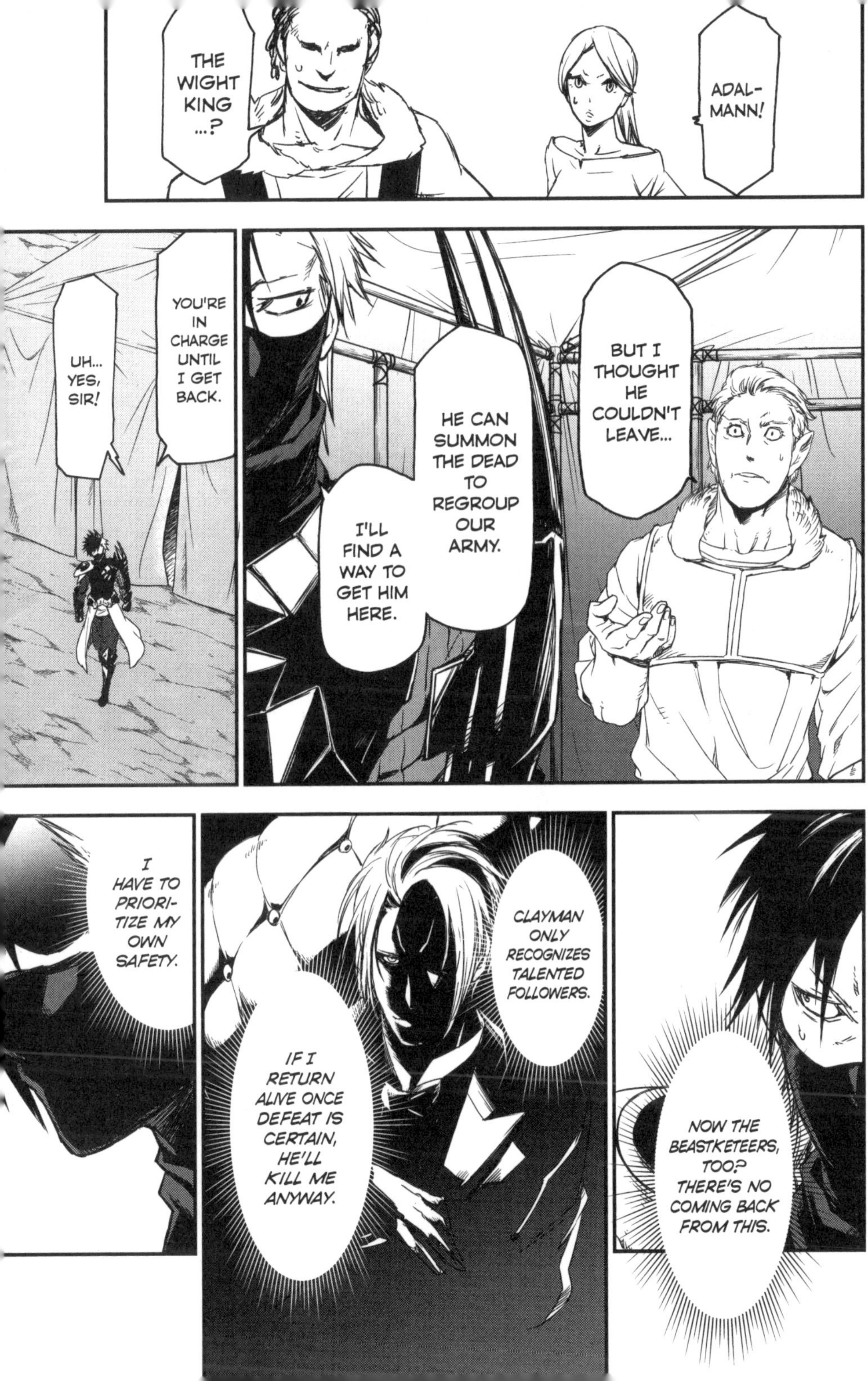
ADAL-MANN!
THE WIGHT KING ...?
BUT I THOUGHT HE COULDN'T LEAVE...
HE CAN SUMMON THE DEAD TO REGROUP OUR ARMY.
I'LL FIND A WAY TO GET HIM HERE.
YOU'RE IN CHARGE UNTIL I GET BACK.
UH... YES, SIR!
NOW THE BEASTKETEERS, TOO? THERE'S NO COMING BACK FROM THIS.
CLAYMAN ONLY RECOGNIZES TALENTED FOLLOWERS.
IF I RETURN ALIVE ONCE DEFEAT IS CERTAIN, HE'LL KILL ME ANYWAY.
I HAVE TO PRIORI-TIZE MY OWN SAFETY.

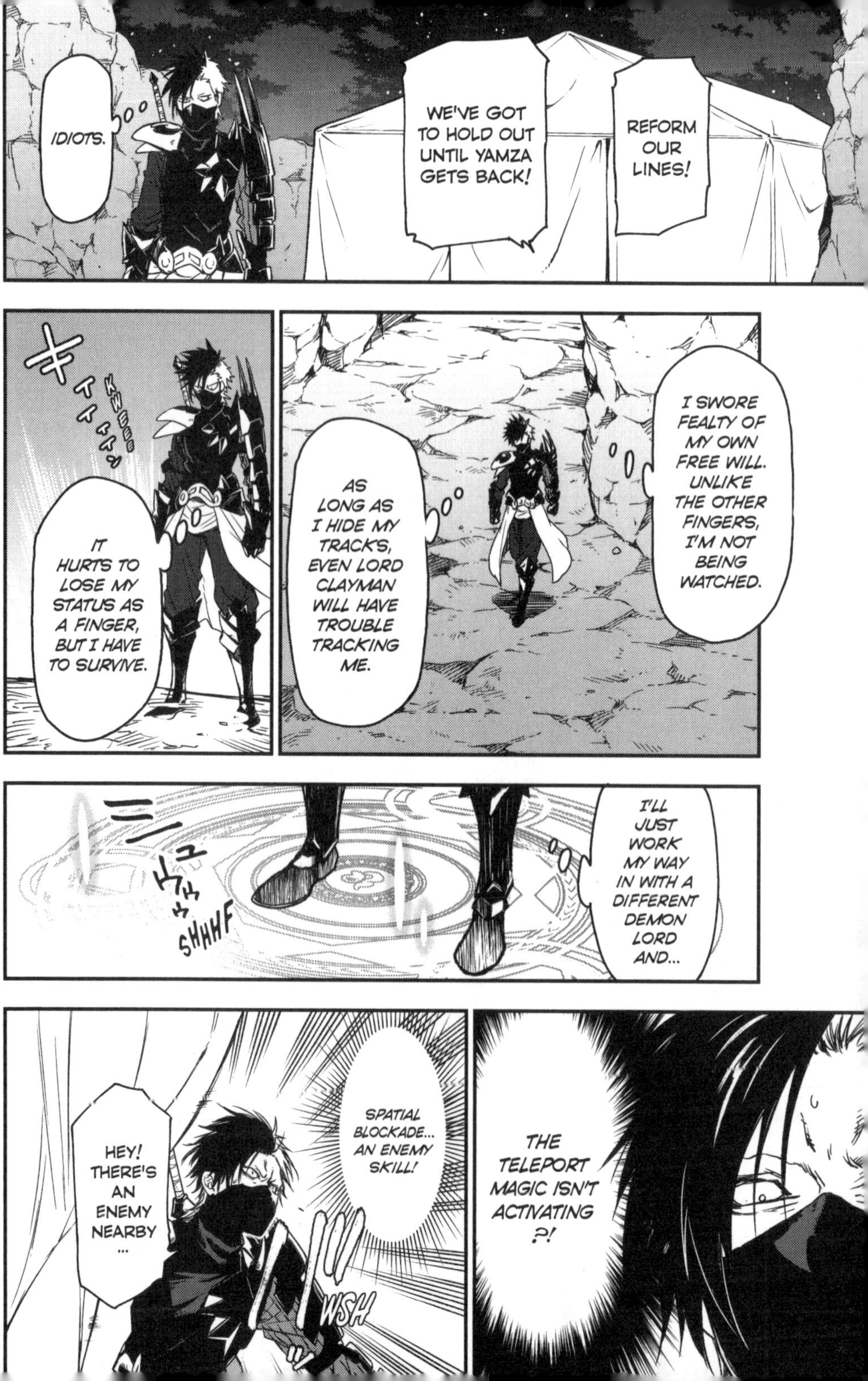
REFORM OUR LINES!
WE'VE GOT TO HOLD OUT UNTIL YAMZA GETS BACK!
IDIOTS.
I SWORE FEALTY OF MY OWN FREE WILL. UNLIKE THE OTHER FINGERS, I'M NOT BEING WATCHED.
AS LONG AS I HIDE MY TRACKS, EVEN LORD CLAYMAN WILL HAVE TROUBLE TRACKING ME.
KWEEE
IT HURTS TO LOSE MY STATUS AS A FINGER, BUT I HAVE TO SURVIVE.
I'LL JUST WORK MY WAY IN WITH A DIFFERENT DEMON LORD AND...
SHHHF
THE TELEPORT MAGIC ISN'T ACTIVATING?!
SPATIAL BLOCKADE... AN ENEMY SKILL!
HEY! THERE'S AN ENEMY NEARBY...
WSH

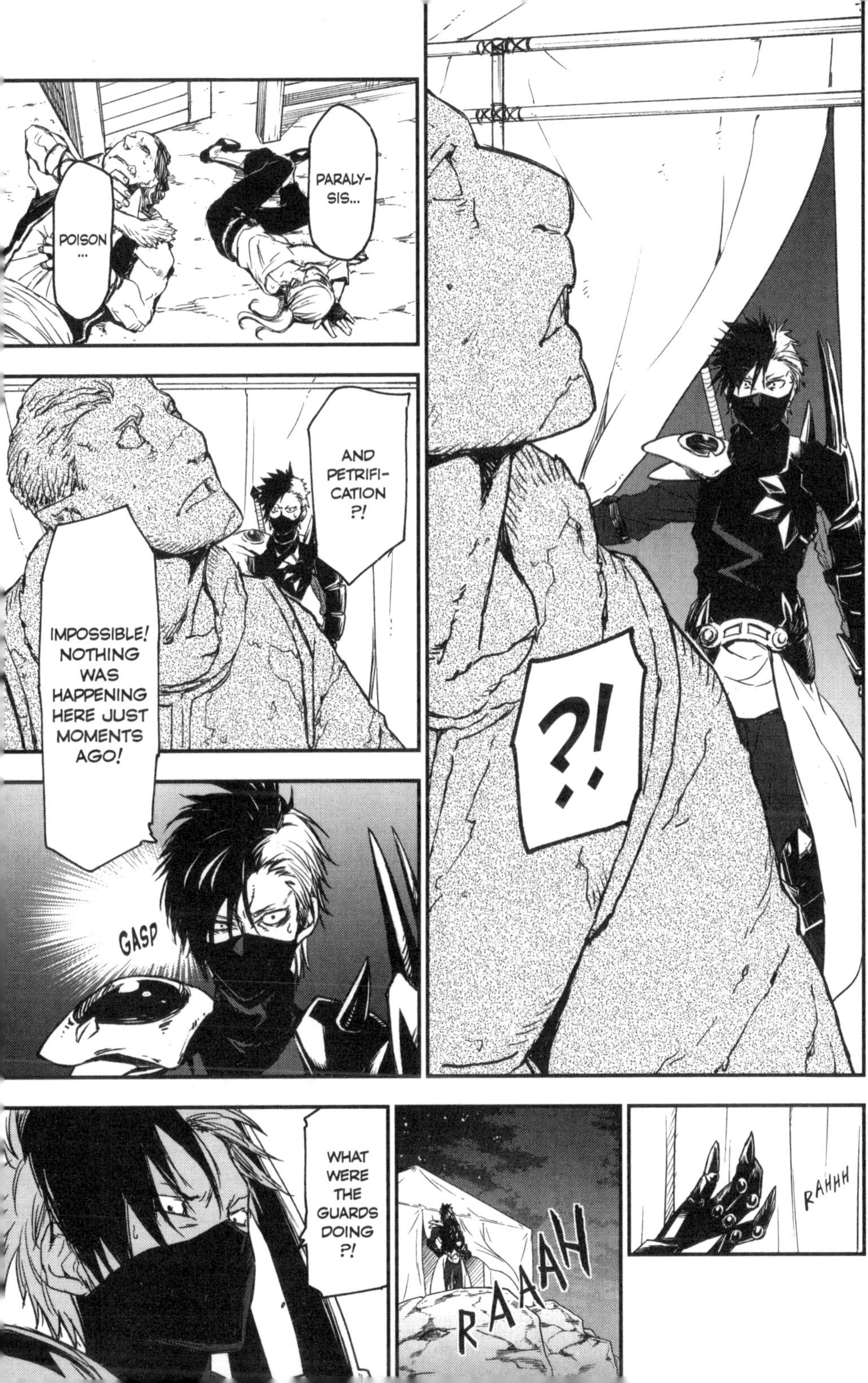
?!
PARALY-SIS...
POISON...
AND PETRIFI-CATION?!
IMPOSSIBLE! NOTHING WAS HAPPENING HERE JUST MOMENTS AGO!
GASP
RAHHH
RAAAH
WHAT WERE THE GUARDS DOING?!

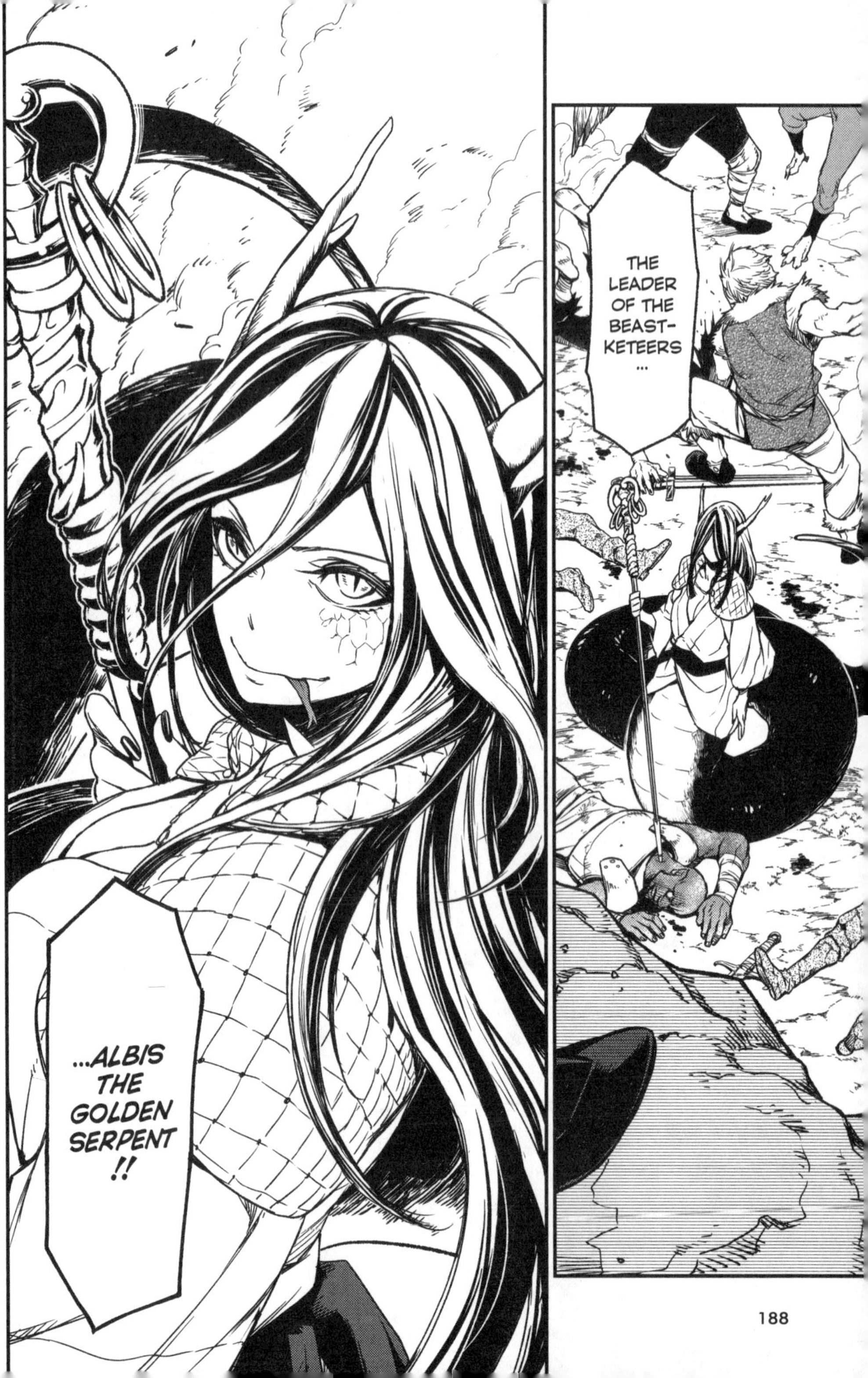
THE LEADER OF THE BEAST-KETEERS ...
...ALBIS THE GOLDEN SERPENT !!

Reincarnate
in Volume 18?

→YES

NO

AFTER THE MONSTER-AND-MAN SUMMIT

SO YOUR BODY IS A HOMUNCULUS? REALLY?
YES. MERELY A VESSEL FOR MY SPIRITUAL BODY TO INHABIT.
THAT MUST BE THALION CRAFTSMANSHIP.
You look human to me!
I'M HUMBLED BY YOUR PRAISE...
...BUT I AM SLIGHTLY REGRETTING IT NOW.
THIS HAS BEEN A VERY WORTHWHILE EVENT.
I WOULD HAVE LIKED TO EXPERIENCE IT IN THE FLESH.
That's nice.
MOST IMPORTANTLY...
I MISSED OUT ON A CHANCE FOR A REAL HUG FROM EREN!!
I hate this fake body!!
You're the best, Dad!!
ARTIFICIAL BODY

*See Vol. 16

LIST OF ACKNOWLEDGMENTS

AUTHOR:
Fuse-sensei

CHARACTER DESIGN:
Mitz Vah-sensei

ASSISTANTS:
Muraichi-san
Daiki Haraguchi-san
Masashi Kiritani-sensei
Taku Arao-sensei

Everyone at the editorial department

AND YOU!!

『Dark Blacksmith』

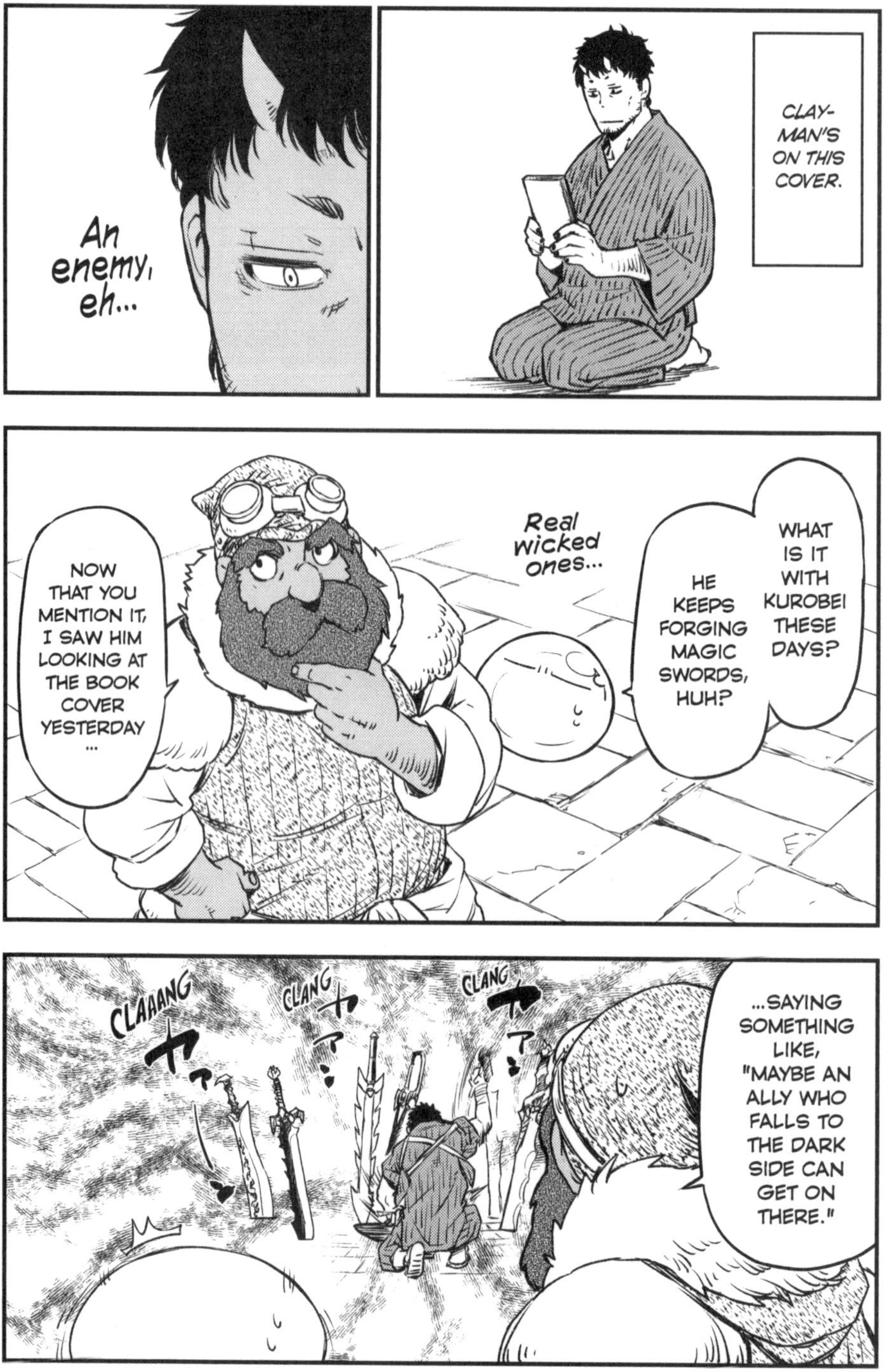
CLAY-MAN'S ON THIS COVER.
An enemy, eh...
WHAT IS IT WITH KUROBEI THESE DAYS?
HE KEEPS FORGING MAGIC SWORDS, HUH?
Real wicked ones...
NOW THAT YOU MENTION IT, I SAW HIM LOOKING AT THE BOOK COVER YESTERDAY...
...SAYING SOMETHING LIKE, "MAYBE AN ALLY WHO FALLS TO THE DARK SIDE CAN GET ON THERE."
CLANG
CLANG
CLAAANG

Grapes from Tempest
"Blue Tempest"

The more brilliant the blue color,
the more prized they are.

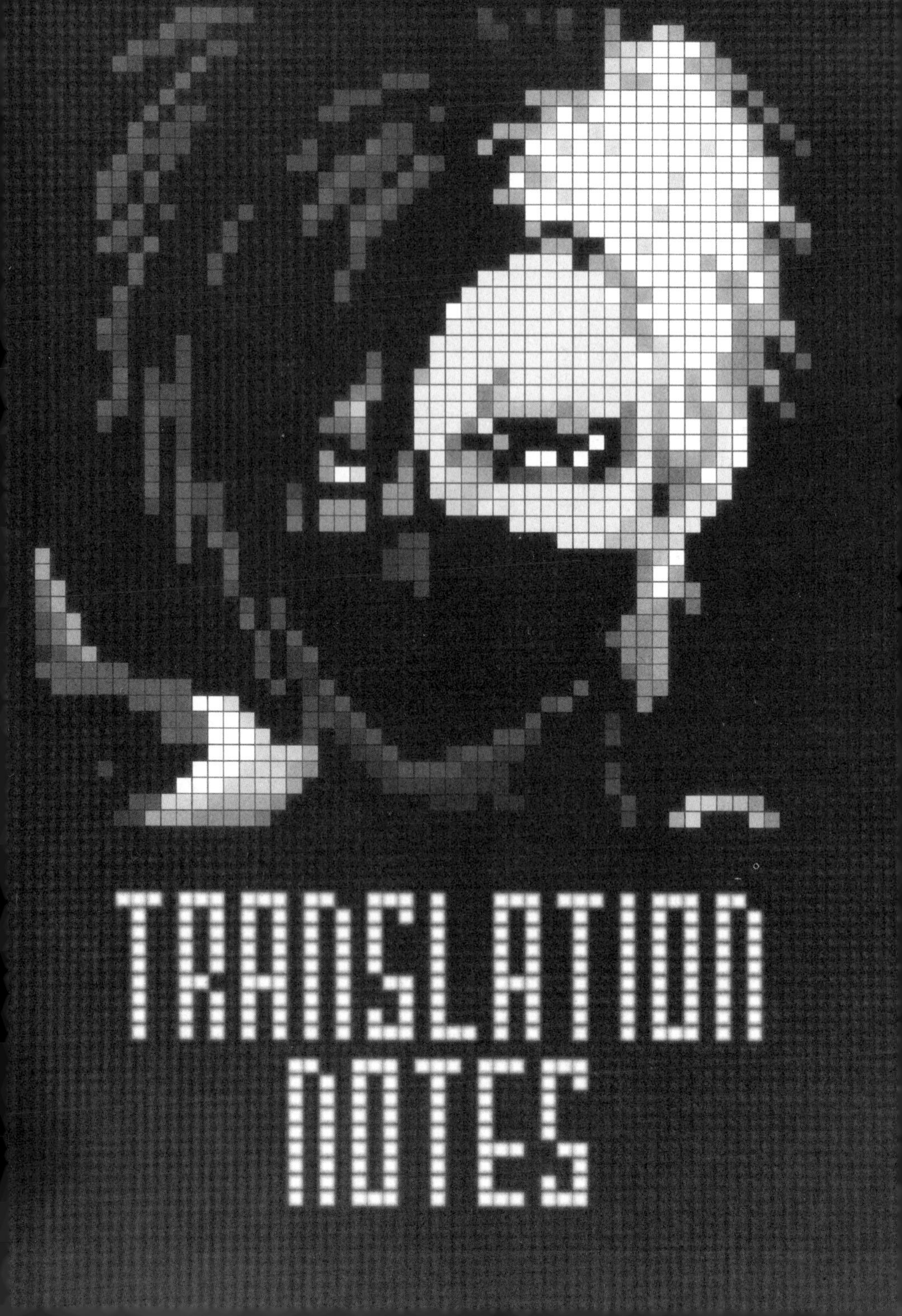

TRANSLATION NOTES

WALPURGIS

page 42

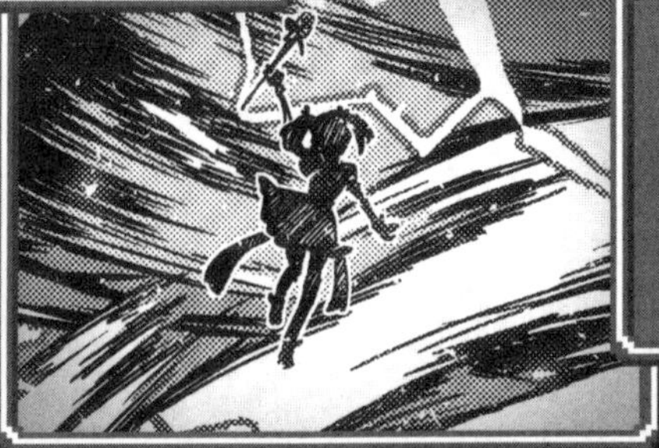

Walpurgisnacht, or "Walpurgis Night," is an event observed in Europe near the spring equinox, a night of bonfires and dancing to drive off evil spirits, because the devil is said to prowl the earth that night. Rimuru's vision suggests that he's remembering the anime series *Madoka Magica*, where Walpurgisnacht refers to a particularly dangerous and powerful witch.

NOT A SCAM

page 57

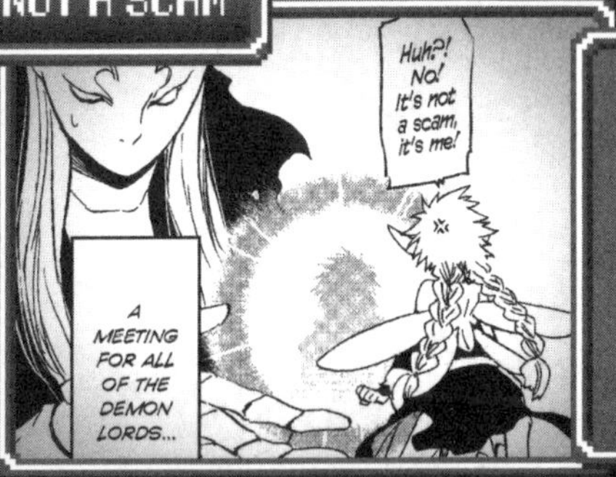
Huh?! No! It's not a scam, it's me!
A MEETING FOR ALL OF THE DEMON LORDS...

This exchange between Ramiris and Guy references an infamous telephone scam in Japan known as the "*Ore, Ore*" (lit. "It's me, it's me!") scam, where fraudsters con elderly people (or ancient Demon Lords, in this case?) over the phone by pretending to be a relative in need of money. They would hurriedly and vaguely identify themselves as "it's me!", as if the target is meant to know who the caller is, and use that urgency to confuse the target into compliance.

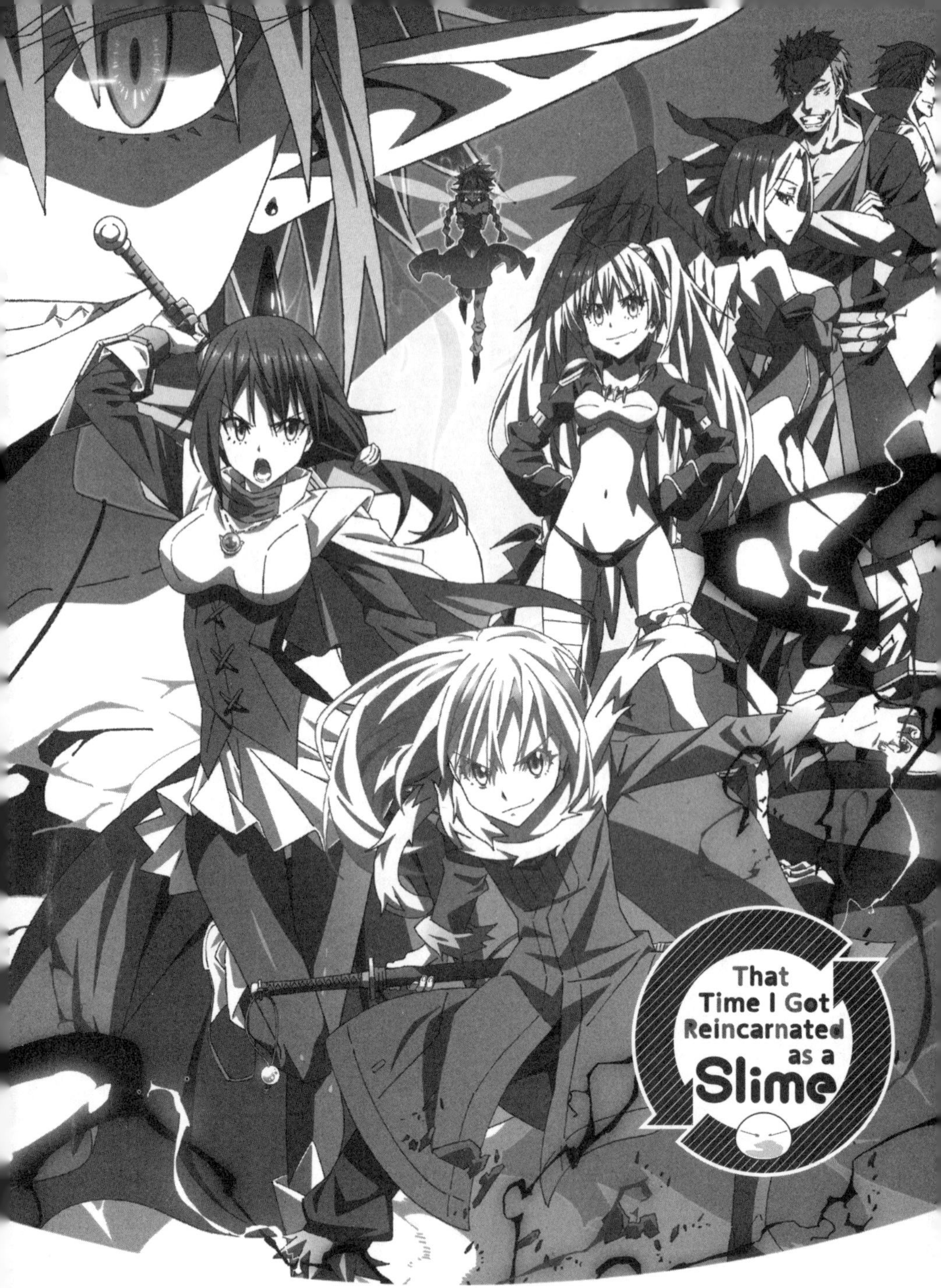
That Time I Got Reincarnated as a Slime

The boys are back, in 400-page hardcovers that are as pretty and badass as they are!

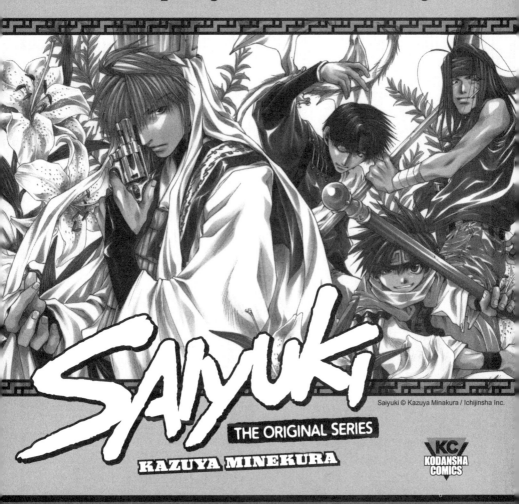

Saiyuki © Kazuya Minakura / Ichijinsha Inc.

SAIYUKI
THE ORIGINAL SERIES
KAZUYA MINEKURA

"AN EDGY COMIC LOOK AT AN ANCIENT CHINESE TALE." —YALSA

Genjo Sanzo is a Buddhist priest in the city of Togenkyo, which is being ravaged by yokai spirits that have fallen out of balance with the natural order. His superiors send him on a journey far to the west to discover why this is happening and how to stop it. His companions are three yokai with human souls. But this is no day trip — the four will encounter many discoveries and horrors on the way.

FEATURES NEW TRANSLATION, COLOR PAGES, AND BEAUTIFUL WRAPAROUND COVER ART!

Young characters and steampunk setting, like *Howl's Moving Castle* and *Battle Angel Alita*

Beyond the Clouds © 2018 Nicke / Ki-oon

A boy with a talent for machines and a mysterious girl whose wings he's fixed will take you beyond the clouds! In the tradition of the high-flying, resonant adventure stories of Studio Ghibli comes a gorgeous tale about the longing of young hearts for adventure and friendship!

EDENS ZERO

エデンズゼロ

HIRO MASHIMA IS BACK! JOIN THE CREATOR OF *FAIRY TAIL* AS HE TAKES TO THE STARS FOR ANOTHER THRILLING SAGA!

EDENS ZERO © Hiro Mashima/Kodansha, Ltd.

A high-flying space adventure! All the steadfast friendship and wild fighting you've been waiting for...IN SPACE!

At Granbell Kingdom, an abandoned amusement park, Shiki has lived his entire life among machines. But one day, Rebecca and her cat companion Happy appear at the park's front gates. Little do these newcomers know that this is the first human contact Granbell has had in a hundred years! As Shiki stumbles his way into making new friends, his former neighbors stir at an opportunity for a robo-rebellion... And when his old homeland becomes too dangerous, Shiki must join Rebecca and Happy on their spaceship and escape into the boundless cosmos.

KC KODANSHA COMICS

A dark and sexy body-horror action manga perfect for fans of *Prison School* and *High School of the Dead*!

Shuichi Kagaya is a smart kid, and most smart kids his age would be thinking about college. Shuichi is also a monster, and he's smart enough to know that monsters don't go to college. But after he uses his monstrous form to save his classmate Claire Aoki, it doesn't matter what his plans for the future were, because he's not the one making the decisions anymore. Now that the seductive, sadistic Claire knows Shuichi's secret, she's got her own ideas about what a monster is good for—because he's not the first monster she's met...

GLEIPNIR

"You and me together...we would be unstoppable."

Futaro Uesugi is a second-year in high school, scraping to get by and pay off his family's debt. The only thing he can do is study, so when Futaro receives a part-time job offer to tutor the five daughters of a wealthy businessman, he can't pass it up. Little does he know, these five beautiful sisters are quintuplets, but the only thing they have in common...is that they're all terrible at studying!

THE QUINTESSENTIAL QUINTUPLETS

negi haruba

ANIME OUT NOW!

Knight of the ice ©Yayoi Ogawa/Kodansha Ltd.

SKATING THRILLS AND ICY CHILLS WITH THIS NEW TINGLY ROMANCE SERIES!

A rom-com on ice, perfect for fans of *Princess Jellyfish* and *Wotakoi*. Kokoro is the talk of the figure-skating world, winning trophies and hearts. But little do they know... he's actually a huge nerd! From the beloved creator of *You're My Pet* (*Tramps Like Us*).

Chitose is a serious young woman, working for the health magazine *SASSO*. Or at least, she would be, if she wasn't constantly getting distracted by her childhood friend, international figure skating star Kokoro Kijinami! In the public eye and on the ice, Kokoro is a gallant, flawless knight, but behind his glittery costumes and breathtaking spins lies a secret: He's actually a hopelessly romantic otaku, who can only land his quad jumps when Chitose is on hand to recite a spell from his favorite magical girl anime!

THE SWEET SCENT OF LOVE IS IN THE AIR! FOR FANS OF OFFBEAT ROMANCES LIKE *WOTAKOI*

Sweat and Soap © Kintetsu Yamada / Kodansha Ltd.

In an office romance, there's a fine line between sexy and awkward... and that line is where Asako — a woman who sweats copiously — meets Koutarou — a perfume developer who can't get enough of Asako's, er, scent. Don't miss a romcom manga like no other!

Magus of the Library

Mitsu Izumi

MITSU IZUMI'S STUNNING ARTWORK BRINGS A FANTASTICAL LITERARY ADVENTURE TO LUSH, THRILLING LIFE!

Young Theo adores books, but the prejudice and hatred of his village keeps them ever out of his reach. Then one day, he chances to meet Sedona, a traveling librarian who works for the great library of Aftzaak, City of Books, and his life changes forever...

KC KODANSHA COMICS

‹ KAMOME ›
SHIRAHAMA

Witch Hat Atelier

A magical manga
adventure for
fans of Disney
and Studio
Ghibli!

Witch Hat Atelier © Kamome Shirahama/Kodansha Ltd.

The magical adventure that took Japan by storm is finally here, from acclaimed DC and Marvel cover artist Kamome Shirahama!

In a world where everyone takes wonders like magic spells and dragons for granted, Coco is a girl with a simple dream: She wants to be a witch. But everybody knows magicians are born, not made, and Coco was not born with a gift for magic. Resigned to her un-magical life, Coco is about to give up on her dream to become a witch...until the day she meets Qifrey, a mysterious, traveling magician. After secretly seeing Qifrey perform magic in a way she's never seen before, Coco soon learns what everybody "knows" might not be the truth, and discovers that her magical dream may not be as far away as it may seem...

KC
KODANSHA
COMICS

A SMART, NEW ROMANTIC COMEDY FOR FANS OF *SHORTCAKE CAKE* AND *TERRACE HOUSE!*

A romance manga starring high school girl Meeko, who learns to live on her own in a boarding house whose living room is home to the odd (but handsome) Matsunaga-san. She begins to adjust to her new life away from her parents, but Meeko soon learns that no matter how far away from home she is, she's still a young girl at heart — especially when she finds herself falling for Matsunaga-san.

A Kodansha Comics Trade Paperback Original
That Time I Got Reincarnated as a Slime 17 copyright © 2021 Fuse / Taiki Kawakami
English translation copyright © 2021 Fuse / Taiki Kawakami

Published in the United States by Kodansha Comics, an imprint of
Kodansha USA Publishing, LLC, New York.

Publication rights for this English edition arranged through
Kodansha Ltd., Tokyo.

First published in Japan in 2021 by Kodansha Ltd., Tokyo
as *Tensei Shitara Suraimu Datta Ken*, volume 17.

ISBN 978-1-64651-232-4

Original cover design by Saya Takagi (RedRooster)

Printed in the United States of America.

www.kodansha.us

1st Printing
Translation: Stephen Paul
Lettering: Evan Hayden
Editing: Vanessa Tenazas
Kodansha Comics edition cover design by Phil Balsman

Publisher: Kiichiro Sugawara

Director of publishing services: Ben Applegate
Associate director of operations: Stephen Pakula
Publishing services managing editors: Alanna Ruse, Madison Salters
Production managers: Emi Lotto, Angela Zurlo